BALA LAKE

IT'S ALL HERE

The great appeal of bed and breakfasting comes from the go-anywhere freedom you'll enjoy. And Wales is the best place in which to enjoy it. You can head for the hills, explore the coastline, get away from it all in a sleepy hamlet, or stay right in the swing of things at a colourful seaside resort. Each day can bring a refreshing change of scene – especially in Wales, where there's so much to see.

ALL CHANGE

Wales could well have been purpose-built for touring. A sweeping, sandy seashore soon rises into rocky mountains. Green valleys lead to empty moorlands. Spectacular lakelands suddenly appear amongst bare hillsides and thick forests. Tiny coves are unexpectedly etched into the coastline close to vast beaches.

There are new sights to see each day when you're out and about in Wales. And this variety isn't just confined to the scenery. There's an amazing diversity of places to visit – everything from tiny craft workshops to towering castles, historic houses to new, all-weather attractions, wildlife parks to woollen mills.

BRECON BEACONS

TRADITIONAL TIMES

The crafts tradition in Wales is as strong as ever. On your travels call in at a woollen mill where traditionally patterned Welsh weaves are still produced. Or take home a piece of pottery, jewellery or woodturning from one of the many craft workshops dotted throughout Wales. At places like Corris, Ruthin and Hay-on-Wye, there are even craft villages where craftspeople of different specialisations work in one location.

Castles are the one thing you simply can't miss. Over 100 are open to visitors, so you're never far from powerful medieval fortresses and romantic ruins. There's mighty Conwy Castle, for example, part of a complete medieval township ringed by sturdy walls. And it's also worth seeking out evocative ruins deep in the country, such as Cilgerran on its wooded bluff above the looping River Teifi.

ATTRACTIONS FOR ALL

Wales's castles come in all shapes and sizes – and the same can be said for the kaleidoscopic range of attractions here. There are parks dedicated to wildlife, butterflies and the countryside, narrow-gauge railways and spectacular showcaves and forest visitor centres.

MUSEUM OF THE WOOLLEN INDUSTRY, DREFACH FELINDRE

CONWY CASTLE

EVENTFUL TIMES

There's so much happening in Wales during 1990. Folk festivals and antique fairs, guided walks and sheepdog trials, market days and sporting events, medieval pageants and Victorian celebrations are all part of a busy events scene. Towns, cities, resorts and villages the length and breadth of Wales will be staging colourful, entertaining events throughout the year. Here are a handful to whet your appetite.

NORTH WALES

FEBRUARY
24	The Children's Society Welsh Centenary Year Thanksgiving Service, Bangor Cathedral, Bangor

MARCH
22	Auriol String Quartet, Theatr Clywd, Mold

APRIL
13	Prestatyn Soul Music Weekend, Pontins Holiday Centre, Prestatyn Sands
15	Bach's St John's Passion, Theatr Clwyd, Mold
25	Llŷn and District Agricultural Show

MAY
5-7	Llandudno Victorian Extravaganza
5-7	Gala 1990, Ffestiniog Railway, Porthmadog

JULY
3-8	Llangollen International Music Eisteddfod

AUGUST
4-18	Menai Strait Regattas

SEPTEMBER
8	Trawsfynydd Agricultural Show

OCTOBER
5	Gwyl Werin, Caernarfon

NOVEMBER
2-4	Prestatyn Soul Weekend, Pontins Holiday Centre, Prestatyn Sands
3-14 December	Christmas Crafts, Ruthin Craft Centre
9-11	General Portfolio Llandudno

MID WALES

25 November 1989 – 13 January 1990	George Chapman: A Retrospective, Aberystwyth Arts Centre

1990

JUNE
9	11th Man Versus Horse Marathon, Llanwrtyd Wells

JULY
23-26	Royal Welsh Show, Builth Wells

AUGUST
4-5	Dyfi Two Day Enduro, Aberangell, Machynlleth
4-11	Llanwrtyd Wells Festival Week
18-26	Llanrindod Wells Victorian Festival

SEPTEMBER
18-21	10th Welsh International Four Days Walks, Llanwrtyd Wells

SOUTH WALES

JANUARY
20	Wales v France, Cardiff Arms Park

FEBRUARY
17	Accordian Day in Wales, Patti Pavilion, Swansea

MENAI STRAIT REGATTAS

EVENTFUL TIMES

MARCH
24 — Bach – St. Mark's Passion, St. Mary's Priory Church, Abergavenny, Gwent

MAY
4-7 — The 8th Llantrisant Festival, Cross Keys Hotel, Llantrisant, Mid Glamorgan

JUNE
13-20 — Saundersfoot Edwardian Week
14-17 — Mumbles Victorian Festival, Mumbles, Swansea
16 — Jazz Festival, Welsh Folk Museum, St. Fagans, Nr Cardiff
24-30 — Pontypridd Flower and Music Festival
30-8 July — Llantwit Fardre Festival

JULY
2-5 — European Tope Angling Championships, Tenby
7 — Machen Agricultural Show, Machen, Gwent
14 — Day of the Valleys, Welsh Folk Museum, St. Fagans, Nr Cardiff
14-22 — Welsh Proms, St. David's Hall, Cardiff
26 — Royal Air Force Brawdy 1990, Haverfordwest
28 — Barry Carnival 10km Road Race, Barry, South Glamorgan

AUGUST
2 — Gower Show, Swansea Airport, Swansea
4-11 — Royal National Eisteddfod, Bryn Bach Park, Rhymney Valley
3 — Fishguard Show
17-19 — Pontardawe International Music Festival, Pontardawe, West Glamorgan

SEPTEMBER
1-2 — Llanelli Flower Festival
15 — Battle of Britain Air Day '90 – RAF St. Athan, Barry, South Glamorgan
15-3 October — Cardiff Festival of Music 1990

29-30 — Harvest Festival, Welsh Folk Museum, St. Fagans, Nr Cardiff

OCTOBER
1 — South Wales Shire Horse Society Show and Sale, Abergavenny, Gwent
1-20 — Swansea Music Festival
6-13 — Cardiff Literature Festival (Provisional)

DECEMBER
20 — Dunvant Male Choir – Christmas Carol Concert, Brangwyn Hall, Swansea

1991
OCTOBER
30 — Rugby Union World Cup 1991, Cardiff Arms Park

EUROPEAN TOURISM YEAR

EUROPEAN YEAR OF TOURISM 1990

1990 has been designated European Tourism Year by the European Community and some of its aims are to encourage cultural tourism, foster youth travel and lengthen the tourist season.

To celebrate European Tourism Year, we in Wales have produced a map in conjunction with Inter Rail, the International Youth Hostel Federation and many of the other tourist boards in Europe showing major sites of Celtic interest and Celtic festivals throughout Europe.

We hope that your stay in Wales will stimulate an interest in a culture that has its roots in the mists of time.

TIPS FOR TRAVELLERS

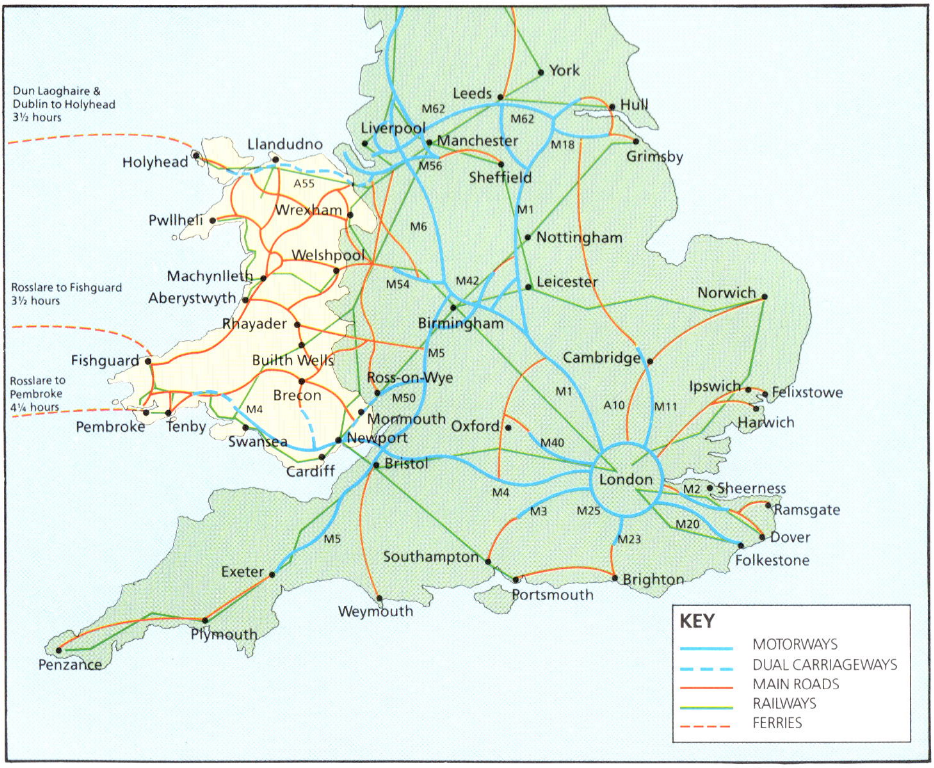

By Car	Miles	Journey Time
London to Cardiff	155	2½ hours
Leicester to Swansea	186	3½ hours
Birmingham to Aberystwyth	119	3 hours
Manchester to Llandudno	83	2 hours
Bristol to Llandudno	83	4½ hours
York to Llangollen	132	3 hours

By Express Coach	Journey Time
London to Cardiff	2¾ hours
Birmingham to Swansea	3¼ hours
Manchester to Llandudno	3 hours
Bristol to Carmarthen	3½ hours
Nottingham to Cardiff	4½ hours
Sheffield to Rhyl	4 hours

By Train	Journey time
London to Cardiff	1¾ hours
London to Llandudno	3¾ hours
London to Fishguard	4 hours
Birmingham to Swansea	3¼ hours
Wolverhampton to Aberystwyth	3 hours
Portsmouth to Swansea	4½ hours
York to Cardiff	4½ hours

By Sea	Sailings Daily (High Season)	Voyage Time
Dun Laoghaire to Holyhead	2	3½ hours
Dublin to Holyhead	2	3½ hours
Rosslaire to Fishguard	3	3½ hours
Cork to Swansea	1	10 hours
Rosslaire to Pembroke Dock	2	4¼ hours

TALYLLYN

Getting to Wales is quick and easy, trouble-free and inexpensive. You'll enjoy your holiday right from the start, without the worries of airport delays and the seemingly inevitable frustrations of long-distance travel. And when you arrive, you'll find that Wales is a grand touring country.

BY CAR

The map on these pages says it all. Look at the way in which the motorway system gives fast, direct access into Wales. What you mightn't be aware of is the westward extension of motorway and dual carriageway routes into South and North Wales. Thanks to ambitious road improvement schemes, it's now a clear run from London almost all the way to Tenby, while the new A55 Expressway avoids many of the old bottlenecks along the popular North Wales coast. Similar improvements to roads into Mid Wales from the M5/M6 via the M54, make for quick and easy access, especially from the Midlands. With a wealth of quiet roads and country lanes, car touring within Wales is a breath of fresh air to those living in the busier parts of Britain.

BY COACH

Coach travel is nowadays a really comfortable experience. Modern coaches have refreshments, a hostess service, videos, air-conditioning and on-board toilets – and ticket prices are very reasonable indeed. Express services link Wales with almost all major towns and cities in England and Scotland. Details from your local travel agent or National Express office.

If you want to travel the length of Wales, take the north-south Traws Cambria Service. It runs for over 200 miles on a daily schedule linking Bangor with Cardiff, calling at places such as Caernarfon, Aberystwyth and Carmarthen. A second Traws Cambria route operates a daily summer service between Liverpool, Wrexham and Cardiff.

Other Welsh services include Crosville Wales's limited-stop Cymru Coastliner between Wrexham and Bangor (via Chester), calling at the major North Wales resorts, with further services on to Holyhead and Porthmadog. This company also operates a Cambrian Express service between North and Mid Wales and the North-west of England.

One of the best ways to see the country is on a day of ½-day excursion run by local coach companies. Tourist Information Centres and local bus stations will have all the details.

If you want to combine coach and rail travel within North and Mid Wales, then ask about the unlimited-travel Rover tickets available (see the 'By rail' section).

Major operators serving Wales are:
National Welsh, 33 West Canal Wharf, Cardiff, South Glamorgan CF1 5DB. Tel. (0222) 376262
Crosville Wales Ltd, Imperial Buildings, Glan y Mor Road, Llandudno Junction, Gwynedd. Tel. (0492) 592111
South Wales Transport, 1 Plymouth Street, Swansea, West Glamorgan SA1 3QF. Tel. (0792) 475511

BY RAIL

British Rail's 125 InterCity service is a real distance shrinker – less than 2 hours from London (Paddington) to Cardiff and less than 3 hours to Swansea. Services also link Cardiff with Birmingham, Sheffield, York and Newcastle; and Swansea with West and Central Wales. There is a fast regular service from London (Euston) calling in at the North Wales resorts. This coast is also served by direct services from Manchester and the West Midlands.

Travelling around by train in Wales is a delight. The Cambrian Coast service from Machynelleth to Pwllheli and Aberystwyth are highly scenic lines. So too are the Heart of Wales (from Shrewsbury to Swansea via Craven Arms) and the Conwy Valley (from Llandudno Junction to Blaenau Ffestiniog) Lines. Ask about the money-saving unlimited-travel Rover and Ranger fares available, some of which include the use of bus services. Your local Rail Travel Centre will have all the details. No visit to Wales is complete without a trip on a narrow-gauge railway. Most are members of the Great Little Trains of Wales – contact the Great Little Trains of Wales, Wharf Station, Tywyn, Gwynedd (Tel. 0654-710472) for details.

BY SEA

Crossing the Irish Sea is easy. Four services operate: Dublin to Holyhead (B&I), Dun Laoghaire to Holyhead (Sealink British Ferries), Rosslare to Pembroke Dock (B&I) and Rosslare to Fishguard (Sealink British Ferries).

GREAT-VALUE ACCOMMODATION

Bed and breakfast accommodation has a tradition of offering great value (with a maximum price of only £14 per person, it certainly applies to the places listed in this guide). A quick glance through these pages will also confirm the excellent choice of B&Bs available – you can pick and choose from a wide range of family guest houses, friendly farmhouses and comfortable hotels.

ABOUT THIS GUIDE

This style of holiday accommodation, like all others, has to move with the times. Today's travellers expect high standards in addition to good value. They want reassurance about the accommodation before making a booking. They want reliable information on facilities and amenities.

The information on these pages reflects all these considerations. Our classification and award schemes, fully explained here, are designed to help you find the place that fits your requirements. It's worth taking a few minutes to study the information. You'll end up with a clear idea of the way in which the accommodation is presented in this guide – and, what's more important, you'll know that you can make a booking in complete confidence.

ALL CHECKED OUT . . . TO HELP YOU CHOOSE

For a start, every single establishment in this guide has been thoroughly checked by the Wales Tourist Board – so there's no uncertainty about standards. We then classify them into different categories so that you can choose the place best suited to your tastes and budget. Please note, though, that the descriptive wording and symbols in the accommodation advertisements have been provided by the proprietor. It should also be noted that our classifications were correct at the time of publication. Inspections are on-going and improvements made by establishments could have resulted in a higher classification since publication.

'CROWNS' – YOUR GUIDE TO FACILITIES

Crowns are the basis of a nationwide classification system for 'serviced' accommodation. It's simplicity itself. The higher the crown rating, the greater the *range* of equipment, facilities and services on offer. You should bear in mind that crowns are a measure of facilities available, *not* quality – a lower classification does not imply lower standards or a lack of quality in comparison to an establishment with more crowns. Please remember to check with establishments concerning the present range of facilities. The Crowns are only a guide and many establishments will offer facilities beyond their particular classification.

L

'Listed'. Clean and comfortable accommodation, though the range of facilities and services may be limited.

Better equipped accommodation, with a wider range of facilities, including washbasins in all bedrooms and a lounge area.

Accommodation offering a more extensive range of facilities and services (the latter in particular), including early morning tea/coffee and calls.

The range of facilities increases with at least one-third of bedrooms with en-suite WC and bath or shower, plus easy chair and full-length mirror in all bedrooms.

An even wider range of facilities and services. Colour TV, radio and telephone in all bedrooms. At least three-quarters of bedrooms with en-suite WC and bath or shower.

The highest classification for serviced accommodation, with an extensive range of facilities and services, including room service, night porter and laundry service. All bedrooms with WC, bath and shower.

AWARD-WINNING RURAL GUEST HOUSES AND FARMHOUSES

Long gone are the days when a guest house or farmhouse simply hung a 'bed & breakfast' sign on the gate and hoped for the best. Standards can now equal those at many a hotel.

The coveted Wales Tourist Board Award recognises and rewards the best rural guest houses and farmhouses. Award-winners have superior standards in furnishings, facilities, comfort and surroundings – in short, that unmistakable 'plus' factor. Look out for the distinctive award symbol next to the chosen few in the accommodation listings. It's a sure sign of something extra-special.

TRY A TASTE OF WALES

Sampling the local cuisine is one of the treats of staying anywhere different. Chefs in Wales are lucky enough to have a wonderful range of fresh, local produce to work with – everything from Welsh lamb to a rich variety of seafoods, succulent salmon and trout to a wide choice of garden-fresh vegetables. And there's an abundance of quality local cheeses that have been compared to the finest in France.

Taste of Wales – Blas ar Gymru helps visitors discover the best in Welsh cooking. Taste of Wales restaurants and eating places serve dishes inspired not only by the goodness of traditional Welsh cuisine, but also by the new, creative, lighter approach to cooking. Welsh cooking used to conjure up images of lamb, leeks, laverbread and little else. Nowadays, you shouldn't be surprised if Welsh rarebit has been replaced by Welsh cheese pâté with red wine, or shellfish pancake in lobster sauce, or even venison and wild mushrooms.

Many restaurants, hotels, inns and farmhouses throughout Wales are members of the Taste of Wales scheme. Look out for the Taste of Wales – Blas ar Gymru sign on your travels. Members advertising in this guide have the TW symbol in their entry. All members are listed in the new *Taste of Wales* book (published by Jarrold), produced with the support of the Wales Tourist Board, and available from Tourist Information Centres and all good bookshops.

HOW TO BOOK

ENQUIRIES

Just a reminder to make things easier all round. When booking a room – or simply making an enquiry – always state:
★ the dates you wish to stay, with any alternatives;
★ how many people are in your party;
★ whether you have any special requirements, such as vegetarian or other diets, terms for children, facilities for pets and so on.

BOOKING DIRECT

Telephone or write to the place of your choice. If you 'phone, remember to send a follow-up letter of confirmation.

BOOKING FORMS AND CENTRAL RESERVATIONS

You can, if you wish, use the booking forms provided at the back of this guide, where you'll also find details of Holidays Wales reservations. Simply complete the appropriate form and send it direct to the accommodation of your choice or, where applicable, to Holidays Wales reservations.

ONE CALL COVERS IT ALL

Everyone is looking for something different from their holiday and you will probably have questions to ask before making your final choice. Holidays Wales Limited provides a free reservation and help service for the Wales Tourist Board. All of the accommodation showing the symbol 🅷 can be booked through Holidays Wales.

There's almost no question they can't answer, and no contract they can't arrange for you. Holidays Wales can fix your peace-of-mind insurance, car hire, trips and excursions, children's cots etc, multi-centre and touring holidays, sports, pastimes, permits, bicycles – the lot! They can even offer a travel service, timetables and tickets for rail, coach, ferry and air travel.

Their staff are highly trained and look forward to helping you make your holiday in Wales a memorable one.

Call (0792) 645555.

Or write – Holidays Wales, PO Box 40, Swansea, West Glamorgan, SA1 1PX

PRICES

There's nothing more expensive in this guide than the per person price of only £14 a night! That's the top, high-season price – you'll find that most rates quoted are even less expensive. Single and double B&B rates are given for low and high seasons. Single is for one person in a single room, double is for two people sharing a double or twin room. Prices quoted in this guide were supplied to the Wales Tourist Board during June/August 1989. So do check all prices and facilities before confirming your booking. All prices include VAT at the current rate.

DEPOSITS

Most places will ask for a deposit when a telephone or written reservation is being made. Some establishments may request payment in advance from clients, particularly at hotels when no written and confirmed reservation has been made.

LATE ARRIVALS

If you've booked in advance and are arriving late, a thoughtful 'phone call to the place in which you're staying will be much appreciated.

CANCELLATIONS AND INSURANCE

When you confirm a holiday booking, bear in mind that you are entering a legally binding contract which entitles the proprietor to compensation if you fail to take up the accommodation. It's always wise to arrange holday insurance to cover you for cancellation and other unforseen eventualities. If you do have to alter your travel plans, always advise the holiday operator or proprietor immediately.

TOURIST INFORMATION CENTRES

We have a network of Tourist Information Centres throughout Wales. They offer a bed-booking service and major centres also run a book-a-bed-ahead scheme which means you can make for your destination safe in the knowledge you have somewhere to stay. Turn to the back of this guide for a full list of centres.

FURTHER INFORMATION

Please get in touch with us if you need any further advice or information, including more details on minimum standards and the Crown and award schemes. Contact Wales Tourist Board, Dept. TCAM, Davis Street, Cardiff, CF1 2FU.

KEY TO SYMBOLS

H	Bookable through Holidays Wales reservations
P	Car parking/garage facilities
🐕	Dogs accepted by arrangement
✗	Facilities provided for non-smokers
✗	Evening meal provided by prior arrangement
TW	Taste of Wales member

SARN PARK TOURIST INFORMATION CENTRE

USING THIS GUIDE

It's easy to find your way around this book. The remainder of the guide is filled with B&B accommodation – guest houses, farmhouses and hotels. First, we divide the accommodation up into three main regions – North, Mid and South Wales – which are colour coded. Each region is then divided into smaller areas so that you can turn immediately to the specific part of Wales that interests you. It's all explained here on the map and index.

Within each small area, the resorts, towns and villages are listed alphabetically with their accommodation. Each place has a map reference enabling you to pinpoint its location on the detailed gridded maps at the back of the book.

NORTH WALES
1. Isle of Anglesey
2. North Wales Coast Resorts
3. Llŷn – Snowdon's Peninsula
4. Snowdonia Mountains & Coastline
5. Clwyd Countryside & Heritage

MID WALES
6. Meirionnydd
7. Ceredigion
8. Montgomeryshire
9. Heart of Wales

SOUTH WALES
10. Pembrokeshire
11. The Coastline and Vales of Dyfed
12. Brecon & the Beacons
13. Swansea, Mumbles & Gower
14. Cardiff & the South Wales Coast
15. Vale of Usk & Wye Valley
16. South Wales Valleys

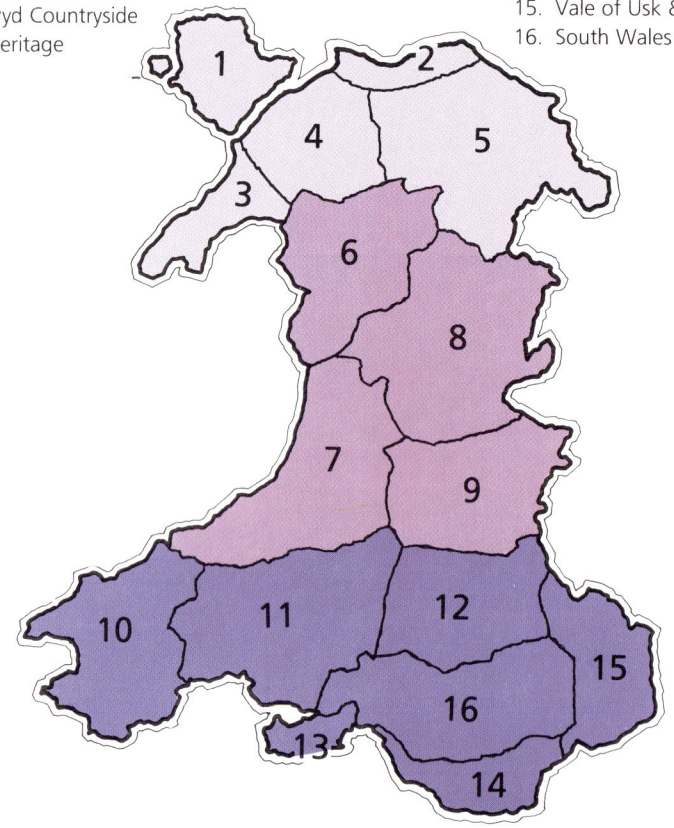

NORTH WALES

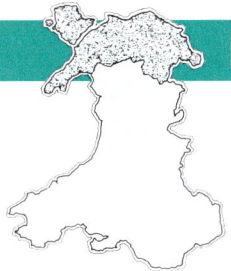

When you're on a B&B break or holiday in North Wales, it's worth getting a good map. There's so much to discover in the dramatically beautiful north. Want to spend a few days in the mountains? Then head for the huge Snowdonia National Park, a rocky, roller-coaster terrain of sharp ridges, steep-sided valleys and tumbling falls. Perhaps you'd prefer a gentler landscape? Then explore the maze of country lanes that criss-cross Clywd's rolling hills and green vales.

What about the coast? North Wales's well-known resorts and sandy beaches are as appealing as ever. Looking for something a little quieter? The answer must be the Isle of Anglesey's peaceful shores or the Llŷn Peninsula's wild beauty.

North Wales is made for exploration. Take a drive up into the clouds from Beddgelert along the lovely Nant Gwynant Pass, a route which skirts the shoulder of Snowdon. Discover the hidden lakelands above Llanrwst or follow exhilarating roads which crest the wide, open spaces of the Clwydian moors. There are B&Bs everywhere – in little stone-built villages, market towns, and out on their own in the heart of the country.

There's a wealth of good B&B accommodation along the coast. The popular resorts of Llandudno, Colwyn Bay, Rhyl and Prestatyn are ideal holiday centres with all kinds of up-to-the-minute attractions (Llandudno's super dry ski slope and Rhyl's Sun Centre and 240 ft high Sky Tower for example). Llandudno also boasts the biggest choice of hotels and guest houses in Wales, so you'll be spoilt for choice.

If you want to get away from it all, then seek out the peaceful shores of the Isle of Anglesey or the Llŷn Peninsula. Both areas are officially designated as being of 'Outstanding Natural Beauty' – a description which is confirmed by anyone who knows Anglesey's sandy shoreline or Llŷn's spectacular cliff-backed coast. The places to stay here are mostly small and friendly – make for charming, castle-crowned Criccieth, for example, or the pretty sailing centre of Beaumaris.

NANT GWYNANT, SNOWDONIA

ISLE OF ANGLESEY

It's always possible to find a quiet stretch of sands away from it all on this lovely island. Anglesey's 125-mile shoreline represents the unhurried face of the North Wales coast. Its resorts and sailing centres are small – stay at handsome Beaumaris or pretty little Moelfre – but there's nothing diminutive about the island's many attractions.

Take to the beach in a big way along Newborough Warren's vast sands and dunes. At Beaumaris, visit the last – and some say greatest – of North Wales's chain of mighty medieval castles. The National Trust's magnificent Plas Newydd mansion is full of treasures, while Pili Palas is filled with exotic butterflies from all over the world. The biggest thing of all on Anglesey is the longest place name in the world (here shortened to a humble Llanfair P.G.), where you'll find a correspondingly large, high-quality crafts shop specialising in woollens and tweeds.

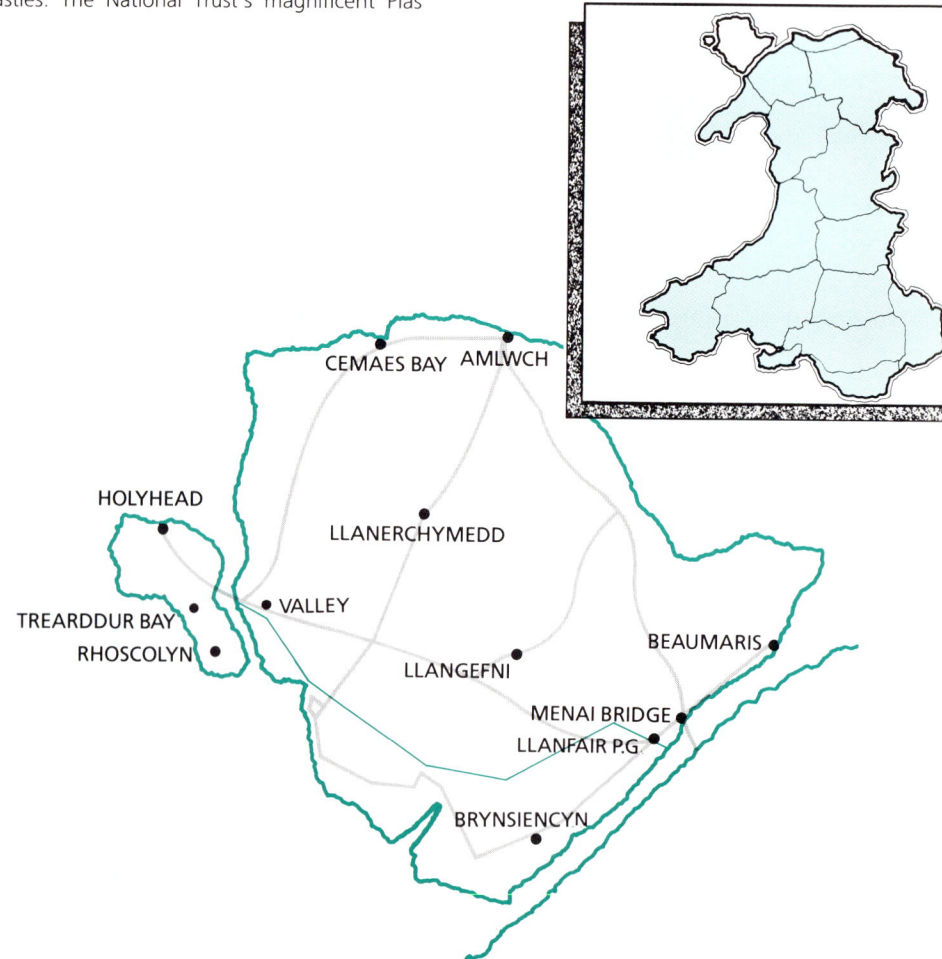

AMLWCH Map Ref Ac1

Quaint Anglesey port, market town and holiday resort. Superb coastal scenery and excellent boating. Golf course, heated indoor swimming pool.

Guest Houses

Fron Dirion

Penrhyd, Amlwch, Gwynedd, LL68 9TN
Tel: (0407) 830688

Small four bedroom family run guest house in own grounds, lovely views of sea and countryside. Ideal location for touring Anglesey. All bedrooms hot and cold, shaver points. Central heating. Separate tables in dining room. TV lounge. Parking space. Early morning tea available if required. Near fishing, golf, swimming amenities, Angora spinning craft. Fire certificate.

P	SINGLE PER PERSON B&B	DOUBLE FOR 2 PERSONS B&B	🛏	4
🐕			📺	
✗	MIN £ | MAX £ \n 13.00	MIN £ | MAX £ \n 24.00	OPEN 1-12	

BEAUMARIS Map Ref Ae3

Beautifully sited Anglesey coastal resort with splendid 13th Century castle. 15th century Tudor House, Victorian Gaol, enchanting Museum of Childhood and the new "Beaumaris Eperience". Yachting centre wth golf course and excellent fishing; 6th century Penmon Priory nearby. Ideal touring centre for Snowdonia with superb views of mountains across Menai Strait.

Guest Houses

Môr-Awel

Llangoed, Beaumaris, Gwynedd, LL58 8NP
Tel: (024878) 826   L

Bed and breakfast, optional evening meal by prior arrangement. Good home cooking. Situated in quiet friendly village. 2 family, 1 double, 2 bathrooms, 1 bathroom with shower. Beach, riding stable, golf, fishing, boat and coarse fishing available, all these amenities can be reached in a few minutes by car.

P	SINGLE PER PERSON B&B	DOUBLE FOR 2 PERSONS B&B	🛏	3
🍴			📺	
✗	MIN £ | MAX £ \n 11.00	MIN £ | MAX £ \n 18.00	OPEN 1-12	

Dinmor

Penmon, Beaumaris, Anglesey, Gwynedd LL58 8SN
Tel: (0248) 810488

Victorian farmhouse in an Area of Outstanding Natural Beauty. Superb views of coastline and Snowdonia. Delicious home cooked vegetarian food and home baked bread. En-suite rooms available. 5 riding ponies for guests with some experience. Many charted walks from the house. Sailing by arrangement. Large sunny garden. Log fires, shelves of books, warm and welcoming.

H 🍴	SINGLE PER PERSON B&B	DOUBLE FOR 2 PERSONS B&B	🛏	5
P ✗			📺	2
🐕	MIN £ | MAX £ \n 11.50 | 11.50	MIN £ | MAX £ \n 24.00 | 28.00	OPEN 1-12	

Farmhouses

Plas Cichle

Beaumaris, Anglesey, Gwynedd, LL58 8PS
Tel: (0248) 78395

This beautiful period farmhouse set in over 200 acres close to the historic town of Beaumaris and the Menai Straits, offers accommodation in spacious, well appointed double or family rooms with private bathrooms and beverage facilities. Emphasis on home cooked local produce. Ideal for exploring Anglesey and Snowdonia. Farmhouse Award 1989. Brochure available.

H	SINGLE PER PERSON B&B	DOUBLE FOR 2 PERSONS B&B	🛏	3
P			📺	3
✗	MIN £ | MAX £	MIN £ | MAX £ \n 26.00 | 26.00	OPEN 2-10	

BRYNSIENCYN Map Ref Ad4

Anglesey hamlet on shores of Menai Strait, looking across to Snowdonia. Bodowyr burial chamber, Plas Newydd stately home and Anglesey Sea Zoo nearby.

Farmhouses

Plas Trefarthen

Brynsiencyn, Anglesey, Gwynedd, LL61 6SZ
Tel: (0248) 73379

Plas Trefarthen stands in 200 acres of land on the shore of the beautiful Menai Strait in an area of outstanding natural beauty with glorious views of Snowdonia. Furnished to a very high standard, spacious bedrooms with en-suite bathrooms, colour TV and tea making facilities. The farm is arable with cattle and sheep. Ideal touring base for visiting sandy beaches, Plas Newydd and Penrhyn Castle, National Trust houses. Home cooking using farm produced meat and vegetables. Full size snooker table. Welsh welcome guaranteed. Self catering available. Send SAE for brochure.

H	SINGLE PER PERSON B&B	DOUBLE FOR 2 PERSONS B&B	🛏	5
P			📺	5
✗	MIN £ | MAX £ \n 14.00	MIN £ | MAX £ \n 28.00	OPEN 1-12	

Tyddyn Goblet

Brynsiencyn, Anglesey, Gwynedd
Tel: (024873) 296

Character farmhouse set back 200 yards from A4080 road. Ground floor suite, double and twin bedroom, shower room and toilet. First floor bedroom and bathroom. Good food, all home cooked. Free range eggs. Convenient for North Wales coast and Snowdonia and many of Anglesey's main attractions. Brochure Mrs Williams.

H ✗	SINGLE PER PERSON B&B	DOUBLE FOR 2 PERSONS B&B	🛏	3
P			📺	
🐕	MIN £ | MAX £ \n 8.50 | 9.50	MIN £ | MAX £ \n 17.00 | 19.00	OPEN 1-12	

BEAUMARIS CASTLE, ISLE OF ANGLESEY

CEMAES BAY
Map Ref Ac1

Quaint, unspoilt Anglesey village with stone quay, boating, fishing and swimming.

HOLYHEAD Map Ref Aa2

Stands on Holy Island, linked by causeway to Anglesey. Port for Irish ferries. Sailing centre and sailing school. Sea angling, cliff and hill walking. RSPB centre; enjoy the sight of sea birds and coastal flora on walk down 365 steps to South Stack lighthouse.

Roselea

26 Holborn Road, Holyhead, Anglesey, Gwynedd LL65 2AT
Tel: (0407) 4391

Homely guest house within five minutes ferry, station, bus station, beaches and golf course. Walking distance town centre. Good home cooking. Hot and cold in bedrooms, tea, coffee and refreshments available. Also evening meal if required. Private TV lounge. Nature reserve, park and leisure centre, ten minutes from Roselea.

	SINGLE PER PERSON B&B		DOUBLE FOR 2 PERSONS B&B		🛏	3
	MIN £	MAX £	MIN £	MAX £		
	12.00	12.00	19.00	19.00	OPEN 1-12	

Guest Houses

Hafod Country House

Cemaes Bay, Isle of Anglesey, Gwynedd, LL67 0DS
Tel: (0407) 710500

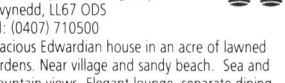

Spacious Edwardian house in an acre of lawned gardens. Near village and sandy beach. Sea and mountain views. Elegant lounge, separate dining room, comfortable bedrooms including two en-suite, all with coffee/tea making facilities. Interesting home cooking using fresh garden produce whenever possible. Past winner North Wales Golden Supercook award. Garden tennis and croquet.

	SINGLE PER PERSON B&B		DOUBLE FOR 2 PERSONS B&B		🛏	3
	MIN £	MAX £	MIN £	MAX £		2
			23.00	26.00	OPEN 1-12	

Treddolphin Guest House

Beach Road, Penrhyn, Cemaes Bay, Anglesey, Gwynedd LL67 0ET
Tel: (0407) 710388

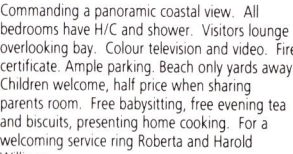

Commanding a panoramic coastal view. All bedrooms have H/C and shower. Visitors lounge overlooking bay. Colour television and video. Fire certificate. Ample parking. Beach only yards away. Children welcome, half price when sharing parents room. Free babysitting, free evening tea and biscuits, presenting home cooking. For a welcoming service ring Roberta and Harold Williams.

	SINGLE PER PERSON B&B		DOUBLE FOR 2 PERSONS B&B		🛏	8
	MIN £	MAX £	MIN £	MAX £		8
	11.00	11.00	18.00	18.00	OPEN 1-12	

Farmhouses

Tyddyn Llwyd

Llanfwrog, Holyhead, Anglesey, Gwynedd LL65 4YN
Tel: (0407) 730639

Get away from it all in the peace and quiet of a secluded farmhouse in unspoilt north west Anglesey, near beautiful sandy beaches. Spacious family accommodation. Comprising one double bedded and one bunk bedded room with own shower and toilet facilities. Colour TV. Good home cooking. Only ten miles from ferry port of Holyhead.

	SINGLE PER PERSON B&B		DOUBLE FOR 2 PERSONS B&B		🛏	2
	MIN £	MAX £	MIN £	MAX £		1
	9.00	9.50	18.00	19.00	OPEN 5-10	

Guest Houses

Hendre

Porth-y-Felin Road, Holyhead, Anglesey, Gwynedd LL65 1AH
Tel: (0407) 2929

Situated opposite park, within few minutes of car ferry, quiet location with uninterrupted views of Holyhead Mountain. Large tastefully furnished rooms, centrally heated, vanity units, tea/coffee facilities. TV in all rooms, one en-suite. TV lounge, dining room. Private parking. Excellent home cooking using all fresh produce. SAE for brochure.

	SINGLE PER PERSON B&B		DOUBLE FOR 2 PERSONS B&B		🛏	3
	MIN £	MAX £	MIN £	MAX £		1
	12.00	14.00	20.00	26.00	OPEN 1-12	

Min-y-Don

2 Newry Fawr, Holyhead, Gwynedd, LL65 1LB
Tel: (0407) 2718

All rooms have H & C, tea, coffee making facilities, TV, 5 bedrooms, 3 with own showers. Open all year. 3 minutes from car ferry. 100 meters from promenade and beach. Short stroll from town centre. Ideal walking, birdwatching, fishing, golf, diving. Nice beaches nearby. Evening meal if required. Laundry facilities available. Baby sitting service available.

	SINGLE PER PERSON B&B		DOUBLE FOR 2 PERSONS B&B		🛏	5
	MIN £	MAX £	MIN £	MAX £		2
	12.00	12.00	20.00	20.00	OPEN 1-12	

Oakleigh

4 Walthew Avenue, Holyhead, Gwynedd, LL65 1AF
Tel: (0407) 2941

Convenient for ferry, railway and bus stations. Situated on the seafront, we offer double, twin and single bedrooms, television lounge, washbasins in bedrooms, central heating, full english breakfast. Handy for town, park, fishing, golf course nearby and off road parking for car and a warm friendly welcome for all our guests.

	SINGLE PER PERSON B&B		DOUBLE FOR 2 PERSONS B&B		🛏	3
	MIN £	MAX £	MIN £	MAX £		
	10.00		20.00		OPEN 1-12	

Wavecrest

93 Newry Street, Holyhead, Gwynedd, LL65 1HU
Tel: (0407) 3637

Friendly, comfortable, family run guest house. Ideal for break of journey en-route to Ireland. Only two minutes drive from ferry, town centre and yards from beach. Good home cooking. All rooms have H & C, tea making facilities, TV, video service, radio alarms and furnished to high standard. Large family room with shower and video.

	SINGLE PER PERSON B&B		DOUBLE FOR 2 PERSONS B&B		🛏	4
	MIN £	MAX £	MIN £	MAX £		
	10.00	12.00	19.00	22.00	OPEN 1-12	

LLANERCHYMEDD
Map Ref Ac2

Central Anglesey village with easy access to island's beaches. Visit Din Llugwy, prehistoric remains of fortified village.

Farmhouses

Drws y Coed

Llanerchymedd, Anglesey, Gwynedd, LL71 8AD
Tel: (0248) 470473

With wonderful panoramic views of Snowdonia, this extremely well appointed farmhouse is situated in beautiful wooded countryside in the centre of Anglesey. It's a 450 acre working farm, beef, sheep and arable. All bedrooms are en-suite with TV, radio and beverage facilities. Central heating. Good food, games room. WTB Farmhouse Award. FHG Diploma Award.

	SINGLE PER PERSON B&B		DOUBLE FOR 2 PERSONS B&B		🛏	4
	MIN £	MAX £	MIN £	MAX £		4
	14.00		28.00	28.00	OPEN 1-12	

LLANFAIR P.G.
Map Ref Ad3

Famous for its full 58-letter name of Llanfairpwllgwyngyllgogerychwyrndrobwllllantysiliogogogoch, which means "St. Mary's church by the white aspen near the violent whirlpool and St. Tysilio's church by the red cave". Fine craft centre; Plas Newydd stately home nearby. 90ft Marquess of Anglesey column; Bryn Celli Ddu burial chamber.

Guest Houses

Carreg Goch
Llanedwen, Llanfairpwll, Anglesey, Gwynedd LL61 6EZ
Tel: (0248) 73315
Carreg Goch stands back from A4080 coast road and is 1 mile from the National Trust property of Plas Newydd. The ground floor guest suite consists of double and twin bedrooms with shared bathroom/shower. All rooms have french windows opening onto private patio. Glorious views of Snowdonia. Convenient for beaches and mountains. Home cooking.

P X	SINGLE PER PERSON B&B		DOUBLE FOR 2 PERSONS B&B		🛏	2
	MIN £	MAX £	MIN £	MAX £		
	10.00	10.00	20.00	20.00	OPEN 3-11	

Sarn Faban Guest House
Penmynydd Road, Llanfair P. G., Anglesey, Gwynedd LL61 5AZ   [L]
Tel: (0248) 712410
Situated one mile off Menai Bridge. Easy access to expressway en route to Ireland, Central for all locations. Five bedrooms, centrally heated including family rooms. Television lounge. Warm Welsh welcome with good home cooking. Brochure available.

H ½ P X 🐕	SINGLE PER PERSON B&B		DOUBLE FOR 2 PERSONS B&B		🛏	5
	MIN £	MAX £	MIN £	MAX £		
	10.00	10.00	20.00	20.00	OPEN 1-12	

CALL Holidays (0792) 645555

LLANGEFNI Map Ref Ad3

Market town and shopping centre, Anglesey's administrative "capital". Fine touring base; all the island's coastline is within 15-20 mile radius. Many prehistoric sites nearby. Theatre and sports centre. Trout fishing in nearby Cefni reservoir.

Guest Houses

Argraig
Llangristiolus, Bodorgan, Isle of Anglesey, Gwynedd, LL62 5PW 👑
Tel: (0248) 724390
Situated in a rural setting with panoramic views of Anglesey and Snowdonia. ½ mile (0.8km) west of A5 trunk road on B4422. Ideal for ferry traffic or touring. Family room, double room, both with H & C, central heating, tea/coffee making, dining room, lounge, TV. Children welcome, reductions for under twelves. A warm Welsh welcome awaits you.

H P	SINGLE PER PERSON B&B		DOUBLE FOR 2 PERSONS B&B		🛏	2
	MIN £	MAX £	MIN £	MAX £		
	9.00	10.00	18.00	20.00	OPEN 1-12	

Farmhouses

Tre'rddol Farm
Llanerchymedd, Anglesey, Gwynedd, LL71 7AR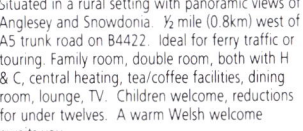
Tel: (0248) 470278
A welcome assured at this former historic 17th century manor house of character. Now a 200 acre working farm, centrally situated in a peaceful rural setting, off the B5109, 6 miles from Llangefni-Holyhead. Spacious en-suite bedrooms. Laundry facilities. Evening dinner optional. Free riding for children. SAE for brochure.

H X P 🐕	SINGLE PER PERSON B&B		DOUBLE FOR 2 PERSONS B&B		🛏	4
	MIN £	MAX £	MIN £	MAX £		4
		14.00		24.00	28.00	OPEN 1-11

MENAI BRIDGE
Map Ref Ad3

First town motorists enter on Anglesey after crossing Telford's graceful Suspension Bridge (built 1826) over the Menai Strait. Grand views of Snowdonia on mainland. Tegfryn Gallery has work by contemporary Welsh artists; Pili Plas butterfly world nearby.

Guest Houses

Bryn Aethwy
Menai Bridge, Anglesey, Gwynedd, LL59 5HS 👑
Tel: (0248) 712228
Spoil yourself in the sumptuous surroundings of a secluded house once owned by the Marquis. Breathtaking views over the straits, lovely gardens, some rooms en-suite, all rooms colour television and drink making facilities. From £12 B&B. Ideal spot for touring centre. Entrance to Bryn Aethwy bottom of Pentraeth Road.

H P ½	SINGLE PER PERSON B&B		DOUBLE FOR 2 PERSONS B&B		🛏	3
	MIN £	MAX £	MIN £	MAX £		2
		12.00		24.00		OPEN 1-12

Bwthyn
5 Bryn Afon, Menai Bridge, Anglesey, Gwynedd LL59 5HA   [L]
Tel: (0248) 713119
Century-old terraced house offers warm, welcoming non- smoking accommodation 1 minute from sparkling straits, with quiet woodland walks around the shore. Comfortable lounge (open fire, TV/video,) double/twin, guest's bathroom, CH. Delicious food. Fishing, shops, pubs, restaurants 5 minutes walk. Rail, coaches 2 miles. Easy access beautiful beaches, countryside, Snowdonia. Come as guests, leave as friends.

H X P ½	SINGLE PER PERSON B&B		DOUBLE FOR 2 PERSONS B&B		🛏	2
	MIN £	MAX £	MIN £	MAX £		
	9.75	9.75	15.50	15.50	OPEN 1-12	

PLAS NEWYDD, ISLE OF ANGLESEY

RHOSCOLYN
Map Ref Ab3

Picturesque sandy bay near Holyhead. Coastal walks, safe swimming, excellent sailing facilities in nearby Trearddur Bay.

Guest Houses

The Old School
Rhoscolyn, Nr Holyhead,
Isle of Anglesey, Gwynedd LL65 2RQ
Tel: (0407) 741593

Minutes from the lovely Rhoscolyn and Trearddur Bay beaches. Diving, fishing and nature walks. Country guest house with beautiful views all round. High standard of accommodation. The guest rooms have colour TV, radio/alarm, hot/cold, tea/coffee facilities and central heating. A magnificent lounge with log burning stove and colour TV. We offer a choice of lovely breakfasts.

P	SINGLE PER PERSON B&B		DOUBLE FOR 2 PERSONS B&B		🛏	3
🐕	MIN £	MAX £	MIN £	MAX £	📅	
	9.50		19.00		OPEN 3-11	

TREARDDUR BAY
Map Ref Aa2

Holiday spot on Holy Island, near Holyhead. Ample accommodation, golden sands, golf, sailing, fishing, swimming.

Hotels

Highground Hotel
Off Ravenspoint Road, Trearddur Bay,
Isle of Anglesey, Gwynedd LL65 2YY
Tel: (0407) 860078

Magnificent panoramic coastal views are a feature of Highground, the perfect setting for family holidays, sporting activities, or relaxing breaks. A family run, licensed hotel, Highground offers a warm and friendly atmosphere where the personal touch counts. All bedrooms have colour televisions and coffee/tea facilities. En-suite rooms available. Access and Visa payment welcomed.

P	SINGLE PER PERSON B&B		DOUBLE FOR 2 PERSONS B&B		🛏	7
X	MIN £	MAX £	MIN £	MAX £	📅	2
	12.50	14.00	25.00	28.00	OPEN 1-12	

CALL Holidays WALES (0792) 645555

Guest Houses

Moranedd Guest House
Trearddur Road, Trearddur Bay,
Anglesey, Gwynedd LL65 2UE
Tel: (0407) 860324

Moranedd is a lovely house with a sun patio overlooking three quarters of an acre of superb gardens. Only five minutes stroll to the beach, shops, sailing and golf clubs. Bedrooms are large and centrally heated with wash basins and tea making facilities. Residents lounge with TV. Licensed dining room. AA and RAC Listed.

H X	SINGLE PER PERSON B&B		DOUBLE FOR 2 PERSONS B&B		🛏	6
P 🐕	MIN £	MAX £	MIN £	MAX £	📅	
	11.00		22.00	26.00	OPEN 1-12	

VALLEY
Map Ref Ab2

Small village on A5, near Holyhead and Anglesey's many sandy beaches.

Farmhouses

Ty Mawr
Valley, Anglesey, Gwynedd, LL65 3HH
Tel: (0407) 740235

The house is large, spacious and tastefully furnished with period furniture, providing comfortable bedrooms with H & C, tea making facilities, colour television. Surrounded by 250 acres of beautiful countryside with views of Snowdonia, minutes from good sandy beaches, four miles from Holyhead car ferry to Ireland. Friendly welcome and personal attention from Mrs Anne Lloyd.

P	SINGLE PER PERSON B&B		DOUBLE FOR 2 PERSONS B&B		🛏	4
🐕 ♿	MIN £	MAX £	MIN £	MAX £	📅	
	11.00	12.00	22.00	24.00	OPEN 3-11	

TREARDDUR BAY, ANGLESEY

NORTH WALES COAST RESORTS

This popular coast stretches from Conwy at one end to Prestatyn at the other. At medieval Conwy, it's difficult to pick the most impressive sight – is it the towering castle or the craggy backcloth of mountains behind? Elegant Llandudno, with its memories of *Alice in Wonderland*, is a resort of rare character. It's a place where period charm (the resort's ornate Victorian architecture is a delight) goes hand-in-hand with up-to-the-minute appeal.

Colourful Colwyn Bay and lively Rhyl are two ever-popular family resorts. The sands are great, the entertainments endless and, like Llandudno, the resorts are ideally located for touring Snowdonia. Don't miss the Welsh Mountain Zoo at Colwyn Bay, and when in Rhyl make the most of the guaranteed good climate at the imaginative Sun Centre on the seafront. Sandy Prestatyn also has an action-packed entertainments scene, enhanced even further by the excellent Nova Centre.

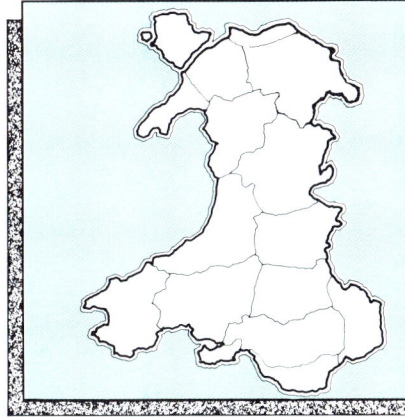

ABERGELE Map Ref Bd4

Convenient centre for exploring the popular coastal resorts. Wooded walks nearby. 18-hole golf course, livestock market. Miles of sand at nearby Pensarn.

Guest Houses

Bryn Elwy

Tower Way, Abergele, Clwyd, LL22 7AY [L]
Tel: (0745) 824314

A friendly welcome awaits you in quiet situation, but central for touring North Wales' beauty spots. Walking, fishing and golf. Parking, TV lounge, good food, every comfort. Highly recommended. Reduced rates for children sharing. Tea and coffee facilities. Two ground floor bedrooms.

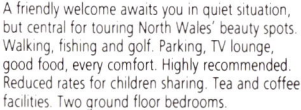

H	SINGLE PER PERSON B&B		DOUBLE FOR 2 PERSONS B&B		🛏	3
P					📺	
♨	MIN £	MAX £	MIN £	MAX £		
	10.00	11.00	18.00	20.00		OPEN 1-12

The Haven Guest House

Towyn Road, Belgrano, Abergele, Clwyd LL22 9AB
Tel: (0745) 823534

Cliff and Barbara Pilley welcome you to the Haven. A friendly guest house with single, double and family rooms having central heating, hot and cold water, shaving points, tea and coffee making facilities, all ingredients supplied. Lounge with colour TV; dining room has separate tables. Access to rooms and lounge at all reasonable times.

H	SINGLE PER PERSON B&B		DOUBLE FOR 2 PERSONS B&B		🛏	4
P					📺	
🐕	MIN £	MAX £	MIN £	MAX £		
		9.00		18.00		OPEN 1-12

Farmhouses

Bryn Car Farm

Betws-yn-Rhos, Abergele, Clwyd, LL22 8DB
Tel: (049260) 605

17th century farmhouse situated in peaceful surroundings and one mile from the village of Betws-yn-Rhos and within easy reach of the popular towns of Colwyn Bay, Llandudno and Conwy. Separate dining room and oak beamed TV lounge. Ideal for touring, walking, pony trekking and golf. Separate toilet and shower. H & C all rooms.

P	SINGLE PER PERSON B&B		DOUBLE FOR 2 PERSONS B&B		🛏	3
♨					📺	
×	MIN £	MAX £	MIN £	MAX £		
			20.00	23.00		OPEN 2-11

COLWYN BAY Map Ref Bb4

Attractive bustling seaside resort. Promenade amusements. Good touring centre for Snowdonia and Anglesey. Leisure centre, Eirias Park, Dinosaur World, Mountain Zoo, theatre. Golf, tennis, riding and other sports. Wide range of hotels and guest houses.

Hotels

Green Lawns Hotel

Bay View Road, Colwyn Bay, Clwyd, [L]
LL29 8DW
Tel: (0492) 530952

Close to sea front and town centre. Open all year. Hot and cold water in all rooms, some with en-suite showers. Lounge with colour television. Restaurant, 2 bars and ballroom. Central heating. Touring centre for Snowdonia and Anglesey. Parking readily available. Leisure Centre, Dinosaur World and Mountain Zoo and other attractions are close.

H ×	SINGLE PER PERSON B&B		DOUBLE FOR 2 PERSONS B&B		🛏	14
P					📺	6
♨	MIN £	MAX £	MIN £	MAX £		
	10.00	12.00	20.00	28.00		OPEN 1-12

Haven Villa Private Hotel

Hillside Road, Colwyn Bay, Clwyd,
LL29 7EL
Tel: (0492) 531931

Small family run hotel. Certificate of Merit for good food, hygiene, Heartbeat Wales Award. Full central heating, payphone, licensed. No smoking areas. Home cooking, menus- English/continental breakfast, health foods on request, baby listening service. Room service on request, plus many more amenities. Please send SAE for further details. M A & C H Smith proprietors.

P	SINGLE PER PERSON B&B		DOUBLE FOR 2 PERSONS B&B		🛏	5
♨					📺	
×	MIN £	MAX £	MIN £	MAX £		
	8.50	10.00	17.00	20.00		OPEN 1-12

Northwood Hotel

47 Rhos Road, Rhos on Sea,
Colwyn Bay, Clwyd LL28 4RS
Tel: (0492) 49931

Detached family run hotel. Prime situation in centre of Rhos on Sea. 175 yards promenade. Most bedrooms en-suite, all with colour television, tea/coffee making facilities and radio/radios. Noted for excellent food. Wide choice of menu at breakfast and dinner. Ideal touring base. Licensed bar. Private parking. Special mini break rates for dinner/bed/breakfast.

H ♨	SINGLE PER PERSON B&B		DOUBLE FOR 2 PERSONS B&B		🛏	13
P ×					📺	10
🐕	MIN £	MAX £	MIN £	MAX £		
	12.00	14.00	24.00	28.00		OPEN 1-12

Southlea Hotel

4 Upper Promenade, Colwyn Bay,
Clwyd, LL28 4BS
Tel: (0492) 532004

Highly recommended 8 bedroomed licensed hotel, central heated, colour TV lounge, pleasant cocktail bar, superb traditional meals served in beamed dining room. All bedrooms H & C, radios, baby listening, teasmades. AA, RAC listed. WTB 2 Crowns. Hosts to theatre stars. Dogs welcome. Special off season breaks. Ideal centre for touring beautiful North Wales. 75 yards sea.

P ×	SINGLE PER PERSON B&B		DOUBLE FOR 2 PERSONS B&B		🛏	8
🐕					📺	
♨	MIN £	MAX £	MIN £	MAX £		
	11.00	12.00	22.00	24.00		OPEN 1-12

St Margarets Hotel

Princes Drive, Colwyn Bay, Clwyd,
LL29 8RP
Tel: (0492) 532718

Edwardian hotel renowned for value and warm hospitality. Two minutes from promenade. Coach station 200 yards. Licensed bar, car park, central heating. TV, tea making facilities, baby listening all bedrooms. En-suite rooms available. High standard of cuisine and service guaranteed. Special diets by arrangement. RAC. Les Routiers. Full Christmas and New Year programme.

P	SINGLE PER PERSON B&B		DOUBLE FOR 2 PERSONS B&B		🛏	14
🐕					📺	7
×	MIN £	MAX £	MIN £	MAX £		
	12.00	14.00	24.00	28.00		OPEN 1-12

Guest Houses

Crossroads

Coed Pella Road, Colwyn Bay, Clwyd,
LL29 7AT
Tel: (0492) 530736

Family run, well established Victorian guest house with considerable charm and relaxing atmosphere, although in the town centre there are scenic views of the mountains and woods. All bedrooms have hot drinks and colour TV facilities, heating. The only guest house approved for accommodation in the borough by Les Routiers. Good Value Guide.

🐕	SINGLE PER PERSON B&B		DOUBLE FOR 2 PERSONS B&B		🛏	4
×					📺	
	MIN £	MAX £	MIN £	MAX £		
	8.50	9.50	17.00	19.00		OPEN 1-12

Farmhouses

Plas Newydd Farm

Llanddulas, Abergele, Clwyd, LL22 8HH
Tel: (0492) 516038

17th century farmhouse in lovely Dulas Valley, 1½ mile A55 and sea. Ideal for touring coast and countryside. Bedrooms of a high standard. Evenings can be spent in beamed sitting room with log fire and TV. Bed and Breakfast £10. Exit A55 Llanddulas through village turn right Beulagh Avenue for 1¼ miles along leafy lane.

P	SINGLE PER PERSON B&B		DOUBLE FOR 2 PERSONS B&B		🛏	3
					📺	
	MIN £	MAX £	MIN £	MAX £		
	10.00	10.00	15.00	15.00		OPEN 4-10

CONWY   Map Ref Bb4

Historic town with mighty castle and complete medieval town walls on river bank. Dramatic estuary setting. Many ancient buildings, Telford Suspension Bridge, popular fish quay, waymarked footpaths. Golf, pony trekking, Butterfly House, aquarium, pleasure cruisers. Touring centre for Snowdonia with good range of accommodation.

Guest Houses

Angorfa Guest House

25 Cadnant Park, Conwy, Gwynedd, LL32 8PR
Tel: (0492) 593280

Friendly guest house in residential area within level walking distance to town. H & C all bedrooms. Ample toilet facilities. Double, twin, family rooms. TV lounge. Separate tables in dining room. Fire certificate. Central heating. Parking on premises. Reductions for children sharing. Small pets accepted. Ideal touring centre. SAE please for reply. Mrs Sian Williams.

P	SINGLE PER PERSON B&B	DOUBLE FOR 2 PERSONS B&B	🛏	3
🐕	MIN £	MAX £	MIN £	MAX £	🚗
			20.00	20.00	OPEN 1-11

Cyfnant

Henryd Road, Conwy, Gwynedd, LL32 8HW
Tel: (0492) 592442

A friendly welcome and good home cooking awaits you at "Cyfnant". Comfortable double, twin, family bedrooms have shower, wash basin and TV. Our licensed guest house is a short walk from Conwy Castle, harbour and town. Ideal base for golf, fishing, sailing, riding, walking. AA listed. Fire certificate. Parking. Reduced rates for children.

H	SINGLE PER PERSON B&B	DOUBLE FOR 2 PERSONS B&B	🛏	5
P				🚗	4
✕	MIN £	MAX £	MIN £	MAX £	
	12.00	12.00	21.00	22.00	OPEN 3-10

CALL Holidays (0792) 645555

Glyn

Old Mill Road, Capelulo, Penmaenmawr, Gwynedd LL34 6TB
Tel: (0492) 622889   [L]

Historic country house below Sychnant Pass. Four acres of bluebell woods, tennis court and gardens. Superb access to mountain walking, bird watching and deserted sandy beach. Guided walks and tours to your itinerary. Separate guest lounge with TV. Packed lunches, laundry service and evening meal available, plus baby sitting. Why not come and relax with us?

H	🍴	SINGLE PER PERSON B&B	DOUBLE FOR 2 PERSONS B&B	🛏	3
P	✕	MIN £	MAX £	MIN £	MAX £	🚗
🐕		10.00	13.00	20.00	26.00	OPEN 1-12

Gwern Borter Country Manor

Ro-wen, Conwy, Gwynedd, LL32 8YL
Tel: (0492) 650360

Idyllic rural setting in 9 acres of beautiful grounds and gardens. A truly perfect spot for exploring the beauty and history of North Wales. Horse riding and cycles available. Period design bedrooms have colour TV, tea making, radio/alarms and hair dryers. Delicious country cooking from our kitchen garden. A warm welcome and happy holiday awaits you. Phone for brochure.

H	✕	SINGLE PER PERSON B&B	DOUBLE FOR 2 PERSONS B&B	🛏	4
P						2
🐕				20.00	28.00	OPEN 1-12

Llys Gwilym Guest House

3 Mountain Road, Cadnant Park, Conwy, Gwynedd LL32 8PU
Tel: (0492) 592351

Friendly guest house makes ideal base for Snowdonia and coastal day visits. Short walk to Conwy and Castle. Single, double and family rooms with hot and cold, shaver points. Colour TV lounge. Separate dining room, licensed bar. AA listed. Fire certificate held. Evening meals by arrangement. Central heating. Parking. Highly recommended. Resident proprietors Mr & Mrs Field.

H	✕	SINGLE PER PERSON B&B	DOUBLE FOR 2 PERSONS B&B	🛏	7
P						1
🐕		MIN £	MAX £	MIN £	MAX £	
		10.50	11.00	20.00	21.00	OPEN 1-12

The Old Ship Guest House

28 High Street, Lancaster Square, Conwy, Gwynedd   LL32 8DE
Tel: (0492) 596445

Relaxation and comfort assured in delightful 16th century surroundings. Situated within Conwy's historic town walls, close to all amenities. All bedrooms have central heating, colour televisions, hand basins, tea and coffee facilities. Some rooms have private shower and toilet. We pride ourselves on the quality of our substantial home cooked breakfasts. Warm welcome guaranteed.

P	✕	SINGLE PER PERSON B&B	DOUBLE FOR 2 PERSONS B&B	🛏	6
🍴						2
		MIN £	MAX £	MIN £	MAX £	
		12.00		24.00		OPEN 1-12

Farmhouses

Garth Fawr Farm

Llangystennin, Llandudno Junction, Gwynedd, LL31 9JF
Tel: (0492) 44646

Sandy beaches with a backdrop of mountains make this farmhouse an ideal base from which to enjoy the attractions of North Wales. Bodnant Garden nearby. Inland Snowdonia offers exciting drives and wonderful walking. Guests have private TV lounge. Central heating in all rooms. Full Welsh breakfast and evening refreshments. Contact Mrs Margaret Williams.

P	SINGLE PER PERSON B&B	DOUBLE FOR 2 PERSONS B&B	🛏	3
🍴	MIN £	MAX £	MIN £	MAX £	🚗
	9.00	10.00	18.00	20.00	OPEN 4-10

Henllys Farm

Llechwedd, Conwy, Gwynedd, LL32 8DJ
Tel: (0492) 593269

In the heart of beautiful countryside. Ideally placed for touring Snowdonia and North Wales coast, 1½ miles from Conwy. Colour TV lounge, two bathrooms both with showers, one double, one family room, wash-basins, tea and coffee making facilities. Evening meal available. Good home cooking fresh produce. 150 acre mixed working farm. SAE Mrs C Roberts.

H	✕	SINGLE PER PERSON B&B	DOUBLE FOR 2 PERSONS B&B	🛏	2
P						
🐕		MIN £	MAX £	MIN £	MAX £	
		9.50	11.00	19.00	22.00	OPEN 3-11

CONWY CASTLE

25

LLANDUDNO
Map Ref Bb3

Premier coastal resort of North Wales with everything the holidaymaker needs. Two beaches, spacious prom, Victorian pier, excellent shops, wide selection of hotels and guest houses. Donkey rides, Punch and Judy, ski slope, Alice in Wonderland exhibition. Visit the Great Orme with its Marine Drive and ride the Cabin Lift and tramway. Conference centre. Many daily coach excursions.

Hotels

The Ashby
31 Church Walks, Llandudno, Gwynedd, LL30 2HL
Tel: (0492) 75608
Comfortable family run hotel located between both shores. Close to all amenities and attractions including golf, ski-ing, beaches and shopping. Spacious rooms with en-suite facilities, colour TV and beverage makers. Good home cooked food and varied menu. Twin, double and family rooms available. Daily, weekly and mini break terms. Reductions for groups and senior citizens.

SINGLE PER PERSON B&B		DOUBLE FOR 2 PERSONS B&B		🛏	8
MIN £	MAX £	MIN £	MAX £		8
12.00		24.00		OPEN 1-12	

Brannock Hotel
36 St David's Road, Llandudno, Gwynedd, LL30 2UH
Tel: (0492) 77483
Situated between both shores, close to shops, railway station, etc. Car parking. Central heating. Separate tables. Open all year (except Christmas). Colour TV and tea/coffee making facilities in all rooms. Some rooms en-suite. Varied home cooking with choice of menu. Access to rooms at all times. Senior citizens discount. AA and RAC Listed.

SINGLE PER PERSON B&B		DOUBLE FOR 2 PERSONS B&B		🛏	8
MIN £	MAX £	MIN £	MAX £		3
10.00	11.00	20.00	22.00	OPEN 1-12	

Branstone
14 Llewelyn Avenue, Llandudno, Gwynedd, LL30 2ER
Tel: (0492) 76448
Situated within easy reach of Ski Slope, beach shops, our family managed hotel is licensed and has a reputation for good food prepared by chef proprietor. 5 course evening dinner available optional. Hot and cold, shaver points, bedside lights all rooms. Own keys, access all times. Midday and evening snacks. Full central heating. Your comfort our priority.

SINGLE PER PERSON B&B		DOUBLE FOR 2 PERSONS B&B		🛏	8
MIN £	MAX £	MIN £	MAX £		
9.50	10.00	18.00	19.00	OPEN 1-12	

Britannia Hotel
Promenade, Llandudno, Gwynedd, LL30 1BG
Tel: (0492) 77185
Situated on the main Promenade commanding excellent views of Llandudno's bay and Great Orme headland. Evening dinner available during summer season. Attractive bedrooms with colour TV, tea, coffee facilities and heating, some en-suite bedrooms, shower, toilets on all floors. Close to Conference Centre and theatre. Shops nearby. Ideal for touring Snowdonia. Ground floor bedroom.

SINGLE PER PERSON B&B		DOUBLE FOR 2 PERSONS B&B		🛏	9
MIN £	MAX £	MIN £	MAX £		6
10.00	14.00	20.00	26.00	OPEN 1-12	

Carmel Private Hotel
17 Craig y Don Parade, Llandudno, Gwynedd, LL30 1BG
Tel: (0492) 77643
3 Crowns highly recommended small private hotel situated on the sea front between the two Ormes. All pleasant bedrooms have colour TV, tea/coffee making facilities. All with either sea or mountain views. Full central heating, full fire certificate. Evening meal optional. Free car park to rear of hotel approached from Carmen Sylva Road.

SINGLE PER PERSON B&B		DOUBLE FOR 2 PERSONS B&B		🛏	10
MIN £	MAX £	MIN £	MAX £		5
9.50	10.00	19.00	24.00	OPEN 4-12	

Cumberland Hotel
North Promenade, Llandudno, Gwynedd
Tel: (0492) 76379
Promenade close to all amenities overlooking beautiful Llandudno Bay. Long or short breaks. Children rates, family rooms, central heated, fire certificate, licensed bar, TV lounge, en-suite, wc shower, baths. Chef cuisine. Evening meals. Colour TV, baby listening, radio intercom, tea and coffee, 13 amp socket all rooms.

SINGLE PER PERSON B&B		DOUBLE FOR 2 PERSONS B&B		🛏	19
MIN £	MAX £	MIN £	MAX £		4
11.00	12.50	22.00	25.00	OPEN 3-11	

Hollybank Hotel
9 St David's Place, Llandudno, Gwynedd, LL30 2UG
Tel: (0492) 78521
Central Res: (0792) 645555
Family run private hotel. Centrally situated on level ground, "garden" area of town close to all amenities. Parking, central heating, payphone. Comfortable single, double, family rooms, with colour TV, beverage facilities, hot and cold, some en-suite. Excellent home cooking, separate tables. Special rates for children sharing with parents. Christmas details on request.

SINGLE PER PERSON B&B		DOUBLE FOR 2 PERSONS B&B		🛏	7
MIN £	MAX £	MIN £	MAX £		4
10.00	10.00	20.00	23.00	OPEN 4-10	

Karden House Hotel
16 Charlton Street, Llandudno, Gwynedd, LL30 2AN
Tel: (0492) 79347
Conveniently situated close to beach, main shopping area, coach and railway stations. A caring fiendly service offers you good home cooking, centrally heated, single, double and family rooms. Special rates for children sharing with adults. Tea/coffee facilities in all rooms. Separate lounge. Licensed bar. Open all year including Christmas, New Year breaks.

SINGLE PER PERSON B&B		DOUBLE FOR 2 PERSONS B&B		🛏	11
MIN £	MAX £	MIN £	MAX £		
10.50	13.00	21.00	26.00	OPEN 1-12	

Mariners Lee
9 Clarence Road, Craig-y-Don, Llandudno, Gwynedd LL30 1TA
Tel: (0492) 77513
Small friendly family run hotel, situated on level ground close to the beach, bowling green, theatre, tennis courts, swimming pool, park and conference centre. All bedrooms have colour television, H & C, tea/coffee facilities. Access to room all day. Residential licence. Full central heating. Packed lunches on request. Phone or write for our colour brochure.

SINGLE PER PERSON B&B		DOUBLE FOR 2 PERSONS B&B		🛏	7
MIN £	MAX £	MIN £	MAX £		
8.50	9.50	17.00	19.00	OPEN 3-10	

LLANDUDNO

Westbourne Private Hotel

8 Arvon Avenue, Llandudno, Gwynedd,
LL30 2DY
Tel: (0492) 77450
All bedrooms contain central heating, colour TV and tea making. Some also en-suite including one twin ground floor. Very central hotel, licensed, chef proprietor, excellent food with choice and friendly quick service, separate dining dining tables. Discount for pensioners off season. Well recommended by satisfied, regular, returning guests. Phone or SAE Doris or George.

🐕 ✗	SINGLE PER PERSON B&B		DOUBLE FOR 2 PERSONS B&B		🛏	13
	MIN £	MAX £	MIN £	MAX £		3
	12.00	12.50	24.00	25.00	OPEN 3-9	

Westdale Hotel

37 Abbey Road, Llandudno, Gwynedd,
LL30 2EH
Tel: (0492) 77996
The Westdale is a pleasant, comfortable hotel. Friendly atmosphere, personal service with good traditional home cooking. Situated on the level, facing Haulfre Gardens. Easy walking distance to shops and beaches. 12 bedrooms, 1 ground floor, some en-suite, teamakers, heated, TV lounge, bar, car park. Evening meal when requested. Fire certificate, 2 Crowns. RAC listed.

H ✗ P 🐕	SINGLE PER PERSON B&B		DOUBLE FOR 2 PERSONS B&B		🛏	12
	MIN £	MAX £	MIN £	MAX £		3
	11.50	12.00	23.00	28.00	OPEN 3-10	

Guest Houses

Bryn Hazel Guest House

10 Harcourt Road, Craig-y-Don,
Llandudno, Gwynedd LL30 1TW
Tel: (0492) 75098
Friendly guest house in quiet tree lined road, on level ground. Adjacent bowling green, tennis courts and park. Short distance beach, shops, entertainments. Colour television lounge. Full central heating. Full fire certificate. Single, double, family rooms available. Reductions for children. Christmas special package. Details on request. Open all year. Your comfort assured. Sorry no pets.

✗	SINGLE PER PERSON B&B		DOUBLE FOR 2 PERSONS B&B		🛏	7
	MIN £	MAX £	MIN £	MAX £		
	8.00	8.50	16.00	17.00	OPEN 1-12	

Bryn Rosa

16 Abbey Road, Llandudno, Gwynedd,
LL30 2EA
Tel: (0492) 78215
A warm welcome awaits you at Bryn Rosa family run hotel, near pier, shops and Happy Valley. Central heating. Colour TV, tea making in all rooms. Some en-suite. Open all year. We offer a choice of menu in a pretty dining room with separate tables and good home cooking. Free car park. Children and dogs welcome. Special rates early and late. Mini breaks. Access and Visa.

P ✗ 🐕 ♿	SINGLE PER PERSON B&B		DOUBLE FOR 2 PERSONS B&B		🛏	7
	MIN £	MAX £	MIN £	MAX £		4
	10.00	11.50	20.00	23.00	OPEN 1-12	

Canberra Guest House

6 St Seiriols Road, Llandudno,
Gwynedd, LL30 2YY
Tel: (0492) 75959
Small family guest house situated on the level in the garden area of Llandudno. Central for railway and bus terminal, also town and entertainment and beaches. Tea making facilities in all rooms. Colour TV in lounge. Good home cooking with evening meal optional. Off street parking.

P ✗	SINGLE PER PERSON B&B		DOUBLE FOR 2 PERSONS B&B		🛏	4
	MIN £	MAX £	MIN £	MAX £		1
	8.50	9.00	17.00	18.00	OPEN 1-11	

Dolwen Guest House

7 St Mary's Road, Llandudno,
Gwynedd, LL30 2UB
Tel: (0492) 77757
Small privately owned and managed guest house, conveniently situated for beach and shops. Separate tables in dining room, TV lounge, hot and cold in bedrooms and central heating. Highly recommended. Good home cooking, children welcome, twin bedded, double bedded and family rooms available, all with shaving points.

🐕 ✗	SINGLE PER PERSON B&B		DOUBLE FOR 2 PERSONS B&B		🛏	4
	MIN £	MAX £	MIN £	MAX £		
	8.50	9.50	17.00	19.00	OPEN 4-10	

Glenavon Guest House

27 St. Mary's Road, Llandudno,
Gwynedd, LL30 2UB
Tel: (0492) 77687
Glenavon Guest House is situated in the garden area of the town. It is central for both shores. Yet only a few minutes from the town, station and all amenities. First class cuisine and service. Our guests comfort and welfare is our priority. Evening dinner available if required. Come and join us.

H ✗	SINGLE PER PERSON B&B		DOUBLE FOR 2 PERSONS B&B		🛏	5
	MIN £	MAX £	MIN £	MAX £		
	9.50	9.50	19.00	19.00	OPEN 3-10	

Marine View

116 Penrhyn Beach East, Penrhyn Bay,
Gwynedd, LL30 3RW
Tel: (0492) 45903
Penrhyn Bay lies between Rhos-on-Sea and Llandudno (only five minutes drive). Peaceful area. Good position, house overlooks the sea to the rear with the Little Orme's head alongside. Suitable for bird watching, fishing, touring. Open all year. Rooms have TV, hot and cold, shaver point. Lounge with balcony and TV. Guests invited to feel "at home".

H P ✗	SINGLE PER PERSON B&B		DOUBLE FOR 2 PERSONS B&B		🛏	3
	MIN £	MAX £	MIN £	MAX £		
	9.50	11.50	19.00	23.00	OPEN 1-12	

Mostyn Guest House

75 Church Walks, Llandudno,
Gwynedd, LL30 2HD
Tel: (0492) 78020/878020
A warm and friendly welcome awaits you at our licensed guest house. Ideally situated close to the North Shore beach, pier, ski slope, Happy Valley gardens and main shopping area. All ages catered for with ground floor twin room. Family double and single rooms available. Good home cooking, vegetarians catered for.

H ✗	SINGLE PER PERSON B&B		DOUBLE FOR 2 PERSONS B&B		🛏	7
	MIN £	MAX £	MIN £	MAX £		
	10.00	10.00	20.00	20.00	OPEN 1-12	

Tideways

51 Bryniau Road, West Shore,
Llandudno, Gwynedd, LL30 2EZ
Tel: (0492) 70543
A friendly welcome awaits you in our small and very comfortable guest house, situated near to West shore. Ideal for touring North Wales. Full breakfast, TV lounge, hot/cold, tea/coffee facilities in bedrooms. Double, family rooms available. Fire certificate held. Highly recommended by previous guests.

♿	SINGLE PER PERSON B&B		DOUBLE FOR 2 PERSONS B&B		🛏	4
	MIN £	MAX £	MIN £	MAX £		
		9.50		17.00	OPEN 3-10	

PRESTATYN Map Ref Be3

Family seaside resort in Clwyd, with good selection of holiday centres. Entertainment galore at superb Nova Centre including heated pools and aqua shute. Sailing, swimming on long, sandy coastline.

Hotels

Hawarden House Hotel

13-15 Victoria Road, Prestatyn, Clwyd, LL19 7SW
Tel: (0745) 4226   L

Small, privately owned hotel. English breakfast, TV, hot and cold all bedrooms. Pay phone, central heating. Close to beach, Nova Sun Centre and shops. Tea and coffee on request, late key. Children are welcome. Good food, warm welcome. Ideal base for touring North Wales and beautiful countryside close by.

H ⚒	SINGLE PER PERSON B&B	DOUBLE FOR 2 PERSONS B&B	🛏	6
P ✕				
🐕	MIN £ / MAX £ 10.00 / 10.00	MIN £ / MAX £ 18.00 / 18.00	OPEN 1-12	

Guest Houses

Roughsedge House

26-28 Marine Road, Prestatyn, Clwyd, LL19 7HD
Tel: (07456) 87359

Centrally situated for town centre, bus/railway stations and Offa's Dyke footpath. Close to beaches, Pontins, Presthaven Sands and the Nova complex. Offering friendly service, home cooking, special diets and choice of menu. Residential licence. Pleasant rooms, H/C, tea/coffee facilities, some with TV, central heated, open fires in winter. Families welcome. Brochure available.

P	SINGLE PER PERSON B&B	DOUBLE FOR 2 PERSONS B&B	🛏	10
✕				
	MIN £ / MAX £ 8.00 / 9.00	MIN £ / MAX £ 16.00 / 18.00	OPEN 1-12	

St. Edwards Guest House

69 Marine Road, Prestatyn, Clwyd, LL19 7HA
Tel: (07456) 3994   L

A warm welcome awaits you at St Edwards, with top quality home cooking. All rooms are centrally heated with hot and cold water and shaver point. Five minutes from town centre, beach, nearby snooker hall, golf courses and leisure complex. We will collect you if you arrive by rail or coach.

H ✕	SINGLE PER PERSON B&B	DOUBLE FOR 2 PERSONS B&B	🛏	5
P				
🐕	MIN £ / MAX £ 10.00	MIN £ / MAX £ 20.00	OPEN 1-12	

RHOS-ON-SEA Map Ref Bc4

Village linking Llandudno and Colwyn Bay with promenade, beach, golf, water skiing, puppet theatre.

Hotels

Stanton House Hotel

33 Whitehall Road, Rhos-on-Sea, Colwyn Bay, Clwyd, LL28 4ET
Tel: (0492) 44363   👑👑

Family licensed hotel. Open all year. Central heating, bedrooms en-suite with tea making and TV available. Reading and TV lounge. Beach 150yds approx. Ideal base for Snowdonia, Conwy, Bodnant Garden. Excellent cuisine. Half board terms available. Special terms for children sharing room with parents. Private car parking. Send for a colour brochure. AA*.

H ⚒	SINGLE PER PERSON B&B	DOUBLE FOR 2 PERSONS B&B	🛏	10
P ✕				
🐕	MIN £ / MAX £ 13.00 / 14.00	MIN £ / MAX £ 26.00 / 28.00	OPEN 1-12	3

Guest Houses

The Cedar Tree

27 Whitehall Road, Rhos-on-Sea, Colwyn Bay, Clwyd LL28 4HW
Tel: (0492) 45867   👑👑

Comfortable friendly guest house, 300 yards promenade. Convenient Snowdonia National Park, Bodnant, Conwy, Colwyn Bay, railway/coach stations within 1 mile. Private parking. En-suite facilities all bedrooms, central heating, tea/coffee making facilities. Family rooms available. Special rates for children sharing parents room. Excellent cuisine, separate tables. Attractive lounge with colour television. Fire certificate. Weekly terms available. Excellent value.

P	SINGLE PER PERSON B&B	DOUBLE FOR 2 PERSONS B&B	🛏	7
🐕				7
✕	MIN £ / MAX £ 11.00 / 13.00	MIN £ / MAX £ 22.00 / 26.00	OPEN 1-11	

Croma

50A Rhos Road, Rhos-on-Sea, Colwyn Bay, Clwyd LL28 4RS
Tel: (0492) 49423   👑👑

Luxury ground floor twin en-suite with colour television and tea/coffee making facilities. Vegetarians, vegans catered for. Sauna facility available. Lovely position close to shops and seafront. Set in quiet private gardens. Pets by arrangement. Family run providing personal service. Telephone Mrs Vyner.

H ⚒	SINGLE PER PERSON B&B	DOUBLE FOR 2 PERSONS B&B	🛏	1
P ✕				1
🐕	MIN £ / MAX £	MIN £ / MAX £ 25.00 / 27.00	OPEN 1-12	

RHYL Map Ref Bd4

Fun-packed coast resort offering all-round entertainment. The Suncentre "indoor beach" with swimming pool, surfing pool and slides together with new 240ft Sky Tower are the major attractions; big funfair, Marine Lake park, Butterfly World, safe swimming, sailing. Extensive holiday caravan parks. Ideal seaside resort for the whole family.

Guest Houses

Beechroyde

27 Palace Avenue, Rhyl, Clwyd, LL18 1HS
Tel: (0745) 350159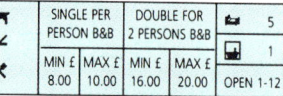

Situated only seven doors from promenade, close to all amenities, popular west end. Good home cooking, separate tables, evening dinner and snacks available. Shaver points, hot and cold all rooms. Own door keys, access at all times. TV lounge. Full central heating. Open all year. Reduced rates early and late season. Mrs Maureen Lawrence.

🐕	SINGLE PER PERSON B&B	DOUBLE FOR 2 PERSONS B&B	🛏	5
⚒				1
✕	MIN £ / MAX £ 8.00 / 10.00	MIN £ / MAX £ 16.00 / 20.00	OPEN 1-12	

RHYL SUNCENTRE

LLŶN – SNOWDON'S PENINSULA

The Llŷn Peninsula is another of North Wales's 'Areas of Outstanding Natural Beauty'. The accolade applies to the spectacular coastline fringing this narrow finger of land that points straight into the sea from Snowdonia. At times – around the charming little resorts of Criccieth, Pwllheli and Nefyn – the coast has a gentle, sandy character. But along other parts of this peaceful peninsula, mountains take a shuddering plunge into the sea as land meets water along a curtain of cliffs.

Llŷn is a peninsula of storm-tossed headlands and sheltered bays. It is a resilient, remote part of Wales where traditional ways live on, and where the old ports of Porthmadog and Abersoch have found new life as busy sailing centres.

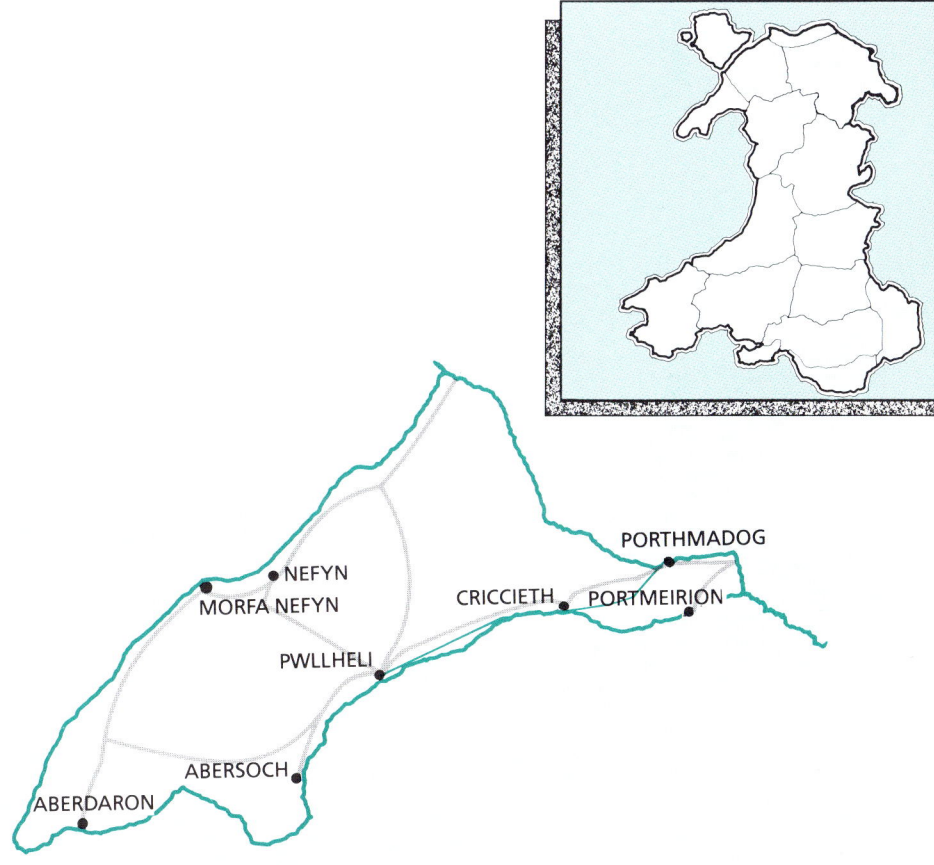

ABERDARON
Map Ref Aa5

Small picturesque village on tip of Llŷn Peninsula. Pilgrims making for Bardsey Island, clearly seen across Bardsey Sound, used to rest at Y Gegin Fawr, now a cafe and souvenir shop.

Guest Houses

Bryn Môr

Aberdaron, Pwllheli, Gwynedd, LL53 8BS
Tel: (0758) 86344

Bryn Môr is a family run guest house overlooking the bay and village. 3 minutes from the beach. Ample parking space. Full English breakfast, evening meal optional. Comfortable lounge with colour television, separate dining room. Bedrooms have hot and cold water, strip lights, shaver points. Access available at all times. Bathroom, shower facilities. Scenic views from rooms. Sorry no pets.

	SINGLE PER PERSON B&B		DOUBLE FOR 2 PERSONS B&B			5
	MIN £	MAX £	MIN £	MAX £		
	10.00	10.00	20.00	20.00	OPEN 1-12	

Carreg Plâs Guest House

Aberdaron, Pwllheli, Gwynedd, LL53 8LH
Tel: (075886) 308

17th century manor house in secluded wooded grounds, two miles from Aberdaron, close to Whistling Sands beach. Ideal base for exploring lovely coastline, largely National Trust owned. Single, double and family rooms available with wash basins, shaver points, tea making facilities. Colour TV. Evening meals with high standard of home cooking. Special reductions for children.

	SINGLE PER PERSON B&B		DOUBLE FOR 2 PERSONS B&B			7
	MIN £	MAX £	MIN £	MAX £		
	12.00	14.00	24.00	28.00	OPEN 1-12	

ABERSOCH
Map Ref Ac5

Dinghy sailing and windsurfing centre with safe sandy beaches. Superb coastal scenery with easy walks. Pony trekking, golf, fishing and sea trips.

Hotels

Belmont (Private) Hotel

Lôn Sarn Bach, Abersoch, Gwynedd, LL53 7EE
Tel: (075881) 2121

Friendly family run licensed hotel near beach and village. Single, double, family rooms available. Special rates for children. Well stocked bar, guest lounge with colour television, patio, car park. Fresh home cooking, vegetarian and special diets available. Optional evening meal (four courses). Bargain breaks, mini weekend offers. Golf, sailing, fishing, walking and riding nearby.

	SINGLE PER PERSON B&B		DOUBLE FOR 2 PERSONS B&B			6
	MIN £	MAX £	MIN £	MAX £		
	12.00	14.00	24.00	28.00	OPEN 1-12	

Guest Houses

Aberview

Lôn Garmon, Abersoch, Pwllheli, Gwynedd LL53 7UG
Tel: (075881) 3452

Aberview is ideally situated away from noise and crowds. One minute beach with beautiful views overlooking the harbour. Comfortable lounge with colour television, tea and coffee facilities in rooms, hot and cold and shaver points. Fire certificate. Excellent cooking and a warm welcome awaits you at Aberview. Brochure available Mrs J Read.

	SINGLE PER PERSON B&B		DOUBLE FOR 2 PERSONS B&B			6
	MIN £	MAX £	MIN £	MAX £		1
	9.00	11.00	18.00	22.00	OPEN 1-12	

Angorfa Guest House

Lôn Sarn Bach, Abersoch, Gwynedd, LL53 7EB
Tel: (075881) 2967

Village situated, family run friendly guest house. Sea views, water sports, safe sandy beaches, golf and horse riding within minutes. Bedrooms have tea/coffee, wash basins and shaver points, TV/video lounge, central heating. High quality home cooked evening meal (optional), full English breakfast, both freshly prepared. Fire certificate. Self catering available. For brochure send SAE to Chris Stanworth.

	SINGLE PER PERSON B&B		DOUBLE FOR 2 PERSONS B&B			4
	MIN £	MAX £	MIN £	MAX £		
			20.00		OPEN 1-12	

Berwyn Guest House

Lôn Golff, Abersoch, Pwllheli, Gwynedd LL53 7EF
Tel: (075881) 2392

One minute away from the beach and golf course, Berwyn is ideally situated in a peaceful location yet very central. Comfortable centrally heated rooms have colour television and H & C. Home cooked evening meals available with restful lounge in which to relax. A warm welcome awaits you at Berwyn. Full fire certificate. Ample private parking.

	SINGLE PER PERSON B&B		DOUBLE FOR 2 PERSONS B&B			5
	MIN £	MAX £	MIN £	MAX £		1
			19.00		OPEN 1-12	

Llysfor Guest House

Abersoch, Nr Pwllheli, Gwynedd, LL53 7AL
Tel: (075881) 2248

We are a well established family run guest house. AA/RAC listed. Our aim is to please and make your stay pleasant. Kettle, hot and cold and shaver points all bedrooms. Comfortable dining room. Home cooking. Cosy lounge, colour TV. Free parking own grounds. 1 minute to beach. Enquiries Mrs F Hiorns.

	SINGLE PER PERSON B&B		DOUBLE FOR 2 PERSONS B&B			7
	MIN £	MAX £	MIN £	MAX £		
	12.50		25.00		OPEN 4-10	

Pengwern

Lôn Sarn Bach, Abersoch, Gwynedd, LL53 7ER
Tel: (075881) 3301

Pengwern is beautifully situated in its own grounds on the edge of Abersoch, with sea and mountain views. Peaceful yet only 10 minutes walk to shops and beach. All rooms have central heating, hot and cold, and tea making facilities. Colour TV in lounge. Excellent home cooking. Ample parking. Reduced rates for children.

	SINGLE PER PERSON B&B		DOUBLE FOR 2 PERSONS B&B			5
	MIN £	MAX £	MIN £	MAX £		
			20.00	26.00	OPEN 1-12	

Tan y Foel

Mynytho, Pwllheli, Gwynedd, LL53 7RL
Tel: (0758) 740807

Quiet country cottage with superb views overlooking St. Tudwal's Islands, Abersoch and Hell's Mouth. Bedrooms have hot and cold water with tea making facilities. Shower and WC for sole use of guests. Centrally heated. Bunks for children. Within easy reach of sailing, golf, riding, walking. Ring Sylvia Dale for particulars. Assured of friendly welcome.

	SINGLE PER PERSON B&B		DOUBLE FOR 2 PERSONS B&B			3
	MIN £	MAX £	MIN £	MAX £		
	10.50	12.00	17.00	24.00	OPEN 2-11	

Tŷ Draw Guest House

Lôn Sarn Bach, Abersoch, Pwllheli,
Gwynedd LL53 7EL
Tel: (075881) 2647

Beautiful guest house with sea and mountain views, set in attractive gardens, in a quieter part of the village. Ideal centre for all activities. Single, double and family rooms all with vanitory units. Comfortable lounge with TV. Tea/ coffee facilities. Fresh aga cooked food. Special diets catered for. Large and secure car/boat park. For brochure contact Jean and Peter Collins.

H	SINGLE PER PERSON B&B	DOUBLE FOR 2 PERSONS B&B	🛏	7
P				
X	MIN £ 10.00	MAX £	MIN £ 20.00	MAX £	🚗	OPEN 4-9

CRICCIETH Map Ref Ad7

Ideal family resort, with safe beach and seafront hotels. Romantic ruined castle overlooking sea. Salmon and sea trout in nearby rivers and lakes. Festival of Music and the Arts in June.

Hotels

Glyn-y-Coed Hotel

Porthmadog Road, Criccieth, Gwynedd,
LL52 0HP
Tel: (0766) 522870

Lovely Victorian house overlooking sea, mountains and castle. AA/RAC listed. Cosy bar. Highly recommended cooking, catering for special diets. En-suite bedrooms with tea/coffee facilities. Full central heating. Parking in grounds. Children welcome. Moderate rates. Golf, fishing. Special parties catered for. SAE please for brochure.

H	SINGLE PER PERSON B&B	DOUBLE FOR 2 PERSONS B&B	🛏	10
P				7
X	MIN £ 12.50	MAX £ 14.00	MIN £ 25.00	MAX £ 28.00	OPEN 1-11

Min-y-Gaer Hotel

Porthmadog Road, Criccieth, Gwynedd,
LL52 0HP
Tel: (0766) 522151

A pleasant, licensed hotel, conveniently situated near the beach with delightful views of the Cardigan Bay coastline. 10 comfortable rooms (9 en-suite) are all heated and have a colour TV and tea/coffee making facilities. An ideal base for touring Snowdonia. Reduced rates for children. Ample car parking. AA/RAC listed. Brochure on request.

H X	SINGLE PER PERSON B&B	DOUBLE FOR 2 PERSONS B&B	🛏	10
P				9
🐕	MIN £ 12.00	MAX £	MIN £ 24.00	MAX £	OPEN 3-10

Guest Houses

Moelwyn Restaurant

27/29 Mona Terrace, Criccieth,
Gwynedd, LL52 0HG
Tel: (0766) 522500

A pretty Victorian restaurant with five bedrooms, all with superb sea views and tea/coffee making facilities. Some en-suite. Lounge bar, residents lounge. Chef/proprietor specialises in local seafood and delicious sauces. Children catered for. Situated directly on the seafront. Well established and known for fine food and a warm atmosphere.

🐕	SINGLE PER PERSON B&B	DOUBLE FOR 2 PERSONS B&B	🛏	5
🍴				3
X	MIN £ 13.50	MAX £	MIN £ 27.00	MAX £	OPEN 4-11

Preswylfa Guest House

4 Castle Terrace, Criccieth, Gwynedd,
LL52 0DY
Tel: (0766) 522829

Small licensed guest house, facing castle and bay. Fine food, personal service, TV lounge. Accommodation - meals as required. Centre Welsh heritage and Great Little Trains of Wales near Snowdonia. Visa, Access.

H 🍴	SINGLE PER PERSON B&B	DOUBLE FOR 2 PERSONS B&B	🛏	5
P X				
🐕	MIN £ 9.50	MAX £ 13.00	MIN £ 19.00	MAX £ 26.00	OPEN 1-12

Rhoslyn

8 Marine Terrace, Criccieth, Gwynedd,
LL52 0EF
Tel: (0766) 522685

Family run sea front guest house. Home cooked meals, tea and coffee facilities all rooms. Packed lunches. Guest lounge with colour TV. Reduced rates senior citizens selected weeks. Full gas central heating, table licence. Ideal centre for touring Snowdonia and Llŷn Peninsula. Brochure on request Crad and Jill Powell.

P	SINGLE PER PERSON B&B	DOUBLE FOR 2 PERSONS B&B	🛏	7
🐕				
X	MIN £ 10.00	MAX £ 10.50	MIN £ 20.00	MAX £ 21.00	OPEN 1-12

Tŷ Newydd

Llanystumdwy, Criccieth, Gwynedd,
LL52 0LW
Tel: (0766) 522811

Tŷ Newydd last home of Lloyd George, set in 3½ acres of its own grounds. Spacious rooms, superb views of sea and mountains. TV lounge, tea and coffee making facilities. Home-made cooking. Ideal holiday venue for families with children. Pets by arrangement. Brochure available. Open all year. Special winter rates.

H	SINGLE PER PERSON B&B	DOUBLE FOR 2 PERSONS B&B	🛏	3
P				
🐕	MIN £ 10.00	MAX £ 14.00	MIN £ 20.00	MAX £ 28.00	OPEN 1-12

Farmhouses

Trem-yr-Eifl Farm

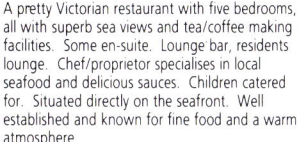

Rhoslan, Criccieth, Gwynedd,
LL52 0NW
Tel: (0766) 522320

Come and stay in our comfortable farmhouse in a beautiful converted old stone barn. We are 2½ miles from Criccieth. Comfortable spacious rooms, 2 doubles, 1 family all with hot and cold water, also bathroom with shower. Separate tables, television lounge. Ideally located for touring Snowdonia and the Llŷn Peninsula.

P	SINGLE PER PERSON B&B	DOUBLE FOR 2 PERSONS B&B	🛏	3
🐕				
	MIN £ 10.00	MAX £ 12.00	MIN £ 17.00	MAX £ 20.00	OPEN 3-10

MORFA NEFYN Map Ref Ab6

Popular Llŷn Peninsula seaside village with extensive sandy beaches, between little harbour of Porthdinllaen and resort of Nefyn. Set against mountainous backdrop of Garn Boduan.

Hotels

Lion Hotel

Tudweiliog, Pwllheli, Gwynedd,
LL53 8ND
Tel: (075887) 244

Les Routiers approved for good value and a warm welcome. Village inn offering good food and facilities. Two rooms en-suite or hot and cold, tea/coffee etc. in all rooms. Full bar licence. Bar meals and restaurant meals at reduced rates. Extensive menu lunchtimes and evenings. Beaches, golf, riding at reasonable distances. Large garden and courtyard barbecues. Block bookings welcome.

H X	SINGLE PER PERSON B&B	DOUBLE FOR 2 PERSONS B&B	🛏	5
P				2
🐕	MIN £ 12.50	MAX £ 14.00	MIN £ 23.00	MAX £ 26.00	OPEN 1-12

CALL Holidays 0792) 645555

31

NEFYN
Map Ref Ab6

Old fishing village on Llŷn Peninsula perched above sweeping bay. Two miles of sand, safe swimming, sailing and fishing.

Hotels

Old Rectory Hotel

Boduan, Pwllheli, Gwynedd, LL53 6DT
Tel: (0758) 720923/721363

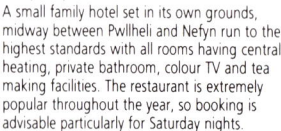

A small family hotel set in its own grounds, midway between Pwllheli and Nefyn run to the highest standards with all rooms having central heating, private bathroom, colour TV and tea making facilities. The restaurant is extremely popular throughout the year, so booking is advisable particularly for Saturday nights.

	SINGLE PER PERSON B&B	DOUBLE FOR 2 PERSONS B&B		4
	MIN £	MAX £	MIN £	MAX £		4
	14.00		28.00		OPEN 1-12

Three Herrings

Well Street, Nefyn, Gwynedd,
LL53 6HW
Tel: (0758) 720864

Olde worlde licensed restaurant with accommodation, good food with wide choice of menu, bar service. Three double rooms, two with extra bed if required, hot and cold, (one room en-suite), shaver points, central heating, TV and tea/coffee making facilities. Large car park nearby. Close to unspoilt beaches, boating, fishing.

	SINGLE PER PERSON B&B	DOUBLE FOR 2 PERSONS B&B		3
	MIN £	MAX £	MIN £	MAX £		1
	11.00	12.00	20.00	21.00	OPEN 3-10

PORTHMADOG
Map Ref Ae7

Harbour town and shopping centre named after William Madocks, who built mile-long Cob embankment. Steam narrow-gauge Ffestiniog Railway runs to Blaenau Ffestiniog, with its slate caverns. Also Welsh Highland Railway. Pottery, maritime museum; Portmeirion Italianate village nearby.

Hotels

Owen's Hotel

71 High Street, Porthmadog, Gwynedd,
LL49 9EU
Tel: (0766) 512098

Small, family hotel in the centre of Porthmadog, under personal supervision of resident proprietors Lena and Edwin Owen. Some rooms en-suite with colour TV and beverage facilities at higher rate. Ffestiniog and Welsh Highland narrow gauge railways five minutes walk. Easy reach of Snowdonia and many lovely beaches. Children welcome. Central heating. AA listed.

	SINGLE PER PERSON B&B	DOUBLE FOR 2 PERSONS B&B		10
	MIN £	MAX £	MIN £	MAX £		7
	13.00	13.00	24.00	24.00	OPEN 3-10

Guest Houses

7 Brittania Terrace

Porthmadog, Gwynedd, LL49 9NB
Tel: (0766) 513073

Situated in Porthmadog directly opposite Ffestiniog Steam Railway. Two minutes town centre. Exceptional views harbour and railway. Keys to rooms. Come and go as you wish. Colour TV's, sinks, free tea/coffee facilities. Shower. Home from home atmosphere. Biggest best breakfast. Open all year. Reduced rates October to April.

	SINGLE PER PERSON B&B	DOUBLE FOR 2 PERSONS B&B		2
	MIN £	MAX £	MIN £	MAX £		
	9.00	11.00	18.00	22.00	OPEN 1-12

Gwydryn

Beach Road, Morfa Bychan,
Porthmadog, Gwynedd LL49 9YA
Tel: (0766) 512420

Situated between Cardigan Bay and Snowdonia Mountain range. Morfa Bychan is 2 miles from Porthmadog and Ffestiniog Narrow Gauge Railway, 5 minutes walk to a sandy beach, golf course close by. Fishing, riding locally. Lounge with TV. Separate dining room. Comfortable 5 bedrooms, 1 family room. Hot and cold. Ample car parking space. Cedarwood chalets to let.

	SINGLE PER PERSON B&B	DOUBLE FOR 2 PERSONS B&B		5
	MIN £	MAX £	MIN £	MAX £		
	9.50	12.50	17.00	24.00	OPEN 1-12

35 Madoc Street

Porthmadog, Gwynedd, LL49 9BU
Tel: (0766) 512843

Friendly welcome for all. Good home cooking, heating in all rooms, TV lounge, tea/coffee making facilities. Keys supplied. Special rates for children. Shops, buses, trains, cinema nearby. Ideally situated for visiting Portmeirion Italiante village. The mountains of Snowdonia, the Ffestiniog Railway Steam Trains and the lovely sandy beaches are near. Open all year. Proprietor Mrs R Skellern.

	SINGLE PER PERSON B&B	DOUBLE FOR 2 PERSONS B&B		2
	MIN £	MAX £	MIN £	MAX £		
	9.00	10.00	18.00	20.00	OPEN 1-12

49 Madog Street

Porthmadog, Gwynedd, LL49 9BU
Tel: (0766) 513107

Ideally situated for touring Snowdonia, visiting the Ffestiniog Railway and local beaches, within easy reach of town centre, convenient for buses and railway stations. Homely atmosphere, good cooking. Children always welcome. Central heating in all rooms. Ample parking nearby. Open all the year round. Contact Mrs G Roberts.

	SINGLE PER PERSON B&B	DOUBLE FOR 2 PERSONS B&B		4
	MIN £	MAX £	MIN £	MAX £		
	8.50	10.00	17.00	20.00	OPEN 1-12

The Oakleys Guest House

The Harbour, Porthmadog, Gwynedd,
LL49 9AS
Tel: (0766) 512482

Situated on the harbour in Porthmadog. Licensed. An excellent base for exploring Snowdonia, Portmeirion and the beaches of Llŷn Peninsula, taking in Pwllheli, Abersoch and Criccieth. Fishing, sea trout, salmon, golf course nearby. Spacious free car park. Comfortable lounge. Informal holiday atmosphere. Two bedrooms with showers, one bedroom en-suite. Electric blankets. Contact Mr & Mrs A H Biddle, proprietors.

	SINGLE PER PERSON B&B	DOUBLE FOR 2 PERSONS B&B		8
	MIN £	MAX £	MIN £	MAX £		1
	11.00	13.00	22.00	24.00	OPEN 3-11

Treforris

Garth Road, Porthmadog, Gwynedd,
LL49 9BN
Tel: (0766) 512853

Friendly run well established Victorian house. Perfect centre for exploring Snowdonia Mountains and beaches. 18 hole golf gourse nearby. Separate sitting room and television lounge. Five letting bedrooms, hot and cold all bedrooms. Central heating. Fire certificate.

	SINGLE PER PERSON B&B	DOUBLE FOR 2 PERSONS B&B		5
	MIN £	MAX £	MIN £	MAX £		
	12.00	12.00	20.00	20.00	OPEN 1-12

Tŷ Newydd

30 Dublin Street, Tremadog,
Porthmadog, Gwynedd LL49 9RH
Tel: (0766) 512553

Two double bedrooms, private showers, colour TV, tea making facilities. One double, one twin with no showers. All rooms have own table in dining room. TV lounge. Private car park. Central to all parts of Snowdonia National Park, Ffestiniog Railway, beaches. Reductions for weekly bookings.

	SINGLE PER PERSON B&B	DOUBLE FOR 2 PERSONS B&B		4
	MIN £	MAX £	MIN £	MAX £		
	12.00		20.00		OPEN 3-10

Farmhouses

Cefn Uchaf Country Guest House

Garndolbenmaen, Porthmadog,
Gwynedd, LL51 9PJ
Tel: (076675) 239
Modernised farmhouse in 12½ acres.
Comfortable lounge central heating, log fires.
Bedrooms with H & C, TV, tea/ coffee making
facilities. Fire certificate. Excellent food. Special
diets catered for. Railways, castles, beaches and
many other attractions close by. Friendly farm
animals. Pets welcome. Special rates for children.
Please contact Anne or Chris Easton for brochure.

	SINGLE PER PERSON B&B	DOUBLE FOR 2 PERSONS B&B		9
	MIN £ 11.75	MAX £ 13.75	MIN £ 23.50	MAX £ 27.50		2 OPEN 1-12

Tyddyn Du Farm

Gellilydan, Blaenau Ffestiniog,
Gwynedd, LL41 4RB
Tel: (0766) 85281
Delightful 17th century historic farmhouse on a
working farm in Snowdonia. Just off the A470.
An ideal base for exploring North Wales.
Inglenook in lounge, beams and exposed
stonework throughout. Some en-suite rooms,
private family unit, all with tea/coffee facilities and
TV. Non-smoking areas. Wholesome food. Pet's
area. Within easy reach of many tourist
attractions. Homely welsh atmosphere. Telephone
or SAE for brochures please.

	SINGLE PER PERSON B&B	DOUBLE FOR 2 PERSONS B&B		4
	MIN £ 11.00	MAX £ 14.00	MIN £ 22.00	MAX £ 28.00		3 OPEN 2-11

PWLLHELI Map Ref Ac7

Small resort big in appeal to sailors; 200 craft are moored in its outer Harbour. Promenade, shopping, golf. River and sea fishing. Starcoast World, Pwllheli nearby.

Guest Houses

Ashlea

Pen-y-Bryn, Mynytho, Pwllheli,
Gwynedd LL53 7SE
Tel: (0758) 740110
"Home from home". Friendly welcome assured.
Quiet situation between Pwllheli and Abersoch.
Ideal for beaches, boating, surfing, fishing, bird
watching, touring, walking, pony trekking, or just
to "get away from it all" 2 en-suite, 1 shared
amenities. Colour TV, tea/coffee, heating. Easy
reach of Snowdonia, Caernarfon, Bangor,
Portmeirion, Llandudno, Anglesey etc.

	SINGLE PER PERSON B&B	DOUBLE FOR 2 PERSONS B&B		3
	MIN £	MAX £	MIN £	MAX £ 27.00		2 OPEN 2-10

Ty'n-y-Park Country Guest House

Rhiw, Pwllheli, Gwynedd LL53 8AA
Tel: (075888) 228
18th century ex-farmhouse with wealth of
exposed beams, 16 acres private grounds. All
rooms comfortably furnished with private shower,
toilet, tea/coffee facilities and colour TV. Good
home cooking, home grown produce. Adventure
play area, badminton court, sunbed facilities.
Abundance birds and wild flowers. Popular sailing
and walking. Reduced rates children. Special
winter breaks.

	SINGLE PER PERSON B&B	DOUBLE FOR 2 PERSONS B&B		3
	MIN £ 9.00	MAX £ 12.00	MIN £ 18.00	MAX £ 24.00		3 OPEN 1-12

Farmhouses

Bryn Crin

Pwllheli, Gwynedd, LL53 5UD
Tel: (0758) 612494
One family room, one double room, both with
wash-basins. One room with two single beds.
Sitting room. Farm commands magnificent views
over Snowdonia and Cardigan Bay. Full breakfast.
Within easy reach of safe sandy beaches and
places of historical interest and leisure facilities.
Half a mile from the centre of Pwllheli in secluded
position.

	SINGLE PER PERSON B&B	DOUBLE FOR 2 PERSONS B&B		3
	MIN £ 9.50	MAX £	MIN £ 19.00	MAX £		OPEN 4-10

Gwynfryn Farm Holidays

(B) Pwllheli, Gwynedd, LL53 5UF
Tel: (0758) 612536
Our organic farm is ideally positioned 1¼ miles
from Pwllheli giving easy access to Snowdonia, 3
castles, slate/ copper mines, unrivalled beauty of
Llŷn's heritage coast. The four visitors taken have
their own dining/sitting room, and no time limits.
Playroom, playground for children (reduced rates).
One double and twin both with wash-basins.
Relax, unwind, enjoy peace tranquility.

	SINGLE PER PERSON B&B	DOUBLE FOR 2 PERSONS B&B		2
	MIN £ 20.00	MAX £	MIN £ 24.00	MAX £		OPEN 1-12

Mathan Uchaf Farm

Boduan, Pwllheli, Gwynedd, LL53 8TU
Tel: (0758) 720487
Mathan Uchaf is a family farm with 80 dairy cows
set in open countryside, 1 mile off main road.
Large lawn makes a safe area for children. Guests
can watch milking, feed pigs and calves, collect
eggs. Two friendly dogs who like to play ball, a
shetland pony to ride and play. Double and
family room with wash basins and 1 twin bedded
room. Dining room, lounge with colour TV. A
warm welcome and good farmhouse cooking.

	SINGLE PER PERSON B&B	DOUBLE FOR 2 PERSONS B&B		3
	MIN £ 11.00	MAX £ 14.00	MIN £ 22.00	MAX £ 28.00		OPEN 5-10

Nantcol Welsh Pony Stud

Tyn-y-Mynydd Farm, Boduan, Pwllheli,
Gwynedd LL58 8PZ
Tel: (0758) 720311
Situated midway between Porthmadog and
Abersoch, offering a wealth of beaches, harbours,
coastal walks. Nantcol is a famous Welsh pony
stud, bred from champions. Bed and breakfast
and evening meal available at the farmhouse.
Enquiries to Mrs Gwen Cooke.

	SINGLE PER PERSON B&B	DOUBLE FOR 2 PERSONS B&B		2
	MIN £ 10.00	MAX £	MIN £ 20.00	MAX £		OPEN 1-12

PWLLHELI HARBOUR

SNOWDONIA MOUNTAINS AND COAST RESORTS

The highest peaks in England and Wales are to be found here – not that you'll have to look far for them. Mount Snowdon, the rugged heart of the Snowdonia National Park, dominates the horizon. Roads venture into these mountains only hesitantly. For a really memorable motoring experience, drive through the old slate town of Llanberis then up along the rocky Llanberis Pass, descending along precipitous Nant Gwynant to Beddgelert.

Llanberis, always popular as a base for walkers and climbers, is also a centre of great attractions. Visit the National Slate Museum, Padarn Country Park, Dolbadarn Castle and the "Underground Giant" – Dinorwig Power Station. Or take a ride on the Llanberis Lake Railway or the famous Snowdon Mountain Railway.

Pretty Beddgelert, like everything else in this area, is dwarfed by the ever-present mountains. Even mighty Caernarfon Castle, Wales's most famous fortress, seems subdued by its surroundings. Bangor's Penrhyn Castle is a fabulous re-creation, built by a 19th-century slate baron (take a look at charming Bangor Pier, restored to its original splendour, while you're there). At Blaenau Ffestiniog you can go underground at Llechwedd Slate Caverns and Gloddfa Ganol Slate Mine. And if you want a bird's-eye view of those mountains, then hop on a flight from the new Caernarfon Air Museum.

BANGOR Map Ref Ae3

Compact cathedral city of character overlooking the Menai Strait; gateway to Anglesey and the Ogwen Valley, with university college and 6th century cathedral. Attractions include Theatre Gwynedd, Penrhyn Castle, museum and art gallery and exquisitely renovated pier. Heated swimming pool, yachting and fishing.

Guest Houses

Yr Elen
Bryn, Llandegai, Bangor, Gwynedd, LL57 4LD
Tel: (0248) 364591
B & B, two bedrooms with adjacent bathroom on ground floor. Touring centre for Snowdonia, Anglesey, North Wales coast. TV, teasmade in bedrooms. Own keys.

P / H	SINGLE PER PERSON B&B	DOUBLE FOR 2 PERSONS B&B	🛏	2
	MIN £	MAX £	MIN £	MAX £	
	14.00		20.00	22.00	OPEN 3-10

Farmhouses

Goetre Isaf Farmhouse

Caernarfon Road, Bangor, Gwynedd, LL57 4DB
Tel: (0248) 364541
Superb country situation, magnificent views. Although isolated, only two miles from Bangor's mainline station. Ideal touring centre for the mountains and castles of Snowdonia, Isle of Anglesey and the beaches of the Llŷn Peninsula. Imaginative farmhouse cooking, special diets accommodated, vegetarians welcome. All bedrooms with dial-phone facilities. Stabling by arrangement.

H / P X / 🐕 TW	SINGLE PER PERSON B&B	DOUBLE FOR 2 PERSONS B&B	🛏	3 / 1
	MIN £	MAX £	MIN £	MAX £	
	12.00	14.00	20.00	28.00	OPEN 1-12

Tros y Waen Holiday Farm
Pentir, Bangor, Gwynedd, LL57 4EF
Tel: (0248) 364448
Superbly situated working farm in the heart of Snowdonia, with easy access to lovely beaches and coastal resorts. Children encouraged to participate in daily working of farm. Tea/coffee facilities. TV lounge, good home cooking, clothes washing facilities. 1 shower room, 1 bathroom separate. Radius 7 miles, golf, horse riding, fishing, mountains, shopping centres, beaches, theatre, leisure centre. Open all year.

H X / P / ✕	SINGLE PER PERSON B&B	DOUBLE FOR 2 PERSONS B&B	🛏	4
	MIN £	MAX £	MIN £	MAX £	
	9.50	10.50	19.00	21.00	OPEN 1-12

BEDDGELERT Map Ref Ae6

Village romantically set amid glorious mountain scenery, with Nant Gwynant Valley to the east and rocky Aberglaslyn Pass to the south. Snowdonia's grandeur all around; Wordsworth made a famous dawn ascent of Mount Snowdon from here. Marvellous walks; links with lengendary dog named Gelert.

Guest Houses

Ael-y-Bryn
Caernarfon Road, Beddgelert, Gwynedd, LL55 4YB
Tel: (076686) 310
Ael-y-Bryn is a detached house with beautiful views across the River Colwyn and Moel Hebog Mountain, yet only 3 minutes walk from village centre. All rooms have vanity units, shaver points. Guests own lounge with TV and log fire, mountain climbers/children welcome. Free baby sitting most nights. Good home cooking. Packed lunches available. Vegetarians welcome.

H / P / X	SINGLE PER PERSON B&B	DOUBLE FOR 2 PERSONS B&B	🛏	3
	MIN £	MAX £	MIN £	MAX £	
	12.00		18.00	24.00	OPEN 1-12

Colwyn
Beddgelert, Gwynedd
Tel: (076686) 276
18th century cottage guest house. Warm, cosy and friendly. Beamed lounge, log fire in original stone fireplace. Overlooking river in centre of picturesque village surrounded by mountains. Spectacular scenery, winter and summer. Perfect base for touring Snowdonia's valleys, lakes and forests. Small shops/inns/cafes in village. Central heating. Small bar. "Real" food to prior order. Walkers welcome. Group rates off season.

H / P X / 🐕	SINGLE PER PERSON B&B	DOUBLE FOR 2 PERSONS B&B	🛏	6 / 2
	MIN £	MAX £	MIN £	MAX £	
	10.00	14.00	20.00	28.00	OPEN 1-12

Glan Gwynant Country Guest House
Nantgwynant, Beddgelert, Gwynedd, LL55 4NW
Tel: (076686) 440
Ken and Sylvia Harper welcome you to their comfortable Victorian home, enjoying panoramic views over Lake Gwynant. Peaceful atmosphere (no TV)! Varied menus, residents licence. Bedrooms include H & C, tea/coffee, elegant lounge/log fire. Fishing. Private parking. Ideal base for touring North Wales, both inland and its beautiful coast. Many excellent walks. Children over twelve welcome.

X	SINGLE PER PERSON B&B	DOUBLE FOR 2 PERSONS B&B	🛏	4 / 1
	MIN £	MAX £	MIN £	MAX £	
	11.00		22.00		OPEN 1-12

Plas Colwyn Guest House
Beddgelert, Gwynedd, LL55 4UY
Tel: (076686) 458
Explore the beauty of Snowdonia, then come back to a warm welcome with Lynda and John Osmond. We offer good home cooking, open fires, colour TV lounge and private parking. The bedrooms are cosy, some en-suite. All centrally heated, H & C and refreshment facilities. Vegetarians welcome. We are also licensed and non smoking.

P X / 🐕 / ✕	SINGLE PER PERSON B&B	DOUBLE FOR 2 PERSONS B&B	🛏	6 / 2
	MIN £	MAX £	MIN £	MAX £	
	10.00	13.00	20.00	26.00	OPEN 1-12

BEDDGELERT

BETHESDA Map Ref Ae4

Small town on busy A5, 4 miles from Bangor. Famous for its Penrhyn Quarries, open for visits April-Sept by arrangement. Magnificent scenery of Snowdonia National Park all around.

Farmhouses

Maes Caradog Farm

Nant Ffrancon, Bethesda, Gwynedd, LL57 3DQ
Tel: (0248) 600266
Farmhouse in the Snowdonia National Park, one mile off the A5 between Capel Curig and Bethesda. Ideally placed for walking and climbing. Hot and cold, shaving points in both rooms. Good home cooking. Reduced rates for children. Car Park on forecourt.

P X	SINGLE PER PERSON B&B		DOUBLE FOR 2 PERSONS B&B		🛏	2
	MIN £	MAX £	MIN £	MAX £		
	9.00	10.00	18.00	20.00	OPEN 1-12	

BETWS GARMON Map Ref Ad5

Village 4 miles from Caernarfon. Good centre for pony trekking and walks in Snowdon's foothills. Hafoty house has rock gardens with flowering shrubs and trees beside waterfalls.

Guest Houses

Bryn Gloch Guest House

Betws Garmon, Caernarfon, Gwynedd, LL54 7YY
Tel: (0286) 85216
Converted traditional Welsh farmhouse on fringe of Snowdonia National Park in beautiful Vale of Betws Garmon. 2 miles to Mount Snowdon, 4 miles Caernarfon, 30 minutes drive to Anglesey and Llŷn Peninsula. Colour TV and tea making facilities in all rooms, most with H & C washbasins. Bar and restaurant.

H P X	SINGLE PER PERSON B&B		DOUBLE FOR 2 PERSONS B&B		🛏	3
	MIN £	MAX £	MIN £	MAX £		
	10.50	11.00	20.00	22.00	OPEN 3-9	

BETWS-Y-COED Map Ref Bb6

Wooded village where three rivers meet. Good hotels and guest houses, close to best mountain area of Snowdonia. Tumbling rivers and waterfalls emerge from a tangle of treetops. Trout fishing, craft shops, golf course, railway and motor museum. Nature trails very popular with hikers; Swallow Falls a must.

Hotels

Coed-y-Fron

Vicarage Road, Betws-y-Coed, Gwynedd, LL24 0AD
Tel: (06902) 365
Coed-y-Fron is a lovely Victorian building in the middle of the village. It has a superb outlook over Betws-y-Coed, which is the premier touring centre for Snowdonia. Residents lounge with TV. Dining room. Six bedrooms, 2 en-suite, plus 2 extra bathrooms, all with H & C, central heating, tea and coffee. Fire certificate held.

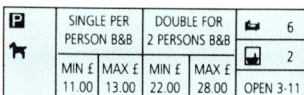

P 🐕	SINGLE PER PERSON B&B		DOUBLE FOR 2 PERSONS B&B		🛏	6
	MIN £	MAX £	MIN £	MAX £		2
	11.00	13.00	22.00	28.00	OPEN 3-11	

Plas Derwen Hotel

Betws-y-Coed, Gwynedd, LL24 0AY
Tel: (06902) 388
Standing alongside the turbulent River Llugwy, the hotel is set in the heart of this renowned picturesque village. Family run, very clean and comfortable accommodation, with excellent value for money licensed restaurant. Colour television, tea and coffee facilities, with heating to all rooms (some en-suite). Children at reduced rates welcome. Free parking. Brochure from resident proprietors Len and Ann Williams.

P 🐕 X	SINGLE PER PERSON B&B		DOUBLE FOR 2 PERSONS B&B		🛏	11
	MIN £	MAX £	MIN £	MAX £		6
			27.00		OPEN 1-12	

Silver Fountain Inn

(A5) Pentrefoelas Road, Betws-y-Coed, Gwynedd, LL24 0HF
Tel: (06902) 341
A friendly inn on A5, 1½ miles east of Betws-y-Coed, open all year. Traditional british breakfast. Good food available every lunch time and evening in bar or restaurant. Family room available with discounts for children. Ample car parking. An ideal base for walking, climbing or exploring beautiful North Wales. Pets by arrangement only.

P 🐕 🍴	SINGLE PER PERSON B&B		DOUBLE FOR 2 PERSONS B&B		🛏	2
	MIN £	MAX £	MIN £	MAX £		
	12.00		24.00		OPEN 1-12	

Guest Houses

Awelon

Plas Isa, Llanrwst, Gwynedd, LL26 0EE
Tel: (0492) 640047
Small family run guest house on the outskirts of Llanrwst 150 yards from A470, 4 miles from Betws-y-Coed. Private parking. Double, family/twin bedrooms, bedside lights, tea makers and central heating. Convenient for touring coast and Snowdonia. Clean, friendly accommodation. Food plentiful. Bed/breakfast, dinner optional. Off season reductions. Pets welcome.

HW X P 🐕	SINGLE PER PERSON B&B		DOUBLE FOR 2 PERSONS B&B		🛏	2
	MIN £	MAX £	MIN £	MAX £		
			18.00		OPEN 3-10	

Bryn Eglwys

Penmachno, Gwynedd, LL24 0TY
Tel: (06903) 424
Old stone house, recently renovated, centre peaceful but lively village, beautiful valley two miles from A5. Double, twin bedrooms, luxury bathroom, central heating, residents' lounge. Display fabric art, patchwork soft furnishings. Traditional English, Wholefood or American-style breakfasts available. Special diets arranged. Excellent centre touring, walking, horse riding, fishing, photography or taking it easy.

H 🍴 P X	SINGLE PER PERSON B&B		DOUBLE FOR 2 PERSONS B&B		🛏	2
	MIN £	MAX £	MIN £	MAX £		
	11.00	14.00	20.00	28.00	OPEN 1-12	

Bryn Glo

Capel Curig, Betws-y-Coed, Gwynedd, LL24 0DT
Tel: (06904) 215
A traditional Welsh cottage, recently refurbished, situated in picturesque location on A5 between Betws-y-Coed and Snowdon. Excellent centre mountain climbing, walking, fishing and touring. All rooms have central heating. Ample car parking space. Home cooked meals and packed lunches available by arrangement. Highly recommended by visitors from overseas as well as U.K.

P X	SINGLE PER PERSON B&B		DOUBLE FOR 2 PERSONS B&B		🛏	2
	MIN £	MAX £	MIN £	MAX £		
	12.00		18.00	24.00	OPEN 1-12	

Bryn Llewelyn

Holyhead Road, Betws-y-Coed, Gwynedd, LL24 0BN
Tel: (06902) 601
Attractive detached house with private parking at rear. Situated on A5 near village centre. Beautiful views of Betws-y-Coed. Friendly, relaxed atmosphere. Forest and lake walks from doorstep. Ideal for hiking, climbing and touring Snowdonia. All rooms are centrally heated and have tea and coffee making facilities. Showers, bath, TV lounge. Open all year.

H P X	SINGLE PER PERSON B&B		DOUBLE FOR 2 PERSONS B&B		🛏	7
	MIN £	MAX £	MIN £	MAX £		1
	9.00	13.00	18.00	26.00	OPEN 1-12	

Craig Dinas Guest House

Dinas Hill, Betws-y-Coed, Gwynedd,
LL24 0HF
Tel: (06902) 254

Charming country house in 4 acres of secluded wooded grounds. Spectacular views of Lledr Valley and forests with mountains beyond. All rooms with tea/coffee making facilities, central heating, colour TV, log fires. Ample parking. Forest walks direct from house. Ideal touring centre. Close to amenities. Fire certificate held.

SINGLE PER PERSON B&B		DOUBLE FOR 2 PERSONS B&B			6
					2
MIN £	MAX £	MIN £	MAX £		
10.00	12.00	20.00	28.00	OPEN 4-9	

Mount Pleasant

Holyhead Road, Betws-y-Coed,
Gwynedd, LL24 0BN
Tel: (06902) 502

Small comfortable guest house ideally situated in the pretty village of Betws-y-Coed. Pretty, cosy bedrooms have colour TV, drinks facilities, heating and wash-basins. All rooms have woodland views. Home cooked evening meals available booked and we are licensed. Vegetarians catered for. Special weekly and group rates, we welcome children of all ages. Car parking available.

SINGLE PER PERSON B&B		DOUBLE FOR 2 PERSONS B&B			5
MIN £	MAX £	MIN £	MAX £		
9.00	14.00	18.00	22.00	OPEN 1-12	

Ty'n-y-Celyn House

Llanrwst Road, Betws-y-Coed,
Gwynedd, LL24 0HD
Tel: (06902) 202

A large Victorian guest house situated in a quiet elevated position in Snowdonia National Park. Beautiful views overlooking the picturesque village of Betws-y-Coed. Ideal touring centre. Nearby golf course. Convenient for fishing, riding, walking. Eight bedrooms, centrally heated, all with colour television, en-suite and tea and coffee making facilities. Licensed. Ample parking.

SINGLE PER PERSON B&B		DOUBLE FOR 2 PERSONS B&B			8
					8
MIN £	MAX £	MIN £	MAX £		
		28.00		OPEN 4-10	

Eirianfa

15-16 Castle Road, Dolwyddelan,
Nr Betws-y-Coed, Gwynedd LL25 0NX
Tel: (06906) 360

Homely guest house in Snowdonia National Park, between Betws-y-Coed and Blaenau Ffestiniog. All rooms remote controlled colour TV, central heating, tea/coffee facilities, laundry/drying service. Ideal for fishing salmon/trout, climbing, horse riding, hiking. Central for touring Snowdonia, coastal resorts, slate mines etc. Double en-suite, twin bedded, family rooms. Evening meals optional. Reduction for children and long stay.

SINGLE PER PERSON B&B		DOUBLE FOR 2 PERSONS B&B			3
					1
MIN £	MAX £	MIN £	MAX £		
9.50	9.50	19.00	25.00	OPEN 1-12	

Pen-y-Banc

Cefn Brith, Cerrigydrudion, Clwyd,
LL21 9TW
Tel: (049082) 479

Situated in the quiet hamlet of Cefn Brith, Pen-y-Banc stands in an elevated setting with beautiful panoramic views over open countryside, within easy reach of main tourist areas of Bala, Snowdonia, Clocaenog Forest and North Wales coast. Open all year. Single, double and family room. Tea and coffee facilities and children welcome. Local fishing, walking, pony trekking etc.

SINGLE PER PERSON B&B		DOUBLE FOR 2 PERSONS B&B			3
MIN £	MAX £	MIN £	MAX £		
9.00	10.00	18.00	20.00	OPEN 1-12	

Farmhouses

Maes Gwyn Farm

Pentrefoelas, Betws-y-Coed, Gwynedd,
LL24 0LR
Tel: (06905) 668

Maes Gwyn is a 17th century farmhouse. Good touring centre for North Wales. Famous Betws-y-Coed only six miles on the edge of Snowdonia National Park, also the woollen mills, slate mines, pony trekking and many other places of interest. One family and one double bedroom. Bathroom with shower, good home cooking.

SINGLE PER PERSON B&B		DOUBLE FOR 2 PERSONS B&B			2
MIN £	MAX £	MIN £	MAX £		
10.00	12.00	20.00	24.00	OPEN 4-11	

The Ferns

Betws-y-Coed, Gwynedd, LL24 0AN
Tel: (06902) 587

Situated in the beautiful Snowdonia National Park. Ideal for walking, climbing, fishing, golf or just relaxing in the scenic countryside. Open all year. Central heated, tea and coffee making facilities in all rooms, double, single, twin and family rooms, en-suite available. Good home cooking, dinner available. We look forward to welcoming you.

SINGLE PER PERSON B&B		DOUBLE FOR 2 PERSONS B&B			9
					3
MIN £	MAX £	MIN £	MAX £		
10.00	14.00	20.00	28.00	OPEN 1-12	

Tan Dinas Guest House

Coedcynhelier Road, Betws-y-Coed,
Gwynedd, LL24 0BL
Tel: (06902) 635

Lovely country Victorian house, delightfully situated in three acres of woodland gardens, offering peace and seclusion yet only 500 yards from village centre and short walk to Swallow Falls. Spacious comfortable, centrally heated rooms, all with H & C, 2 en-suite, tea/coffee facilities. Large car park, splendid views and log fires. Satellite TV. Non smokers only.

SINGLE PER PERSON B&B		DOUBLE FOR 2 PERSONS B&B			6
					2
MIN £	MAX £	MIN £	MAX £		
11.00	14.00	21.00	28.00	OPEN 1-12	

Royal Oak Farmhouse

Betws-y-Coed, Gwynedd, LL24 0AH
Tel: (06902) 427/632

Old water mill set in five acres on a pretty meander of the river Llugwy. Quiet peaceful seclusion but only three minutes walk from village centre. Just two pretty bedrooms, bathroom with shower, TV lounge with open log fire. Fishing available from grounds. Golf course close by.

SINGLE PER PERSON B&B		DOUBLE FOR 2 PERSONS B&B			2
MIN £	MAX £	MIN £	MAX £		
		19.00	20.00	OPEN 4-11	

Ty-Coch Farm & Trekking Centre

Penmachno, Betws-y-Coed,
Gwynedd, LL25 0HJ
Tel: (06903) 248

Situated in Gwydyr forest in heart of Snowdonia National Park. All rooms private bath/shower. Tea making facilities. Central heating. Pony trekking optional. Attractive holiday resort. Betws-y-Coed a short drive away. Very quiet area. Car essential. Good base for touring, walking, golf, fishing, slate mines, castles etc. Excellent meals served. Many recommendations WTB Award.

SINGLE PER PERSON B&B		DOUBLE FOR 2 PERSONS B&B			4
					4
MIN £	MAX £	MIN £	MAX £		
10.50	11.50	21.00	23.00	OPEN 2-11	

Llyspeiran

15 Llwyn Brith, Betws Road, Llanrwst,
Gwynedd LL26 0HH
Tel: (0492) 641673

Enjoy a homely and friendly welcome with home cooking, in a modern bungalow on a small private estate 150 yards from A470. Llanrwst is a market town, ideally situated to explore Snowdonia and its beauty or the seashores. 1 double, 1 twin, bathroom, shower, toilet. Ideal for the disabled. Golf, mountaineering, motoring, walking, fishing. B & B from £9.

SINGLE PER PERSON B&B		DOUBLE FOR 2 PERSONS B&B			2
MIN £	MAX £	MIN £	MAX £		
9.00		18.00		OPEN 1-12	

Tan-y-Cyrau

Betws-y-Coed, Gwynedd, LL24 0BL
Tel: (06902) 653

Peace and quiet and glorious views are what to expect at Tan-y-Cyrau. An elevated unique alpine style house situated on a private forestry road only 5 minutes from village. Superb walks from house. Delightful rooms, two have own wc's. All have colour TV's, heating, wash basins, tea/coffee facilities. Lovely secluded garden. Non smokers only.

SINGLE PER PERSON B&B		DOUBLE FOR 2 PERSONS B&B			3
MIN £	MAX £	MIN £	MAX £		
10.50	13.50	25.00	27.00	OPEN 1-12	

BETWS-Y-COED CONTINUED

Tyddyn Gethin Farm

Penmachno, Betws-y-Coed, Gwynedd, LL24 OPS
Tel: (06903) 392

Always a welcome at Tyddyn Gethin, clean and comfortable, good home cooking, near to Conwy Falls and Woollen Mill, very central for touring. Dining room, sitting room, bathroom, shower, three bedrooms, hot and cold in bedrooms, 200 yards off B4406, 1/2 mile from village Penmachno, 3½ miles from Betws-y-Coed.

P X ☂ ✂	SINGLE PER PERSON B&B		DOUBLE FOR 2 PERSONS B&B		🛏	3
	MIN £	MAX £	MIN £	MAX £		
	10.50	11.50	21.00	23.00	OPEN 1-12	

BLAENAU FFESTINIOG Map Ref Ba7

One-time centre of the Welsh slate industry, now a tourist town with two cavernous slate quarries open to visitors. Narrow-gauge Ffestiniog Railway runs from Porthmadog. Nearby Stwlan Dam, part of hydro-electric scheme, reached through marvellous mountain scenery.

Guest Houses

Afallon

Manod Road, Blaenau Ffestiniog, Gwynedd, LL41 4AE
Tel: (0766) 830468

Situated in Snowdonia National Park, family run guest house with good food, homely clean accommodation. TV, central heating all rooms. Separate shower, toilet, bathroom. Slate mines, narrow gauge railways, castles, walks, fishing, golfing, sandy beaches within easy reach. Dinner by prior arrangement. Dogs by arrangement. Children reduced rates. A Welsh welcome awaits all guests.

H ✂ P X ☂	SINGLE PER PERSON B&B		DOUBLE FOR 2 PERSONS B&B		🛏	3
	MIN £	MAX £	MIN £	MAX £		
	9.00	11.00	18.00	22.00	OPEN 1-12	

Gwynfryn

Gellilydan, Blaenau Ffestiniog, Gwynedd, LL41 4EA
Tel: (076685) 225

Detached house of character in the centre of a quiet village of Gellilydan, lovely scenery. Ideal base for exploring Snowdonia. Plenty of places to visit. One double, one family bedrooms with wash-basins, shaver points, tea/coffee facilities. Full central heating, TV lounge. Dining room with separate tables. Plenty of good food and a homely friendly welcome awaits all guests.

H ✂ P ☂	SINGLE PER PERSON B&B		DOUBLE FOR 2 PERSONS B&B		🛏	2
	MIN £	MAX £	MIN £	MAX £		
	9.50	10.50	19.00	21.00	OPEN 1-12	

Ty'n-y-Coed

Rhiwbryfdir, Blaenau Ffestiniog, Gwynedd, LL41 3HS
Tel: (0766) 830782

Set in its own spacious grounds, Ty'n-y-Coed is privately owned. Situated in the heart of Snowdonia just ten minutes walk from the mountain town of Blaenau Ffestiniog. Good home cooking, choice of menu. H & C all rooms, TV lounge/dining room. 2 singles, family and double with four poster bed. Parking available, warm welcome awaits.

H ✂ P X ☂	SINGLE PER PERSON B&B		DOUBLE FOR 2 PERSONS B&B		🛏	4
	MIN £	MAX £	MIN £	MAX £		
	10.50	13.50	21.00	27.00	OPEN 1-12	

CAERNARFON Map Ref Ad4

Dominated by magnificent 13th century castle, most famous of Wales's medieval fortresses. Segontium Roman Fort and Museum. Popular sailing, old harbour, market square, Lloyd George statue. Holiday centre at gateway of Snowdonia.

Hotels

Gorffwysfa Hotel

St David's Road, Caernarfon, Gwynedd, LL55 1BH
Tel: (0286) 2647

Former Victorian rectory situated in superior residential area. Magnificent views Menai Straits and Anglesey. En-suite rooms, tea/coffee facilities, radio, colour TV, lounge, bar facilities. Pool, games etc. Special rates for children. Infants free. Wide choice of menu. Large breakfast. Special breaks available. Ideal activity/touring centre for Snowdonia/Llŷn/Anglesey. Parking on site.

H ✂ P X ☂	SINGLE PER PERSON B&B		DOUBLE FOR 2 PERSONS B&B		🛏	7
						4
	MIN £	MAX £	MIN £	MAX £		
	13.00	14.00	21.00	28.00	OPEN 1-12	

Menai Bank Hotel

North Road, Caernarfon, Gwynedd, LL55 1BD
Tel: (0286) 673297

Family run AA* and RAC*. Easy walking distance town centre and Castle. Extensive views over Menai Strait to Anglesey. Clean comfortable bedrooms with tea/coffee facilities. Colour TV, en-suite rooms available, restaurant, bar food, well stocked bar, lounge, pool table, pay phone. Hotel car park. Bargain breaks, early and late season. Ring now for colour brochure/tariff.

P ☂ X	SINGLE PER PERSON B&B		DOUBLE FOR 2 PERSONS B&B		🛏	15
						9
	MIN £	MAX £	MIN £	MAX £		
	14.00		24.00		OPEN 1-11	

Menai View Hotel

North Road, Caernarfon, Gwynedd, LL55 1BD
Tel: (0286) 4602

Small private hotel overlooking beautiful Menai Strait, close to town centre, harbour and castle. Central for Llŷn beaches, Anglesey and Snowdonia Mountain. Family rooms. All rooms with colour TV, tea/coffee, central heating, some with sea view. Licensed restaurant. Lounge bar. Menu and wine list available. Reduced rates for 3 or more nights. Fire certificate.

☂ X	SINGLE PER PERSON B&B		DOUBLE FOR 2 PERSONS B&B		🛏	6
	MIN £	MAX £	MIN £	MAX £		
	11.00	14.00	22.00	28.00	OPEN 1-12	

Guest Houses

Caer Siddi

Llanddeiniolen, Caernarfon, Gwynedd, LL55 3AD
Tel: (0248) 670462

Georgian vicarage peaceful rural setting surrounded by trees, glorious views to Snowdon, Caernarfon Bay and the Rivals. Ideally located for Gwynedd attractions, 4 miles to Caernarfon. Fully modernised, warm, spacious accommodation. Colour TV lounge. Childrens price reductions. Farmhouse breakfast, 3 course evening meals, home cooking and baking. Tea making facilities. Fire certificate. WTB Farmhouse and GH Award.

H X P ☂	SINGLE PER PERSON B&B		DOUBLE FOR 2 PERSONS B&B		🛏	2
	MIN £	MAX £	MIN £	MAX £		
	11.00	11.00	22.00	22.00	OPEN 1-12	

Chatham Farmhouse

Llandwrog, Caernarfon,
Gwynedd, LL54 5TG
Tel: (0286) 831257

Croeso, welcome to our peaceful guest house. Relax amid the glorious scenery of Snowdonia and its coastline. Enjoy our free range eggs and home made bread during a lazy breakfast, home grown, organic vegetables as part of wholesome meals. Kettles, wash basins in comfortable, pretty bedrooms. Perfect touring base, beach three miles, good bird watching area.

	SINGLE PER PERSON B&B	DOUBLE FOR 2 PERSONS B&B		3
	MIN £	MAX £	MIN £	MAX £	
	10.00	12.00	20.00	24.00	OPEN 4-10

Dingle Nook

Dinas Dinlle, Llandwrog,
Caernarfon,
Gwynedd LL54 5TW
Tel: (0286) 830457

All accommodation at ground level. Facilities include hot and cold water, shaver points, tea/coffee facilities in all rooms. Separate lounge. Parking facilities. Beach within short walking distance. Ideally situated for Caernarfon, Snowdonia.

	SINGLE PER PERSON B&B	DOUBLE FOR 2 PERSONS B&B		3
	MIN £	MAX £	MIN £	MAX £	
	10.00	14.00	20.00	28.00	OPEN 3-10

Gwynant

Stryd Ganol, Saron, Bethel,
Nr Caernarfon, Gwynedd   LL55 1YP
Tel: (0248) 670029

Gwynant in the village of Bethel is beautifully placed as a base from which to enjoy a holiday in Snowdonia, Anglesey and North West Wales. Comfortable accommodation, 2 bedrooms with bathroom en-suite. Adequate parking facilities. Walking climbing, sailing, canoeing, windsurfing, fishing, birdwatching, castles, museums, craft centres, horse riding all within reasonable distance.

	SINGLE PER PERSON B&B	DOUBLE FOR 2 PERSONS B&B		4
	MIN £	MAX £	MIN £	MAX £	2
	10.00	14.00	24.00	28.00	OPEN 1-12

Marianfa

St David's Road, Caernarfon, Gwynedd,
LL55 1EL
Tel: (0286) 5589

Marianfa is a Victorian guest house of character situated five minutes from the town centre. Caernarfon is an ideal place to drive from for touring North Wales, inland and coastal. All rooms have hot and cold. Colour television and tea and coffee facilities. Double, twin and family rooms with reduced rates for children. Why not try us!

	SINGLE PER PERSON B&B	DOUBLE FOR 2 PERSONS B&B		5
	MIN £	MAX £	MIN £	MAX £	
			20.00	22.00	OPEN 1-12

Meirion Guest House

Victoria Road, Caernarfon, Gwynedd,
LL55 2RH
Tel: (0286) 3470

Situated on hill overlooking town and Menai Straits. Central for touring Snowdonia, Llŷn Peninsula and Anglesey. Open all year. Shaver points in bedrooms. Shower in bathroom. Single, double and family rooms available with special rates for children. Cot and high chair available. Hot and cold in single. Television lounge. Dogs by arrangement.

	SINGLE PER PERSON B&B	DOUBLE FOR 2 PERSONS B&B		3
	MIN £	MAX £	MIN £	MAX £	
	10.00	10.00	17.00	18.00	OPEN 1-12

Swn-y-Fenai

8 Church Street, Caernarfon, Gwynedd,
LL55 1SW
Tel: (0286) 2633

Small family guest house. Situated within town walls in a quiet street. Adjacent to castle and promenade. Tastefully decorated throughout. All bedrooms, TV, H & C, tea/coffee making facilities. Family room with special rates for children. Bathroom with shower. Separate shower and toilet. All amenities, public car park and bus station. Central for many tourist attractions.

	SINGLE PER PERSON B&B	DOUBLE FOR 2 PERSONS B&B		4
	MIN £	MAX £	MIN £	MAX £	
	8.50	10.00	17.00	20.00	OPEN 1-12

Tal Menai Guest House

Bangor Road, Caernarfon, Gwynedd,
LL55 1TP
Tel: (0286) 2160

In its own grounds on A487 to Bangor, wide views over Menai Strait and Anglesey. Central heating. Hot and Cold in bedrooms. Bathroom with shower. Tea/coffee making facilities. One twin en-suite. Evening meals on request, vegetarian and special diets catered for. Non smoking TV lounge and dining room. Reduction for children, weekly bookings and senior citizens. No pets. French/Welsh spoken.

	SINGLE PER PERSON B&B	DOUBLE FOR 2 PERSONS B&B		5
	MIN £	MAX £	MIN £	MAX £	1
	12.00	12.50	22.00	24.00	OPEN 1-11

Ty'n Llwyn Cottage

Llanllyfni, Caernarfon,
LL54 6RP
Tel: (0286) 881526

Situated on a quiet country road, half mile off the A487 Caernarfon to Porthmadog road. Beautiful Welsh stone cottage with attractive garden. Good home cooked food, large dining room with open fire, lounge with colour TV. Two en-suite bedrooms, one ground floor, other two with wash basins and shaver points, all rooms with heating.

	SINGLE PER PERSON B&B	DOUBLE FOR 2 PERSONS B&B		4
	MIN £	MAX £	MIN £	MAX £	2
	11.00	14.00	22.00	28.00	OPEN 3-11

Wallasea Guest House

21 Segontium Terrace, Caernarfon,
Gwynedd, LL55 2PH
Tel: (0286) 3564

RAC listed. Georgian terrace house circa 1828. 2 minutes walk town centre. Overlooking River Seiont, castle and Menai Strait. Cot, high chair available. Colour TV lounge. Fire certificate, tea/coffee facilities in bedrooms optional. Ideal base for touring Snowdonia, Llŷn Peninsula, Anglesey. Fully modernised throughout. Shower room. All bedrooms centrally heated, shaver points. B & B from £10 per person.

	SINGLE PER PERSON B&B	DOUBLE FOR 2 PERSONS B&B		4
	MIN £	MAX £	MIN £	MAX £	
	12.00	12.00	20.00	22.00	OPEN 1-12

The Welsh Kitchen

St. David's Road, Caernarfon, Gwynedd,
LL55 1BH
Tel: (0286) 2012

The Cook's Welsh so the food's great! Freshly prepared tasty meals, home-baked bread and delicious desserts. Pretty bedrooms with colour TV, tea/coffee making facilities, one room en-suite, with open log and coal fire plus fixed heating. Situated ¼ mile from Caernarfon Castle in quiet road, and 8 miles outside Snowdonia National Park. Little ones welcome!

	SINGLE PER PERSON B&B	DOUBLE FOR 2 PERSONS B&B		3
	MIN £	MAX £	MIN £	MAX £	1
	12.50	12.50	25.00	25.00	OPEN 4-10

The White House

Llanfaglan, Caernarfon,
Gwynedd, LL54 5RA
Tel: (0286) 673003

A large detached house in its own grounds overlooking the sea and Snowdonia. We have 2 bedrooms with private facilities at indicated prices plus 3 en-suite rooms. All have tea making facilities and colour television. Guests may use the lounge, swimming pool and gardens. Ideally situated for ornithologists, walking, windsurfing, golf and Welsh castles.

	SINGLE PER PERSON B&B	DOUBLE FOR 2 PERSONS B&B		5
	MIN £	MAX £	MIN £	MAX £	3
	14.00	14.00	28.00	28.00	OPEN 1-12

Farmhouses

Bron Rhiw

Lôn-y-Buarth, Fron, Caernarfon,
Gwynedd LL54 7RB
Tel: (0286) 880069

Self contained 18th century stone cottage completely detached from main cottage, but all set within 2 acre smallholding in peaceful countryside overlooking panoramic views of Caernarfon Bay and Anglesey. Cottage has all mod cons and can be used in compelte privacy. Full breakfast with freshly laid eggs brought to your cottage each morning.

	SINGLE PER PERSON B&B	DOUBLE FOR 2 PERSONS B&B		1
	MIN £	MAX £	MIN £	MAX £	1
	12.50	12.50	25.00	25.00	OPEN 1-12

CAERNARFON CONTINUED

Farmhouses

Cae Mawr Farm

Bontnewydd, Caernarfon, Gwynedd, LL54 7YE
Tel: (0286) 830520

Stone farmhouse three miles from Caernarfon, set in beautiful peaceful countryside, with unspoilt woodland, adjoining good trout river. Two lounges, colour television, separate dining room and tables with tea making facilities. Two bathrooms, central heating, log fires. Wholesome home cooking. Homely atmosphere and a warm welcome assured. Central for many tourist attractions. Reductions for children.

	SINGLE PER PERSON B&B		DOUBLE FOR 2 PERSONS B&B			3
	MIN £	MAX £	MIN £	MAX £		
	10.00	12.00	20.00	24.00		OPEN 1-12

Pantiau Farm

Rhosgadfan, Caernarfon, Gwynedd, LL54 7LD
Tel: (0286) 830002

All rooms en-suite with central heating, TV, tea facilities, radio/clock. We are a small mountain farm 4 miles from Caernarfon. We offer peace and tranquility of the mountains yet easy access to the natural beauties and commercial attractions North Wales has to offer. Home baking a speciality. "Small but beautiful". Kennels available by arrangement

	SINGLE PER PERSON B&B		DOUBLE FOR 2 PERSONS B&B			3
						3
	MIN £	MAX £	MIN £	MAX £		
	12.00	14.00	22.00	24.00		OPEN 2-11

Pengwern

Saron, Llanwnda, Caernarfon, Gwynedd, LL54 5UH
Tel: (0286) 830717

Charming spacious farmhouse of character set in 130 acres of land, beautifully situated between mountains and sea. Well appointed bedrooms all with en-suite or private bathrooms. The land runs down to Foryd Bay and is noted for its bird life. Situated 3 miles from Dinas Dinlle beach. Jane - Mrs Jones' daughter has a cookery diploma and provides all the excellent meals. Wales Tourist Board Farmhouse Award.

	SINGLE PER PERSON B&B		DOUBLE FOR 2 PERSONS B&B			3
						2
	MIN £	MAX £	MIN £	MAX £		
	14.00	14.00	24.00	28.00		OPEN 3-10

Rhyddallt Ganol Farm

Caeathro, Caernarfon, Gwynedd, LL55 2TH
Tel: (0286) 2085

Caernarfon 2½ miles. A warm welcome awaits you at Rhyddallt Ganol amidst the peace and quietness of a beautiful garden. 2 double, 1 twin room available. Hot and cold all rooms, evening meal optional.

	SINGLE PER PERSON B&B		DOUBLE FOR 2 PERSONS B&B			3
	MIN £	MAX £	MIN £	MAX £		
	9.00		18.00			OPEN 4-12

Tyddyn Perthi Farm

Tan-y-Maes, Portdinorwic, Gwynedd, LL56 4UQ
Tel: (0248) 670336

A working dairy farm where guests will find a warm welcome, very comfortable accommodation and excellent meals. "A Taste of Wales" member". Situated just off A487 between the historic town of Caernarfon and university city of Bangor, makes this farmhouse and ideal base to explore the numerous delights of this beautiful area. Contact Mrs Barbara Lewis.

	SINGLE PER PERSON B&B		DOUBLE FOR 2 PERSONS B&B			2
	MIN £	MAX £	MIN £	MAX £		
	13.50	14.00	27.00	28.00		OPEN 3-10

Tŷ Mawr Farmhouse

Saron, Llanwnda, Caernarfon, Gwynedd LL54 5UH
Tel: (0286) 830091

Outstanding farmhouse of great character dating from 1600's with modern civilised comforts. Three pretty bedrooms, each with en-suite bathroom or shower room, superb views, period furniture, centrally heated, richly carpeted. Delicious breakfasts, traditional British or wholefoods, vegetarians welcomed. Tranquil, sunny position, easy to find, good tarmac access, ample parking. Close to Caernarfon and unspoilt coastline.

	SINGLE PER PERSON B&B		DOUBLE FOR 2 PERSONS B&B			3
						3
	MIN £	MAX £	MIN £	MAX £		
			24.00	28.00		OPEN 1-12

CAPEL CURIG
Map Ref Ba6

Village ringed by Snowdon's mountains, with accommodation and craft shops. Great favourite with climbers. Good walking and fishing.

Guest Houses

Llugwy Guest House

Capel Curig, Nr Betws-y-Coed, Gwynedd, LL24 OES
Tel: (06904) 218

Located in centre of village five miles from Snowdon. Ideal for walking, climbing, fishing, boating, beaches, small trains, castles, artificial ski slope. Two public lounges, one with TV. Beamed dining room. Drying room, central heating and wonderful mountain views from each bedroom. A warm welcome for everyone. Small parties specially catered for.

	SINGLE PER PERSON B&B		DOUBLE FOR 2 PERSONS B&B			6
	MIN £	MAX £	MIN £	MAX £		
	11.00	12.00	20.00	22.00		OPEN 1-12

LLAN FFESTINIOG
Map Ref Ba7

The village stands on a high bluff looking towards the sea, neighbour of Blaenau Ffestiniog, once slate capital of the world. Explore underground slate caverns or ride the Ffestiniog Narrow Gauge Railway.

Guest Houses

Pen y Banc

27 Ty'n-y-Maes, Llan Ffestiniog, Gwynedd, LL41 4NW
Tel: (0766 76) 2474

Good village bed and breakfast in sylvan surroundings, overlooking the beautiful Vale of Ffestiniog, with its famous litte railway. Comfortable and ample. Tea/coffee making facilities. TV. Meals by arrangement. Great scenery, lakes, waterfalls, mountains, long sandy beaches, Harlech Castle and Portmeirion nearby. Ideal photography, fishing, walking and bird watching. Only problem, too much choice.

	SINGLE PER PERSON B&B		DOUBLE FOR 2 PERSONS B&B			2
	MIN £	MAX £	MIN £	MAX £		
	14.00	14.00	24.00	24.00		OPEN 1-12

LLANBERIS
Map Ref Ae4

Popular centre for walkers and climbers; least difficult (3½ miles) walk to Snowdon summit starts here. For easy ride up take Snowdon Mountain Railway. Also Llanberis Lake Railway, slate industry museum, Oriel Eryri interpretive centre and Padarn Country Park.

Hotels

Alpine Lodge Hotel

1 High Street, Llanberis, Caernarfon, Gwynedd LL55 4EN
Tel: (0286) 870294

A lovely little country house style hotel recommended by Les Routiers in the Guide to Britain. Alpine Lodge is situated at the quieter Caernarfon end of Llanberis with views of the lake and mountains. The bar and restaurant, open to residents only, provides a wide choice of food and wines. Large private car park.

	SINGLE PER PERSON B&B		DOUBLE FOR 2 PERSONS B&B			8
	MIN £	MAX £	MIN £	MAX £		
	11.00	13.00	22.00	26.00		OPEN 1-12

Dolafon Hotel

High Street, Llanberis, Gwynedd,
LL55 4SU
Tel: (0286) 870993

Pleasant family hotel in its own grounds. Close by foot route to Snowdon. Four en-suites two family rooms with colour TV, tea/coffee facilities all rooms. Comfortable lounge, residents bar, open all year. Rambling, climbing, groups welcome. An ideal base for touring or exploring our lakes and local amenities including lakeside and mountain railway. Canoe hire.

	SINGLE PER PERSON B&B	DOUBLE FOR 2 PERSONS B&B		9
	MIN £ / MAX £ 10.50 / 11.00	MIN £ / MAX £ 21.00 / 26.00		4 OPEN 1-12

Glyn Afon Hotel

High Street, Llanberis, Gwynedd,
LL55 4HA
Tel: (0286) 872528

At the foot of Mount Snowdon. Only 10 minutes walk from Snowdon Mountain railway. A Two Crown family run hotel with a high standard of service, complimented with a hearty breakfast at realistic prices. Vegetarians welcome. All bedrooms fully central heated with hot/cold, colour television and tea/coffee making facilities. Off street car park. Dogs by arrangement.

	SINGLE PER PERSON B&B	DOUBLE FOR 2 PERSONS B&B		8
	MIN £ / MAX £ 10.50 / 12.50	MIN £ / MAX £ 21.00 / 25.00		OPEN 1-12

Mount Pleasant Hotel

High Street, Llanberis, Gwynedd,
LL55 4HA
Tel: (0286) 870395

Friendly family run hotel in Snowdonia. Ideal for walking, climbing and touring North Wales. Single, double, twin and family rooms, hot and cold, tea/coffee making facilities, most with private shower, en-suite available. Central heating. Separate dining room, TV lounge and well stocked bar. Evening meals, bar snacks and à la carte menu. Special rates for children and parties.

	SINGLE PER PERSON B&B	DOUBLE FOR 2 PERSONS B&B		7
	MIN £ / MAX £ 11.00 / 14.00	MIN £ / MAX £ 22.00 / 28.00		1 OPEN 1-12

Guest Houses

Hafod y Gwynt Guest House

Nant Gwynant, Caernarfon, Gwynedd,
LL55 4NS
Tel: (0286) 871057

Situated in the heart of Snowdonia, next door to famous Climbing Inn, one mile from start of Pyg and Miners track up Snowdon. Fly fishing in own lake. One family room en-suite, log fire, central heting, TV room, good home cooking, guided walks and climbing by arrangement. Fantastic views.

	SINGLE PER PERSON B&B	DOUBLE FOR 2 PERSONS B&B		3
	MIN £ / MAX £ 10.50 / 11.50	MIN £ / MAX £ 21.00 / 23.00		1 OPEN 1-12

Lakeside

Llanrug, Caernarfon, Gwynedd,
LL55 4ED L
Tel: (0286) 870065

A magnificent country home set in six acres of beautiful gardens and woodlands on the shores of a private lake shared only with peacocks and pheasants. The accommodation is to an exceptionally high standard and within its setting perhaps makes it one of the finest in Snowdonia. Accommodation for disabled available. Telephone for brochure.

	SINGLE PER PERSON B&B	DOUBLE FOR 2 PERSONS B&B		3
	MIN £ / MAX £ 14.00	MIN £ / MAX £ 28.00 / 28.00		OPEN 1-12

LLANFAIRFECHAN
Map Ref Ba4

Quiet resort offering hill walking, pony trekking, mountain scenery, yachting, fishing. Safe swimming. Fine views across bay to Puffin Island and Anglesey; golf course.

Guest Houses

The Towers

Promenade, Llanfairfechan, Gwynedd,
LL33 0DA L
Tel: (0248) 680012

Magnificent old manor house standing in its own private lawned grounds on the sea front below the slopes of Snowdonia. Superb views of Anglesey and Menai Strait. Ideally situated for castles, Snowdonia, golf, fishing and touring. Climbing guides available. Large private car park. All rooms with private en-suite facilities. Superb lounge with colour TV.

	SINGLE PER PERSON B&B	DOUBLE FOR 2 PERSONS B&B		3
	MIN £ / MAX £ 14.00 / 14.00	MIN £ / MAX £ 20.00 / 28.00		3 OPEN 1-12

LLANRWST Map Ref Bb6

Attractive town where crystal-clear river rolls through lush meadows; chief shopping centre of Upper Conwy Valley. Handsome bridge designed by Indigo Jones in 1636. Gwydir Park has bowling, putting and children's playground. Good range of accommodation. Bodnant Garden 8 miles away.

Hotels

Corn-u-Copia Hotel

Bridge Street, Llanrwst, Gwynedd,
LL26 0ET L
Tel: (0492) 640275

Corn-u-Copia originally a 16th century post house, now converted to a comfortable family hotel is surrounded by the beauty of Conwy Valley. Whilst the market town of Llanrwst steeped in history offers immense interest for tourists. Llanrwst is central to all of Snowdonia and the coast. New for 1990, all rooms en-suite, centrally heated.

	SINGLE PER PERSON B&B	DOUBLE FOR 2 PERSONS B&B		10
	MIN £ / MAX £ 10.50 / 14.00	MIN £ / MAX £ 21.00 / 28.00		4 OPEN 1-12

Guest Houses

The White Cottage

Maenan, Llanrwst, Gwynedd, LL26 0UL
Tel: (0492) 640346

Situated in the beautiful Conwy Valley, 2 miles north of Llanrwst (A470). All bedrooms have open views. Hot and cold and central heating. Ample parking. Colour TV, bathroom with shower. Stroll in country or woodland or relax in lovely garden. Good home cooking and warm welcome from Kathleen and Tony Isherwood.

	SINGLE PER PERSON B&B	DOUBLE FOR 2 PERSONS B&B		3
	MIN £ / MAX £ 20.00	MIN £ / MAX £ 20.00		OPEN 1-12

WALES *It's magic*

SNOWDON AND LLYNNAU MYMBYR

LLANRWST CONTINUED
Farmhouses

Maes-y-Garnedd

Capel Garmon, Llanrwst, Gwynedd,
LL26 ORR
Tel: (06902) 428
140 acre mixed farm situated in Capel Garmon (2 miles off A5). Beautiful scenery and excellent walks. An ideal centre for touring Snowdonia and within easy reach of beaches. One double and one family bedroom. S.A.E. for brochure. AA listed. Children welcome. A warm and friendly welcome awaits you. Washbasins in bedrooms. Evening meal optional.

H P ✕	SINGLE PER PERSON B&B		DOUBLE FOR 2 PERSONS B&B		🛏	2
	MIN £	MAX £	MIN £	MAX £	OPEN 4-10	
	11.00	12.00	20.00	24.00		

Pennant Farm

Melin-y-Coed, Llanrwst, Gwynedd,
LL26 OTR
Tel: (0492) 640529
Pennant is a lovely old farmhouse, situated on the side of the beautiful Conwy Valley, above the historic town of Llanrwst, 4 miles north of Betws-y-Coed. Spectacular views of the Eryri mountains, including Snowdon. Parking, TV lounge. Baby intercom service. Cot available on request. Bathroom and separate shower-room. Send SAE for further information.

H ✕ P ✕ 🐕	SINGLE PER PERSON B&B		DOUBLE FOR 2 PERSONS B&B		🛏	3
	MIN £	MAX £	MIN £	MAX £	OPEN 1-12	
	10.00	12.00	18.00	22.00		

PENMAENMAWR   Map Ref Ba4

Small coast resort below mighty headland which posed immense challenges to road and rail engineers. Sailing, water skiing, safe swimming, golf. On edge of Snowdonia National Park.

Guest Houses

Cynlas

Fernbrook Road, Penmaenmawr,
Gwynedd, LL34 6ED
Tel: (04929) 623491
Central Res: (0492) 530478
Welcome to Cynlas. Comfortable accommodation. All rooms have wash hand basins, shaving points, free tea/coffee facilities. Reduced rates children sharing parents room. Colour TV lounge. Cleanliness, friendliness and good food assured. Enclosed parking, gardens. Sea and mountain views. Beautiful new promenade, lovely safe bathing, beach ideal for children, free buckets and spades for children. An ideal base for all North Wales.

H ✕ P ✕	SINGLE PER PERSON B&B		DOUBLE FOR 2 PERSONS B&B		🛏	3
	MIN £	MAX £	MIN £	MAX £	OPEN 3-9	
	9.50	10.00	18.00	20.00		

TREFRIW   Map Ref Bb5

Woollen mill village on west side of Conwy Valley, with Trefriw Wells Spa. Lakes at Llyn Crafnant and Llyn Geirionnydd, both local beauty spots. Good walking country.

Guest Houses

Crafnant Guest House

Trefriw, Llanrwst, Gwynedd, LL27 0JH
Tel: (0492) 640809
Charming, family run Victorian guest house in beautiful Conwy Valley, Snowdonia. In picturesque village of Trefriw, famous for Woollen Mill, Roman Spa Waters and Lakes. Non-smoking, traditional and vegetarian breakfast, private parking, drying facilities, central heating. All bedrooms hot and cold, TV, hair dryer, tea/coffee, shaver point. Some en-suite. Reduced rates for children.

H ✕ P ✕	SINGLE PER PERSON B&B		DOUBLE FOR 2 PERSONS B&B		🛏	6
					🚿	2
	MIN £	MAX £	MIN £	MAX £	OPEN 1-12	
	11.00	13.50	22.00	27.00		

Llys Caradog Guest House

Trefriw, Gwynedd, LL27 0RQ
Tel: (0492) 640919
A friendly welcome awaits you in our large stone built guest house and tea room. Mountains, lakes, rivers, coast all within easy reach. Central heating, coal fires, showers, drying room, TV lounge. Home cooking. Family, twin bedded or bunk rooms available. Small groups welcome, (walkers, schools, special needs etc).

P ✕ 🐕	SINGLE PER PERSON B&B		DOUBLE FOR 2 PERSONS B&B		🛏	4
					🚿	2
	MIN £	MAX £	MIN £	MAX £	OPEN 1-12	
	7.00	9.00	14.00	18.00		

SYCHNANT PASS

42

CLWYD COUNTRYSIDE AND HERITAGE

Clwyd's green hills and vales are steeped in history. Ruthin is renowned for its medieval buildings (not to mention its medieval banquets). The shell of a spectacularly located castle guards Llangollen, the pretty riverside home of the International Musical Eisteddfod, held each July. Denbigh still has reminders of its days as a fortress town, while Holywell's name comes from its ancient well, one of the traditional 'Seven Wonders of Wales'.

Bodelwyddan Castle, winner of the 'Museum of the Year' award in 1989, is home to a superb collection of 19th-century works of art from the National Portrait Gallery. Erddig Hall, near Wrexham, is the National Trust's supreme example of 'upstairs, downstairs' living. Clwyd's wealth of history and heritage spreads itself across a lovely landscape. Take time off to explore the Clwydian Hills, the heather-covered Hiraethog moorlands and the undiscovered Berwyn Mountains.

CORWEN   Map Ref Be7

Pleasant market town in Vale of Edeyrnion. Liverstock mart held regularly. Fishing in river Dee, swimming pool, good walks.

Hotels

Corwen Court Private Hotel

London Road, Corwen, Clwyd, LL21 0DP
Tel: (0490) 2854
Situated on the A5. Converted old police station and courthouse. Six prisoners' cells now single bedrooms. Hot and cold in each. Double bedrooms have bathroom en-suite. Lounge with colour TV and dining room with separate tables where Magistrates once presided. Centrally heated. Fire certificate. AA listed. Convenient base for touring North Wales.

P	SINGLE PER PERSON B&B		DOUBLE FOR 2 PERSONS B&B		🛏	10
🐕	MIN £	MAX £	MIN £	MAX £	🍽	4
X	11.00	12.00	22.00	24.00	OPEN 3-12	

Guest Houses

Pen-y-Bont Fawr

Cynwyd, Corwen, Clwyd, LL21 0ET
Tel: (0490) 2226
Comfortable centrally heated guest house set amidst beautiful unspoilt countryside, away from the crowds, yet convenient to the A5. A good base from which to explore North and Mid Wales, or just to relax. Delicious freshly prepared meals, wholefood or vegetarian. Guided walking or cycling holidays arranged. Please send for our brochure.

H X	SINGLE PER PERSON B&B		DOUBLE FOR 2 PERSONS B&B		🛏	5
P	MIN £	MAX £	MIN £	MAX £	🍽	
✁	13.00		24.00		OPEN 1-12	

Tyn Llidiart

Carrog Road, Corwen, Clwyd, LL21 9RS
Tel: (0490) 2729
Welcome to Tyn Llidiart a country house set in the Dee Valley, by the River Dee and overlooking the Berwyn Mountains. Rooms are en-suite with colour TV, tea/coffee making facilities, also hairdriers and complimentary shampoos. We are a very central base for the coast and countryside. All our rooms are very tastefully furnished.

P	SINGLE PER PERSON B&B		DOUBLE FOR 2 PERSONS B&B		🛏	2
🐕	MIN £	MAX £	MIN £	MAX £	🍽	2
	12.00	12.00	24.00	24.00	OPEN 3-10	

Farmhouses

Cae Crwn Farm

Bryneglwys, Corwen, Clwyd, LL21 9NF
Tel: (049085) 243   L
Pleasantly situated with beautiful views. Two attractive bedrooms, one with vanitory unit. Both having radios, tea/ coffee facilities. Guests sitting room with TV. Separate dining room. Ducks goats and ponies to interest the children. Scenic carriage drives and pony rides, Llangollen, Ruthin, Bala and coast within easy reach. SAE for brochure.

P	SINGLE PER PERSON B&B		DOUBLE FOR 2 PERSONS B&B		🛏	2
🐕	MIN £	MAX £	MIN £	MAX £	🍽	
X	8.50	9.50	17.00	19.00	OPEN 1-12	

DENBIGH   Map Ref Be5

Castled town in Vale of Clwyd, with much historic interest. Pony trekking, riding, fishing, golf, tennis and bowls. Indoor heated swimming pool. Centrally located for enjoying the rolling hills of Clwyd - a rich farming area full of small, attractive villages.

Hotels

Saracens Head Hotel

Llansannan, Clwyd, LL16 5HH
Tel: (074577) 212
Set in beautiful surroundings yet within easy reach of the North Wales coast and Snowdonia. Comfortable bedrooms with H & C, shaver points and tea making facilities. Residents lounge with colour TV, 20 cover restaurant, bar snacks available at all times. Breaks for fishing, shooting, riding and sailing arranged through the hotel. Real fires, real ale.

H X	SINGLE PER PERSON B&B		DOUBLE FOR 2 PERSONS B&B		🛏	6
P	MIN £	MAX £	MIN £	MAX £	🍽	
🐕	14.00	14.00	28.00	28.00	OPEN 1-12	

Guest Houses

Cayo Guest House

74 Vale Street, Denbigh, Clwyd, LL16 2BW
Tel: (07457) 2686
Excellent position for touring coast, Snowdonia or walk on the Berwyns and Offa's Dyke. Golf courses and excellent fishing nearby. TV lounge, central heating, family rooms, food bought fresh daily. Farmhouse butter and meats served. Licensed.

H	SINGLE PER PERSON B&B		DOUBLE FOR 2 PERSONS B&B		🛏	5
🐕	MIN £	MAX £	MIN £	MAX £	🍽	
X	11.00		22.00		OPEN 1-12	

Farmhouses

College Farm

Peniel, Denbigh, Clwyd, LL16 4TT
Tel: (074570) 276
Mixed farm in peaceful surroundings 2½ miles Denbigh just off B4501. Bedrooms have wash basins. Good centre for touring North Wales. Sailing, fishing, walking nearby. Families welcome. Good home cooking with vegetables from our organic garden and free range eggs. You are assured of a warm welcome by the bilingual Parry family. Farmhouse Award.

H ✁	SINGLE PER PERSON B&B		DOUBLE FOR 2 PERSONS B&B		🛏	2
P X	MIN £	MAX £	MIN £	MAX £	🍽	
🐕	10.00	11.00	20.00	22.00	OPEN 4-11	

FLINT   Map Ref Cb4

Town on Dee Estuary with oldest charter in Wales (1284) and Shakesperian connections: its castle is mentioned in "Richard 11"

Farmhouses

Oakenholt Farm

Chester Road, Flint, Clwyd, CH6 5SU
Tel: (03526) 3264
Comfortable homely fifteenth century Welsh farmhouse on working sheep and dairy farm. Lovely location ideal for touring North Wales, Chester. Two double, one twin, hot and cold, tea coffee. Central heating, beamed TV lounge, guest bathroom. Children welcome, safe play area and lovely garden. Come and see the cows being milked and other seasonal jobs. No smoking.

H X	SINGLE PER PERSON B&B		DOUBLE FOR 2 PERSONS B&B		🛏	3
P	MIN £	MAX £	MIN £	MAX £	🍽	
✁	10.00		20.00		OPEN 1-12	

GLYN CEIRIOG   Map Ref Eb1

Vale of Ceiriog village in foothills of Berwyns. Ideal for pony trekking and walks. Ceiriog Memorial Institute a "must" for lovers of Welsh poetry. Visitors welcome at nearby Chwarel Wynne slate quarry and museum.

Guest Houses

Glan Deg

High Street, Glyn Ceiriog, Llangollen, Clwyd LL20 7EG
Tel: (069172) 8905

Comfortable accommodation in the beautiful Ceiriog Valley. Central heating, hot and cold water, TV in bedrooms. Guest sitting room with tea making facilities. Home cooking, special menus on request, fresh garden produce. Splendid walking area, pony trekking establishments nearby. Many places of natural beauty and historic interest within easy reach. Two Crown rating.

P	SINGLE PER PERSON B&B		DOUBLE FOR 2 PERSONS B&B		🛏	2
X	MIN £	MAX £	MIN £	MAX £	📷	
	9.00	9.00	18.00	18.00	OPEN 1-12	

GLYNDYFRDWY
Map Ref Ca7

Owain Glyndwr - the Glendower of Shakespeare - prince of Wales and visionary, was born here in the 14th century; a mound 1½ miles west of village is said to be the site of his manor. Several hotels in area specialising in salmon and trout fishing.

Guest Houses

Bryngwenallt

Glyndyfrdwy, Corwen, Clwyd, LL21 9BN
Tel: (049083) 340   L

Family guest house situated in quiet country lane, ten minutes drive from A5 at Glyndyfrdwy. Beautiful views of Berwyn Mountains and Dee Valley. Single rooms and double room available (twin beds). Central heating, tea and coffee making facilities. Separate dining room. Cooked breakfast optional. Ideally situated for touring and walking holidays, fishing and canoeing.

H	SINGLE PER PERSON B&B		DOUBLE FOR 2 PERSONS B&B		🛏	3
P	MIN £	MAX £	MIN £	MAX £	📷	
	9.50	11.00	19.00	22.00	OPEN 4-10	

HOLYWELL Map Ref Cb4

Place of pilgrimage for centuries, the 'Lourdes of Wales' with St Winifred's Holy Well. Remains of Basingwerk Abbey (1131) nearby. New Leisure Centre with swimming pools. Greenfield Valley Heritage Park and Grange Cavern Military Museum.

Guest Houses

The Hall

Lygan y Wern, Pentre Halkyn, Holywell, Clwyd CH8 8BD   L
Tel: (0352) 780215

Conveniently situated on A55 15 miles Chester, 70 miles Holyhead. Open all year, self contained centrally heated accommodation in recently reconstructed 18th century cottages, comprising 5 bedrooms, 2 bathrooms, dining room and sitting room. Lovely grounds, children welcome. Good local hotels and pubs for evening meal nearby.

H	SINGLE PER PERSON B&B		DOUBLE FOR 2 PERSONS B&B		🛏	5
P	MIN £	MAX £	MIN £	MAX £	📷	
🐕	11.00	12.00	22.00	24.00	OPEN 1-12	

Farmhouses

Greenhill Farm

Bryn Celyn, Holywell, Clwyd, CH8 7QF
Tel: (0352) 713270

Greenhill is a timber framed farmhouse modernised to include 3 family rooms (one en-suite), twin and double bedrooms, all with tea making facilities. We have an oak beamed lounge and panelled dining room. Also games/utility room with washing facilities and snooker table. Children are especially welcome to watch the milking.

H	SINGLE PER PERSON B&B		DOUBLE FOR 2 PERSONS B&B		🛏	5
P					📷	1
X	MIN £	MAX £	MIN £	MAX £		
	11.00		22.00		OPEN 3-11	

LLANDRILLO Map Ref Ea2

Between Bala and Corwen in the Vale of Edeyrnion and sheltered by the Berwyn Mountains, this peaceful village has angling and walking as its most popular activities.

Guest Houses

Bod Erw Guest House

Bod Erw, Llandrillo, Corwen, Clwyd, LL21 0SN
Tel: (049084) 261

Elegant Edwardian house set in beautiful Dee Valley on edge of Snowdonia National Park. Enjoy the superb views from our large windows. Popular centre for walking and climbing, fishing, water saports. Full English breakfast, evening meal by arrangement, or join our impromptu outdoor barbecues. Children very welcome (discount). Mrs Jones.

H ✂	SINGLE PER PERSON B&B		DOUBLE FOR 2 PERSONS B&B		🛏	3
P X	MIN £	MAX £	MIN £	MAX £	📷	
🐕	12.50		25.00		OPEN 1-12	

LLANGOLLEN
Map Ref Ec1

Romantic town on salmon-filled Dee, famous for its International Musical Eisteddfod; singers and dancers from 30 countries come here every July. Browse through its little shops; stand on 14th century stone bridge. Pottery, weavers, Canal Museum, Plas Newydd stately home (of Ladies of Llangollen fame); golf course. Standard gauge steam railway. Valle Crucis Abbey in superb setting 2 miles away. Castell Dinas Bran overlooks town.

Guest Houses

Dinbren House

Dinbren Road, Llangollen, Clwyd, LL20 8TF
Tel: (0978) 860593

Lovely old house set in 2½ acre garden. Beautiful view across the Dee Valley yet within easy walking distance of Llangollen. Large comfortable bedrooms with central heating, wash-basins, tea and coffee making facilities and TV. Family room available. Guests own bathroom and shower rooms. Friendly atmosphere and a warm welcome.

H ✂	SINGLE PER PERSON B&B		DOUBLE FOR 2 PERSONS B&B		🛏	4
P	MIN £	MAX £	MIN £	MAX £	📷	
🐕	10.00	11.00	20.00	22.00	OPEN 1-12	

LLANGOLLEN CONTINUED

Guest Houses

Fron Deg

Abbey Road, Llangollen, Clwyd, LL20 8EF
Tel: (0978) 860126

Attractive Regency style detached house in idyllic surroundings, on A542, 12 minutes walk from town centre. Large rooms with views, central heating, with tea and coffee, television included. Guests own bathroom and shower, family room, child reductions. Longer stay reductions. Ideal base for walkers, canoeists, anglers or for touring North Wales and border country.

H	SINGLE PER PERSON B&B	DOUBLE FOR 2 PERSONS B&B	🛏	4
P	MIN £	MAX £	MIN £	MAX £	
	11.00	12.00	22.00	24.00	OPEN 1-12

Glanafon

Abbey Road, Llangollen, Clwyd, LL20 8SS
Tel: (0978) 860725

Victorian family run guest house overlooking River Dee and 10 minutes walk from Llangollen town centre. Spacious comfortable twin and double, family bedrooms with hot/cold, tea and coffee facilities. Lovely views. Guests own lounge. Private parking. Children welcome and with reduced rates. Ideally situated for fishing, walking, golfing, canoeing, pony trekking, touring.

H	SINGLE PER PERSON B&B	DOUBLE FOR 2 PERSONS B&B	🛏	3
P	MIN £	MAX £	MIN £	MAX £	
	10.00	12.00	20.00	24.00	OPEN 1-12

The Grange

Grange Road, Llangollen, Clwyd, LL20 8AP
Tel: (0978) 860366

Attractive country house of character in large, secluded and tranquil gardens offering good clean accommodation. Spacious, comfortable, twin and double or family bedrooms with washbasins, tea/coffee facilities and central heating. Luxury guest bathroom. Colour TV lounge. Within easy walking distance of town with its many varied eating places. Child reductions. Parking in grounds.

H	SINGLE PER PERSON B&B	DOUBLE FOR 2 PERSONS B&B	🛏	2
P	MIN £	MAX £	MIN £	MAX £	
			24.00	28.00	OPEN 1-12

Hillcrest

Hill Street, Llangollen, Clwyd, LL20 8EU
Tel: (0978) 860208

Victorian house with large garden, situated 400 yards from the town centre. Ideal for walks, fishing, cycling and central for touring. Plas Newydd 200 yards away. Open all year. Hot and cold; shaver points all bedrooms, double, twin and family rooms available with special rates for children. Good home cooking. Television lounge. Central heating.

H	SINGLE PER PERSON B&B	DOUBLE FOR 2 PERSONS B&B	🛏	3
P	MIN £	MAX £	MIN £	MAX £	
		13.00		23.00	OPEN 1-12

The Old Vicarage

Froncysyllte, Llangollen, Clwyd, LL20 7YR
Tel: (0978) 823018

Attractive 17th century period house situated at the head of the Vale of Llangollen beside the River Dee. Peaceful secluded outstanding views. Twin, double and family bedrooms. En-suite toilets and basins. Bathroom, shower room, hot drinks, TV and heating in bedrooms. Spacious accommodation. Comfortable friendly atmosphere. Gardens. Local inns offering bar and restaurant meals.

H	SINGLE PER PERSON B&B	DOUBLE FOR 2 PERSONS B&B	🛏	3
P	MIN £	MAX £	MIN £	MAX £	
	10.00	12.00	20.00	24.00	OPEN 1-12

Whitegate

Grange Road, Llangollen, Clwyd, LL20 8AP
Tel: (0978) 860960

The perfect base from which to explore Llangollen and North Wales. Whitegate is an attractive Edwardian family house, set on the edge of Llangollen, adjacent to Plas Newydd, long renowned as the home of "The Ladies of Llangollen". All bedrooms have hot and cold water, central heating. Ample parking. Children welcome. TV lounge.

H	SINGLE PER PERSON B&B	DOUBLE FOR 2 PERSONS B&B	🛏	3
P	MIN £	MAX £	MIN £	MAX £	
	12.00	15.00	20.00	22.00	OPEN 1-12

Farmhouses

Cae Madoc Farm

Llandegla, Wrexham, Clwyd, LL11 3BD
Tel: (097888) 270

Do you like log fires, good food, separate tables? Our farm is high in the hills between Llangollen and Ruthin (Horseshoe Pass) road, situated on the A5104, 1 mile from A525 junction. All bedrooms H & C, central heating, tea making facilities. Separate guests bathroom, sitting, dining rooms. Central for Snowdonia, Chester. Riding, clay pigeon shooting nearby. Mrs Del Crossley.

H ✗	SINGLE PER PERSON B&B	DOUBLE FOR 2 PERSONS B&B	🛏	3
P	MIN £	MAX £	MIN £	MAX £	
	10.00	12.00	20.00	24.00	OPEN 1-12

Dee Farm

Rhewl, Llangollen, Clwyd, LL20 7YT   L
Tel: (0978) 861598

An old farmhouse, west of Llangollen on the River Dee in a beautiful quiet valley with superb views. Facilities include a separate bathroom, sitting room for guests, tea and coffee. A good pub is within 200 yards for meals. Ideal for walking, fishing and touring and bird watching.

H	SINGLE PER PERSON B&B	DOUBLE FOR 2 PERSONS B&B	🛏	2
P	MIN £	MAX £	MIN £	MAX £	
	10.00		20.00		OPEN 1-12

Fron Goch Farmhouse Holidays

Cynwyd, Corwen, Clwyd, LL21 0NA
Tel: (049084) 418

An old farmhouse lying under the Berwyn Mountains, Fron Goch has lovely views from the upper Dee Valley. Log fires, hot showers and a comfortable sitting room. Eggs and vegetables from our garden. Optional evening meal with delicious home cooking. Plenty of maps, books and advice on the wide range of local activities available.

P ✗	SINGLE PER PERSON B&B	DOUBLE FOR 2 PERSONS B&B	🛏	3
🐕	MIN £	MAX £	MIN £	MAX £	1
	14.00		24.00	28.00	OPEN 1-12

Maes-yr-Ychain Farm

Llantysilio, Llangollen, Clwyd, LL20 8DB   L
Tel: (0978) 861381

Pat and John Hammond welcome you to their comfortable centuries old farmhouse home in a secluded setting with magnificent views over the Dee Valley and Berwyn Mountains. Lounge, dining room, double, twin (with wash-basin) and single bedrooms. Guests bathroom. Good food, free range eggs and home baked bread. Tastefully decorated and centrally heated throughout. Brittany Ferries Recommended.

P	SINGLE PER PERSON B&B	DOUBLE FOR 2 PERSONS B&B	🛏	3
🐕	MIN £	MAX £	MIN £	MAX £	
	10.00		20.00		OPEN 4-10

Saith Daran Farm

Llandegla, Wrexham, Clwyd, LL11 3BA
Tel: (097888) 685

A dairy farm beautifully situated near the top of the Horseshoe Pass at the junction of the A5104 and A542 ideal for touring North Wales coast, Snowdonia and Chester. Relax and enjoy the lovely surroundings in the conservatory. Bedrooms have delightful views, showers, en-suite, tea making facilities, shaver points, electric blankets and clock/radios. Please contact Mrs Pat Thompson.

H	SINGLE PER PERSON B&B	DOUBLE FOR 2 PERSONS B&B	🛏	2
P	MIN £	MAX £	MIN £	MAX £	1
✗	12.00	12.50	24.00	25.00	OPEN 1-12

Ty'n Celyn

Tyndwr, Llangollen, Clwyd, LL20 8AR
Tel: (0978) 861117

Spacious oak beamed traditional Welsh farmhouse with glorious views 1½ miles from Llangollen centre. Ideal situated for golf, fishing, horse riding, canoeing and walking. Double, twin or family bedrooms all en-suite with tea/coffee making facilities. Ample parking space. Guests lounge with log fire and colour TV. Childrens reductions. Short breaks at regular rates.

H	SINGLE PER PERSON B&B	DOUBLE FOR 2 PERSONS B&B	🛏	3
P	MIN £	MAX £	MIN £	MAX £	3
✗			24.00	26.00	OPEN 1-12

LLANRHAEADR YM MOCHNANT Map Ref Eb3

Pastoral clam befits the village where Bishop William Morgan translated the Bible into Welsh in the 1580s. Some small hotels and guest houses, popular with pony trekkers. Best known today for proximity to highest waterfall in Wales, Pistyll Rhaeadr (240ft) - one of the "Severn Wonders of Wales".

Guest Houses

Llys Morgan Guest House

Llanrhaeadr ym Mochnant, Oswestry, Salop, SY10 0JZ

Llys Morgan is an historic house where the bible translation was done in 1588. It is an ideal spot for all country pursuits. Ideally situated for local beauty spots. Good home cooking with local produce. Quiet and peaceful. Hot and cold in all bedrooms. Some rooms en-suite. Children welcome. Family rooms available.

H ✕ P ✝	SINGLE PER PERSON B&B		DOUBLE FOR 2 PERSONS B&B		🛏	6
					🛏	3
	MIN £	MAX £	MIN £	MAX £		
	10.00	12.00	20.00	24.00	OPEN 1-12	

MOLD Map Ref Cb5

County town of Clwyd, on edge of Clwydian Range. Theatr Clwyd offers wide range of entertainment. Friendly inns, good walks, church with animal frieze. Visit Daniel Owen Centre, memorial to "the Dickens of Wales". Open markets Mondays and Fridays; golf course.

Guest Houses

Alyn Bank Guest House

Wrexham Road, Pontblyddyn, Mold, Clwyd CH7 4HG
Tel: (0352) 770275

Two twin rooms en-suite, shower & toilet. Family room with hot and cold facilities. Bathroom. Large well kept garden overlooking River Alyn and golf course. Free trout fishing. Good evening meals 5 minutes walk. Chester 10 miles. Theatre Clwyd. Coast and mountains easy distance. Guest lounge with TV, central heating in all rooms.

P ✝ ✻	SINGLE PER PERSON B&B		DOUBLE FOR 2 PERSONS B&B		🛏	3
					🛏	1
	MIN £	MAX £	MIN £	MAX £		
	12.50		22.00	26.00	OPEN 1-12	

Tan y Bryn Guest House

100 High Street, Mold, Clwyd, CH7 1BH   L
Tel: (0352) 3902

Family run guest house situated at top end of main street. Convenient for Theatre Clwyd, Shire Hall and Law Courts. Single, double and family rooms with special rates for children. TV in all rooms. Residential licence, car parking, central heating, fire certificate, tea/coffee making facilities available on request.

H P ✝	SINGLE PER PERSON B&B		DOUBLE FOR 2 PERSONS B&B		🛏	7
	MIN £	MAX £	MIN £	MAX £		
	10.00	14.00	20.00	24.00	OPEN 1-12	

Farmhouses

Hill Farm

Llong, Mold, Clwyd, CH7 4JP   L
Tel: (0244) 550415

Georgian house on 300 acre dairy farm, situated between Mold and Chester. Ideal for touring Snowdonia, coast and National Trust properties. Golf, riding, fishing nearby. Large selection of eating places. Central heating, large bedrooms with H & C, guests own sitting room with drink making facilities. Traditional farmhouse breakfasts with choice. AA listed.

H P ✻	SINGLE PER PERSON B&B		DOUBLE FOR 2 PERSONS B&B		🛏	3
	MIN £	MAX £	MIN £	MAX £		
	13.00	14.00	22.00	26.00	OPEN 1-12	

Leeswood Old Hall Farm

Wrexham Road, Mold, Clwyd, CH7 4HF   L
Tel: (0352) 770228

A friendly welcome to this family run dairy farm. The large 18th century house set in landscaped gardens overlooks parkland and Alyn Valley, Mold two miles. Chester ten miles. Use of two bathrooms. Visitors lounge with television. Reductions for children and longer visits.

H ✻ P ✝	SINGLE PER PERSON B&B		DOUBLE FOR 2 PERSONS B&B		🛏	3
	MIN £	MAX £	MIN £	MAX £		
	10.00	10.50	19.00	20.00	OPEN 4-10	

NORTHOP Map Ref Cb5

Historic town of Northop with late 15th century St. Peter's Church built by Margaret Beaufort. Close by is Ewloe Castle circa 1210 AD - a Welsh castle built by Llewellyn The Great.

Farmhouses

Groes Farm

Northop, Mold, Clwyd, CH7 6AG   L
Tel: (035286) 322

Central for Chester and North Wales. Working sheep farm with secluded 17th century beamed farmhouse overlooking Dee Estuary. 2 miles from motorway at Northop. Log fires, central heating in all rooms, TV. Use of family living room or guest sitting room. Tea and biscuits on arrival. First class breakfast. Good evening food at nearby inns.

H ✻ P ✕ ✝	SINGLE PER PERSON B&B		DOUBLE FOR 2 PERSONS B&B		🛏	2
	MIN £	MAX £	MIN £	MAX £		
	10.00	11.00	20.00		OPEN 1-12	

PISTYLL RHAEADR

RUTHIN   Map Ref Ca6

Attractive and historic market town noted for its fine architecture; curfew is still rung nightly! Many captivating old buildings. Hill-top town square where medieval days are held weekly in season. Medieval banquets in Ruthin Castle. Ancient St. Peter's Church has beautiful gates and carved panels. Good range of small shops; craft centre with workshops. Ideal base for Vale of Clwyd.

Guest Houses

Argoed Guest House

Mwrog Street, Llanfwrog, Ruthin, Clwyd LL15 1LG
Tel: (08242) 3407
Telex: 94070162 HALL G
Fax: (08242) 4924

An attractive, timbered house, fully centrally heated, with ample parking facilities. Single, double, twin-bedded and en-suite rooms available. Lounge with TV. Shower and baths available. Beautiful garden with own stream. Commanding superb views of Clwydian Hills. Situated within easy walking distance of Historic Ruthin, Brittany Ferries recommended. Member of award winning B & B (GB) organisation.

P	SINGLE PER PERSON B&B		DOUBLE FOR 2 PERSONS B&B		🛏	3
	MIN £	MAX £	MIN £	MAX £	🛁	1
	13.80	13.80	27.60	27.60	OPEN 1-12	

Eyarth Station

Llanfair D C, Ruthin, Clwyd,
LL15 2EE
Tel: (08242) 3643

Former railway station now beautifully converted commended country guest house. Outdoor pool, TV lounge. Family suite PB, five bedrooms en-suite. Private Parking. 3 minutes drive medieval banquet at Ruthin Castle. Central for Snowdonia, Llangollen, Chester. Ideal centre for / 3day stop over. Magnificent views, close to many excellent golf courses. Best B & B in Wales 88. AA merit award. Brittany Ferries recommended. BTA commended.

H ✕	SINGLE PER PERSON B&B		DOUBLE FOR 2 PERSONS B&B		🛏	6
P ✕					🛁	5
🐕	MIN £	MAX £	MIN £	MAX £	OPEN 1-12	
				28.00		

Gorffwysfa

Llanfair D C, Ruthin, Clwyd, LL15 2UN
Tel: (08242) 2432

Spacious country house set in peaceful rural surroundings. 1½ miles from Ruthin. Ideal location for exploring North Wales. Within easy reach of Snowdonia, Llangollen, Chester and National Trust properties of Erddig, Chirk Castle and Bodnant Garden. All rooms with private bath or en-suite, WC, shower, TV and tea/coffee facilities. Car parking available. No smoking requested.

H ✕	SINGLE PER PERSON B&B		DOUBLE FOR 2 PERSONS B&B		🛏	3
P ✕					🛁	3
🐕	MIN £	MAX £	MIN £	MAX £	OPEN 1-12	
	14.00		28.00			

Woodlands

Llanbedr D C, Ruthin, Clwyd, LL15 1UT   L
Tel: (08242) 3751

Welcome to our home. Situated in its own grounds. Comfortable homely lounge, breakfast room, two double rooms. Guest own bathroom, central heating throughout. Tea and coffee facilities. Superb views over the Vale of Clwyd, medieval Ruthin, country walks, Chester, North Wales coast and Snowdonia. Reduced weekly rates

P ✕	SINGLE PER PERSON B&B		DOUBLE FOR 2 PERSONS B&B		🛏	2
	MIN £	MAX £	MIN £	MAX £	OPEN 4-10	
			22.00	24.00		

Farmhouses

Ffynogion Farm

Llanfair Dyffryn Clwyd, Ruthin, Clwyd   L
Tel: (08242) 2851

Situated in the beautiful Vale of Clwyd, Ffynogion is a dairy farm on the outskirts of the medieval town Ruthin. The listed farmhouse dates back to the 16th century. Both double rooms have tea and coffee making facilities. There is a comfortable panelled lounge with colour television. Full farmhouse breakfast. Ample parking space.

P	SINGLE PER PERSON B&B		DOUBLE FOR 2 PERSONS B&B		🛏	2
🐕	MIN £	MAX £	MIN £	MAX £	OPEN 3-10	
				18.00		

ST. ASAPH   Map Ref Be4

City of smallest cathedral in Britain, scene of annual North Wales Music Festival; information in Cathedral Museum. Prehistoric Cefn Caves nearby. Pleasantly sited on river Elwy in verdant Vale of Clwyd.

Farmhouses

Pen-y-Bryn Farm

Bod Erw, St. Asaph, Clwyd, LL17 0LF   L
Tel: (0745) 583213

A warm welcome awaits you at this working farm situated a mile west of St. Asaph, 200 yards off A55. Centrally located for touring North Wales. Hot and cold in one family and double rooms with additional single room. 2 bathrooms, shower, central heating throughout. Guests own TV lounge, full breakfast. Children welcome with reductions. Send SAE to Mrs B Williams.

H	SINGLE PER PERSON B&B		DOUBLE FOR 2 PERSONS B&B		🛏	4
P					🛁	
🐕	MIN £	MAX £	MIN £	MAX £	OPEN 1-12	
	8.00	10.00	16.00	20.00		

Plas Penucha

Caerwys, Mold, Clwyd, CH7 5BH
Tel: (0352) 720210

Welcome to this 16th century farmhouse, altered over succeeding centuries but retaining sense of history and serenity in comfortable surroundings. Extensive gardens overlooking Clwydian Hills. Twin bedroom with shower, double and single with wash basins. Spacious lounge with Elizabethan panelling. Full central heating. Two miles A55. Ideal touring centre for North Wales. Brochure from Nest Price.

H ✕	SINGLE PER PERSON B&B		DOUBLE FOR 2 PERSONS B&B		🛏	4
P					🛁	
✕	MIN £	MAX £	MIN £	MAX £	OPEN 1-12	
	11.00	11.00	22.00	22.00		

ST ASAPH CATHEDRAL

WREXHAM Map Ref Cc6

Busy industrial and commercial town, gateway to North Wales. St. Giles' Church has graceful tower and altar piece by Yelihu Yale, of Yale University fame. Visit Erddig Hall stately home nearby. Good shopping; industrial museum at neighbouring Bersham. Museum, art gallery, swimming pool, golf.

Bridge House
Penley, Wrexham, Clwyd, LL13 0LY L
Tel: (097873) 763
A modernised farmhouse in rural Brookside setting with open views across the countryside. Between A525 and A539. Ideal for visiting attractions on Welsh/Shropshire/Cheshire border. North Wales coast, Snowdonia and Llangollen. 1 double, 2 twin bedded rooms with tea/coffee facilities, TV, central heating, parking. Bathroom complete with separate shower also toilet. Bed and breakfast, evening meal by arrangement.

H X	SINGLE PER PERSON B&B		DOUBLE FOR 2 PERSONS B&B		🛏	3
P						
✗	MIN £	MAX £	MIN £	MAX £		
	13.00	13.00	24.00	24.00	OPEN 1-12	

Mill House
Higher Wych, Malpas, Cheshire, SY15 7JR
Tel: (0948) 73362
Modernised mill house on Clwyd/Cheshire border in peaceful rural surroundings with a stream running through the garden. The house is centrally heated with a log fire in the lounge. One bedroom has an en-suite shower/wc. All bedrooms have washbasins, radio and tea making facilities. Children and senior citizens reductions.

H X	SINGLE PER PERSON B&B		DOUBLE FOR 2 PERSONS B&B		🛏	2
P					🛏	1
♒	MIN £	MAX £	MIN £	MAX £		
	10.00	10.00	20.00	20.00	OPEN 1-12	

Guest Houses

Brackenwood
67 Wynnstay Lane, Marford, Wrexham, Clwyd LL12 8LH L
Tel: (097883) 2866
Attractive family guest house with large garden to rear in quiet residential area. Children very welcome. All rooms have central heating and tea making facilities, some have vanity units, one has private toilet and wash basin. Good home cooking. Evening meals on request. Packed lunches. Telephone available. Easy reach Chester, Wrexham, Manchester and North Wales.

H ♒	SINGLE PER PERSON B&B		DOUBLE FOR 2 PERSONS B&B		🛏	5
P X					🛏	1
🐕	MIN £	MAX £	MIN £	MAX £		
	13.00	14.00	24.00	26.00	OPEN 1-12	

Grove Guest House
36 Chester Road, Wrexham, Clwyd, LL11 2SD
Tel: (0978) 354288
Grove guest house gives a friendly service. Close to town centre. Detached house with twelve rooms, some en-suite. Central heating, tea and coffee facilities and TV in all rooms. Tennis, swimming, golf, horse riding nearby. Large car park. Reasonable terms.

P	SINGLE PER PERSON B&B		DOUBLE FOR 2 PERSONS B&B		🛏	12
🐕					🛏	2
♒	MIN £	MAX £	MIN £	MAX £		
	10.50	12.50	21.00	25.00	OPEN 1-12	

Farmhouses

Buck Farm
Hanmer, Clwyd, SY14 7LX
Tel: (094874) 339
Buck Farm on the A525, A warm welcoming and cosy Tudor farmhouse is a good touring base for North Wales, Cheshire, Shropshire, Staffordshire. We provide vegetarian or vegan and meat meals on request, always make our own muesli, granola, hotcakes and wonderful vegetable soups (sans msg). French spoken. Library, music, cycle shelter. No smoking. AA Listed. Farmhouse Award.

H ♒	SINGLE PER PERSON B&B		DOUBLE FOR 2 PERSONS B&B		🛏	4
P X						
🐕	MIN £	MAX £	MIN £	MAX £		
	11.50	13.00	23.00	27.00	OPEN 1-12	

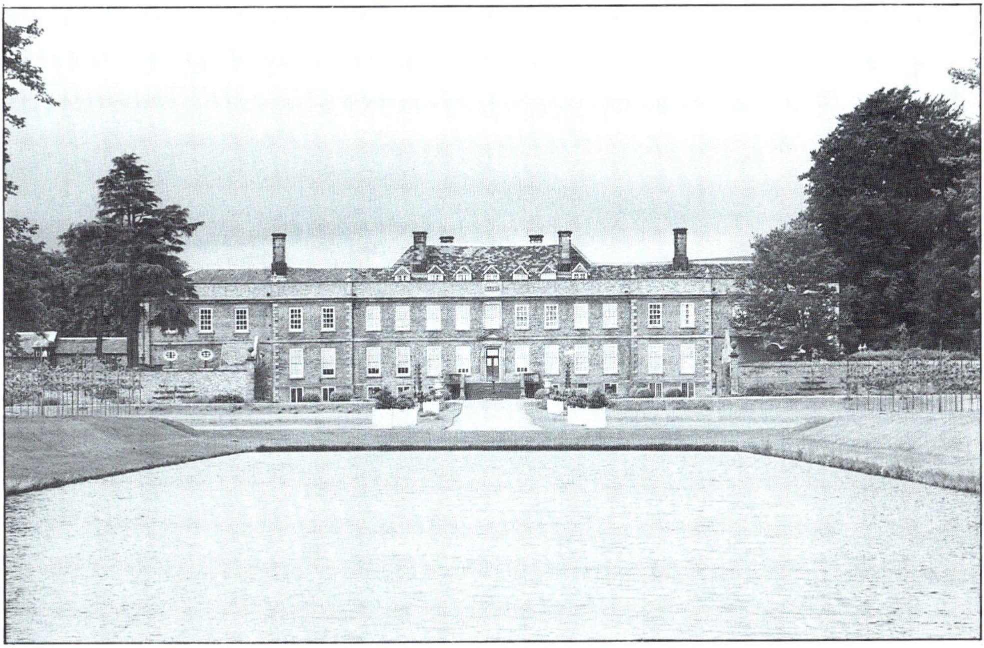

ERDDIG (NATIONAL TRUST), NEAR WREXHAM

MID WALES

This is Wales at it's greenest and most peaceful. There's a view from the aptly named Precipice Walk above Dolgellau that captures the character of this unhurried, unspoilt region. The path is high on the flanks of a narrow valley, looking out against a backcloth of round-shouldered mountains to the snaking, sandy Mawddach Estuary and the sea.

Mid Wales's mixture of green uplands and sandy bays casts a special spell. It's a wonderful touring area, with traffic-free roads which wind their way through vales and forests before climbing into mountain solitudes. Characterful B&Bs are scattered throughout the region. Stay at a low-ceilinged old inn where the locals meet. Spend a few days at a farmhouse in the heart of the country. Explore the coast from one of Mid Wales's charming resorts or historic sailing ports. Or choose a traditional market town were the farmers congregate each week to buy and sell.

You won't want to rush around in Mid Wales. Take your time and you'll discover some of its many secrets. Soak up the scenery at the lovely Cregennen Lakes in the foothills of mighty Cader Idris. Take the Bwlch y Groes road from Dinas Mawddwy (the most spectacular mountain road in Wales and not for the faint-hearted!) to the forest-ringed waters of remote Lake Vyrnwy. And see if you can find Pistyll Rhaeadr, Wales's highest waterfall, hidden away in deepest border country.

These are just some of Mid Wales's many gems. Much of the Snowdonia National Park extends southwards into the region (all the way to Machynlleth, in fact), and westwards to the shores of Cardigan Bay. Along this coast there are three outstandingly beautiful estuaries where wooded slopes sweep down to a sandy shoreline rich in wildlife (the old signal box on the banks of the Mawddach at Penmaenpool is now a bird observatory).

The resorts along the bay complement their peaceful surroundings perfectly. The largest is modestly sized Aberystwyth, a charming seaside town with a well-preserved Victorian seafront and good selection of B&B accommodation. Other attractive places to stay on the coast and in the country include Barmouth, Dolgellau, Welshpool, Llandrindod Wells, Machynlleth, Aberaeron and New Quay.

ELAN VALLEY RESERVOIR

MEIRIONNYDD

The mountains sweep down to the sea all along Meirionydd's coastline. The view from the ramparts of Harlech Castle captures the essence of this highly scenic slice of Wales – the fortress stands on a rocky outcrop between the Snowdonia National Park's peaks and the sands of Cardigan Bay.

There are more dramatic encounters between mountain and sea along the Mawddach and Dyfi Estuaries. To enjoy the best of Meirionydd's coast and country, stay at places like Barmouth and Aberdovey. Or head inland for the forests, lakes, and hills around dark-stoned Dolgellau and mountain-ringed Bala. Meirionydd's many attractions include the Bala Lake Railway and the Talyllyn narrow-gauge lines (the latter being the longest-serving of Wales's little railways – Talyllyn celebrates its 125th anniversary in 1990). Try the exciting new dry ski slope at Trawsfynnd, visit Fairbourne's 'Butterfly Safari', and call in at the Corris Crafts Centre where many different craftspeople work.

ABERDOVEY/ABERDYFI   Map Ref Db6

Dinghy sailors' paradise on the Dyfi Estuary. All watersports, thriving yacht club, good inns looking out over the bay and 18-hole golf club links. Superb views towards hills and mountains.

Guest Houses

Brodawel Guest House

Tywyn Road, Aberdovey, Gwynedd, LL35 0SA
Tel: (065472) 347
Quiet convenient guest house close to championship golf links and excellent bathing beach. Private parking. Five minutes to village railway station, tennis and bowling.

P X 🐕 ✕	SINGLE PER PERSON B&B		DOUBLE FOR 2 PERSONS B&B		🛏	6
	MIN £	MAX £	MIN £	MAX £		3
			24.00		OPEN 3-12	

Cartref Guest House

Aberdovey, Gwynedd, LL35 0NR
Tel: (065472) 273
Cartref is an attractive, detached, family run guest house renowned for our cuisine and a relaxed, friendly atmosphere. Situated on the sea front, providing comfortable, spacious bedrooms some of which are en-suite, TV, tea/coffee making facilities. We are one of the few properties in Aberdovey offering private car parking facilities.

P 🐕 ✕	SINGLE PER PERSON B&B		DOUBLE FOR 2 PERSONS B&B		🛏	7
	MIN £	MAX £	MIN £	MAX £		3
	12.00	12.00	23.00	23.00	OPEN 1-12	

Plas Dyfi

Pennal, Machynlleth, Powys, SY20 9LB
Tel: (065475) 688
On A493 between Machynlleth and Aberdyfi. South facing in two acres with glorious views overlooking Dyfi Estuary. All rooms with hot and cold water, razor and electrical points, hot drinks and colour TV facilities, central heating throughout. Children over ten welcome. Sorry no pets. Plenty of parking space. Evening meals by arrangement.

H X P ✕	SINGLE PER PERSON B&B		DOUBLE FOR 2 PERSONS B&B		🛏	3
	MIN £	MAX £	MIN £	MAX £		
	11.00	12.00	22.00	24.00	OPEN 3-10	

CALL Holidays (0792) 645555

1 Trefeddian Bank

Aberdyfi, Gwynedd, LL35 0RU
Tel: (065472) 487
Small friendly guest house in quiet, elevated situation. Panoramic views over golf course, beach and Cardigan Bay. Comfortable TV lounge, sun lounge, sun bathing terrace. All bedrooms have storage heaters, H & C, shaver sockets, tea making facilities. Parking. Reductions for children. Good food, evening meal by arrangement. Sorry no smoking in the house, except in the sun lounge.

P ✕ ✕	SINGLE PER PERSON B&B		DOUBLE FOR 2 PERSONS B&B		🛏	3
	MIN £	MAX £	MIN £	MAX £		
	10.00	10.00	20.00	20.00	OPEN 1-12	

Farmhouses

Gogarth Hall

Pennal, Machynlleth, Powys, SY20 9LB
Tel: (0654) 75235
A warm family welcome awaits you at our farm situated 5 miles from Machynlleth, 4 miles from Aberdovey beach. Wonderful views overlooking the Dovey Estuary. Fishing, shooting, watersports, scenic walks. Ron and Deilwen offer traditional Welsh bed and breakfast and evening meal. Private lounge, dining room, bathroom. Bedrooms with wash basins and tea making facilities. Utility and playroom when wet. Ron and Deilwen warmly welcome you their home to meet the family and enjoy a working farm holiday. Reduced rates for children. baby sitting service. Please send for brochure. In early 1990 telephone will be (0654) 791235.

H P ✕	SINGLE PER PERSON B&B		DOUBLE FOR 2 PERSONS B&B		🛏	2
	MIN £	MAX £	MIN £	MAX £		
	10.50	11.50	21.00	23.00	OPEN 1-12	

WALES It's magic

BALA   Map Ref De2

Tree-lined main street has interesting little shops and charming hotels. Narrow-gauge railway runs one side of Bala Lake, 4 miles long and ringed with mountains. Golf, sailing, fishing - a natural touring centre for Snowdonia.

Hotels

Fronddderw Private Hotel

Stryd-y-Fron, Bala, Gwynedd, LL23 7YD
Tel: (0678) 520301
Fronddderw is a charming period mansion set on the hillside overlooking the town of Bala with magnificent views of the Berwyn mountains and Bala Lake. All rooms have hot and cold, central heating, tea and coffee making facilities. TV lounge with colour TV. Ample free parking. Dinner optional. Excellent value.

H X P ✕	SINGLE PER PERSON B&B		DOUBLE FOR 2 PERSONS B&B		🛏	8
	MIN £	MAX £	MIN £	MAX £		2
	10.00	11.00	20.00	26.00	OPEN 1-12	

New Inn Hotel

Llangynog, Oswestry, Shropshire, SY10 0EX
Tel: (069174) 229
Small, privately owned and managed hotel, open all year. In quiet situation, but central for North and Mid Wales beauty spots and walks. Single, double and family rooms, some en-suite, centrally heated, H & C all rooms. Special rates for children. Bar and restaurant meals. Ample car parking. TV lounge. Fire certificate granted. AA listed.

H X P 🐕	SINGLE PER PERSON B&B		DOUBLE FOR 2 PERSONS B&B		🛏	7
	MIN £	MAX £	MIN £	MAX £		2
	14.00	14.00	28.00	28.00	OPEN 1-12	

Guest Houses

Pen-Isa'r-Llan

Llanfor, Bala, Gwynedd, LL23 7DW
Tel: (0678) 520507
Situated half a mile outside Bala on the A494. An attractive large country house with spacious accommodation. Tea and coffee in all bedrooms, some en-suite with colour TV. Licensed. Sunbed, sauna, gymnasium, pool table and pony trekking. Reduced rates for children sharing parents room. Parties catered for. Fire certificate held.

P 🐕 ✕	SINGLE PER PERSON B&B		DOUBLE FOR 2 PERSONS B&B		🛏	7
	MIN £	MAX £	MIN £	MAX £		3
	13.50	13.50	27.00	27.00	OPEN 1-12	

Penybryn Farm Guest House

Sarnau, Bala, Gwynedd, LL23 7LH
Tel: (06783) 297
Farm guest house accommodation, B & B or B & B and evening meal. Six bedrooms, two bathrooms, hot and cold water in all bedrooms. Colour television in lounge. Delicious food. Home cooking, high standard. Fire certificate and Farmhouse Award holder. Own lake for fishing. Marvellous views overlooking Berwyn Mountains. Terms with SAE on request.

H P ✕	SINGLE PER PERSON B&B		DOUBLE FOR 2 PERSONS B&B		🛏	6
	MIN £	MAX £	MIN £	MAX £		
	12.00	14.00	20.00	24.00	OPEN 2-11	

Plas Teg Guest House

Tegid Street, Bala, Gwynedd, LL23 7EN
Tel: (0678) 520268

Early nineteenth century town house with six large family rooms furnished with antiques. Coffee and tea making facilities in all rooms. Good home cooking with vegetables from the garden. Ample car parking for twelve cars. Within minutes walk of the town and the lake and all water sport activities. Dogs very welcome.

	SINGLE PER PERSON B&B		DOUBLE FOR 2 PERSONS B&B			6
	MIN £	MAX £	MIN £	MAX £	OPEN 1-12	
	12.50	12.50	25.00	25.00		

Farmhouses

Eirianfa Farm

Sarnau, Bala, Gwynedd, LL23 7LH
Tel: (06783) 389

Mixed farm 3 miles from Bala on A494. Family, double, twin bedded rooms, all with wash basins, C/H, tea/coffee facilities. Dining, sitting room with TV. Bathroom separate toilet and shower. Good home cooked food served. Private trout lake. Ideal centre for touring North/Mid Wales. Children welcomed.

	SINGLE PER PERSON B&B		DOUBLE FOR 2 PERSONS B&B			3
	MIN £	MAX £	MIN £	MAX £	OPEN 3-10	
	11.00	13.00	20.00	22.00		

Erw Feurig Farm Guest House

Cefnddwysarn, Bala, Gwynedd, LL23 7LL
Tel: (06783) 262

Beautifully situated facing the Berwyn mountains. Extremely comfortable and spacious family, double and twin bedrooms one on the ground floor. Tea/coffee making facilities. Full central heating and keys. Excellent breakfasts and dinners served. TV in separate lounge. Families welcome with cot and high chair available. Private fishing in own lake. Children at reduced rates.

	SINGLE PER PERSON B&B		DOUBLE FOR 2 PERSONS B&B			4
	MIN £	MAX £	MIN £	MAX £	OPEN 3-10	
	11.00	12.00	22.00	24.00		

Melin Meloch Mill

Llanfor, Bala, Gwynedd, LL23 7DP
Tel: (0678) 520101

Unique 13th century water mill with an oak galleried interior and many interesting features. We provide a good standard of comfort and hospitality. Melin Meloch stands on the banks of the River Dee, close to Bala Lake and town and within easy reach of North Wales, many tourist attractions.

	SINGLE PER PERSON B&B		DOUBLE FOR 2 PERSONS B&B			3
	MIN £	MAX £	MIN £	MAX £	OPEN 1-12	
			23.00	25.00		

Rhydydefaid Farm

Frongoch, Bala, Gwynedd, LL23 7NT   L
Tel: (0678) 520456

Traditional Welsh stone farmhouse, three miles from Bala on A4212 road. One family bedroom with shower, one twin bedroom, both with wash-basins, tea/coffee facilities. Oak beamed lounge, inglenook fireplace. Central heating. Welsh welcome awaits you. Beautiful countryside, ideal centre for keen anglers, walkers, canoeists, sailing and touring Snowdonia.

	SINGLE PER PERSON B&B		DOUBLE FOR 2 PERSONS B&B			2
						1
	MIN £	MAX £	MIN £	MAX £	OPEN 3-10	
	9.50	12.00	19.00	22.00		

Tair Felin Farm

Frongoch, Bala, Gwynedd, LL23 7NS   L
Tel: (0678) 520763

A warm welcome awaits you at Tair Felin Farm situated three miles north of Bala on A4212 road and in the Snowdonia National Park. Convenient for sailing, trekking, walking, walking, golfing etc. Lounge with colour TV. Comfort and good home cooking. Working farm with sheep and cattle. Ideal for touring North and Mid Wales.

	SINGLE PER PERSON B&B		DOUBLE FOR 2 PERSONS B&B			2
	MIN £	MAX £	MIN £	MAX £	OPEN 3-10	
			20.00	23.00		

Talybont Isa Farm

Rhyduchaf, Bala, Gwynedd, LL23 7SD
Tel: (0678) 520234

Talybont Isa is ideally situated for touring North and Mid Wales with varied interests in the Bala area. Fishing, walking, golf, windsurfing, sailing, pony trekking. Two ground floor bedrooms make the farmhouse suitable for the disabled guest. A warm welcome and good farm cooking awaits you here. Tea/coffee facilities provided.

	SINGLE PER PERSON B&B		DOUBLE FOR 2 PERSONS B&B			3
	MIN £	MAX £	MIN £	MAX £	OPEN 1-11	
	12.50	14.00	20.00	24.00		

BARMOUTH Map Ref Db4

Golden sands and miles of wonderful mountain and estuary walks nearby. Promenade, funfair, pony rides on beach. Lifeboat house, RNLI Museum and HQ of Merioneth Yacht Club. A thriving holiday town with good shops and inns. Excellent parking on seafront.

Hotels

The Sandpiper

7 Marine Parade, Barmouth, Gwynedd, LL42 1NA
Tel: (0341) 280318

The Sandpiper is superbly situated on Barmouth sea front. There is free parking outside and we are a short, level walk from the station. Most rooms have en-suite facilities. Television and free tea/coffee in all rooms. Ground floor bedroom available. Residential licence. Central heating. Brochure from Susan and John Palmer.

	SINGLE PER PERSON B&B		DOUBLE FOR 2 PERSONS B&B			11
						7
	MIN £	MAX £	MIN £	MAX £	OPEN 4-10	
	12.50	13.50	21.00	27.00		

Guest Houses

Endeavour Guest House

Marine Parade, Barmouth, Gwynedd, LL42 1NA
Tel: (0341) 280271

Open all year. Good food, choice of menus. Colour TV's, showers, tea making in all family and double rooms. Access at all times. Happy atmosphere. Reasonable terms. Pets welcome by prior arrangement. Children welcome.

	SINGLE PER PERSON B&B		DOUBLE FOR 2 PERSONS B&B			9
						3
	MIN £	MAX £	MIN £	MAX £	OPEN 1-12	
	11.50	12.50	23.00	26.00		

Hendre y Plentyn

3 Hendre Villas, Barmouth, Gwynedd, LL42 1PW   L
Tel: (0341) 281284

Victorian house in quiet cul-de-sac overlooking park. Short easy walks to beach and shops. Spacious rooms, vanity units, tea/coffee facilities, TV lounge, separate dining room. Good home cooking. Packed lunches, special diets. Access 24 hours, easy parking. Special rates for families, senior citizens, clubs, schools, and special needs groups accommodated. Current Gwynedd fire authority certificate.

	SINGLE PER PERSON B&B		DOUBLE FOR 2 PERSONS B&B			6
	MIN £	MAX £	MIN £	MAX £	OPEN 1-12	
	9.50	11.00	19.00	22.00		

BARMOUTH CONTINUED

Guest Houses

Pen Parc Guest House

Park Road, Barmouth, Gwynedd, LL42 1PH
Tel: (0341) 280150
A small guest house in a quiet situation overlooking bowling and putting greens and tennis courts, yet only four minutes from sea. H & C in all rooms. Tea making facilities. All bedrooms on first floor. We pride ourselves on good food and personal service. Open all year. Walkers welcome. Sorry no children or pets.

P	SINGLE PER PERSON B&B		DOUBLE FOR 2 PERSONS B&B			4
	MIN £	MAX £	MIN £	MAX £		
X	10.00	11.00	20.00	22.00	OPEN 1-12	

Farmhouses

Llwyndu Farmhouse

Llanaber, Barmouth, Gwynedd, LL42 1RR
Tel: (0341) 280144
Beautiful old listed 17th century farmhouse north of Barmouth with wonderful views over Cardigan Bay. Beaches nearby. Family/double rooms, all en-suite, beverage facilities. Magnificent oak beamed lounge, inglenook fireplaces, super food including vegetarian. Licensed. Les Routiers Recommended. AA Listed. Winter breaks including candlelit dinners and complimentary wine. For a relaxing break contact Peter or Paula Thompson.

P	SINGLE PER PERSON B&B		DOUBLE FOR 2 PERSONS B&B			6
	MIN £	MAX £	MIN £	MAX £		6
X			28.00		OPEN 1-11	

DINAS MAWDDWY
Map Ref Dd4

Mountain village famed for its salmon and trout fishing and marvellous walks. On fringe of Snowdonia National Park. Visit the extensive Meirion woollen mill and visitor centre with craft shop, tea shop etc.

Farmhouses

Bryncelyn Farm

Dinas Mawddwy, Machynlleth, Powys, SY20 9JA
Tel: (06504) 289
Bryncelyn Farm is in peaceful valley of Cywarch at the foot of Aran Fawddwy, set amidst some of the finest sceneries. An excellent centre to enjoy surrounding North and Mid Wales. Within easy reach of coast and market town of Machynlleth. Log fire. Generous home cooked meals. Tea and coffee making facilities, en-suite, also spacious bedrooms with heating. The Edwards family offers you a homely holiday in a comfortable farmhouse. The farm is two miles from Dinas Mawddwy, good road to farm.

H	SINGLE PER PERSON B&B		DOUBLE FOR 2 PERSONS B&B			2
P X						2
	MIN £	MAX £	MIN £	MAX £		
	11.00				OPEN 1-12	

Bryn Sion Farm

Cwm Cywarch, Dinas Mawddwy, Machynlleth, Powys SY20 9JG
Tel: (06504) 251
A welcome awaits you at Bryn Sion Farm, situated at the foot of Aran Fawddwy 1½ miles from the village of Dinas Mawddwy. Fishing and shooting on farm. Two double bedrooms both with H & C and tea making facilities. Ample car parking. Reduction for children. Cot and high chair available. Good meals provided. Log fires in sitting room.

H X	SINGLE PER PERSON B&B		DOUBLE FOR 2 PERSONS B&B			2
P						
	MIN £	MAX £	MIN £	MAX £		
	8.50	10.00	17.00	20.00	OPEN 1-12	

DOLGELLAU Map Ref Dc4

Handsome stone-built small town which seems to have grown naturally out of the mountains. Interesting shops, pubs, cafes; good hotel, guest house and farmhouse accommodation. Excellent base for touring coast and countryside.

DOLGELLAU

Guest Houses

Dwy Olwyn

Coed y Fronallt, Dolgellau, Gwynedd, LL40 2YG
Tel: (0341) 422822
A comfortable guest house situated in an acre of landscaped gardens, boasting magnificent views of the Cader Idris Mountain range in a peaceful position, yet only 10 minutes walk from the town within the Snowdonia National Park. Close to all amenities. Good home cooking, parking, lounge with colour TV, evening meals if desired, hot and cold all bedrooms.

H	SINGLE PER PERSON B&B		DOUBLE FOR 2 PERSONS B&B			3
P X						1
	MIN £	MAX £	MIN £	MAX £		
	10.00		19.00		OPEN 3-11	

Esgair Wen Newydd

Garreg Feurig, Llanfachreth Road, Dolgellau, Gwynedd LL40 2YA
Tel: (0341) 423952
Spacious new bungalow. Magnificent Cader Idris mountain views. Dolgellau 10 minutes walk. Very quiet. High standard of home cooking. Comfort, cleanliness, personal attention assured. Two double, one twin, wash-basins, shaver points, electric blankets, tea/coffee facilities. Guest bathroom, shower, C/H. Evening meals. Ideal walking, touring, bird watching, gold panning, narrow gauge railways, beaches, ski slope. No smoking.

H X	SINGLE PER PERSON B&B		DOUBLE FOR 2 PERSONS B&B			3
P						
	MIN £	MAX £	MIN £	MAX £		
	13.50		23.00		OPEN 1-12	

Floreat

Llanelltyd, Dolgellau, Gwynedd, LL40 2SU
Tel: (0341) 422358
Floreat is situated in the Snowdonia National Park overlooking the Cader Idris mountain range and Mawddach Estuary. It stands in its own landscaped grounds and peaceful position. Close to sandy beaches, gold mines, narrow gauge railways and numerous walks. Ample parking, lounge with colour TV, separate dining area. Warm welcome and good home cooking.

H	SINGLE PER PERSON B&B		DOUBLE FOR 2 PERSONS B&B			3
P X						
	MIN £	MAX £	MIN £	MAX £		
	10.00		20.00		OPEN 4-10	

Fronoleu Farm Restaurant

Tabor, Dolgellau, Gwynedd, LL40 2PS
Tel: (0341) 422361
Secretly situated, a place of wild beauty stands Fronoleu. This old converted farmhouse offers four comfortable bedrooms, three double rooms, two of which can be family rooms and a single or twin room. All have TV, tea/coffee making facilities and vanity units. The licensed stable restaurant serves an à la carte menu every evening.

H X	SINGLE PER PERSON B&B		DOUBLE FOR 2 PERSONS B&B			4
P						
	MIN £	MAX £	MIN £	MAX £		
	12.50	14.00	24.00	28.00	OPEN 1-12	

Y Goedlan

Brithdir, Dolgellau, Gwynedd, LL40 2RN
Tel: (0341) 423131

This old vicarage with adjoining farm offers peaceful accommodation in pleasant rural surroundings. Ideally placed on B4416 road for walks, sea and mountains. Spacious double, twin and family rooms, all with tea, coffee making facilities. H & C, central heating, colour TV lounge, shower, two conveniences, parking. Comfort with homely atmosphere. Hearty breakfast. Reductions for children. Dolgellau 2 miles.

P	SINGLE PER PERSON B&B	DOUBLE FOR 2 PERSONS B&B	🛏	3
	MIN £	MAX £	MIN £	MAX £	
	9.50		19.00	21.00	OPEN 1-11

Herongate

Arthog, Nr Dolgellau, Gwynedd, LL39 1BJ
Tel: (0341) 250349

Herongate is situated at the water's edge of the beautiful Mawddach Estuary in a lovely area. Especially suitable for those seeking a holiday off the beaten track in a peaceful place with comfort and delightful views. Bedrooms all attractive with hot and cold water and shaving points. Comfortable lounge with colour television. Ample parking.

P ✗	SINGLE PER PERSON B&B	DOUBLE FOR 2 PERSONS B&B	🛏	3
	MIN £	MAX £	MIN £	MAX £	
	11.00	11.00	20.00	21.00	OPEN 5-9

Heulwen

Llanfachreth, Gwynedd, LL40 2UT
Tel: (0341) 423085

Heulwen is situated outside the quaint village of Llanfachreth, surrounded by beautiful views. It is an ideal centre for exploring the Snowdonia National Park. Hearty breakfasts, warm and homely bedrooms, lounge with colour TV and large patio to while away the long summer evenings, all help to make your stay a memorable one.

H ✗ P 🐾	SINGLE PER PERSON B&B	DOUBLE FOR 2 PERSONS B&B	🛏	3
	MIN £	MAX £	MIN £	MAX £	
	10.00		19.00		OPEN 3-10

Ivy House

Finsbury Square, Dolgellau, Gwynedd, LL40 1RF
Tel: (0341) 422535

Country town guest house offering attractive accommodation. A welcoming atmosphere and good food. Residential licence for the cellar bar. Full central heating. All bedrooms TV, tea and coffee facilities. Evening meals or bar snacks optional, idyllic walking and touring centre, maps and information available.

🐾 ✗	SINGLE PER PERSON B&B	DOUBLE FOR 2 PERSONS B&B	🛏	6
	MIN £	MAX £	MIN £	MAX £	3
				25.00	OPEN 1-12

Llwyn Talcen

Brithdir, Dolgellau, Gwynedd, LL40 2RY [L]
Tel: (034141) 276

Situated in an acre of rhododendron and azaelia gardens. Llwyn Talcen offers a warm welcome, outstanding views, together with peace and quiet. Ideal centre for hill walkers and nature lovers. We offer good fresh food, organic whenever possible. Traditional and vegetarian fare available. Reduced rates for children. Ample parking.

H P ✗	SINGLE PER PERSON B&B	DOUBLE FOR 2 PERSONS B&B	🛏	2
	MIN £	MAX £	MIN £	MAX £	
	9.00	10.50	18.00	21.00	OPEN 1-12

Farmhouses

Cyfannedd Uchaf

Arthog, Dolgellau, Gwynedd, LL39 1LX [L]
Tel: (0341) 250526

We promise you fantastic views. Comfortable farmhouse with spacious rooms overlooking the Mawddach Estuary, excellent mountain and valley walking, drying facilities. Ideal for those seeking seclusion. Homely food, complimentary tea tray, all rooms. Children over 14 welcome, regret no pets. Brochure Mrs Anna Tovey. Come and share our hospitality, phone now. Fishing and pony trekking nearby.

P ✗	SINGLE PER PERSON B&B	DOUBLE FOR 2 PERSONS B&B	🛏	3
	MIN £	MAX £	MIN £	MAX £	
			22.00		OPEN 1-12

Tyddynmawr Farmhouse

Islawrdref, Cader Road, Dolgellau, Gwynedd LL40 1TL
Tel: (0341) 422331

It's paradise! Honestly! A warm welcome awaits you in this lovingly restored 18th century farmhouse. Beams, log fires. Each bedroom has superb mountain views. En-suite available. We farm the magnificent mountain of Cader Idris and have waterfalls, slate mines, caves and fishing on mountain lake on farm. We offer peace, tranquility and seclusion.

H P	SINGLE PER PERSON B&B	DOUBLE FOR 2 PERSONS B&B	🛏	2
	MIN £	MAX £	MIN £	MAX £	1
	12.00	13.00	24.00	26.00	OPEN 1-12

DYFFRYN ARDUDWY Map Ref Da3

Pleasant village near coast on Barmouth-Harlech road, set between sea and mountains. Caravan sites nearby.

Guest Houses

Cromlech

Dyffryn Ardudwy, Gwynedd, LL44 2EP [L]
Tel: (03417) 485

Small guest house offering good food and homely atmosphere, situated midway between Harlech and Barmouth in Dyffryn village. Half hour walk to the unspoilt beaches through woods and sand-dunes. Ideal base for visiting Snowdonia, convenient for public transport, outstanding walks and golden beaches. Ample parking and large garden overlooking open fields. Vegetarian cooking available.

H ✗ P 🐾	SINGLE PER PERSON B&B	DOUBLE FOR 2 PERSONS B&B	🛏	4
	MIN £	MAX £	MIN £	MAX £	
	9.00	12.00	17.00	24.00	OPEN 1-12

FAIRBOURNE Map Ref Db4

Quiet resort with 2 miles of sand south of Mawddach Estuary. Railway buffs travel far to go on its 1' 3" gauge railway. Shops and accommodation. Car parks. Butterfly farm.

Guest Houses

Bryn-y-Mor Guest House

Llwyngwril, Gwynedd, LL37 2JQ
Tel: (0341) 250043

A warm welcome is extended at this quiet family run guest house overlooking the sea with private car park. This Victorian house has large light bedrooms, two double, one twin, electric heating, usual facilities. Central for touring, trains, buses, holiday sports, trekking, etc. Hot drinks available at all times. Friendly service in a pleasant village.

P ✗ 🐾 ✗	SINGLE PER PERSON B&B	DOUBLE FOR 2 PERSONS B&B	🛏	3
	MIN £	MAX £	MIN £	MAX £	
			18.00	22.00	OPEN 1-11

Einion House

Friog, Fairbourne, Gwynedd, LL38 2NX
Tel: (0341) 250644

Pleasant family run guest house, comfortably furnished and with homely atmosphere. Restaurant and residential licence. Fire certificate. All bedrooms have tea making facilities, clock/radios and hairdryers. Beautiful sea and mountain views. Children welcome. Pets by arrangement. Set in an area of exceptional scenery within easy reach of beaches, castles and great little trains.

H ✗ P 🐾	SINGLE PER PERSON B&B	DOUBLE FOR 2 PERSONS B&B	🛏	8
	MIN £	MAX £	MIN £	MAX £	2
	12.50	14.00	25.00	28.00	OPEN 1-12

HARLECH   Map Ref Da2

Small, stone-built town dominated by remains of 13th century castle - site of Owain Glyndwr's last stand. Dramatically set on a high crag, the castle commands a magnificent panorama of rolling sand dunes, sea and mountains. Home of 18-hole Royal St David's Golf Club. Shell Island nearby; theatre and swimming pool.

Guest Houses

Abbott House
Llandanwg, Harlech, Gwynedd, LL46 2SB
Tel: (034123) 483
Detached house, close to Harlech with its famous castle. Near sixth century church. Centrally heated, colour televisions, wash basins every room. Reduced rates for children. Local activities, trekking, sailing, wind surfing, fishing, Great Little Trains of Wales. Near station. Modern flat also available. Warm welcome assured.

SINGLE PER PERSON B&B		DOUBLE FOR 2 PERSONS B&B			3
MIN £	MAX £	MIN £	MAX £		
9.00	15.00	18.00	22.00		OPEN 1-12

Aris Guest House
Pen y Bryn, Harlech, Gwynedd, LL46 2SL
Tel: (0766) 780409
Aris is a small friendly guest house situated in a very quiet spot immediately above Harlech village. Magnificent views over Castle, beach and Snowdonia. All four bedrooms are tastefully furnished, H & C, teamakers, television, electric blankets, central heating. Ample parking. Good food using garden produce, fish is our speciality. Vegetarians welcome.

SINGLE PER PERSON B&B		DOUBLE FOR 2 PERSONS B&B			4
MIN £	MAX £	MIN £	MAX £		
10.00	10.00	20.00	20.00		OPEN 1-12

Arundel
High Street, Harlech, Gwynedd, LL46 2YE
Tel: (0766) 780637
Situated 100 yards above Harlech Castle with beautiful views of golf course, Tremadog Bay and Snowdonia Mountains. Central for touring North Wales. Lovely sandy beach. Ample parking. Full central heating. Bathroom with separate shower, separate toilet. Home from home atmosphere.

SINGLE PER PERSON B&B		DOUBLE FOR 2 PERSONS B&B			3
MIN £	MAX £	MIN £	MAX £		
		19.00	22.00		OPEN 1-12

Fron Deg
Llanfair, Harlech, Gwynedd, LL46 2RS
Tel: (0766) 780448
Very conveniently located within ½ mile walking distance of centre of Harlech. Offering Championship Golf. Famous castle and splendid views. Fron Deg has 3 centrally heated rooms, "good wholesome cooking". Ideal for the country life, walking, fishing, riding. Enquiries to Mrs Ann E Jones.

SINGLE PER PERSON B&B		DOUBLE FOR 2 PERSONS B&B			3
MIN £	MAX £	MIN £	MAX £		
10.00	11.00	20.00	22.00		OPEN 1-12

Glan-y-Gors
Llandanwg, Harlech, Gwynedd, LL46 2SD
Tel: (034123) 410
House with 2 acres of land situated 400 yards from sandy beach. Close to Harlech Castle and golf club. Presenting good home cooking. Welsh speaking family. Homely and relaxed atmosphere. Train station within walking distance. Beautiful views of mountains. 1 family, 1 double, 1 twin bedroom. Electric blankets and central heating for winter months. Evening meal optional. Reduced rates for children.

SINGLE PER PERSON B&B		DOUBLE FOR 2 PERSONS B&B			3
MIN £	MAX £	MIN £	MAX £		
9.00		18.00			OPEN 1-12

TAL-Y-LLYN   Map Ref Dc5

Lakeside village below Cader Idris mountain, ideally placed for fishing and walking. Narrow-gauge Talyllyn Railway, which runs to a nearby halt, connects with Tywyn.

Farmhouses

Dolffanog Fach
Tal-y-Llyn, Tywyn, Gwynedd, LL36 9AJ
Tel: (065473) 235
Dolffanog is situated near Tal-y-Llyn Lake at the foot of Cader Idris. Bedrooms with wash-basins, shaver points, heating tea/coffee facilities. Lounge with colour TV, comfort and good home cooking. Fire certificate granted. Ample car parking. Ideal centre for touring, walking or fishing. Games room with full size snooker table and dart board. Contact Mrs Meirwen Pughe. New telephone number 1990 (0654) 761235.

SINGLE PER PERSON B&B		DOUBLE FOR 2 PERSONS B&B			3
MIN £	MAX £	MIN £	MAX £		
11.00	12.00	22.00	24.00		OPEN 3-10

TRAWSFYNYDD   Map Ref Dc2

In the heartland of Snowdonia National Park, Trawsfynydd stands on the edge of a lake fed by several small streams that tumble down from the mountains. The Trawsfynydd Power Station is near the lake. Plenty of hill walking and fishing.

Farmhouses

Llainwen Farm
Trawsfynydd, Gwynedd, LL41 4TN
Tel: (076687) 242
Situated in Snowdonia National Park. 41 acre mixed farm on bus route. Farmhouse offering one family bedroom with two double beds and one single bed also double bedroom, both with shaver points and wash basin. Ideal centre for walking, fishing, sightseeing and ski-ing! Reduced rates for children.

SINGLE PER PERSON B&B		DOUBLE FOR 2 PERSONS B&B			2
MIN £	MAX £	MIN £	MAX £		
10.00		20.00			OPEN 4-10

HARLECH CASTLE

TYWYN   Map Ref Da5

Seaside resort on Cardigan Bay, with beach activities, sea and river fishing and golf among its leading attractions. Narrow-gauge Talyllyn Railway runs inland from here and St. Cadfan's Stone and Llanegryn Church are important Christian sites. In the hills stand Castell-y-Bere, a native Welsh castle, and Bird Rock, a haven for birdlife.

Guest Houses

The Old Mill

Aberdovey Road, Tywyn, Gwynedd, LL36 9HS
Tel: (0654) 711832
The Mill is situated on the main A493 Aberdovey Road. 1½ miles from the seaside town of Tywyn, 2½ mile from the picturesque village of Aberdovey. Twin, doubles and family room. Special rates for children up to twelve. Residents lounge with television, video, tea and coffee facilities in all rooms. Restaurant with separate tables. Gardens. Fire certificate.

	SINGLE PER PERSON B&B		DOUBLE FOR 2 PERSONS B&B		🛏	7
	MIN £	MAX £	MIN £	MAX £		
	12.50	13.50	25.00	27.00	OPEN 1-12	

Pant y Neuadd Country House

Aberdyfi Road, Tywyn, Gwynedd, LL36 9HW
Tel: (0654) 711393
Originally the home of Sir Hayden Jones owner of the famous Tal-y-Llyn Railway. The house has been modernised but still retaining its character, oak panelling and log fires. All three rooms have heating, TV's, tea making facilities. All are en-suite. A quiet stroll away from Tywyn and close by to all outdoor pursuits.

	SINGLE PER PERSON B&B		DOUBLE FOR 2 PERSONS B&B		🛏	3
	MIN £	MAX £	MIN £	MAX £		3
	14.00	14.00	24.00	28.00	OPEN 4-10	

WALES *It's magic*

Farmhouses

Hendy Farm

Tywyn, Gwynedd, LL36 9RU
Tel: (0654) 710457
Family run farm situated in Snowdonia National Park with beautiful scenic views, near town and beach. Talyllyn railway nearby. Ideal area for sporting activities. Three spacious double bedrooms, wash basins, tea making facilities television and radio. A warm welcome awaits you in relaxed informal atmosphere, from a welsh speaking family. Contact Anne Lloyd-Jones.

	SINGLE PER PERSON B&B		DOUBLE FOR 2 PERSONS B&B		🛏	3
	MIN £	MAX £	MIN £	MAX £		
	11.00	13.00	20.00	24.00	OPEN 1-12	

Llanllwyda Farm

Llanfihangel-y-Pennant, Tywyn, Gwynedd, LL36 9TW
Tel: (065477) 276
Farmhouse situated in the picturesque valley of Dysynni. Beamed ceiling in dining room/sitting room. Homely atmosphere. Good home cooking. 1 double bedroom, 1 twin bedded bedrooms, 1 family bedroom, 1 bathroom, separate WC and basin. Beach 6 miles away. Excellent bird watching area. Good walks, golf 6 miles away. Farmhouse facing Cader Idris and near Bird Rock where cormorants are nesting. Fishing available River Dysynni 3 minutes from farmhouse.

	SINGLE PER PERSON B&B		DOUBLE FOR 2 PERSONS B&B		🛏	3
	MIN £	MAX £	MIN £	MAX £		
	10.00	12.00	18.00	20.00	OPEN 3-12	

Tan y Coed Ucha

Abergynolwyn, Tywyn, Gwynedd, LL36 9UP
Tel: (0654) 782228
Tan y Coed Ucha is situated on the B4405 road. Tal-y-Llyn Narrow Gauge Railway runs through our land with Dolgoch Falls nearby and the disused quarry above Abergynolwyn, also in easy reach to climb Cader Idris. Modern services, colour TV, log fires when wet and cold. Tea/coffee facilities in bedrooms, 1 family, 1 single, 1 twin bedded. Midweek and weekend breaks available.

	SINGLE PER PERSON B&B		DOUBLE FOR 2 PERSONS B&B		🛏	3
	MIN £	MAX £	MIN £	MAX £		
	9.00	10.00	18.00	20.00	OPEN 3-10	

Tynybryn Farm

Llanfihangel y Pennant, Tywyn, Gwynedd, LL36 9TN
Tel: (065477) 277
Tynybryn set in picturesque countryside. Sitting-dining room. 300 year old farmhouse with stone fireplaces, beams, log fires. Full support to Heart Beat Wales, Taste of Wales. Cader Idris, trout fishing, Bera Castle, Bird Rock, Talyllyn Railway and lake. Welsh speaking family. Swimming pool and sea at Tywyn and Aberdovey. Excellent walks. Pony farm. Tea- coffee facilities in bedroom. Bara brith and Welsh cakes. Also self catering farmhouse, with all modern conveniences. Tranquil, secluded beautiful views, rolling mountains. Bird watching. Full central heating.

	SINGLE PER PERSON B&B		DOUBLE FOR 2 PERSONS B&B		🛏	3
	MIN £	MAX £	MIN £	MAX £		
	10.50	13.00	21.00	26.00	OPEN 1-12	

WINDSURFING, TALYLLYN LAKE

CEREDIGION

Reminders of Wales's traditions and heritage are commonplace in Ceredigion. Aberystwyth preserves its Victorian character – it's even got a camera obscura (a popular amusement in bygone times) and a marvellous 'museum in a music hall'). Aberaeron's handsome Georgian harbour can be viewed from a unique aerial ferry, based on a 19th-century original. At Devil's Bridge (go there by steam train from Aberystwyth), you can see why the dramatic gorge was described in the 19th century as a 'dread chasm'. And New Quay's picturesque stone quayside, now busy with colourful holiday craft, still displays its old table of harbour tolls.

Drovers used to gather in Tregaron's square before setting off with their livestock to markets along the English border. You can trace their footsteps by motoring over Wales's most spectacular drovers' route, the Abergwesyn Pass, a narrow road which winds its way eastwards across the empty 'Roof of Wales'.

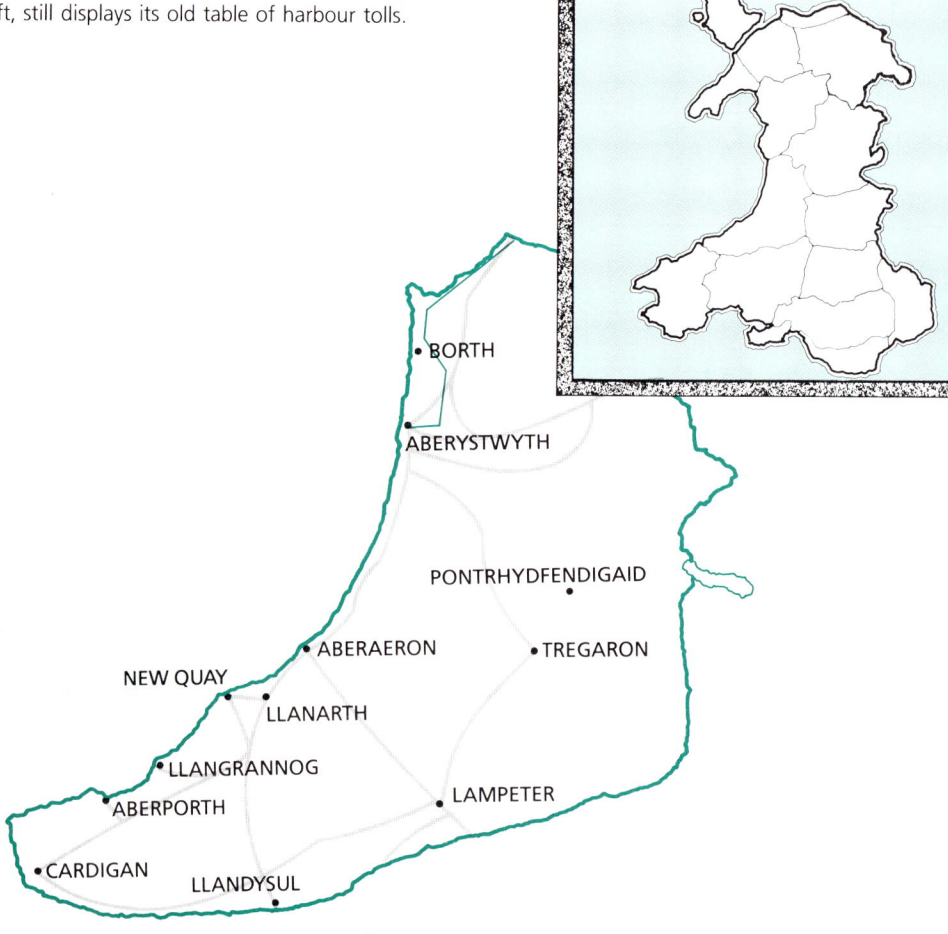

ABERAERON Map Ref Fc4

Most attractive little town on Cardigan Bay, with distinctive Georgian-style architecture. Pleasant harbour, marine aquarium and coastal centre with a re-creation of Aberaeron Express, an extraordinary ariel ferry first built in 1885. Sailing popular; good centre for coast and inland.

Guest Houses

7/8 Bellevue Terrace

Aberaeron, Dyfed, SA46 OBB
Tel: (0545) 570107

Spacious bedrooms overlooking Aberaeron harbour. Facilities for babies and children including babysitting. Special rates for family room. Ground floor facilities for disabled guests. Choice of good home cooking. Beverages always available. Large safe garden and flower filled conservatory to relax in. We enjoy having visitors and provide a really personal service.

SINGLE PER PERSON B&B		DOUBLE FOR 2 PERSONS B&B		🛏	4
MIN £	MAX £	MIN £	MAX £		
12.00	15.00	24.00	24.00	OPEN 1-12	

Llys Aeron Guest House

Lampeter Road, Aberaeron, Dyfed, SA46 0ED
Tel: (0545) 570276

A lovely area to spend a relaxed holiday. Aberaeron sits around a charming harbour. Friendly shops. Good pubs. Llys Aeron has cheerful, comfortable bedrooms, all with wash basins. Breakfast room overlooking garden. Parking on private forecourt. We welcome you and yours including well behaved pets. Aberaeron has marvellous summer sunsets.

SINGLE PER PERSON B&B		DOUBLE FOR 2 PERSONS B&B		🛏	4
MIN £	MAX £	MIN £	MAX £		
10.00	13.00	19.00	23.00	OPEN 1-12	

Mynedfa

4 Queen Street, Aberaeron, Dyfed, SA46 0BX
Tel: (0545) 570712

Warm Welsh welcome awaits you in our guest house. Ideally located for touring countryside, situated within 300 yards from beach, car park, bus stop, town centre, in quiet no through road. Television lounge, central heating. Wash basin, shaver points, tea/coffee facilities in bedrooms. Walking distance to bowling green, tennis courts, swimming pool, riverside walk, fishing.

SINGLE PER PERSON B&B		DOUBLE FOR 2 PERSONS B&B		🛏	3
MIN £	MAX £	MIN £	MAX £		
9.00	10.00	18.00	20.00	OPEN 1-12	

Pontsaeson Guest House

Cross Inn, Llanon, Dyfed, SY23 5NE
Tel: (09746) 410

Traditional 17th century stone Welsh longhouse situated in beautiful countryside with own woodland trout stream. Ideal for artists, bird watchers. H & C, central heating, shaver points all rooms. Tea/coffee facilities. TV lounge. Home cooking. Reduced rates for children sharing/OAP's. One twin, two doubles. Central for touring North/South Wales 3 miles Cardigan coast.

SINGLE PER PERSON B&B		DOUBLE FOR 2 PERSONS B&B		🛏	3
MIN £	MAX £	MIN £	MAX £		
	28.00		28.00	OPEN 1-12	

Tŷ Lon

Ciliau Aeron, Aberaeron, Dyfed, SA48 8DL
Tel: (0570) 470726

Tŷ Lon is a family run guest house set in the beautiful Vale of Aeron. 2½ miles from Aberaeron within easy reach of Cardigan Bay. Local activities include river and sea fishing, horse riding. All bedrooms have wash basins, shaver points, central heating, separate bathroom and toilets. Ample parking space. Food and comfort are our specialities.

SINGLE PER PERSON B&B		DOUBLE FOR 2 PERSONS B&B		🛏	3
MIN £	MAX £	MIN £	MAX £		
10.00	12.00	20.00	24.00	OPEN 1-12	

ABERYSTWYTH Map Ref Fe2

Premier resort of the Cardigan Bay coastline. Fine promenade, cliff railway, camera obscura, pier and many other seaside attractions. University town, lively Arts Centre with theatre and concert hall. National Library of Wales stands commandingly on hillside. Good shopping. Vale of Rheidol narrow-gauge steam line runs to Devil's Bridge Falls.

Hotels

Windsor Private Hotel

41 Queens Road, Aberystwyth, Dyfed, SY23 2HN
Tel: (0970) 612134

Ten bedroomed hotel situated close to sea front and shops, tennis, bowls and golf at rear of premises. All rooms have hot and cold, TV, shaving points, tea/coffee making facilities. Some rooms have private shower. Residential licence and fire certificate in force. Hotel is privately run by proprietors.

SINGLE PER PERSON B&B		DOUBLE FOR 2 PERSONS B&B		🛏	10
MIN £	MAX £	MIN £	MAX £		
11.00	14.00	22.00	28.00	OPEN 1-12	

Guest Houses

Bryn-y-Don

36 Bridge Street, Aberystwyth, Dyfed, SY23 1QB
Tel: (0970) 612011

Close to station and seafront. Tea/coffee making facilities, colour TV, hot and cold all bedrooms. Evening meal optional. Reductions for children, cot, high chair, baby sitting available. Good home cooking. Warm welcome always. Contact Mrs Iona Daniel.

SINGLE PER PERSON B&B		DOUBLE FOR 2 PERSONS B&B		🛏	4
MIN £	MAX £	MIN £	MAX £		
10.00	13.00	18.00	22.00	OPEN 1-12	

Glyn Garth Licensed Guest House

South Road, Aberystwyth, Dyfed, SY23 1JS
Tel: (0970) 615050

Glyn Garth is situated adjacent to south promenade near castle and harbour. All rooms have colour TV, H & C, tea/ coffee making and many with en-suite facilities. Fully centrally heated with a comfortable lounge. This family run guest house is noted for excellent food and service where cleanliness is a high priority. Not recommended for heavy smokers. AA Listed. RAC Acclaimed.

SINGLE PER PERSON B&B		DOUBLE FOR 2 PERSONS B&B		🛏	10
MIN £	MAX £	MIN £	MAX £		6
12.00	14.00	24.00	28.00	OPEN 1-12	

ABERSTWYTH CONTINUED

Guest Houses

Glynwern Guest House

Llanilar, Aberystwyth, Dyfed, SY23 4NY
Tel: (09747) 203 [L]

Glynwern is an attractive house set in its own extensive grounds, with own gardens fronting the River Ystwyth, with free private fishing for guests. Two double bedrooms with washbasins, one twin and two single rooms. Comfortable lounge and pleasant dining room. Central heating. Open all year. Ideal base for peaceful, restful or exploring holiday. No dogs allowed. SAE.

	SINGLE PER PERSON B&B	DOUBLE FOR 2 PERSONS B&B		5
	MIN £	MAX £	MIN £	MAX £	
	14.00	14.00	28.00	28.00	OPEN 1-12

Hemstal Guest House

69 North Parade, Aberystwyth, Dyfed, SY23 2JW
Tel: (0970) 624398

Family run guest house approximately 150 yards from sea front, located in town centre. Hot and cold in all rooms. Central heating. Fire certificate. TV lounge. Bed and breakfast, optional evening meals, very reasonable terms. Homely. Write or telephone for details. Guests personally cared for by proprietors Jean and Elwyn Thomas.

	SINGLE PER PERSON B&B	DOUBLE FOR 2 PERSONS B&B		6
	MIN £	MAX £	MIN £	MAX £	
	12.00			20.00	OPEN 1-12

Linkenma

19 Custom House Street, Aberystwyth, Dyfed, SY23 1JR
Tel: (0970) 617480

Linkenma a small guest house situated 100 yards from south promenade, castle and harbour. Near main shopping centre, rail, bus station. Hot and cold, shaver points all bedrooms. Central heating throughout. TV lounge. Early and late tea or coffee served on request. Highly recommended for good food and friendly atmosphere. Under personal supervision of proprietress.

	SINGLE PER PERSON B&B	DOUBLE FOR 2 PERSONS B&B		3
	MIN £	MAX £	MIN £	MAX £	
	10.00	11.00	19.00	22.00	OPEN 1-12

Llwynhâf

26 Cambrian Street, Aberystwyth, Dyfed, SY23 1NZ
Tel: (0970) 624826

Llwynhâf is a small family guest house, situtated 100 yards from the railway station, bus terminal, car park, and main shopping centre. Remodernised to a very high standard. We provide colour televisions and tea/coffee making facilities in all bedrooms, central heating and separate shower room. Cot and high chair available. Open all year round.

	SINGLE PER PERSON B&B	DOUBLE FOR 2 PERSONS B&B		3
	MIN £	MAX £	MIN £	MAX £	
	10.00	10.00	20.00	20.00	OPEN 1-12

Melford Guest House

20 Mill Street, Aberystwyth, Dyfed, SY23 1HZ
Tel: (0970) 612096

A small, family run guest house situated 200 yards from rail and bus stations and within 400 yards of harbour, castle, promenade and shopping centre. Full central heating throughout. Hot and cold in all rooms, bathroom with shower. Colour TV in residents lounge. Early morning tea or coffee served on request. Homely welcome always.

	SINGLE PER PERSON B&B	DOUBLE FOR 2 PERSONS B&B		3
	MIN £	MAX £	MIN £	MAX £	
	9.00	11.00	18.00	20.00	OPEN 1-12

Myrddin

1 Rheidol Terrace, Aberystwyth, Dyfed, SY23 1JU
Tel: (0970) 612799

Comfortable, friendly family run guest house. Experienced in providing excellent service and good food. 100 yards from south promenade, castle and harbour. All bedrooms have hot and cold, shaver points, and central heating. Colour television lounge. Separate dining room. A warm welcome awaits you. See for yourselves. Brochure available. Please contact Mrs Lisa Bumford.

	SINGLE PER PERSON B&B	DOUBLE FOR 2 PERSONS B&B		3
	MIN £	MAX £	MIN £	MAX £	
	9.00	10.50	18.00	21.00	OPEN 7-9

Myrddin

6 South Marine Terrace, Aberystwyth, Dyfed, SY23 1JX
Tel: (0970) 612031

This is an ideally situated guest house on the south promenade overlooking Cardigan Bay, adjacent to the castle and harbour. Most rooms have sea views, all with hot and cold, colour satellite TV, tea/coffee making facilities. Central heating. Comfortable TV lounge. The Myrddin is well renowned for its home cooking and friendly welcome.

	SINGLE PER PERSON B&B	DOUBLE FOR 2 PERSONS B&B		4
	MIN £	MAX £	MIN £	MAX £	
	11.00	12.00	20.00	24.00	OPEN 1-12

Plas Antaron

Antaron Avenue, Penparcau, Aberystwyth, Dyfed   SY23 1SF
Tel: (0970) 611550

Approximately one mile from town centre. All bedrooms have TV, tea making facilities. Licensed, cot available. Parking. Most rooms en-suite. Double, twin rooms. Two ground floor rooms. Bar meals available. Evening dinner with prior booking. Special rates for children sharing. Reduced rates January to March and October to November.

	SINGLE PER PERSON B&B	DOUBLE FOR 2 PERSONS B&B		10
					7
	MIN £	MAX £	MIN £	MAX £	
		14.00		23.00	OPEN 1-12

Yr Hafod

1 South Marine Terrace, Aberystwyth, Dyfed, SY23 1JX
Tel: (0970) 617579

This comfortable guest house is well known for its fine food and hospitality. It is ideally situated on the south promenade adjacent to the castle and overlooking Cardigan Bay. Most bedrooms with panoramic sea views, all with hot and cold, colour television, tea/coffee making facilities etc. Fully centrally heated. A warm welcome always.

	SINGLE PER PERSON B&B	DOUBLE FOR 2 PERSONS B&B		4
	MIN £	MAX £	MIN £	MAX £	
	11.00	12.00	22.00	24.00	OPEN 1-12

Farmhouses

Cwmergyr Farm

Ponterwyd, Aberystwyth, Dyfed, SY23 3LB
Tel: (097085) 301 [L]

Cwmergyr is a modern farmhouse, among the beautiful Cambrian Mountains, 16 miles east of Aberystwyth off A44. Comfort, good food and warm welcome assured. Two bedrooms with TV and tea/coffee facilities. Guest own bathroom. Lounge/dinner, separate tables, TV, log fire. Children welcome, reduced rates. No pets. Fishing, trekking, beaches, walks, steam railway nearby.

	SINGLE PER PERSON B&B	DOUBLE FOR 2 PERSONS B&B		2
	MIN £	MAX £	MIN £	MAX £	
	10.50	10.50	17.00	20.00	OPEN 2-11

Neuadd Parc Farm

Capel Bangor, Aberystwyth, Dyfed, SY23 3NA
Tel: (097084) 260 [L]

Neuadd Parc 207 acre mixed farm with friesian dairy herd, Welsh section C cob type show ponies, is situated in the picturesque Rheidol Valley, 8 miles Aberystwyth. Victorian style farmhouse, dining room, comfortable lounge with colour TV, 1 twin bedded, 1 family room, 1 double room, 1 bathroom with shower, 1 toilet. Rough shooting and fishing on farm. Ideal for walks and birdwatching. Good plain food served. Homely atmosphere and peaceful holiday.

	SINGLE PER PERSON B&B	DOUBLE FOR 2 PERSONS B&B		3
	MIN £	MAX £	MIN £	MAX £	
	8.50	9.00	17.00	18.00	OPEN 3-10

Tycam Farm

Capel Bangor, Aberystwyth, Dyfed,
SY23 3NA
Tel: (097084) 662

Peaceful dairy/sheep farm in glorious Rheidol Valley, 7½ miles Aberystwyth, only 2½ miles off A44. Real home comfort and farmhouse cooking. Lounge/dining room (separate tables), colour TV. Perfect centre for walking, bird watching, sightseeing, ½ mile superb salmon, sewin, trout fishing on farm, plus nearby lakes. Pony trekking, golf and beaches within easy reach. 2 fine family rooms, 1 double all with central heating, bathroom, toilet etc. Ample car parking.

H	SINGLE PER PERSON B&B		DOUBLE FOR 2 PERSONS B&B		🛏	3
P	MIN £	MAX £	MIN £	MAX £		
X	9.00		18.00		OPEN 1-12	

L

BORTH Map Ref Db7

Popular holiday village with marvellous expanse of firm sands, ideal for beach games. Fine views to north across Dovey Estuary. Golf links, promenade 2 miles long.

Guest Houses

Rock House

Llancynfelyn, Machynlleth, Powys,
SY20 8PU
Tel: (097086) 678

A friendly welcome awaits you in a quiet situation with scenic views, all rooms have hot and cold, shaver points, tea and coffee making facilities, two double rooms have TV. TV lounge, good home cooking, parking. No pets. Seaside resort of Borth 3 miles, ideal for children. Evening meal by prior arrangement only.

P	SINGLE PER PERSON B&B		DOUBLE FOR 2 PERSONS B&B		🛏	3
X	MIN £	MAX £	MIN £	MAX £		
	10.50	12.00	21.00	24.00	OPEN 1-12	

Tŷ-Gwylan Guest House

Francis Road, Borth, Dyfed, SY24 5NJ
Tel: (0970) 871434

Overlooking miles of safe sandy beach, boating, fishing and all water sports. Golf course and pony trekking nearby. Homely atmosphere, friendly welcome awaits you from June and Ron. Double or twin bedded rooms with hot and cold also tea/coffee making facilities, TV etc. Evening meals optional. Special Spring and Autumn breaks. Ample parking.

H	SINGLE PER PERSON B&B		DOUBLE FOR 2 PERSONS B&B		🛏	4
P X	MIN £	MAX £	MIN £	MAX £		
	10.00	12.00	20.00	24.00	OPEN 1-12	

CARDIGAN Map Ref Fa5

Market town close to beaches and resorts. Good shopping facilities, accommodation, inns. Golf and fishing. Base for exploring inland along wooded Teifi Valley and south to the Pembrokeshire Coast National Park.

Guest Houses

Berwyn

St. Dogmaels, Cardigan, Dyfed,
SA43 3HS
Tel: (0239) 613555

Privately situated with magnificent views, overlooking River Teifi. Central for beautiful beaches, country walks, coastal path, golf, fishing, sailing, boat trips, Welsh crafts. Enjoy breakfast with gorgeous views. Relax on two acres delightful grounds. En-suite with TV. Bedrooms with vanity suites, tea/coffee facilities. Central heating. TV lounge. Ample private parking. (Croeso) Welsh welcome.

P	SINGLE PER PERSON B&B		DOUBLE FOR 2 PERSONS B&B		🛏	3
🍴						1
♿	MIN £	MAX £	MIN £	MAX £		
	10.50	12.50	21.00	25.00	OPEN 1-12	

Bingham House

Pendre, Cardigan, Dyfed, SA43 1JU
Tel: (0239) 615190

Small family run guest house in excellent location for shops, countryside and beaches. Tennis, golf, fishing, watersports (including canoeing and jetskis), wildlife park nearby. Friendly atmosphere, good food, tea/coffee making facilities available, hot and cold in all rooms. Separate colour TV lounge, private parking. Open all year. Special weekly rates.

H ♿	SINGLE PER PERSON B&B		DOUBLE FOR 2 PERSONS B&B		🛏	3
P X						1
🍴	MIN £	MAX £	MIN £	MAX £		
	11.00		20.00	26.00	OPEN 1-12	

Brynhyfryd Guest House

Gwbert Road, Cardigan,
Dyfed, SA43 1AE
Tel: (0239) 612861

A comfortable homely stay is assured at our long established guest house. Situated in a pleasant area of Cardigan, within easy walking distance of town centre. Bedrooms have heating, washbasins, tea/coffee facilities. 1 bedroom with en-suite most with colour TV, guests lounge, evening meals, payphone. No problems with parking. AA & RAC listed. WTB guest house Award 1989.

X	SINGLE PER PERSON B&B		DOUBLE FOR 2 PERSONS B&B		🛏	6
						1
	MIN £	MAX £	MIN £	MAX £		
	11.00	12.00	22.00	24.00	OPEN 1-12	

Hendy

Llangoedmor, Cardigan, Dyfed,
SA43 2LH
Tel: (0239) 614117

Hendy is situated in a large garden 1½ miles from Cardigan. The ground floor bedrooms are well furnished and have H & C, tea and coffee making facilities. Meals are served in your own room Ground floor bathroom. Use of laundry facilities if required. Packed lunches are available. Vegetarians welcome. Ample parking. No smoking or pets.

P	SINGLE PER PERSON B&B		DOUBLE FOR 2 PERSONS B&B		🛏	2
🍴						
X	MIN £	MAX £	MIN £	MAX £		
			22.00	25.00	OPEN 1-12	

Maes-a-Môr

Gwbert Road, Cardigan,
Dyfed, SA43 1AE
Tel: (0239) 614929

A friendly welcome awaits you by the Jones family in this attractively decorated Edwardian house. All bedrooms have private facilities with colour TV, tea/coffee facilities available. Centrally heated and double glazed throughout. Separate TV lounge, payphone. Private parking. Centrally situated in the historic market town and ideal for exploring central Wales and the rugged coastal paths. WTB Guest House Award and Hygiene Certificate. Highly recommended by Let's Go Guide to Britain and Ireland.

P X	SINGLE PER PERSON B&B		DOUBLE FOR 2 PERSONS B&B		🛏	3
🍴						3
♿	MIN £	MAX £	MIN £	MAX £		
	14.00	14.00	24.00	28.00	OPEN 1-12	

Trellacca Guest House & Tea Room

Tremain, Cardigan, Dyfed, SA43 1SJ
Tel: (0239) 810730

4 miles north of Cardigan (A487). Ideal base for touring Mid Wales. 1 family room en-suite, 1 double, 2 singles, hot and cold, shaver points, tea/coffee facilities, cots available. Comfortable TV lounge, separate dining room, good home cooking. Payphone. Snooker, darts, table tennis, croquet. Nearest beach Aberporth 2½ miles. Weekly rates and reductions for children.

H X	SINGLE PER PERSON B&B		DOUBLE FOR 2 PERSONS B&B		🛏	4
P						1
♿	MIN £	MAX £	MIN £	MAX £		
	13.00	13.00	26.00	26.00	OPEN 1-12	

CALL Holidays (0792) 645555

LAMPETER Map Ref Fe5

Farmers and students mingle in this distinctive small central Dyfed town, in the picturesque Teifi Valley. Concerts are often held in St. David's University College, and visitors are welcome. Golf and angling, range of small shops and some old inns.

Guest Houses

Min-y-Llan
Llanwenog, Llanybydder, Dyfed, SA40 9UT
Tel: (0570) 480378
Country house in peaceful surroundings with panoramic views. Within easy reach of popular resorts and lively market towns. Central heating throughout. Spacious lounge, TV, separate dining room. One double, two twin bedrooms, washbasins, tea facilities, evening meal by arrangement. Good home cooking, own garden produce. Warm Welsh welcome. Ideal centre for walking, fishing, pony trekking.

H P ×	SINGLE PER PERSON B&B		DOUBLE FOR 2 PERSONS B&B		🛏 3
	MIN £	MAX £	MIN £	MAX £	
	10.00	11.00	20.00	22.00	OPEN 3-9

Penwern Old Mills
Cribyn, Lampeter, Dyfed, SA48 7QH L
Tel: (0570) 470762
Welcome to this former rural Woollen Mill set in a quiet valley alongside a small stream. Penwern offers homely accommodation, evening meal optional, packed lunches by arrangement, large comfortable lounge, television, central heating. Cot and highchair available. Well behaved pets welcomed. Non smokers preferred. Trout lakes nearby. Many Mid Wales attractions within reasonable distance.

H ½ P × 🐾	SINGLE PER PERSON B&B		DOUBLE FOR 2 PERSONS B&B		🛏 3
	MIN £	MAX £	MIN £	MAX £	
	8.50	8.50	16.00	16.00	OPEN 1-12

Strachan House
Pencarreg, Llanybydder, Dyfed, SA40 9QG L
Tel: (0570) 480973
A warm welcome awaits you in quiet situation but central for touring Mid Wales beauty spots. ½ hour from coast road. Walking, golfing, riding, fishing arranged. TV lounge. Good food. Every modern comfort. Tea and coffee facilities. Twin beds and double beds available. Quiet village with very old church and country pub. Horse sales every month.

H × P 🐾	SINGLE PER PERSON B&B		DOUBLE FOR 2 PERSONS B&B		🛏 4
					2
	MIN £	MAX £	MIN £	MAX £	
	8.00	12.00	15.00	22.00	OPEN 1-12

Farmhouses

Abermeurig Mansion
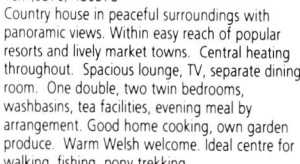
Lampeter, Dyfed, SA48 8PP
Tel: (0570) 470216
Listed ancestral home between Lampeter and Aberaeron off A487 road on B4337. 4 poster and canopy bedrooms, two bedrooms en-suite, shower room, hot and cold with shaver points, tea making facilities. Good home cooking, separate tables. Near pony trekking, woollen mills, golf course 8 miles. BTA commended. Wales Tourist Board Award, 3 Crowns. Come and enjoy real hospitality, fishing, shooting, varied wild life.

H TW P ½	SINGLE PER PERSON B&B		DOUBLE FOR 2 PERSONS B&B		🛏 3
					2
	MIN £	MAX £	MIN £	MAX £	
	14.00		28.00		OPEN 1-12

Bryncastell Farm

Llanfair Road, Lampeter, Dyfed, SA48 8JY
Tel: (0570) 422447
"Croeso" John, Beti and Siân welcome you to our 140 acre working farm. Commanding panoramic views across the Teifi Valley to Cambrian Mountains. Twin, double, family bedrooms, private bathrooms, beverage facilities. TV, clock/radio. Warm Welsh welcome. Excellent cuisine. WTB Farmhouse Award 2 Crowns. Activities, fishing, shooting, water divining, bird watching. 1 mile Lampeter, 20 minutes to coast.

H TW P ×	SINGLE PER PERSON B&B		DOUBLE FOR 2 PERSONS B&B		🛏 2
					2
	MIN £	MAX £	MIN £	MAX £	
	11.00	14.00	22.00	28.00	OPEN 1-12

Brynog Mansion
Felinfach, Lampeter, Dyfed, SA48 8AQ
Tel: (0570) 470266
Brynog is a 200 year old mansion with 200 acres, situated in the beautiful Vale of Aeron midway between Lampeter and the seaside resort of Aberaeron, 3/4 miles off A482 main road and villages of Felinfach and Ystrad Aeron. Rough shooting, fishing, birdwatching, riverside walks. Modern amenities. En-suite bedrooms. WTB Farmhouse Award. Tea making facilities. Full Welsh breakfast and a warm welcome.

H TW P × 🐾	SINGLE PER PERSON B&B		DOUBLE FOR 2 PERSONS B&B		🛏 5
					2
	MIN £	MAX £	MIN £	MAX £	
	12.00	14.00	24.00	28.00	OPEN 1-12

Nantymedd Farm

Llanfair, Lampeter, Dyfed, SA48 8JZ
Tel: (057045) 208
Your ideal country holiday in beautiful surroundings. Free trout and salmon fishing on the River Teifi. Within easy driving distance to the seaside resorts of Aberaeron and New Quay. Trekking centre nearby. Good home cooked food. Two double rooms available with special rates for children.

H ½ P × 🐾	SINGLE PER PERSON B&B		DOUBLE FOR 2 PERSONS B&B		🛏 2
	MIN £	MAX £	MIN £	MAX £	
		18.00		20.00	OPEN 1-11

LLANARTH Map Ref Fc4

Village in heart of Welsh cob country, 2½ miles from seaside town of New Quay. Fine sandy bays and choice of bracing headland walks along the coast.

Guest Houses

Cartref
12 Cae Martha, Llanarth, Dyfed, SA47 0RQ L
Tel: (0545) 580524
A friendly welcome awaits you in quiet situation in Mid Wales. Ideal for touring, walking or fishing. 2 miles to local beach. TV/radio, tea/coffee making facilities both rooms. Sorry no facilities for small children. Non smokers only.

P ½ ×	SINGLE PER PERSON B&B		DOUBLE FOR 2 PERSONS B&B		🛏 2
					1
	MIN £	MAX £	MIN £	MAX £	
	8.00	10.00	19.50	23.00	OPEN 1-12

Farmhouses

Parc Farm
Derewen Gam (Oakford), Llanarth, Dyfed, SA47 0RX L
Tel: (0545) 580390
Traditional farmhouse quietly secluded midway between Aberaeron and New Quay. Ideal for walking, touring, bird watching, riding. Good home cooking. 3 bedrooms, 2 with washbasins, shaving points. Central heating, lounge with colour TV, dining room, licensed bar. Friendly atmosphere. Clean level site in unspoilt countryside.

H P × 🐾	SINGLE PER PERSON B&B		DOUBLE FOR 2 PERSONS B&B		🛏 3
	MIN £	MAX £	MIN £	MAX £	
	9.00	12.00	18.00	24.00	OPEN 1-12

LLANDYSUL Map Ref Fc6

Pleasant Teifi-side village in an area rich with woollen mills where visitors are welcome. Salmon fishing very popular; canoeing at certain times of year.

Guest Houses

Pellorwel

Bwlch-y-Groes, Ffostrasol, Llandysul, Dyfed SA44 5JX [L]
Tel: (023975) 226

We offer friendly, informal hospitality in our Victorian style home, situated in a small village on the A486 in very pretty countryside yet convenient for Cardiganshire resorts and the beautiful mountainous scenery of Mid Wales. Single, twin and double/family rooms available. Good home cooking using own garden produce in season. Off road parking.

P	SINGLE PER PERSON B&B		DOUBLE FOR 2 PERSONS B&B		🛏	3
✕	MIN £	MAX £	MIN £	MAX £		
	10.00	12.00	20.00	24.00	OPEN 1-12	

Plas Cerdin

Ffostrasol, Llandysul, Dyfed, SA44 4TA
Tel: (023975) 329

Relax and enjoy the peaceful, friendly atmosphere of our modern split-level house, situated 350 yards from A486 Llandysul-New Quay road. Large TV lounge with panoramic views. Three double bedrooms (two with en-suite shower/ toilet), two single rooms, all with wash basins, shaver points. Good fresh food. Tea/coffee facilities available. Ample parking.

P	SINGLE PER PERSON B&B		DOUBLE FOR 2 PERSONS B&B		🛏	5
✕	MIN £	MAX £	MIN £	MAX £		2
	10.50	12.00	21.00	24.00	OPEN 1-12	

Farmhouses

Broniwan

Rhydlewis, Llandysul, Dyfed, SA44 5PF
Tel: (023975) 261

Attractive stone built farmhouse in delightful position near Cardiganshire coast. Ideal for bird watching, walkers, fishermen. Three pretty bedrooms with radio/alarms. One en-suite. Sitting room with books and log fire, dining room with lovely views, excellent meals including vegetarian. Packed lunches by arrangement. Quiet pets accepted. No smoking please. 10 minutes from River Teifi, 40 minutes from M4. Mrs Carole Jacobs.

H ✕	SINGLE PER PERSON B&B		DOUBLE FOR 2 PERSONS B&B		🛏	3
P ✕	MIN £	MAX £	MIN £	MAX £		1
🐾 TW	11.00	13.00	22.00	26.00	OPEN 1-12	

LLANGRANNOG Map Ref Fb4

Popular with children as a safe summer holiday beach, this is an ideal base for touring the Cardigan Bay coast - a typical little seaside village.

Farmhouses

Hendre Farm

Llangrannog, Llandysul, Dyfed, SA44 6AP
Tel: (023978) 342

Welcome to our lovely period farmhouse overlooking the sea. The house is comfortable and stylish throughout. Excellent meals are served. One bedroom has en-suite facilities. We are 2 miles from Ceredigion's Heritage coastline with its sandy beaches and coastal footpaths, and 1 mile from Wales' newest dry ski-slope. WTB farmhouse Award. Brochure from Mrs Bethan A Williams. New telephone number from March 1990 (0239) 654342.

H	TW	SINGLE PER PERSON B&B		DOUBLE FOR 2 PERSONS B&B		🛏	3
P	✕						1
✕		MIN £	MAX £	MIN £	MAX £		
		10.50	13.00	21.00	26.00	OPEN 3-10	

Penlan Fawr Farmhouse

Plwmp, Llandysul, Dyfed, SA44 6HR
Tel: (023975) 205

Farmhouse just off A487 coast road, midway between Aberaeron and Cardigan. Llangrannog beach 4 miles, a warm welcome, very comfortable accommodation and excellent home cooking awaits you on our 200 acre dairy, sheep and shire horse farm. Family and double room with wash basins, tea/ coffee facilities. Brochure from Mrs Fernleigh Smith. (Wales Tourist Board Farmhouse Award.)

H	SINGLE PER PERSON B&B		DOUBLE FOR 2 PERSONS B&B		🛏	2
P						
✕	MIN £	MAX £	MIN £	MAX £		
	11.00	12.00	22.00	24.00	OPEN 3-11	

NEW QUAY Map Ref Fc4

Very pretty holiday and yachting centre on Cardigan Bay popular with campers and caravanners. Boat and fishing trips. Good base for exploring this beautiful coastline.

Guest Houses

Arfon View

Francis Street, New Quay, Dyfed, SA45 9QL
Tel: (0545) 560837

Excellent views over Cardigan Bay to Snowdonia. Situated above New Quay looking down on harbour and village. Quiet and secluded in private grounds. Only five minutes from sea and shops. Ample secure parking. Large rooms with hot and cold, shaver points, TV lounge. Home cooking. Warm Welsh welcome with personal service. Highly recommended.

H ✕	SINGLE PER PERSON B&B		DOUBLE FOR 2 PERSONS B&B		🛏	3
P						
✕	MIN £	MAX £	MIN £	MAX £		
	9.50	12.50	19.00	23.00	OPEN 4-10	

Caerllyn

Gilfachreda, New Quay, Dyfed, SA45 9SP
Tel: (0545) 580121

Large comfortable cottage, valley setting, large garden 1½ miles New Quay, ten minutes walk to sandy beaches. Tea making, television, wash basins, shaver points, central heating in bedrooms. Large lounge, separate tables. Near riding stables, opportunities for sailing, swimming, walking, relaxing. Many nearby cafes, restaurants. Good position for touring all Cardigan Bay. Friendly atmosphere.

H	SINGLE PER PERSON B&B		DOUBLE FOR 2 PERSONS B&B		🛏	3
🐾	MIN £	MAX £	MIN £	MAX £		
	9.50	10.50	19.00	21.00	OPEN 1-11	

Neuadd Wen

Llanarth, Dyfed, SA47 0NH
Tel: (0545) 580316

Luxury peaceful bungalow in elevated situation with superb views. No passing traffic. Lovely woodland/riverside walks, New Quay beaches two miles. Spacious comfortable rooms, bathrooms en-suite, remote control colour TV. No limit free tea/coffee facilities. Safe for children, free pony rides. Breakfast fit for a king, happy welcome atmosphere. Satisfaction guaranteed, highly recommended.

H ✕	SINGLE PER PERSON B&B		DOUBLE FOR 2 PERSONS B&B		🛏	2
P ✕						2
🐾	MIN £	MAX £	MIN £	MAX £		
	12.50	12.50	25.00	25.00	OPEN 1-12	

Pine Lodge

Francis Street, New Quay, Dyfed, SA45 9QL
Tel: (0545) 560698

Peacefully set in quiet grounds overlooking Cardigan Bay. Completely refurbished. All rooms have washbasins, colour TV, tea/coffee facilities, central heating, private parking. Sea views. Five minutes from beach and shops. Cot available. Personal service. Highly recommended.

H	SINGLE PER PERSON B&B		DOUBLE FOR 2 PERSONS B&B		🛏	3
P						1
✕	MIN £	MAX £	MIN £	MAX £		
	12.00	12.00	24.00	24.00	OPEN 3-10	

NEW QUAY CONTINUED

Farmhouses

Llwynwermod Farm

Maenygroes, New Quay,
Dyfed, SA45 9JR
Tel: (0545) 560083

The farmhouse one mile from New Quay is next to National Trust land with footpath to an unspoilt beach. Reception rooms have log fires and views over Cardigan Bay. Each bedroom central heated, tea/coffee facilities, private shower/bath. Whatever the weather we offer cosy accommodation and wholesome food in comfortable friendly surroundings. WTB Farmhouse Award.

H		SINGLE PER PERSON B&B		DOUBLE FOR 2 PERSONS B&B		🛏	3
P	TW	MIN £	MAX £	MIN £	MAX £	🚗	3
🐾	✕		13.00	22.00	26.00	OPEN 1-12

Nanternis Farm

Nanternis, New Quay, Dyfed,
SA45 9RP
Tel: (0545) 560181

In peaceful hamlet well placed for touring and variety of activities. 2½ miles New Quay, 1½ miles Cwm Tudu. Comfortable guest lounge with open log fire, colour TV. Separate dining room, guest bathroom with separate toilet. Bedrooms have wash basins and drink making facilities. Central heating throughout. Two charming stone self-catering cottages available in farmyard. Brochure available.

H	✕	SINGLE PER PERSON B&B		DOUBLE FOR 2 PERSONS B&B		🛏	2
P		MIN £	MAX £	MIN £	MAX £	🚗	
✓			18.00		22.00	OPEN 4-9

PONTRHYD-FENDIGAID Map Ref Ga3

Large village on the upper reaches of the Teifi in a pastoral area full of rivers and small lakes. Best-known Welsh Medieval poet, Dafydd ap Gwilym, lies buried beneath yew tree in atmospheric ruins of Strata Florida Abbey. A popular eisteddfod is held here annually. Nearest town is Tregaron; pony trekking in surrounding hills; fishing.

Guest Houses

Llysteg

Pontrhydfendigaid, Ystrad Meurig,
Dyfed, SY25 6BB
Tel: (09745) 697

A family run 3 Crown licensed guest house with spacious double, single, family and twin rooms, all attractively furnished with en-suite bathrooms and heaters. We pride ourselves on warm hospitality, good service and excellent home cooking. Tea and home-made cakes on arrival. A homely guest house from which to discover rural Wales. Brochure on request.

H	✕	SINGLE PER PERSON B&B		DOUBLE FOR 2 PERSONS B&B		🛏	7
P		MIN £	MAX £	MIN £	MAX £	🚗	6
🐾		12.00	13.50	27.00	27.00	OPEN 1-12

TREGARON Map Ref Ga3

Small traditional market town offering many pony trekking centres. Anglers and naturalists delight in this area: the great bog nearby is a nature reserve with rare flowers and birds.

Guest Houses

The Edelweiss at Mountain Green

Penuwch, Tregaron, Dyfed, SY25 6QZ
Tel: (097423) 601

The Edelweiss Country Guest House in beautiful position overlooking Cardiganshire countryside yet only 6 miles to Coast. Open throughout year for long or short breaks. Central heating, colour television, hot and cold units every bedroom. Non smokers only. £65 weekly, dinner £5 daily. Delightful alpine garden. Lounge. Parking. Certificate held of The Royal Institute of Public Health and Hygiene.

H	✕	SINGLE PER PERSON B&B		DOUBLE FOR 2 PERSONS B&B		🛏	3
P		MIN £	MAX £	MIN £	MAX £	🚗	
✓		10.00	12.00	20.00	24.00	OPEN 1-12

Glanrhyd Isaf

Stags Head, Llangeitho, Tregaron,
Dyfed, SY25 6QU
Tel: (0974) 298762

A modern bungalow situated on an elevated site surrounded by beautiful countryside. 10 miles from coast. Comfortably furnished, centrally heated. Double room en-suite, TV, tea/coffee facilities, twin bedded room, use of bathroom. Tea/coffee provided. Evening meal by arrangement. Ideal walking, touring, bird watching country. Pony trekking, golf, fishing in area. OS ref. sheet 146. Ref 637 591.

H	✕	SINGLE PER PERSON B&B		DOUBLE FOR 2 PERSONS B&B		🛏	2
P		MIN £	MAX £	MIN £	MAX £	🚗	1
✓		10.50	10.50	23.00	23.00	OPEN 1-12

Neuaddlas Guest House

Tregaron, Dyfed, SY25 6LG
Tel: (0974) 298380

Enjoy the timeless beauty of Mid Wales. Our guest house stands in it's own grounds overlooking the Cors Caron Nature Reserve and nestling beneath the unspoilt Cambrian Mountains. Ideally situated for local beauty spots, attractions and country walks. Bedrooms are tastefully furnished most en-suite, tea/coffee facilities. Splendid views from our dining room and TV lounge. Disabled visitors welcome. Ample car parking.

H	✕	SINGLE PER PERSON B&B		DOUBLE FOR 2 PERSONS B&B		🛏	4
P	TW	MIN £	MAX £	MIN £	MAX £	🚗	3
🐾		12.00	14.00	24.00	28.00	OPEN 1-12

Farmhouses

Hillcroft

Llanddewi Brefi, Dyfed,
SA48 8LH
Tel: (0570) 54300

Two crown with Farmhouse Award. Situated on the B4343 between Tregaron and Lampeter. Hillcroft is a new house set in three acres of lawns on family farm of 200 acres. Home cooking, fishing, pony trekking, golf, bird watching nearby. Twelve miles from sea. Large dining room. TV lounge. Double, twin and single rooms with WHB. Tea facilities. Ample car parking. Details Mrs E Jones.

H	✓	SINGLE PER PERSON B&B		DOUBLE FOR 2 PERSONS B&B		🛏	4
P	✕	MIN £	MAX £	MIN £	MAX £	🚗	
🐾		12.00	14.00	24.00	28.00	OPEN 1-12

MONTGOMERYSHIRE

This area takes in everything from wild, high mountains dotted with isolated stone farmsteads to gentle, fertile border country where you'll see old black-and-white buildings which are typical of the Marches borderlands. Montgomeryshire is farming country through-and-through. Visitors can mingle with farming folk during market days, livestock sales and sheepdog trials.

It's the perfect place for those who like to get a map out and explore tall-hedged country lanes that lead to timeless, tranquil villages. And they might even find remote Pistyll Rhaedr, Wales's highest waterfall, on their travels. Let a narrow-gauge steam train take you on a trip through the hills around Welshpool. And don't miss two castles that couldn't be more different – the National Trust's sumptuous, stately Powis Castle, and Montgomery Castle, a spectacularly located medieval ruin on its rocky perch above a pretty little town.

LAKE VYRNWY
Map Ref Ea3

Man-made lake amid idyllic mountain scenery. Fine walking and pony-trekking country.

Farmhouses

Tynymaes Farm
Llanwddyn, Powys,
SY10 0NN
Tel: (069173) 216
A very warm welcome is extended to all guests at Tynymaes which is a working hill farm situated 2 miles from Lake Vyrnwy. All bedrooms have wash-basins and heating. Good farmhouse fare, dining room and spacious lounge. Homely atmosphere. Excellent base for walking and touring. AA listed and holder of WTB Farmhouse Award. Enquiries to Mrs H A Parry.

H	SINGLE PER PERSON B&B		DOUBLE FOR 2 PERSONS B&B		🛏	3
P					🍴	
✗	MIN £	MAX £	MIN £	MAX £		
	12.00	12.00	22.00	22.00	OPEN 5-10	

LLANBRYNMAIR
Map Ref De5

Scattered mountain-ringed village on Afon (River) Twymwyn, a tributary of the Dyfi. Travel south from here on the B4518 to Llyn (Lake) Clywedog - an inspiring mountain route.

Hotels

Star Inn
Dylife, Staylittle, Llanbrynmair,
Powys SY19 7BW
Tel: (06503) 345
Set in some of Britain's most breathtaking countryside, just off B4518, 9 miles north west of Llanidloes. Ideal for get-away-from-it-all holidays. Pony trekking from own riding stables. Fishing, golfing, sailing and sightseeing nearby. Full central heating. All rooms have hot and cold water, colour TV residents' lounge. Home cooking. Reasonable prices and a warm welcome guaranteed. AA listed.

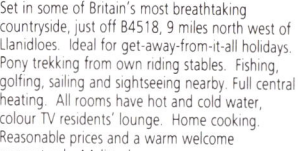

H	✗	SINGLE PER PERSON B&B		DOUBLE FOR 2 PERSONS B&B		🛏	7
P						🍴	2
	🐕	MIN £	MAX £	MIN £	MAX £		
		12.50	14.00	25.00	28.00	OPEN 1-12	

Guest Houses

Cyfeiliog Guest House
Bont Dolgadfan, Llanbrynmair, Powys,
SY19 7BB   [L]
Tel: (06503) 231
Riverside guest house. Beams, log fires, friendly atmosphere with books, maps, information for guests. Centre for bird watching, walking, touring spectacular countryside. 30 minutes to sea. Centrally heated bedrooms, 2 twin, 1 family, visitors bathroom, TV lounge. Home cooked food, wholefoods, vegetarian, special needs catered for. A warm welcome assured in this lovely setting by the River Twymyn.

H	SINGLE PER PERSON B&B		DOUBLE FOR 2 PERSONS B&B		🛏	3
P					🍴	
	MIN £	MAX £	MIN £	MAX £		
	12.50	12.50	21.00	21.00	OPEN 1-12	

LLANDINAM
Map Ref Ea7

Pleasant Severn-side village near Newtown. Home of famous Welsh industrialist David Davies who started out as a sawyer and finished by founding Barry Dock as a coal exporting port.

Hotels

Lion Hotel
Llandinam, Powys, SY17 5BY   [L]
Tel: (068684) 233
Small family hotel in award winning village situated on banks of the River Severn. Fly fishing available, single and twin rooms with wash basins, TV, tea making facilities. Comprehensive home cooking menu. Real ale served in locals bar. 10% reduction on stays 3 nights or more.

H	SINGLE PER PERSON B&B		DOUBLE FOR 2 PERSONS B&B		🛏	4
P					🍴	
✗	MIN £	MAX £	MIN £	MAX £		
	14.00	14.00	25.00	28.00	OPEN 1-12	

Farmhouses

Trewythen
Llandinam, Powys, SY17 5BQ
Tel: (068684) 444
Trewythen is an AA listed, mixed farm set in beautiful countryside situated in the parish of the award winning village of Llandinam. A traditionally beamed farmhouse, comfortably furnished with a warm welcome and good home cooking. Hot and cold, shaver points, tea making facilities in all rooms. Ideal location for touring Mid Wales. Brochure available. New telephone number 1990. (0686688) 444.

H	✂	SINGLE PER PERSON B&B		DOUBLE FOR 2 PERSONS B&B		🛏	2
P	✗					🍴	
	🐕	MIN £	MAX £	MIN £	MAX £		
		11.00	11.00	22.00	22.00	OPEN 5-10	

LLANFAIR CAEREINION
Map Ref Fb5

Pleasant town set amid forest in lovely Vale of Banwy; best known as terminus for narrow-gauge Welshpool and Llanfair Light Railway.

Guest Houses

Carreg Arthur House
Llanfair Caereinion, Welshpool, Powys,
SY21 0DD   [L]
Tel: (0938) 810585
Situated at 1,150 feet above sea level with spectacular views over surrounding countryside. Large modern guest house standing in 3½ acres. 3 bedrooms, one en-suite, lounge with satelite TV. Children half price, babysitting arranged. Pets welcome. Reduced rates for long stays. Very quiet, peaceful location. Lovely for walking, bird spotting, painting, touring Mid Wales.

✗	SINGLE PER PERSON B&B		DOUBLE FOR 2 PERSONS B&B		🛏	3
P					🍴	1
🐕	MIN £	MAX £	MIN £	MAX £		
	9.00	9.00	18.00	18.00	OPEN 1-12	

Old Mill House
Llanfair Caereinion, Powys, SY21 0SB   [L]
Tel: (0938) 810623
On the banks of the River Banwy amongst lovely Welsh hills. Near narrow gauge railway and Powis Castle. Ideal centre for touring Mid Wales, or stop here on your way to the coast. Excellent meals in our licensed restaurant. Tea making facilities and wash basins in rooms.

P	SINGLE PER PERSON B&B		DOUBLE FOR 2 PERSONS B&B		🛏	5
🐕					🍴	1
✗	MIN £	MAX £	MIN £	MAX £		
	10.50	10.50	21.00	21.00	OPEN 1-12	

Farmhouses

Madogs Wells Farm
Llanfair Caereinion, Welshpool, Powys,
SY21 0DE   [L]
Tel: (0938) 810446
Warm welcome and good home cooking await visitors to our small stock rearing hill farm. Situated in quiet secluded valley surrounded by plenty of wildlife, centrally heated farmhouse, colour TV, tea and cake served evenings. Ideal location for touring Mid Wales. Families welcome. Reduced rates for under 12's. Washing facilities.

H	✗	SINGLE PER PERSON B&B		DOUBLE FOR 2 PERSONS B&B		🛏	3
P						🍴	
	🐕	MIN £	MAX £	MIN £	MAX £		
			9.00		18.00	OPEN 1-12	

LLANFYLLIN Map Ref Eb3

Historic small country town in rolling Powys farmlands Lake Vyrnwy and 240ft Pistyll Rhaeadr waterfall are popular beauty spots nearby.

Farmhouses

Delwyn Farm

Derwlwyn Lane, Llanfyllin, Powys, SY22 5LB [L]
Tel: (069184) 249

Delwyn has one family room with washbasin and one twin bedded room with washbasin on first floor. One double bedded room en-suite on the ground floor. Visitors are welcome to enjoy the beauty and peace of the area. Situated 300 yards down Derwlwyn Lane off the A490, right at the southern approach to the town. Ideal for walking, cycling and touring. Warm welcome gauranteed.

H	SINGLE PER PERSON B&B		DOUBLE FOR 2 PERSONS B&B		🛏	3
P						1
🐕	MIN £	MAX £	MIN £	MAX £	OPEN 4-10	
	10.00	10.00	20.00	20.00		

Llettymeirch

Llanfihangel, Llanfyllin, Powys, SY22 5JF 👑👑
Tel: (069184) 639

Come and enjoy a farm holiday in Mid Wales. Self contained unit all ground floor with own bathroom and shower suitable for the disabled. Family room with a superb view. Evening meal optional. Children half price. 7 miles from Llanfyllin on the Lake Vyrnwy B4393. 3 miles from Llanfihangel B4382.

H 🍴	SINGLE PER PERSON B&B		DOUBLE FOR 2 PERSONS B&B		🛏	1
P ✕						1
🐕	MIN £	MAX £	MIN £ 18.00	MAX £	OPEN 1-12	

LLANGURIG Map Ref Gc1

First village on fledgling river Wye, 1000ft up in the mountains. A craft centre and a monastic 14th century church. Good touring centre for lakes and mountains of central Wales. Ideal walking countryside.

Guest Houses

The Old Vicarage

Llangurig, Llanidloes, Powys, SY18 6RN
Tel: (05515) 280

Enjoy the beauty of Mid Wales at our spacious Victorian Vicarage 1000ft up in the mountains. Ideal base for walking, bird watching and touring the lakes and valleys of central Wales. H & C all rooms (some en-suite). Two guest lounges. Pets welcome. Tourist Board Award for comfort and service. Choice of evening meals. Warm welcome gauranteed.

H 🍴	SINGLE PER PERSON B&B		DOUBLE FOR 2 PERSONS B&B		🛏	5
P ✕						2
🐕 📺	MIN £ 12.50	MAX £ 14.00	MIN £ 25.00	MAX £ 28.00	OPEN 1-12	

LLANIDLOES Map Ref Gd1

Historic and attractive market town at confluence of Severn and Clywedog rivers; excellent touring centre. Noted for its 16th century market hall, now a museum, and other fine half-timbered buildings. Interesting shops. Massive Clywedog dam and lake 3 miles away on B4518.

Guest Houses

Hafod Guest House

Llandinam, Powys, SY17 5BA 👑
Tel: (05512) 2527

Secluded country house in large grounds set in lovely wooded valley, one mile off A470, five miles from old market town of Llanidloes. All rooms with washbasins, central heating. Panelled dining room-lounge with colour TV. Vegetarian and special diets. Home cooking. Ground floor bedrooms and facilities. Ideal walking, touring, bird watching, trekking. Children welcome.

H 🍴	SINGLE PER PERSON B&B		DOUBLE FOR 2 PERSONS B&B		🛏	4
P ✕						
🐕	MIN £ 11.00	MAX £ 12.00	MIN £ 22.00	MAX £ 24.00	OPEN 1-12	

MACHYNLLETH
Map Ref Dc5

Historic market town near beautiful Dovey Estuary. Owain Glyndwr's Parliament House is now a museum and brass rubbing centre; next door is the Tourist Information Centre. Ancient and modern meet here; the inventive National Centre for Alternative Technology is 3 miles away, just off the A487 to Dolgellau.

Guest Houses

Pendre Guest House

Maengwyn Street, Machynlleth, Powys, SY20 8EF 👑👑
Tel: (0654) 2088

Georgian style house in ancient market town of Machynlleth. H & C in all spacious bedrooms, TV lounge, parking. Ideal for fishing, bird watching, golf, walks, many miles of golden sand on coast. New town sports and leisure centre to open 1990. WTB Two Crown rated. A warm welcome to all.

| P | SINGLE PER PERSON B&B | | DOUBLE FOR 2 PERSONS B&B | | 🛏 | 3 |
| 🐕 | MIN £ | MAX £ | MIN £ 20.00 | MAX £ 22.00 | OPEN 2-11 | |

Farmhouses

Cefn

Darowen, Machynlleth, Powys, SY20 8NS 👑👑
Tel: (06502) 336/273

Lies at end of small peaceful village amidst beautiful hill farming country. Central for touring North, Mid Wales and West coast. Excellent walking from house. Oak beamed dining/dining room with excellent views. Television, log fires. Bedrooms with wash basins, one family room, one en-suite. Personal attention to comfort. Six miles east of Machynlleth.

H 🍴	SINGLE PER PERSON B&B		DOUBLE FOR 2 PERSONS B&B		🛏	3
P ✕						1
🐕	MIN £ 10.00	MAX £	MIN £ 20.00	MAX £	OPEN 1-12	

MACHYNLLETH CONTINUED

Farmhouses

Cefn Coch Uchaf

Cemmaes Road, Machynlleth, Powys, SY20 8LH
Tel: (06502) 552

16th century farmhouse, mountain location. Excellent country for bird watching, golfing, fishing, dog training, easy access to beaches. Good country fare, vegetarians catered for. Evening meal £5. TV lounge, tea and coffee free on request. Pets welcome. Menu includes pheasant, salmon, game pie, Welsh lamb, pork, chicken. Assorted sweets.

	SINGLE PER PERSON B&B		DOUBLE FOR 2 PERSONS B&B			3
	MIN £	MAX £	MIN £	MAX £		1
	9.50	10.50	19.00	20.00		OPEN 4-10

Gwernstablau Farm

Llanwrin, Machynlleth, Powys, SY20 8QH
Tel: (06502) 262

18th century farmhouse in the Dovey Valley. Beams, log fire when cold. A place to stop and muse. Proprietor always there to welcome guests. Tea/coffee, TV in all rooms. En-suite, lounge, separate dining room with individual tables. Central heating. All for guests use only. Aberdovey 12 miles. Dolgellau 16 miles.

	SINGLE PER PERSON B&B		DOUBLE FOR 2 PERSONS B&B			4
	MIN £	MAX £	MIN £	MAX £		1
	11.00		22.00			OPEN 1-12

Hafan Farm

Aberangell, Machynlleth, Powys, SY20 9ND
Tel: (06502) 375

A warm welcome awaits you at Hafan situated 10 miles from the market town of Machynlleth in the beautiful Dovey Valley and within easy reach of the sea. Excellent centre for walking, touring, cycling and fishing. The house being centrally heated with oak beamed TV lounge. Two bedrooms, 1 family room with washbasin, 1 double room with bathroom. Ample parking space.

	SINGLE PER PERSON B&B		DOUBLE FOR 2 PERSONS B&B			2
	MIN £	MAX £	MIN £	MAX £		1
	10.00		20.00			OPEN 1-12

Mathafarn

Llanwrin, Machynlleth, Powys, SY20 8QJ
Tel: (06502) 226

Henry VII is reputed to have stayed here en-route to the Battle of Bosworth. Now this 16th century elegant country house is part of a working farm. Inglenook log fires, central heating, television lounge. 1 twin private bathroom, one double en-suite, one single. Close to Machynlleth and the beautiful coastline at Aberdovey. Ample parking space.

	SINGLE PER PERSON B&B		DOUBLE FOR 2 PERSONS B&B			3
	MIN £	MAX £	MIN £	MAX £		2
	12.50	12.50	23.00	25.00		OPEN 1-12

MEIFOD Map Ref Eb4

Gentle valley of Vyrnwy river. Rich borderland country.

Farmhouses

Penrhwnin Farmhouse

Trefananney, Meifod, Powys, SY22 6XX
Tel: (069181) 632

Penrhwnin situated close to Llanrhaeadr Water Falls, Montgomery Canal, Offa's Dyke. Golfing, fishing, canoeing. We offer private accommodation, tea making facilities, own TV lounge and dining area. En-suite. Log fire. Relaxed atmosphere. Ideal touring base. Children reduced rates. Evening meal by arrangement, packed lunches.

	SINGLE PER PERSON B&B		DOUBLE FOR 2 PERSONS B&B			3
	MIN £	MAX £	MIN £	MAX £		2
	10.00	12.00	20.00	24.00		OPEN 1-12

MONTGOMERY Map Ref Ec6

Hilltop market town of distinctive Georgian architecture beneath the ruins of a 13th century castle. Offa's Dyke, which once marked the border, runs nearby.

Farmhouses

Little Brompton Farm

Montgomery, Powys, SY15 6HY
Tel: (068681) 371

17th century farmhouse with WTB Farmhouse Award. Situated on B4385, 2 miles east of Georgian town of Montgomery. Double, twin and family bedrooms, some en-suite, all with H & C, shaver points, tea trays. A mixed working farm. Delicious cooking. Personal attention with value for money are our priorities. Brochure Mrs Gaynor Bright. New telephone number 1990 (0686) 668371.

	SINGLE PER PERSON B&B		DOUBLE FOR 2 PERSONS B&B			3
	MIN £	MAX £	MIN £	MAX £		1
	11.00	13.00	22.00	26.00		OPEN 1-12

CALL Holidays Wales (0792) 645555

Pentrehyling Farm

Churchstoke, Montgomery, Powys, SY15 6HU
Tel: (05885) 249

We welcome you to the friendly family atmosphere of our 17th century home, a comfortable border farmhouse, central to the Welsh Marches. Ideal country pursuits. After a good night's sleep, enjoy a hearty breakfast. 1 family, 1 double/twin, 1 single, all with heating, wash-basins, hot drinks. Large comfortable lounge, spacious dining room, separate tables. Car park. Children welcome.

	SINGLE PER PERSON B&B		DOUBLE FOR 2 PERSONS B&B			3
	MIN £	MAX £	MIN £	MAX £		
	11.00	12.00	22.00	24.00		OPEN 1-12

NEWTOWN Map Ref Eb6

Busy Severn Valley market town and one-time home of Welsh flannel industry. Textile history recalled in small museum; another collection centres around Robert Owen, pioneer socialist, who lived here. Solid old buildings, river promenade, street market and the lively Theatr Hafren.

Guest Houses

Greenfields

Kerry, Newtown, Powys, SY16 4LH
Tel: (068688) 596

Situated ¼ mile east of the picturesque village of Kerry on the A489 (approx 3½ miles from Newtown). A warm welcome with home cooking is extended to all guests. All bedrooms have H & C, shaving points, tea/coffee making facilities. Ample parking, lounge with colour TV. Good base for exploring Mid Wales and the Borderlands.

	SINGLE PER PERSON B&B		DOUBLE FOR 2 PERSONS B&B			3
	MIN £	MAX £	MIN £	MAX £		
	10.00	11.00	20.00	22.00		OPEN 1-12

Royston

Pool Road, Newtown, Powys, SY16 1DS
Tel: (0686) 628127

Set back off the Welshpool road, four minutes walk out of Newtown opposite "Little Chef", amid the countryside of Wales. We offer quiet comfortable accommodation with heating in bedrooms if required, also hot and cold water basins, shaving points, TV, tea making facilities. Parking off road for second cars. Good home cooked breakfast. Separate shower room.

	SINGLE PER PERSON B&B		DOUBLE FOR 2 PERSONS B&B			3
	MIN £	MAX £	MIN £	MAX £		
	9.00	9.50	18.00	19.00		OPEN 1-12

Farmhouses

Cwmllwydion Farm

Llandinam, Powys, SY17 5DJ
Tel: (068684) 314
Delightful accommodation overlooking the Severn Valley. Bed and breakfast, evening meal by prior arrangement, home-made and produced food. Personal heating, heating, shower and bath. Separate lounge and dining room. Ideal fishing, walking, touring, situated just off the A470 halfway between Llanidloes and Newtown. Details and brochure from Mrs G Rowlands.

	SINGLE PER PERSON B&B	DOUBLE FOR 2 PERSONS B&B		2
	MIN £	MAX £	MIN £	MAX £	
	13.00	13.00	26.00	26.00	OPEN 1-12

Gate Farm

Llandyssil, Montgomery, Powys, SY15 6LN
Tel: (068688) 625
Stay with a young family on a modern dairy farm situated on a hillside 3 miles from the main Welshpool to Newtown road. Double, twin and family rooms have H & C, tea making facilities and central heating. TV lounge. Reduced rates for children. Pets by arrangement. Guests are assured of homely atmosphere. Brochure Mrs Anwen Lloyd.

	SINGLE PER PERSON B&B	DOUBLE FOR 2 PERSONS B&B		3
					1
	MIN £	MAX £	MIN £	MAX £	
	12.00	12.00	20.00	24.00	OPEN 1-12

Lower Gwestydd Farm

Newtown, Powys, SY16 3AY
Tel: (0686) 626718
Situated 2 miles north of Newtown just off B4568 road. Open all year. Two bedrooms en-suite all bedrooms have tea and coffee facilities. Fully central heating, colour TV lounge. Separate dining room offers "A Taste of Wales". Large garden. Farmhouse award. 200 acres mixed farm. Home produce served when in season. Marvellous views, quiet and peaceful scenic walks.

	SINGLE PER PERSON B&B	DOUBLE FOR 2 PERSONS B&B		3
					2
	MIN £	MAX £	MIN £	MAX £	
	11.50	12.00	23.00	24.00	OPEN 1-12

PENYBONTFAWR
Map Ref Eb3

Village amid forests and lakes, near the spectacular Pistyll Rhaeadr waterfalls. Pony trekking and walking country, with hills and woods all around.

Farmhouses

Penyceunant

Penybontfawr, Oswestry, Shropshire, SY10 0PF
Tel: (069174) 459
Old farmhouse in elevated position above Tanat Valley. Substantial rooms with spectacular views, wash basin, colour TV, easy chair and tea/coffee making facilities. Ideal as a secluded retreat yet well placed for touring. Evening meals only available at weekends. B & B weekly rate six times daily rate. Map loan for walkers. Drying facilities. SAE details.

	SINGLE PER PERSON B&B	DOUBLE FOR 2 PERSONS B&B		2
	MIN £	MAX £	MIN £	MAX £	
	10.00	12.00	18.00	20.00	OPEN 1-12

WELSHPOOL Map Ref Ec5

Old market town of the borderlands, full of character, with half-timbered buildings and welcoming inns. Good shopping centre; golf and angling. Powis Castle is an impressive stately home with a Clive of India museum. Ride the narrow-gauge Welshpool and Llanfair Light Railway.

Guest Houses

Peniarth

10 Cefn Hawys, Red Bank, Welshpool, Powys, SY21 7RH
Tel: (0938) 552324
A warm friendly Welsh welcome awaits you. Detached house situated at the end of a quiet cul-de-sac on the outskirts of a small market town. Ideal for walking and touring. Special rates for children. Parking, central heating.

	SINGLE PER PERSON B&B	DOUBLE FOR 2 PERSONS B&B		3
	MIN £	MAX £	MIN £	MAX £	
	11.00	11.00	22.00	22.00	OPEN 4-10

Springbank Farm

Golfa, Welshpool, Powys, SY21 9AF
Tel: (0938) 554568
Grade 11 listed country residence of character in over six acres situated 1 mile from Welshpool with outstanding views overlooking part of Powis Castle estate. Trout fishing available within 1 mile, golf course 2 miles. 2 en-suite and 1 family room with bathroom adjacent, all with tea/coffee making facilities, TV lounge, central heating.

	SINGLE PER PERSON B&B	DOUBLE FOR 2 PERSONS B&B		3
					2
	MIN £	MAX £	MIN £	MAX £	
	12.00	12.00	24.00	24.00	OPEN 1-12

Tresi-Aur

Brookfield Road, Welshpool, Powys, SY21 7PZ
Tel: (0938) 552430
Two crowns family or double room with own bathroom and shower. Car parking. Children under 14. Central heating. TV, tea or coffee, telephone, open March until October. No smoking. Shaving points. Golf, fishing and pony trekking facilities in area.

	SINGLE PER PERSON B&B	DOUBLE FOR 2 PERSONS B&B		1
	MIN £	MAX £	MIN £	MAX £	
	11.00	11.00	22.00	22.00	OPEN 3-10

Farmhouses

Lower Luggy

Berriew, Welshpool, Powys
Tel: (068685) 389
This beautifully situated farmhouse is recently renovated, full of character with friendly and homely atmosphere. 3 bedrooms, one single, double and family. Comfortable lounge. There are lovely walks along the Rivers Rhiew and Severn and Montgomery Canal. The pretty village of Berriew is only 1½ miles away.

	SINGLE PER PERSON B&B	DOUBLE FOR 2 PERSONS B&B		3
	MIN £	MAX £	MIN £	MAX £	
	11.00	11.00	22.00	24.00	OPEN 1-11

Pentrego Farm

Meifod, Powys, SY22 6DH
Tel: (093884) 353
Pentrego Farm is a spacious 16th century black and white farmhouse on a working farm set in unspoilt countryside, ¼ miles from Meifod village, on the A495 road. Only a car ride away from the many attractions of mid wales and also on the "Glyndwr Way" walk. All bedrooms have magnificent views and wash basins. Friendly family welcome. Good home cooking.

	SINGLE PER PERSON B&B	DOUBLE FOR 2 PERSONS B&B		2
	MIN £	MAX £	MIN £	MAX £	
	11.00	12.50	22.00	25.00	OPEN 1-12

Plas Dwpa

Berriew, Welshpool, Powys, SY21 8PS
Tel: (068685) 298
Situated 1½ miles from the pretty village of Berriew. Working farm, dairy, poultry, enjoying magnificent views. Modern house, one double, twin and family bedroom, with wash-basins, tea/coffee making facilities. Large lounge, colour TV. A warm welcome and good food awaits visitors. Ideal for touring lakes, castles, railways. Brochure on request from Mrs F M Hughes.

	SINGLE PER PERSON B&B	DOUBLE FOR 2 PERSONS B&B		3
	MIN £	MAX £	MIN £	MAX £	
	11.00	12.00	22.00	24.00	OPEN 3-11

WELSHPOOL CONTINUED

Severn Farm

Welshpool, Powys, SY21 7BB
Tel: (0938) 553098

Modernised farmhouse on outskirts of Welshpool commanding superb view of long mountain and Severn Valley. Guests own TV (colour) lounge, central heating, bathroom, shower room. ¾ mile town centre. Ideally situated for Powis Castle, Narrow Gauge Railway, swimming, pony trekking, golf, fishing, canal trips,. Cardigan coast only a short journey.

H X P 🐕	SINGLE PER PERSON B&B		DOUBLE FOR 2 PERSONS B&B		🛏	3
	MIN £	MAX £	MIN £	MAX £		
	12.00	13.00	22.00	24.00	OPEN 1-12	

Upper Pandy Farm

Berriew, Welshpool, Powys, SY21 8PW
Tel: (068685) 338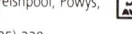

Black and white timbered farmhouse situated 1½ miles from the pretty village of Berriew. Working family farm of 140 acres with beef and sheep. One double or twin bedded room, one family room with washbasins, tea and coffee making facilities. Good food and a warm welcome. Reduced terms for children. Brochure Mrs Elizabeth Jones.

H X P 🐕	SINGLE PER PERSON B&B		DOUBLE FOR 2 PERSONS B&B		🛏	2
	MIN £	MAX £	MIN £	MAX £		
	11.00	12.00	22.00	24.00	OPEN 4-10	

Willows Farm

Halfway House, Shrewsbury, Shropshire, SY5
Tel: (0743) 884233 [L]

Willows Farm is situated on A458 road, Shrewsbury, Welshpool. Beef and sheep farm. Ideal for touring lakes and places of historic interest. Family room, double and twin bedded room. Television lounge.

H X P ✕	SINGLE PER PERSON B&B		DOUBLE FOR 2 PERSONS B&B		🛏	3
	MIN £	MAX £	MIN £	MAX £		
	11.00	12.00	20.00	22.00	OPEN 3-10	

Tynllwyn Farm

Welshpool, Powys, SY21 9BW
Tel: (0938) 553175/553054

A warm welcome awaits you in our family run AA/RAC listed, comfortable friendly farmhouse, peaceful and relaxing in a beautiful part of Mid Wales. 1 mile from the country town of Welshpool. All bedrooms have heating, H/C, colour TV, tea and coffee making facilities. All home cooking. Licensed bar. Out of season bargain breaks available.

H X P TW 🐕	SINGLE PER PERSON B&B		DOUBLE FOR 2 PERSONS B&B		🛏	5
	MIN £	MAX £	MIN £	MAX £		
	14.00	14.00	23.00	23.00	OPEN 1-12	

DOWN ON THE FARM

For something really different, stay on a working farm. On a friendly farmhouse holiday you'll enjoy high standards of comfort, good food and great surroundings.
Our Farm Holidays brochure has all the details. For your free copy, please contact Wales Tourist Board, Dept. WTS, Davis Street, Cardiff CF1 2FU.

POWIS CASTLE

HEART OF WALES

The name accurately reflects the character of this region. The images most closely associated with rural Wales – green, undulating countryside, characterful farming towns, rushing mountain streams, trout- and salmon-rich rivers – all come to life in the Heart of Wales. Pony trekking is popular around Rhayader and Llanwrtyd Wells. Builth Wells hosts the largest agricultural gathering in Wales when the Royal Welsh Show comes to town every July. And at nearby Llandrindod Wells you can – if you are curious enough – still take the spa waters that, according to the locals, cure almost everything.

Genteel Llandrindod is a popular inland resort with an excellent selection of places to stay. It's surrounded by superb scenery – close by, for example, are the Elan Valley lakelands, a spectacular string of man-made lakes within the folds of the untravelled Cambrian Mountains.

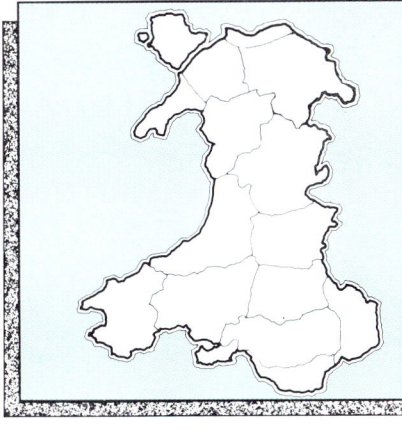

BUILTH WELLS
Map Ref Ge4

Solidly-built old country town which plays host every July to Royal Welsh Agricultural Show. Lovely setting on River Wye amid beautiful hills. Lively sheep and cattle markets. Good shopping for local products, touring centre for Mid Wales and border country. River walk, Wyeside Arts Centre.

Guest Houses

Bron Wye Licensed Guest House

5 Church Street, Builth Wells, Powys, LD2 3BS
Tel: (0982) 553587

Rosalind and Martin Wiltshire welcome you to Bron Wye Christian family run guest house, amidst some of the loveliest countryside nationwide. Two single, two family rooms, TV lounge, dining room, bar, central heating, tea and coffee facilities, evening meals by arrangement. Snacks available. Car parking, cycle parking. Hot and cold all rooms, TV's all bedrooms. Pay phone available. Children and pets welcome. Garden etc.

P / ☂ / X	SINGLE PER PERSON B&B		DOUBLE FOR 2 PERSONS B&B		🛏 4 / 💷
	MIN £	MAX £	MIN £	MAX £	
	10.00	10.00	20.00	20.00	OPEN 1-12

Llanfair Guest House

1 The Strand, Builth Wells, Powys, LD2 3BG
Tel: (0982) 553253

Llanfair is beautifully situated overlooking the park and River Wye. A short walk to the market town of Builth Wells. All rooms have TV, washbasins and tea and coffee making facilities. We have an extensive à la carte restaurant menu, a bar and serve bar meals. We are an excellent centre for touring.

H X / P / ☂	SINGLE PER PERSON B&B		DOUBLE FOR 2 PERSONS B&B		🛏 8 / 💷 4
	MIN £	MAX £	MIN £	MAX £	
	10.00	13.00	20.00	26.00	OPEN 3-12

The Owls

High Street, Builth Wells, Powys, LD2 3AB
Tel: (0982) 552518

Small family run guest house. Home cooking. Bar and friendly welcome. Near to the River Wye and central for touring the beautiful Heart of Wales. Lounge Bar. Sun lounge. Private car park at rear. En-suite rooms available with private bathroom. TV in most rooms. Tea making facilities in all rooms. Central heating. Evening meal available.

P X / ☂ / ✗	SINGLE PER PERSON B&B		DOUBLE FOR 2 PERSONS B&B		🛏 5 / 💷 3
	MIN £	MAX £	MIN £	MAX £	
	10.50	12.00	21.00	24.00	OPEN 1-12

Querida

43 Garth Road, Builth Wells, Powys, LD2 3AR
Tel: (0982) 553642

Querida is within easy reach of town centre. Golf, fishing, sports hall nearby. Excellent walks beside Wye, easy reach of Brecon Beacons, Black Mountains, Elan Valley, pony trekking and Welsh craft shops. TV lounge. Bathroom, shower, two toilets. Tea, coffee making all bedrooms.

H / P / ☂	SINGLE PER PERSON B&B		DOUBLE FOR 2 PERSONS B&B		🛏 3 / 💷
	MIN £	MAX £	MIN £	MAX £	
	10.00	10.50	18.00	19.00	OPEN 1-12

Farmhouses

Disserth Mill

Disserth, Builth Wells, Powys, LD2 3TN
Tel: (0982) 553217 [L]

Take A483 – 3 miles north of Builth. Sign posted to Disserth Mill. Good home cooking, comfortable bedrooms with H & C, central heating. 2 miles to village, 3 miles for swimming etc. Clean meadow with safe brook for children to play.

H ½ / P X / ☂	SINGLE PER PERSON B&B		DOUBLE FOR 2 PERSONS B&B		🛏 3 / 💷
	MIN £	MAX £	MIN £	MAX £	
	11.00	11.00	20.00	20.00	OPEN 4-10

Dollynwydd Farm

Builth Wells, Powys, LD2 3RZ
Tel: (0982) 553660 [L]

17th Century farmhouse 200 acres, beef and sheep. Home cooking, own produce. Four bedrooms, two bathrooms, outstanding area for touring, walking, bird watching, golf and riding. Own trout river, salmon fishing can be arranged. Tennis courts, sports hall with squash courts, bowling, golf all within two miles. We are 1 mile from Builth Wells on B4520, 1st left down quiet farm lane.

H X / P / ☂	SINGLE PER PERSON B&B		DOUBLE FOR 2 PERSONS B&B		🛏 4 / 💷
	MIN £	MAX £	MIN £	MAX £	
	10.00	12.00	20.00	24.00	OPEN 3-10

New Hall Farm Guest House

Llandew Ir Cwm, Builth Wells, Powys, LD2 3RX
Tel: (0982) 552483

Situated 1½ miles from market town of Builth Wells. A warm welcome and good home cooking awaits guests at our comfortable farmhouse. Panoramic views overlooking the Wye Valley and Aberedw Hills. Ideal for walking and touring Mid Wales. Sports centre, golf course and fishing nearby. Central heating, tea making facilities in bedrooms.

P / ½ / X	SINGLE PER PERSON B&B		DOUBLE FOR 2 PERSONS B&B		🛏 6 / 💷 2
	MIN £	MAX £	MIN £	MAX £	
	12.00	14.00	24.00	28.00	OPEN 1-12

Tŷ Isaf Farm

Erwood, Builth Wells, Powys, LD2 3SZ
Tel: (09823) 607

Situated just off A470 near Erwood village. 340 acre working farm overlooking Wye Valley. Ideal spot from which to tour Mid Wales. Good walks beside the Wye, mountains etc. H&C all rooms. TV lounge, tea/coffee making all bedrooms. Evening meals. AA listed. WTB Farmhouse Award. Fishing, golf, swimming nearby.

H X / P TW / ☂	SINGLE PER PERSON B&B		DOUBLE FOR 2 PERSONS B&B		🛏 3 / 💷
	MIN £	MAX £	MIN £	MAX £	
	9.00	10.00	18.00	20.00	OPEN 1-12

ERWOOD
Map Ref Ha5

Pretty wayside village in narrow wooded valley. The good ale in the "local" spired the idea of Punch magazine.

Guest Houses

Old Vicarage

Erwood, Builth Wells, Powys, LD2 3EX [L]
Tel: (09823) 680

Situated just off A470 near Erwood. A most attractive guest house set in own grounds overlooking the unparalleled beauty of the Wye Valley. Three bedrooms all with H & C, shavolites, tea, coffee making facilities, one with colour TV. Guests own lounge. Black Mountains, Brecon Beacons, Elan Valley. Pony trekking, swimming, golf all nearby. Erwood 5 minutes walk away with two homely inns. Children welcome. Central heating. Guests own bathroom with separate toilet. Home grown garden produce produced for meals.

H X / P / ☂	SINGLE PER PERSON B&B		DOUBLE FOR 2 PERSONS B&B		🛏 3 / 💷
	MIN £	MAX £	MIN £	MAX £	
	8.50	9.50	17.00	19.00	OPEN 1-12

LLANDRINDOD WELLS
Map Ref Ge3

Victorian spa town with spacious streets and impressive architecture. You can still take the waters at Rock Park Gardens. A popular inland resort with golf, fishing, bowling, boating and tennis available. Good selection of hotels. Excellent touring centre for Mid Wales hills and lakes. Annual Victorian Festival in August.

Hotels

Drovers Arms

Howey, Llandrindod Wells, Powys,
LD1 5PT
Tel: (0597) 2508
Family run village inn in quiet picturesque location, two minutes south of Llandrindod Wells (A483). Single, double and family bedrooms. Lounge and public bars, real ales, charming 13th century cellar restaurant and patio garden. Delicious bar snacks and à la carte menus offering best local produce and interesting speciality dishes. Golfers! Concessionary green fees available.

SINGLE PER PERSON B&B		DOUBLE FOR 2 PERSONS B&B		3
MIN £	MAX £	MIN £	MAX £	1
12.00	14.00	24.00	28.00	OPEN 1-12

Gwystre Inn

Gwystre, Llandrindod Wells, Powys,
LD1 6RN
Tel: (059787) 650
18th century country inn beautiful country and riverside gardens. Comfortable rooms, full central heating, two bathrooms, residents lounge, dining room. Lounge bar, farmers bar, coffee lounge. Full licence. Morning coffee, lunches, bar food, evening meals served. All home cooking. Ideal for walking, touring, fishing, golf and pony trekking in area. Warm and friendly atmosphere.

SINGLE PER PERSON B&B		DOUBLE FOR 2 PERSONS B&B		5
MIN £	MAX £	MIN £	MAX £	
12.00	14.00	24.00	28.00	OPEN 1-12

Guest Houses

Corven Hall

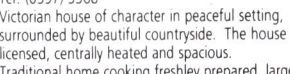

Howey, Llandrindod Wells,
Powys, LD1 5RE
Tel: (0597) 3368
Victorian house of character in peaceful setting, surrounded by beautiful countryside. The house is licensed, centrally heated and spacious. Traditional home cooking freshly prepared, large dining room, TV lounge, bar. Most bedrooms en-suite, tea, coffee facilities. Ground floor accommodation. Ideal walking, touring, bird watching country, fishing, golf in area. WTB Guest House Award. Brochure available. During 1990 (0597) 823368.

SINGLE PER PERSON B&B		DOUBLE FOR 2 PERSONS B&B		7
MIN £	MAX £	MIN £	MAX £	5
11.00	13.50	22.00	27.00	OPEN 1-11

Disserth Guest House

Disserth, Howey,
Llandrindod Wells, Powys
LD1 6NL
Tel: (059789) 277
Nestling in the beautiful Ithon Valley, Disserth provides the ideal touring centre. A warm welcome awaits you. Comfort, hospitality, centrally heated throughout, tea making facilities and good home cooking in peaceful surroundings. Oak beams. Original stone fireplaces, tastefully furnished rooms. Licensed bar, coffee and craft shop. Walking, private trout fishing in this birdwatcher's paradise.

SINGLE PER PERSON B&B		DOUBLE FOR 2 PERSONS B&B		2
MIN £	MAX £	MIN £	MAX £	
10.50	12.00	21.00	22.00	OPEN 2-11

Rhydithon

Dyffryn Road, Llandrindod Wells,
Powys, LD1 6AN
Tel: (0597) 822624
Small family guest house in a quiet side road just off the high street. Hot and cold in rooms, television lounge. Close to all amenities, public car park, non smoking, jacuzzi, sauna, steam room meters. An ideal location for touring the countryside and reservoirs of Mid Wales.

SINGLE PER PERSON B&B		DOUBLE FOR 2 PERSONS B&B		4
MIN £	MAX £	MIN £	MAX £	
9.00	9.50	18.00	19.00	OPEN 1-12

Stredders Vegetarian Guest House

Park Crescent,
Llandrindod Wells, Powys,
LD1 6AB
Tel: (0597) 2186
Stredders rooms have H & C, beverage making facilities, clock radios, remote-control colour TV's and central heating. The guests' lounge has TV, video, stereo and open fire. We are licensed and carry mostly organic wines. Luxurious heated swimming pool, jacuzzi, sauna, steam room available free for guests. We always make your stay comfortable relaxed and memorable.

SINGLE PER PERSON B&B		DOUBLE FOR 2 PERSONS B&B		3
MIN £	MAX £	MIN £	MAX £	
11.00	14.00	22.00	28.00	OPEN 1-12

Sunny Bank Guest House

Ithon Road, Llandrindod Wells, Powys,
LD1 6AS
Tel: (0597) 4977
Relax in the comfort of this elegant Edwardian guest house, family run with an established reputation for excellent food and friendly service. Spacious, attractive rooms all with central heating, colour television, radio, tea/coffee facilities. Traditional and vegetarian cookery, quality wines. Quiet location with views over hills, riverside walks, short stroll to town centre.

SINGLE PER PERSON B&B		DOUBLE FOR 2 PERSONS B&B		4
MIN £	MAX £	MIN £	MAX £	
11.00	12.50	22.00	25.00	OPEN 1-12

Farmhouses

Highbury Farm

Llanyre, Llandrindod Wells, Powys,
LD1 6EA
Tel: (0597) 2716
A small holding situated one mile outside Llandrindod Wells on the edge of the village of Llanyre. A warm welcome awaits you. Comfortable spacious rooms, one double, one family/twin room and one single. Full central heating. Colour TV in lounge. Separate dining room, evening meal optional. Farmhouse award held. AA listed. Brochure and enquiries to Mrs Shirley Evans.

SINGLE PER PERSON B&B		DOUBLE FOR 2 PERSONS B&B		3
MIN £	MAX £	MIN £	MAX £	
9.50	10.50	19.00	21.00	OPEN 4-10

LLANWRTYD WELLS
Map Ref Gc5

One-time spa encircled by hills, now a centre for pony trekking, walking and fishing. Cambrian woollen weaving mill is a popular attraction. For spectacular views explore nearby Abergwesyn Pass/Llyn Brianne area. Mountain Bike Centre.

Guest Houses

Caeglas

Ffos Road, Llanwrtyd Wells, Powys,
LD5 4RS
Tel: (05913) 547
Half mile from town in open countryside with views of nearby Eppynt Hills, has three guest rooms with bathroom and shower room. TV in residents lounge. Downstairs cloakroom. Home cooking, wholemeal bread, free range eggs, own honey. Ideal centre for touring, walking, red kite country. Can book pony trekking, riding, mountain bikes, nearby hotel swimming pool, pitch and putt, lake.

SINGLE PER PERSON B&B		DOUBLE FOR 2 PERSONS B&B		3
MIN £	MAX £	MIN £	MAX £	
11.00	12.00	22.00	24.00	OPEN 1-12

WALES It's magic

CALL Holidays
(0792) 645555

NEW RADNOR
Map Ref Hb3

Ancient town on edge of Radnor forest at foot of Vron Hill. Esgair Nantau falls nearby and Offa's Dyke path. A small, secluded rural town, where countryside activities can be enjoyed.

Hotels

Eagle Hotel
Broad Street, New Radnor, Presteigne, Powys LD8 2SN
Tel: (054421) 208
Friendly village pub in glorious countryside 4 miles from english border on A44. Excellent home cooked food (including vegetarian) served in charming restauarant/coffee-shop. Two comfortable bars with real ale; adjoining games room with TV; five bedrooms (two family) with H & C, tea/coffee facilities. Fire certificate. Open all year including Christmas and New Year.

SINGLE PER PERSON B&B		DOUBLE FOR 2 PERSONS B&B		🛏	5
MIN £	MAX £	MIN £	MAX £		OPEN 1-12
14.00		24.00			

PRESTEIGNE
Map Ref Hc2

Typical black-and-white half-timbered border town with ancient inns; the Radnorshire Arms has secret passages. Pony trekking available - a perfect way of exploring this tranquil wooded countryside.

Guest Houses

Brook Cottage
Lingen, Bucknell, Shropshire, SY7 0DY
Tel: (0544) 267990
Relax or explore the Marches from white painted C1780's brick cottage, 2 acre garden with brook in centre of idyllic Lingen village. 3 miles Presteigne, 15 Ludlow, 22 Hereford, 61 Machynlleth. Full central heating, lashings of hot water. TV lounge, sole use bathroom. Vegetarian, vegan and demi-veg, menus a speciality.

SINGLE PER PERSON B&B		DOUBLE FOR 2 PERSONS B&B		🛏	2
MIN £	MAX £	MIN £	MAX £		OPEN 1-11
12.00	14.00	22.00	24.00		

RHAYADER
Map Ref Gd2

Country town full of character, with inviting inns and Welsh craft products in the shops. Excellent base for exploring mountains and lakes (Elan Valley and Claerwen), with opportunities for pony trekking and fishing.

Hotels

The Horseshoe Inn
Church Street, Rhayader, Powys, LD6 5AT
Tel: (0597) 810982
Under new ownership, this friendly family run pub is situated behind the busy thoroughfare of the small market town of Rhayader, only three miles from the renowned Elan Valley reservoirs. Completely refurbished bedrooms with H & C, tea making facilities, fully heated. Pleasant dining room with varied menu, selection of wines available. Large car park.

SINGLE PER PERSON B&B		DOUBLE FOR 2 PERSONS B&B		🛏	3
MIN £	MAX £	MIN £	MAX £		OPEN 1-12
12.00	14.00	24.00	24.00		

Guest Houses

Brynteg
East Street, Rhayader, Powys, LD6 5EA
Tel: (0597) 810 052
Family run guest house where you can be assured of a very warm welcome and comfortable stay. Central heating, shaving points, hot and cold all rooms. TV lounge, 2 bathrooms with showers, separate tables in dining room. Children half price. 3 miles from beautiful Elan Valley lakes. An ideal centre for touring Mid Wales.

SINGLE PER PERSON B&B		DOUBLE FOR 2 PERSONS B&B		🛏	3
MIN £	MAX £	MIN £	MAX £		OPEN 4-10
		17.00	17.00		

Liverpool House
East Street, Rhayader, Powys, LD6 5EA
Tel: (0597) 810706
Family run guest house where friendliness and service go hand in hand. Centrally heated throughout. Bedrooms have colour television, clock-radio, tea making facilities and most have en-suite. Spacious lounge with colour television. Childrens outdoor play area. Private parking. Ideally central for walking, bird watching and touring. Three miles from the beautiful Elan Valley Reservoirs.

SINGLE PER PERSON B&B		DOUBLE FOR 2 PERSONS B&B		🛏	4
MIN £	MAX £	MIN £	MAX £		3
		20.00	27.00		OPEN 4-10

Ramblemore Holidays
Tre-Garreg, St Harmon, Rhayader, Powys, LD6 5LU
Tel: (059788) 604
What can we offer? A warm friendly welcome in our converted stone barn, rooms en-suite, food is home baked using locally grown organic produce when available. Walking, bird watching and pony trekking, reservoirs and one of Radnorshire's wild life reserves within close proximity. Peace and tranquility. Regretfully we cannot accept smokers, children or pets.

SINGLE PER PERSON B&B		DOUBLE FOR 2 PERSONS B&B		🛏	2
MIN £	MAX £	MIN £	MAX £		2
	26.00		26.00		OPEN 4-10

Farmhouses

Beili Neuadd Farmhouse
Rhayader, Powys, LD6 5NS
Tel: (0597) 810211
An attractive stone built farmhouse set amidst beautiful countryside in a quiet secluded position. Guests are assured of every comfort with central heating, log fires and spacious accommodation in single, double and twin bedded rooms, shower and bathrooms. Good imaginative meals using fresh garden and farm produce. Wales Tourist Board Farmhouse Award.

SINGLE PER PERSON B&B		DOUBLE FOR 2 PERSONS B&B		🛏	2
MIN £	MAX £	MIN £	MAX £		2
11.00		22.00			OPEN 1-12

Downfield Farm
Rhayader, Powys, LD 6 5PA
Tel: (0597) 810 394
Downfield farm is situated one mile east of Rhayader set back off A44 Cross Gates Road, with good clean access, ample parking space surrounded by hills and lake. Fishing, pony trekking and good walking country nearby. All bedrooms with hot and cold water, with coffee and tea making facilities. We extend a warm welcome.

SINGLE PER PERSON B&B		DOUBLE FOR 2 PERSONS B&B		🛏	3
MIN £	MAX £	MIN £	MAX £		
10.00	11.00	19.00	20.00		OPEN 3-11

SOUTH WALES

There's a wide choice of everything – B&B accommodation and scenery – in South Wales. Stay in a city or enjoy the peace and quiet of a farmhouse deep in the hills. You may prefer a clifftop guest house with a tremendous sea view, or one tucked away on a wooded inlet. South Wales is full of contrasts. Within this region there are two national parks (which couldn't be more different in character), Wales's two major cities, the leafy Wye Valley and beautiful border country, traditional hills and vales, and a huge coastline where you'll find everything from colourful resorts to nature reserves.

Firstly, those two national parks: the mountains of the Brecon Beacons and Pembrokeshire's spectacular seashores. The Beacons park is centred around Pen y Fan, at nearly 3,000 ft the highest peak in South Wales. The Beacons' open mountainsides and grassy slopes are ideal for walking and pony trekking. Brecon, Abergavenny and Llandovery are attractive market towns and convenient centres from which to explore the park, though you'll also find a good scattering of B&B accommodation elsewhere.

The Pembrokeshire Coast National Park in the far south-west is one of Europe's finest stretches of untouched coastline. Its rugged, rocky northern shores are dotted with small resorts and places to stay such as the tiny cathedral city of St David's. In the more popular south, there's an excellent choice of holiday accommodation around sandy Tenby and the watersports centre of Saundersfoot.

There's more superb coastline along the Gower Peninsula, the first part of Britain to be declared an 'Area of Outstanding Natural Beauty'. Gower is on the doorstep of Swansea, an attractive city by the sea with a dazzling new marina and Maritime Quarter (and while you're here, don't miss the fresh foods market, the biggest and best in Wales). Cardiff, Wales's capital, is an architecturally magnificent city with a modern shopping complex, Victorian arcades, superb Civic Centre and city-centre castle. More and more visitors are now discovering Cardiff's cosmopolitan charms. And more and more visitors are also discovering the nearby South Wales 'Valleys', an area of unexpected beauty and varied attractions.

MARLOES SANDS

PEMBROKESHIRE

The incomparable coastline around Wales's south-western tip is all within the Pembrokeshire Coast National Park. The park's 225 square miles encompasses secluded coves, towering headlands, huge beaches and tranquil backwaters. Tenby, with its pastel-painted harbourside houses and narrow medieval streets, is a gem of a resort (its three sparkling beaches have won the Keep Britain Tidy organisation's Clean Beaches award).

Together with the neighbouring sailing centre of Saundersfoot, Tenby serves as a popular, picturesque base from which to savour some of Europe's best stretches of coastal splendour. Further west, around Dale, Broad Haven and Newgale, there are more magnificent sands, surfing beaches and walks along a seashore rich in wildlife. The tiny cathedral city of St David's heralds the start of North Pembrokeshire's rocky bays and undiscovered beaches, a savagely beautiful coastline stretching all the way to Cardigan.

BROAD HAVEN
Map Ref Jb5

Sand and green hills cradle this village in the midst of the Pembrokeshire Coast National Park. Good beach, accommodation, shops.

Guest Houses

Anchor House
Broad Haven, Haverfordwest,
Pembrokeshire, Dyfed SA62 3JW
Tel: (0437) 781542
Sanding alongside a magnificent sandy beach, Anchor House is ideally situated for a perfect family holiday.

P	SINGLE PER PERSON B&B		DOUBLE FOR 2 PERSONS B&B			6
🐕	MIN £	MAX £	MIN £	MAX £		
✗	11.00	14.00	22.00	28.00		OPEN 4-9

The Atlantic Club/Guest House
Settlands Hill, Broad Haven,
Haverfordwest, Dyfed SA62 3JY
Tel: (0437) 781589
Situated on the cliff overlooking Broad Haven with panoramic views of the bay. Beach 300 yards down the hill. Safe bathing and popular for wind surfing. The club is open to holiday members. Facilities for children, bar snacks available. Accommodation consists of 2 twin, 1 double bedrooms all with H & C, TV, tea and coffee facilities.

H	SINGLE PER PERSON B&B		DOUBLE FOR 2 PERSONS B&B			3
P	MIN £	MAX £	MIN £	MAX £		
🐕	9.50	9.50	19.00	19.00		OPEN 5-10

Cigfran
7 Atlantic Drive, Broad Haven,
Haverfordwest, Pembrokeshire, Dyfed
SA62 3JA
Tel: (0437) 781460
Welcome to our small family home with a sea view, lazy cat, comfortable beds and wonderful breakfasts. Three pretty guest rooms with TV, easy chairs, tea facilities, for the privacy you probably prefer. Come and go as you wish. Supper tables booked at various recommended places if required. We love you to sing in the shower, but not to smoke in the house, please.

H	SINGLE PER PERSON B&B		DOUBLE FOR 2 PERSONS B&B			3
P	MIN £	MAX £	MIN £	MAX £		
✗	9.00	9.00	18.00	18.00		OPEN 3-10

Glenfield
5 Atlantic Drive, Broad Haven,
Haverfordwest, Pembrokeshire Dyfed
SA62 3JA
Tel: (0462) 781502 L
A warm welcome awaits you at my comfortable guest house with ample home cooked meals and friendly services. Hot and cold in all bedrooms. Tea making facilities in all rooms. Full central heating, colour television. Own key. 300yds to beach and coastal path.

P	SINGLE PER PERSON B&B		DOUBLE FOR 2 PERSONS B&B			4
✗	MIN £	MAX £	MIN £	MAX £		
	9.00	9.00	18.00	18.00		OPEN 1-12

Sea View
Marine Road, Broad Haven,
Haverfordwest, Dyfed, SA62 3JR
Tel: (0437) 781753 L
Situated 50 yards from safe sandy beach. Two family rooms with hot and cold, shaver points and view of the sea, colour TV in each room. Licensed restaurant. 10% discount for three or more nights. Special terms for senior citizens. Open all year with reduced rates from October- March including Christmas and New Year.

H	SINGLE PER PERSON B&B		DOUBLE FOR 2 PERSONS B&B			3
P ✗	MIN £	MAX £	MIN £	MAX £		
🐕	9.50	9.50	19.00	19.00		OPEN 1-12

CROES-GOCH
Map Ref Jb3

Small village, useful spot for touring Pembrokeshire Coast National Park and nearby holiday centres of St. David's and Fishguard.

Farmhouses

Trearched Farm Guest House
Croes-Goch, Haverfordwest,
Dyfed, SA62 5JP
Tel: (0348) 831310
Trearched is an 18th century farmhouse situated down farm drive at lodge entrance off A487 in village. Spacious grounds with small lake. 70 acre arable farm. Footpath link to Tre-fin 2¼ miles. Ideal touring North and South Pembrokeshire. Bird watching, walking, RAC and AA listed. WTB Farmhouse Award. Fire certificate. SAE brochure please or phone.

H	SINGLE PER PERSON B&B		DOUBLE FOR 2 PERSONS B&B			7
P	MIN £	MAX £	MIN £	MAX £		
✗	12.00	14.00	24.00	28.00		OPEN 1-12

CRYMYCH
Map Ref Fa7

Centre of an upland farming area, good walking and hiking on the gentle slopes of the Preseli Hills. Handy for the sandy coves of north Pembrokeshire and Cardigan Bay.

Hotels

Butchers Arms
Tegryn, Llanfyrnach, Dyfed, SA35 0BL
Tel: (023977) 680 L
Traditional village pub set in beautiful countryside near Preseli Mountains and National Park. Good area for walking and fishing. Being one of the highest villages in Pembrokeshire the views from the bar are superb and the garden lovely to sit in. Warm hospitality, good food (evening meals available). Pleasant accommodation assured. C.A.M.R.A. listed.

P	SINGLE PER PERSON B&B		DOUBLE FOR 2 PERSONS B&B			3
✗	MIN £	MAX £	MIN £	MAX £		
	10.00	13.00	20.00	26.00		OPEN 1-12

Guest Houses

Gwelfor Country Guest House
Blaenffos, Crymych, Dyfed, SA37 0HZ
Tel: (0239) 831599
Spectacular Preseli Mountain views from Gwelfor. A friendly family run guest house. Crafts, castles, cromlechs, coastline and Cardigan town close by. All rooms hot/cold, central heating with tea facilities. Residents TV lounge. Excellent traditional fare along with vegetarian cooking, our speciality. Mainly organic home grown vegetables. Situated 6 miles south of Cardigan on A478 Tenby road.

P ✗	SINGLE PER PERSON B&B		DOUBLE FOR 2 PERSONS B&B			4
🐕						2
✗	MIN £	MAX £	MIN £	MAX £		
	13.00		22.00	26.00		OPEN 1-12

WALES
It's magic

DALE
Map Ref Jb6

Sheltered yachting village. Henry VII landed near here and marched on to take the crown at the Battle of Bosworth in 1485. Many good beaches nearby. Skokholm and Skomer islands off-shore - both marvellous havens for sea birds.

Hotels

Post House Hotel
Dale, Haverfordwest, Pembrokeshire, Dyfed SA62 3RE
Tel: (0646) 636201
100 yards from bay in National Park, coastal village of Dale. Seven bedroomed family run licensed hotel. Double and twin rooms, three have en-suite facilities, showers in most others. Residents lounge, colour television, also large conservatory. Good food in very comfortable surroundings. Ideal for walking, sightseeing or visiting islands of Skomer, Skokholm and Grassholm. Closed February.

P	SINGLE PER PERSON B&B		DOUBLE FOR 2 PERSONS B&B		🛏	7
	MIN £	MAX £	MIN £	MAX £		3
X	11.00	11.00	20.00	28.00		OPEN 1-12

Farmhouses

Skerryback Farmhouse
Sandy Haven, St Ishmaels,
Haverfordwest, Dyfed SA62 3DN   L
Tel: (06465) 598
Comfortable traditional Pembrokeshire farmhouse on coastal footpath. 1 double, 1 single room with electric blankets. Tea, coffee facilities. H & C in one bedroom, central heating. TV lounge. Open most of the year.

P	SINGLE PER PERSON B&B		DOUBLE FOR 2 PERSONS B&B		🛏	2
	MIN £	MAX £	MIN £	MAX £		
X	9.50		19.00			OPEN 1-11

DINAS CROSS
Map Ref Jd2

Small village on coast road north of Fishguard, with lovely coastal and hill surroundings. Within the Pembrokeshire Coast National Park and not far from Pentre Ifan Stone Age cromlech.

Farmhouses

Cilwenen Hill Farm
Dinas Cross, Newport, Dyfed, SA42 0XU 👑 👑
Tel: (03486) 239
A warm welcome awaits you at our small holding which is just off main road, with superb views overlooking woodland and beach. Guests are welcome all year in two double, one twin bedded rooms, all with H & C, tea and coffee facilities. Bathroom, separate shower room. Lounge. footpath to beach links National Park coastal path.

H	SINGLE PER PERSON B&B		DOUBLE FOR 2 PERSONS B&B		🛏	3
P X	MIN £	MAX £	MIN £	MAX £		
	11.00		22.00			OPEN 1-12

FISHGUARD
Map Ref Jc2

Lower Fishguard is a cluster of old wharfs and cottages around a beautiful harbour. "Under Milk Wood" with Richard Burton was filmed here in 1971. Shopping in Fishguard town. Good Walks along Pembrokeshire Coastal Path and in the country. Nearby Goodwick is the Irish ferry terminal, with a direct rail link from London. Excellent range of craft workshops in area.

Guest Houses

Bryntirion Guest House
Glanymor Road, Goodwick, Dyfed, SA64 0ER   👑
Tel: (0348) 872189
Two minutes from village, five minutes to Irish cross channel ferry. Single, double and family rooms. Lounge area with colour TV. Full central heating. Ideal centre for golf, fishing, horse riding, walking, beaches and touring Pembrokeshire National Park. All rooms hot and cold water and shaver points. Parking available.

H	SINGLE PER PERSON B&B		DOUBLE FOR 2 PERSONS B&B		🛏	3
P X	MIN £	MAX £	MIN £	MAX £		
	11.00	11.00	22.00	22.00		OPEN 1-12

Cefn y Dre
Fishguard, Dyfed, SA65 9QS   L
Tel: (0348) 874499
Ideally situated touring base within two miles of town centre in secluded country house setting with coach house artist's studio. Open all year with licensed dining room, television lounge, tea making facilities in all bedrooms, two with wash basins, including twin bedded family room. Home cooked evening meals with reduced rates for children.

P	SINGLE PER PERSON B&B		DOUBLE FOR 2 PERSONS B&B		🛏	3
X	MIN £	MAX £	MIN £	MAX £		
			20.00	20.00		OPEN 1-12

Cri'r Wylan
Pen Wallis, Fishguard, Pembrokeshire, Dyfed, SA65 9HR   L
Tel: (0348) 873398
Relax in comfort in homely atmosphere. Attractive rooms, central heating, colour television in lounge. Detached stone house with superb views overlooking Fishguard Bay. Central for Presili Hills and coastal paths, beaches etc. Short stroll town centre. Ample parking, peaceful surroundings. Late night ferry welcome and transport on request. Children very welcome, cot and baby sitting available.

P	SINGLE PER PERSON B&B		DOUBLE FOR 2 PERSONS B&B		🛏	3
	MIN £	MAX £	MIN £	MAX £		
	10.00	12.00	20.00	24.00		OPEN 1-12

Gorwel
21 Vergam Terrace, Fishguard, Dyfed, SA65 9DD   L
Tel: (0348) 873963
Interested in walking, there are miles of National Park paths along whole coastline. Welsh Woollen Mills, pottery making, craft shops. Convenient for Irish ferry. Good home cooking by proprietor. Evening meals optional. Sandy beaches, museums, inns, shops, pony riding. Colour TV in lounge. Parking facilities. Near night ferry.

P	SINGLE PER PERSON B&B		DOUBLE FOR 2 PERSONS B&B		🛏	3
X	MIN £	MAX £	MIN £	MAX £		
		10.00		20.00		OPEN 4-10

Hamilton Guest House
21-23 Hamilton Street, Fishguard, Dyfed, SA65 9HL   👑 👑
Tel: (0348) 873834
A warm welcome extended to our family run guest house with reduced rates for children and babysitting available. Situated in the centre of Fishguard. Good overnight stop for coastal path walkers. Bathroom with separate shower. Drying facilities. Good home cooking including vegetarian dishes with evening meals by prior arrangement. Late night ferry bookings accepted.

H X	SINGLE PER PERSON B&B		DOUBLE FOR 2 PERSONS B&B		🛏	5
P	MIN £	MAX £	MIN £	MAX £		
	10.50	11.50	20.00	22.00		OPEN 1-12

Ivy Bridge

Drim Mill, Dyffryn, Goodwick, Pembrokeshire, Dyfed SA64 0FT
Tel: (0348) 872623 [L]

A warm welcome awaits you at Ivy Bridge. All rooms are en-suite, with colour TV and hot drinks facilities. Try our indoor heated swimming pool, whirlpool, games room and solarium, or relax by the open fire in the lounge. Good home cooking, vegetarian guests welcomed. Ample car parking. Family suite available. Full central heating.

H ⚙ P ✕ 🐕	SINGLE PER PERSON B&B	DOUBLE FOR 2 PERSONS B&B	🛏	6
				6
	MIN £ / MAX £ 14.00	MIN £ / MAX £ 28.00	OPEN 1-12	

Rhos Felen

Scleddau, Fishguard, Dyfed, SA65 9RD
Tel: (0348) 873711 [L]

Country house (licensed) in 3 acres of grounds, with putting green. 2 miles Fishguard and Harbour. CH, guest lounge, Col TV, H & C, shaver points in all bedrooms. Single, double, family rooms, (cots), special rates under twelves. Baby sitting. Tea and coffee always available. Late ferry bookings. Adjoining restaurant open daily for coffees, light lunches, snacks, teas. Home cooking. Large car park.

H ⚙ P ✕ 🐕	SINGLE PER PERSON B&B	DOUBLE FOR 2 PERSONS B&B	🛏	4
	MIN £ 10.00	MAX £ 14.00	MIN £ 20.00	MAX £ 28.00	OPEN 1-12

Stanley House

Quay Road, Goodwick, Fishguard, Dyfed SA64 0BS
Tel: (0348) 873024 [L]

Situated above main entrance road to Fishguard Ferry terminal. Enjoying fine views of bay and Preseli Hills beyond. Ideal centre for National Park, coastal path, bird watching and water sports. Convenient to beach and shops. Providing a personal warm welcome. Comfortable accommodation, lounge, tea and coffee facilities in bedrooms. Special rate children.

H P 🐕	SINGLE PER PERSON B&B	DOUBLE FOR 2 PERSONS B&B	🛏	3
	MIN £ 10.50	MAX £	MIN £ 21.00	MAX £ 21.00	OPEN 1-12

55 West Street

Fishguard, Dyfed, SA65 9NG
Tel: (0348) 873592 [L]

Town house near town centre. Ample parking to rear. Large comfortable rooms all with H & C, central heating and tea making facilities. Television lounge, drying facilities. Near ferry port, 24 hour service. Reductions for children. Golf, fishing-sea and river, riding, excellent sailing facilities and spectacular walks. Reductions for long stay. Vegetarians receive understanding treatment!

P ⚙ ✕	SINGLE PER PERSON B&B	DOUBLE FOR 2 PERSONS B&B	🛏	3
	MIN £ 10.00	MAX £ 10.00	MIN £ 20.00	MAX £ 20.00	OPEN 1-12

Farmhouses

Erw Lon Farm

Pontfaen, Fishguard, Dyfed, SA65 9TS 👑👑
Tel: (0348) 881297

A peacefully comfortable farm of beef and sheep at the foot of the Preseli Hills overlooking the Gwaun Valley in National Park. One twin bedded room and two doubles, one with en-suite, all pretty with hot and cold, shaving points, tea and coffee facilities, bathroom with separate shower room. A real Welsh welcome.

H ✕ P ⚙	SINGLE PER PERSON B&B	DOUBLE FOR 2 PERSONS B&B	🛏	3
				1
	MIN £ 10.00	MAX £ 14.00	MIN £ 20.00	MAX £ 28.00	OPEN 5-11

Gilfach Goch Farmhouse

Garn Gelli Hill, Fishguard, Dyfed, SA65 9SR 👑👑
Tel: (0348) 873871

Superbly positioned smallholding in National Park near coastal path and beaches. 18th century stone built house of character, peacefully surrounded by lawns, flowerbeds, productive gardens. Attractive beamed rooms, inglenook, furnished with antiques. Pretty bedrooms, tea/coffee, H & C, some with TV. 2 bathrooms. Fire certificate. Fishguard 2 miles. A487 to Cardigan.

H ✕ P 🐕	SINGLE PER PERSON B&B	DOUBLE FOR 2 PERSONS B&B	🛏	5
	MIN £ 12.00	MAX £ 14.00	MIN £ 24.00	MAX £ 28.00	OPEN 3-10

FRESHWATER EAST
Map Ref Jd6

Sheltered sandy bay backed by dunes. Good swimming, access for boats, limited car parking.

Motels

East Trewent Farm

Freshwater East, Pembroke, Dyfed, SA71 5LR 👑
Tel: (0646) 672127

Situated on the magnificent Pembrokeshire coast. The rooms are part of a lovely range of old stone farm buildings beautifully converted. Each room has hand basin, tea making facilities, central heating, toilets and showers adjoining. The coastal path runs alongside the land and is ideally situated for walking and the beach. Licensed bar and restaurant.

H ✕ P 🐕	SINGLE PER PERSON B&B	DOUBLE FOR 2 PERSONS B&B	🛏	6
	MIN £ 12.50	MAX £ 12.50	MIN £ 25.00	MAX £ 25.00	OPEN 1-12

Guest Houses

Sea Horses

Freshwater East, Pembroke, Pembrokeshire, Dyfed, SA71 5SLA 👑👑
Tel: (0646) 672405

A welcoming comfortable guest house. Ideal touring centre within Pembrokeshire National Park and close to coastal footpath, castles nearby. The many sandy beaches of Pembrokeshire are within easy reach. Good food and friendly service. All bedrooms have H & C, TV lounge. Parking.

H P ✕	SINGLE PER PERSON B&B	DOUBLE FOR 2 PERSONS B&B	🛏	3
	MIN £ 10.00	MAX £ 12.00	MIN £ 20.00	MAX £ 24.00	OPEN 4-10

GOODWICK   Map Ref Jc2

Sheltered sandy bay below Fishguard town backed by children's play areas. Cross-channel port with regular ferry service from Rosslare in Ireland. Memorial to the last invasion of Britain by the French and the bravery of an extraordinary local woman, Jemima Nicholas.

Guest Houses

Siriole Guest House

Quay Road, Goodwick, Pembrokeshire, Dyfed, SA64 0BS [L]
Tel: (0348) 873203

RAC Listed. On the edge of Fishguard Bay, about ½ mile from Irish Ferry Port, open for late boats. Panoramic views of Preseli hills, on the Pembrokeshire Coastal Path. No children under five years old. Children same rate as adults. No pets, no family rooms. Tea making facilities in bedrooms.

P	SINGLE PER PERSON B&B	DOUBLE FOR 2 PERSONS B&B	🛏	6
	MIN £ 10.00	MAX £ 10.00	MIN £ 20.00	MAX £ 20.00	OPEN 1-12

CALL Holidays (0792) 645555

HAVERFORDWEST
Map Ref Jc5

Ancient town - now a good base for exploring the Pembrokeshire Coast National Park - and the administrative and shopping centre for the area. Medieval churches and narrow streets; museum and art gallery in castle. Graham Sutherland collection in Picton Castle, a few miles east.

Hotels

The Denant Mill Inn
Dreenhill, Dale Road, Haverfordwest, Pembrokeshire Dyfed SA62 3TS
Tel: (0437) 766569

Converted 16th century mill in a "lost world" setting. Seven acres unspoiled woodland, 700 yard trout brook, close Skomer Island, surfing, sailing, golf. Weekly clay pigeon shooting. A la carte restaurant, bar snacks. All rooms central heating and H & C washbasin. Children's play area. Recommended by CAMRA for beers and cooking. Real ale, real food, real hospitality.

H	✕	SINGLE PER PERSON B&B		DOUBLE FOR 2 PERSONS B&B		🛏	8
P						🚗	3
🐕		MIN £ 14.00	MAX £	MIN £ 26.00	MAX £	OPEN 1-12	

Guest Houses

Abbots Leigh
Chapel Road, Keeston, Haverfordwest, Pembrokeshire, Dyfed   SA62 6HL   [L]
Tel: (0437) 710556

Small, friendly establishment with beautiful views of Preseli hills. Swimming, surfing, lovely beaches and the coastal path are nearby. Guest have their own bathroom. There is colour TV and central heating. Special terms for children, baby sitting undertaken. Home grown and home cooked evening meals. One family and one single room.

H	♨	SINGLE PER PERSON B&B		DOUBLE FOR 2 PERSONS B&B		🛏	2
P	✕					🚗	
🐕		MIN £	MAX £ 7.50	MIN £	MAX £ 15.00	OPEN 1-12	

College Guest House
St Thomas Green, Haverfordwest, Dyfed, SA61 1QX
Tel: (0437) 763710

Family run Georgian guest house. H & C, central heating, television. Parking opposite. Ideal touring centre Pembrokeshire. 6 miles beaches, coastal paths, surfing, wind surfing, fishing and many other activities, including golf, reservoir and hill walking.

H		SINGLE PER PERSON B&B		DOUBLE FOR 2 PERSONS B&B		🛏	5
🐕						🚗	
♨		MIN £ 11.00	MAX £ 12.00	MIN £ 22.00	MAX £ 24.00	OPEN 1-12	

The Fold
Cleddau Lodge, Camrose, Haverfordwest, Pembrokeshire, Dyfed SA62 6HY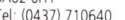
Tel: (0437) 710640

Converted 15th century farmhouse in secluded garden overlooking River Cleddau. Private fishing available. Central to Pembrokeshire coast 6 miles. Two double bedrooms H & C, TV, tea/coffee. Own shower, toilet, separate entrance. Homely welcome as one of the family. WTB 1 Crown. Part of 50 acre estate with gardens, woodlands and river.

H		SINGLE PER PERSON B&B		DOUBLE FOR 2 PERSONS B&B		🛏	2
P						🚗	
♨		MIN £ 9.00	MAX £ 9.00	MIN £ 18.00	MAX £ 18.00	OPEN 1-12	

Redstock Guest House
Johnston, Haverfordwest, Dyfed, SA62 3HN
Tel: (0437) 890287

Mrs Boyett's guest house has been caring for its guests for over 30 years giving excellent value for money, all home comforts. Situated 2 miles from Milford Haven and 4 miles to Haverfordwest, Redstock is very convenient for touring West Wales. Comfort and guests satisfaction is ensured. Ample car parking just off the A4078 past Johnston.

P		SINGLE PER PERSON B&B		DOUBLE FOR 2 PERSONS B&B		🛏	10
🐕						🚗	
✕		MIN £ 12.50	MAX £ 13.50	MIN £ 25.00	MAX £ 27.00	OPEN 1-12	

Farmhouses

Cuckoo Mill Farm
Pelcomb Bridge, Haverfordwest, Dyfed, SA62 6EA   [L]
Tel: (0437) 2139

Situated peacefully in central Pembrokeshire, 2 miles out of Haverfordwest. 6 miles coastline walks, beaches. Mixed livestock working farm. Two comfortable bedrooms with storage heaters. Bathroom with shower, toilet. Lounge with TV and open fire. Personal attention. Good home cooking using home produce. Evening meal at short notice. Children and pets welcome.

H	✕	SINGLE PER PERSON B&B		DOUBLE FOR 2 PERSONS B&B		🛏	2
P						🚗	
🐕		MIN £ 8.50	MAX £ 10.00	MIN £ 17.00	MAX £ 20.00	OPEN 1-11	

Dreenhill Farm
Dale Road, Haverfordwest, Pembrokeshire, Dyfed, SA62 3XG   [L]
Tel: (0437) 764494

Stone built farmhouse standing in pleasant garden in quiet countryside. Farm lane off B4327, 2½ miles from Haverfordwest, 5 miles coast. 3 comfortable bedrooms, 1 twin, 2 single. Extra folding bed. Bedrooms have tea/ coffee trays. Guests own bathroom. Full central heating. Private nature trail. Non smokers. No pets. Reduction over 3 nights.

P		SINGLE PER PERSON B&B		DOUBLE FOR 2 PERSONS B&B		🛏	3
♨						🚗	
		MIN £ 11.00	MAX £ 12.00	MIN £ 22.00	MAX £ 24.00	OPEN 1-12	

LITTLE HAVEN
Map Ref Jb5

Combines with Broad Haven - just over the headland - to form a complete family seaside holiday centre in Pembrokeshire Coast National Park. The village dips down to a pretty sandy beach. Popular spot for sailing, swimming and surfing.

Guest Houses

Valley View
Strawberry Hill, Little Haven, Haverfordwest, Pembrokeshire, Dyfed SA62 3UT   [L]
Tel: (0437) 781227

Comfortable, peaceful bungalow with quiet relaxed atmosphere, views over wooded country. Two twin bedrooms, H & C, shaver points, central heating. Large living room, colour TV. Substantial breakfasts, tea/coffee always available. Easy access to renowned scenic coastal path. 5 minutes walk to picturesque village with sandy beaches. Three excellent pubs and bistro.

P		SINGLE PER PERSON B&B		DOUBLE FOR 2 PERSONS B&B		🛏	2
🐕						🚗	
		MIN £	MAX £	MIN £ 24.00	MAX £ 24.00	OPEN 3-11	

MAENCLOCHOG
Map Ref Je3

Typical Pembrokeshire village, south of Preseli Hills. Llys-y-Fran Reservoir, with its nature trails and sailings, is close by and there is great scope for gentle hill walking.

Guest Houses

Twmpath Guest House
Maenclochog, New Moat, Clunderwen, Dyfed, SA66 7RL   [L]
Tel: (09913) 489

Sixty beaches within easy reach. Doubles, singles, all with H & C and tea facilities. Approved riding stables nearby, ride over the blue stone Preseli Mountains. Several country parks (fishing and sports). Television lounge, inglenook fire on cold evenings. Good home cooking with free packed lunches for children. Happy atmosphere and our personal attention at all times.

H	✕	SINGLE PER PERSON B&B		DOUBLE FOR 2 PERSONS B&B		🛏	4
P						🚗	
♨		MIN £ 9.50	MAX £ 12.00	MIN £ 19.00	MAX £ 24.00	OPEN 1-12	

MARLOES
Map Ref Jb5

A remote sandy stretch of the Pembrokeshire Coast National Park, overlooking Skomer Island - a haven for puffins and other seabirds. Safe for surfing and swimming; boat trips to the island from nearby Martin's Haven.

Guest Houses

The Foxes
Marloes, Haverfordwest, Dyfed, SA62 3AY
Tel: (0646) 527

Single, double, family, twin bedrooms. H & C, washbasins, central heating. Situated centre village. Sandy beaches, boat trips, Skomer-Grassholm bird islands-see puffins nesting. Miles coastal path walks, lovely wild flowers. Children welcome, reduced rates. Licensed restaurant, meals from £1.50. Ample parking. Access rooms all times. Pet welcome. Fire certificate. Tea facilities. HHH recommended.

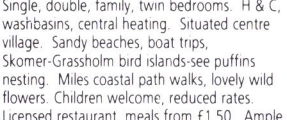

	SINGLE PER PERSON B&B		DOUBLE FOR 2 PERSONS B&B		🛏	5
	MIN £	MAX £	MIN £	MAX £		
	11.00	14.00	22.00	28.00	OPEN 1-12

MILFORD HAVEN
Map Ref Jc6

Important port on edge of Pembrokeshire Coast National Park; Nelson called it one of the best natural harbours he had seen. Fine walks and gardens. Torch Theatre. Excellent touring base.

Hotels

Ferry Inn
Llanstadwell, Neyland, Milford Haven, Dyfed SA73 1EG
Tel: (0646) 600270

Situated on the water's edge, enjoying fine views of the Cleddau Estuary on route of the Pembrokeshire Coastal Path. Our family run Inn has seven bedrooms, dining room, TV lounge, two licensed bars and games room. Children welcome. River front/patio garden. Close to Neyland Marina. Ideal base for touring, fishing, sailing and walking.

	SINGLE PER PERSON B&B		DOUBLE FOR 2 PERSONS B&B		🛏	7
	MIN £	MAX £	MIN £	MAX £		1
	12.00	14.00	24.00	28.00	OPEN 1-12

Farmhouses

Woodson Farm
Lower Thornton, Milford Haven, Dyfed, SA73 3UQ
Tel: (0437) 890358

Situated in a quiet area between Milford Haven and Haverfordwest near many lovely beaches and ideal for walking the coastal path. Sports centre in Milford Haven. Good food and a warm welcome awaits you. Hot and cold water and tea/coffee making facilities in all bedrooms.

	SINGLE PER PERSON B&B		DOUBLE FOR 2 PERSONS B&B		🛏	4
	MIN £	MAX £	MIN £	MAX £		
	12.00	12.00	24.00	24.00	OPEN 3-10

MYNACHLOG-DDU
Map Ref Je3

On southern approach to Preseli Hills. Prehistoric stone circle nearby. Centrally located village for rugged north Pembrokeshire coast and beaches of the south.

Farmhouses

Yethen Isaf
Mynachlog-Ddu, Clunderwen, Pembrokeshire, Dyfed, SA66 7SN
Tel: (09913) 256

Traditional 300 year old farmhouse with inglenook fireplace and beams, enjoying spectacular views within Preseli Hills National Park. 12 miles from coast, working sheep and beef farm. Tea/coffee making facilities all rooms. Bathroom with shower. Ideal centre for discovering secret valleys and empty hills steeped in history. Packed lunches with homely cooking. TV lounge.

	SINGLE PER PERSON B&B		DOUBLE FOR 2 PERSONS B&B		🛏	3
	MIN £	MAX £	MIN £	MAX £		
	14.00	14.00	24.00	28.00	OPEN 1-12

NARBERTH
Map Ref Je5

Small market town, ancient castle remains. Convenient for beaches of Carmarthen Bay and resorts of Tenby and Saundersfoot. Nearby is the multi-activity Oakwood Adventure and Leisure Park.

Guest Houses

Heron's Reach
Landshipping, Narberth, Pembrokeshire, Dyfed SA67 8BE
Tel: (083485) 366

Modern bungalow with two twin bedded en-suite rooms, colour TV, coffee/tea facilities. Adjacent village pub with food available. Car parking. Tidal river, fishing, boating 200 yards. All in Pembrokeshire National Park, an area of beautiful countryside and variety of beaches within easy reach. Landshipping is a quiet peaceful hamlet off the tourist routes.

	SINGLE PER PERSON B&B		DOUBLE FOR 2 PERSONS B&B		🛏	2
	MIN £	MAX £	MIN £	MAX £		2
		10.50		21.00	OPEN 1-12

Traethgwyn Guest House
Robeston Wathen, Narberth, Pembrokeshire, Dyfed, SA67 8EN
Tel: (0834) 860598

A warm welcome awaits you at our small guest house situated on the edge of the Pembrokeshire National Park, close to the Preseli Hills, 8 miles to coast. Home cooking from home grown produce when available. H & C all rooms. Tea/coffee making facilities. TV lounge. Central heating. Country inn nearby. SAE for terms.

	SINGLE PER PERSON B&B		DOUBLE FOR 2 PERSONS B&B		🛏	3
	MIN £	MAX £	MIN £	MAX £		
	9.00	10.00	18.00	20.00	OPEN 2-11

NEWPORT
Map Ref Jd2

Ancient castled village on Pembrokeshire coast. Fine beaches - bass and sea trout fishing. Pentre Ifan burial chamber is close by. Accommodation and restaurants. Backed by heather-clad Preseli Hills.

Hotels

The Salutation Inn
Felindre Farchog, Crymych, Dyfed, SA41 3UY
Tel: (0239) 820564

Beautifully situated in the Pembrokeshire National Park, 5 minutes from Newport beach and the Preseli hills. Facilities nearby include riding, golf, fishing, sailing, birdwatching, walking, canoeing and lazing quietly. Modern and traditional rooms. Pleasant restaurant, good food. A really relaxing place to stay.

	SINGLE PER PERSON B&B		DOUBLE FOR 2 PERSONS B&B		🛏	9
	MIN £	MAX £	MIN £	MAX £		9
	14.00		28.00		OPEN 1-12

NEWPORT CONTINUED

Guest Houses

White Berries

Long Street, Newport, Dyfed, SA42 OTJ L
Tel: (0239) 820458

Spacious private house very close to coastal path and beach, but also near town centre. Ideal for walking, bird watching, boating, swimming, golf, tennis, fishing and riding. Shops and tourist information nearby. Excellent pubs and restaurants within walking distance. Large lounge, TV, central heating, open fire, tea/coffee making facilities in rooms. Children welcome.

	SINGLE PER PERSON B&B		DOUBLE FOR 2 PERSONS B&B		🛏	2
🐕	MIN £	MAX £	MIN £	MAX £		
	10.00	11.50	20.00	22.00	OPEN 1-12	

NEYLAND   Map Ref Jc6

Village, north bank. Milford Haven. Pembroke Castle.

Guest Houses

Church Lakes Guest House

88 Church Road, Llanstadwell, Neyland, Milford Haven, Dyfed SA73 1EA
Tel: (0646) 600840

Comfortable, detached house alongside the Cleddau Estuary foreshore and coastal footpath. Haven views from all rooms and terrace with yachts from nearby Westfield Marina, the Irish ferries, etc. often adding interest. Tea/coffee facilities and H & C in bedrooms. Good food. Near Cleddau Bridge linking Preseli and South Pembrokeshire. Details from Barry and Sylvia Fieldhouse.

	SINGLE PER PERSON B&B		DOUBLE FOR 2 PERSONS B&B		🛏	3
🐕	MIN £	MAX £	MIN £	MAX £		
✗	10.00	10.00	20.00	20.00	OPEN 1-12	

PEMBROKE   Map Ref Jd6

Ancient borough built around Pembroke Castle, birthplace of Henry VII. Fascinating Museum of Romany Crafts and Lore. Sandy bays within easy reach, yachting, fishing - all the coastal activities associated with estuaries. Plenty of things to see and do in the area around.

82

Guest Houses

Chestnut House

Cosheston, Pembroke, Dyfed, SA72 4UD L
Tel: (0646) 685402

A stone built character house, set in a one acre garden with outstanding views. Two double bedrooms have H & C and tea and coffee making facilities, shower room and guests own lounge and dining room. Car parking. Friendly atmosphere, good breakfast, special rates for children. Local beauty spots nearby. No smoking please.

	SINGLE PER PERSON B&B		DOUBLE FOR 2 PERSONS B&B		🛏	2
🍴	MIN £	MAX £	MIN £	MAX £		
			22.00	22.00	OPEN 3-9	

High Noon Guest House

Lower Lamphey Road, Pembroke, Dyfed, SA71 4AB 👑👑
Tel: (0646) 683736/681232

Friendly family run guest house, close to main street, within short drive of beaches, coastal path and historic Pembroke Castle. Facilities for golf, fishing and boating are nearby. Children are welcome at reduced rrates. Some en-suite rooms, open all year. Home cooking, restaurant licence. AA Listed. WTB 2 crowns. Centrall heated, hot and cold all rooms.

H ✗	SINGLE PER PERSON B&B		DOUBLE FOR 2 PERSONS B&B		🛏	9
P						2
🐕	MIN £	MAX £	MIN £	MAX £		
	10.00	12.50	20.00	25.00	OPEN 1-12	

The Old Rectory

Cosheston, Pembroke, Pembrokeshire, Dyfed   SA72 4UJ L
Tel: (0646) 684960

Set in two acre garden. Believed to date from Norman times. The Old Rectory has tastefully furnished bedrooms, spacious lounge with colour TV. Upstairs dining room where home cooked food is served at times to suit. Ideal touring base for National Park, beaches and castles, village walks. Farmyard animals to feed. Special rates for children.

P ✗	SINGLE PER PERSON B&B		DOUBLE FOR 2 PERSONS B&B		🛏	3
🐕	MIN £	MAX £	MIN £	MAX £		
🍴	12.00	13.00	24.00	26.00	OPEN 1-12	

Rosedene

Hodgeston, Pembroke, Dyfed, SA71 5JU L
Tel: (0646) 672586

Large, detached bungalow midway Tenby/Pembroke, 1½ miles Freshwater East beach. Idyllic situation in National Park village green. Well kept grounds. Spectacular coastline, castles, golf, water sports nearby. Family/ doubles (some en-suite). Ground floor rooms with courtesy trays, TV's, H & C. Singles available. Relaxing lounge, separate dining room. Ample parking and unrestricted access. Mini breaks Spring/Autumn. Central heating.

H	SINGLE PER PERSON B&B		DOUBLE FOR 2 PERSONS B&B		🛏	4
P						2
	MIN £	MAX £	MIN £	MAX £		
	12.00	13.50	24.00	27.00	OPEN 1-12	

Farmhouses

Bangeston Farm

Stackpole, Pembroke, Dyfed, SA71 5BX L
Tel: (0646) 683986

Situated three miles from Pembroke. Not far from excellent clean beaches and coastline walks. Homely farmhouse which overlooks coastal area. Good home cooking, hearty breakfasts, tea making facilities in all bedrooms. Comfortable accommodation, separate dining tables, lounge with colour TV, central heating. Family and double rooms available. Peaceful countryside. Why not come and visit?

P	SINGLE PER PERSON B&B		DOUBLE FOR 2 PERSONS B&B		🛏	3
✗	MIN £	MAX £	MIN £	MAX £		
	10.00	10.00	18.00	18.00	OPEN 4-10	

Home Farm

Stackpole, Pembroke, Dyfed, SA71 5DQ L
Tel: (0646) 661244

Relax in comfort at our homely farmhouse, set near idyllic wooded lakeside on the coast path. A short walk to the unspoilt sandy beaches of Broad Haven and Barafundle, Bosherston, lily pools and St. Govans nearby. Ideal base for climbing, fishing, bird watching, walking the coast path. Spacious twin/double/family rooms with hand-basins, TV, tea and coffee. Reduced rates for children. A warm welcome. Croeso cynnes.

H 🍴	SINGLE PER PERSON B&B		DOUBLE FOR 2 PERSONS B&B		🛏	3
🐕	MIN £	MAX £	MIN £	MAX £		
	12.00		19.00	24.00	OPEN 3-10	

Thrustle Mill Farm

Freshwater East, Pembroke, Dyfed, SA71 5LT L
Tel: (0646) 685351

Three bedrooms shared bathroom and shower facility with constant hot water. Forty six acre beef and poultry farm with market garden. Good off road parking for 10 cars. Two miles from beach in warm secluded valley. 1 mile from Pembroke town. Horse riding available, lily ponds and other amenities in our immediate area Woodland Fen.

H	SINGLE PER PERSON B&B		DOUBLE FOR 2 PERSONS B&B		🛏	3
P	MIN £	MAX £	MIN £	MAX £		
🍴	9.50	10.50	19.00	21.00	OPEN 1-12	

West Farm

Castlemartin, Pembroke, Dyfed, SA71 5HW L
Tel: (064681) 234

West Farm is a large dairy farm, five miles south west of Pembroke, two miles from Freshwater west beach. The bedrooms are spacious and comfortable, all have H & C, basins and tea/coffee making facilities. Colour TV in sitting room. Good home cooking. Many beauty spots and sandy beaches within easy reach. Children welcome.

H ✗	SINGLE PER PERSON B&B		DOUBLE FOR 2 PERSONS B&B		🛏	4
P						2
🐕	MIN £	MAX £	MIN £	MAX £		
	10.00	12.00	20.00	24.00	OPEN 3-10	

SAUNDERSFOOT
Map Ref Je6

Popular resort on South Pembrokeshire coast. Picturesque harbour and beach offering holiday activities - swimming, sailing, sea angling and birdwatching. Set on Pembrokeshire Coast National Park footpath.

Hotels

Pleasant Valley House

Pleasant Valley, Stepaside, Saunderfoot, South Pembrokeshire, Dyfed SA67 8NY
Tel: (0834) 813607
Situated in a peaceful wooded valley, aptly named Pleasant Valley. 500 yards from Wisemans Bridge beach, thirty minutes coastal walk into Saunderfoot. We have ample parking facilities, licensed bar and a 32' x 16' swimming pool. Large residential lounge, dining room with separate tables, varied menu. Picturesque surroundings and within easy reach of beautiful sandy beaches.

H	SINGLE PER PERSON B&B	DOUBLE FOR 2 PERSONS B&B		9
P				1
X	MIN £ 10.00	MAX £ 12.00	MIN £ 20.00	MAX £ 24.00	OPEN 3-10

Guest Houses

Belcot

Ragged Staff, Saundersfoot, Dyfed, SA69 9HT L
Tel: (0834) 812769
Tranquility, minutes from harbour and beach. Patios, sun deck, private parking. Open all year. Central heating. Tea and coffee making facilities in all rooms. Warm welcome to this split level ultra modern house.

P	SINGLE PER PERSON B&B	DOUBLE FOR 2 PERSONS B&B		3
X				
	MIN £ 12.50	MAX £ 22.00	MIN £ 22.00	MAX £	OPEN 1-12

Cliff House

Wogan Terrace, Saundersfoot, Pembrokeshire, Dyfed, SA69 9HA
Tel: (0834) 813931
Ideally situated guest house in the heart of this popular seaside resort, we have unrivalled sea views and are only one minute's walk from the beach. Double, twin or family rooms. All rooms have wash basin, shaver point, tea and coffee facilities and central heating. Luxury en-suite facilities in several rooms. Superb cuisine.

	SINGLE PER PERSON B&B	DOUBLE FOR 2 PERSONS B&B		6
X				3
	MIN £	MAX £ 20.00	MIN £	MAX £ 26.00	OPEN 1-12

Edgecombe Guest House

The Ridgeway, Saundersfoot, Dyfed, SA69 9JE
Tel: (0834) 812810
Family guest house 200 yards from beach village and all amenities. Comfortable rooms all with tea making facilities some en-suite, home cooking, heated outdoor swimming pool, life guard in attendance at all times. Children very welcome. Baby sitting arranged. Licensed bar. TV room. Parking.

H	SINGLE PER PERSON B&B	DOUBLE FOR 2 PERSONS B&B		10
P				6
X	MIN £ 9.50	MAX £ 14.00	MIN £ 19.00	MAX £ 28.00	OPEN 3-11

Sandy Hill Guest House

Tenby Road, Saundersfoot, Pembrokeshire, Dyfed SA69 9DR
Tel: (0834) 813165
Small friendly guest house offering bed, breakfast, dinner. Licensed bar, swimming pool, car park. Tea and coffee facilities, colour TV in all guest rooms. AA RAC Listed. Enjoying country aspect but only three minutes drive Saundersfoot beach, five minutes drive Tenby. Personal attention from Peggy and David Edwards.

P	SINGLE PER PERSON B&B	DOUBLE FOR 2 PERSONS B&B		5
X	MIN £ 11.00	MAX £ 12.00	MIN £ 22.00	MAX £ 24.00	OPEN 3-10

Springfield Guest House

St Brides Hill, Saundersfoot, Pembrokeshire, Dyfed SA69 9NP
Tel: (0834) 813518
Small family run guest house overlooking Carmarthen Bay. AA/RAC Listed. 5 minutes walk to beach, shops, harbour. All rooms H & C with shaver points, some en-suite, central heating, colour TV lounge, reading area, tea making facilities. Reduction for children sharing rooms. Full fire certificate held. Warm friendly welcome. Private car park at rear of house.

H	SINGLE PER PERSON B&B	DOUBLE FOR 2 PERSONS B&B		5
P				2
	MIN £ 13.00	MAX £ 14.00	MIN £ 22.00	MAX £ 26.00	OPEN 1-11

Farmhouses

Carne Mountain Farm

Reynalton, Kilgetty, Dyfed, SA68 0PD L
Tel: (0834) 860546
Welcome to Carne Mountain and enjoy the peace of our lovely traditional farmhouse, set amidst 40 acres of lovely countryside. 3½ miles Saundersfoot beach. Delightful home cooking. Lovely beamed sitting room, with log fire, colour TV etc. Separate farmhouse dining room. Pretty bedrooms, centrally heated with wash hand basins, teasmade. SAE to Mrs Holgate for brochure.

H	SINGLE PER PERSON B&B	DOUBLE FOR 2 PERSONS B&B		3
P X				
	MIN £ 8.50	MAX £ 9.50	MIN £ 17.00	MAX £ 19.00	OPEN 1-12

Heatherton Farm

Devonshire Drive, Saundersfoot, Dyfed, SA69 9EE L
Tel: (0834) 813343
Spacious new bungalow situated on dairy farm 2½ miles Saundersfoot, 4 miles Tenby. Riding stables and country pub nearby. Good home cooking. Single, double and family room available. H & C in most rooms, lounge and separate TV lounge, dining room with separate tables. Full size snooker table for guests use. Special rates for children.

H X	SINGLE PER PERSON B&B	DOUBLE FOR 2 PERSONS B&B		3
P				
	MIN £ 10.00	MAX £ 11.00	MIN £ 20.00	MAX £ 22.00	OPEN 6-10

SOLVA
Map Ref Jb4

Pembrokeshire coast village with small attractive harbour and craft shops. Pembrokeshire Coast Path offers good walking. Exotic butterflies at Nectarium.

Guest Houses

Min-yr-Afon

Middle Mill, Solva, Dyfed, SA62 6XD L
Tel: (0437) 721394
Ideally situated for St. David's Peninsula and National Park Coast Path, in Middle Mill, Solva. Every comfort, friendly atmosphere with country cooking. Full central heating, small swimming pool, parking. The bedrooms have H & C, tea/coffee making facilities, we even have a four poster bed. Bed and breakfast, evening meal optional. Packed lunches by arrangement.

	SINGLE PER PERSON B&B	DOUBLE FOR 2 PERSONS B&B		3
X				1
	MIN £ 9.50	MAX £ 12.50	MIN £ 19.00	MAX £ 25.00	OPEN 1-12

The Old Manse

47 High Street, Solva, Haverfordwest, Pembrokeshire Dyfed SA62 6TE L
Tel: (0437) 721553
Pleasant quiet country setting in the lovely village of Solva. Best kept village award holder. Clean, comfortable, spacious rooms with friendly service close to harbour and sea. Ideal for family holidays. Evening meals optional. TV, tea and coffee in all bedrooms. Individual tables in dining room. Home cooking. Diets catered for if required. Iron available.

H	SINGLE PER PERSON B&B	DOUBLE FOR 2 PERSONS B&B		3
P X				
	MIN £ 9.50	MAX £ 10.50	MIN £ 18.00	MAX £ 20.00	OPEN 1-12

SOLVA CONTINUED

Farmhouses

Llanddinog Old Farmhouse

Solva, Haverfordwest, Dyfed, SA62 6NA
Tel: (03483) 224
Peacefully situated in spacious grounds. This 16th century farmstead is ideal for beaches, fishing, riding, walking. Close St. David's, Preseli Mountains. Homely atmosphere. Home produced foodstuffs, local fish. Children's reductions. 1 family, 1 twin, 1 single, wash basins, central heating, colour TV, dining room, picnics, parking, laundry, highchair, cots, dogs accepted. Children's play area. Small animals and birds. Self catering also available. SAE Mrs Griffiths.

H ✗ P ♞	SINGLE PER PERSON B&B		DOUBLE FOR 2 PERSONS B&B		🛏	3
	MIN £	MAX £	MIN £	MAX £	🏠	
	11.00	12.00	22.00	24.00	OPEN 1-12	

Lochmeyler Farm

Pen-y-Cwm, Solva, Haverfordwest,
Pembrokeshire, Dyfed SA62 6LL   [L]
Tel: (03483) 7724
Lochmeyler is a 220 acre dairy farm. Centre for St Davids Peninsula, 4 miles Solva Harbour grid number FM 855275. 11th century farmhouse with 5 en-suite bedrooms all with colour TV, video, telephone, tea making facilities, electric blankets, clock radio, hair dryer. Two lounges (one for non-smokers), log fires early and late season. Children 10 years and over welcomed, choice of menus, vegetarians can be catered for. Brochure - M Jones.

H ⌘ P TW ♞ ✗	SINGLE PER PERSON B&B		DOUBLE FOR 2 PERSONS B&B		🛏	5
	MIN £	MAX £	MIN £	MAX £	🏠	5
	12.50	14.00	25.00	28.00	OPEN 1-12	

ST. DAVID'S Map Ref Ja4

Smallest cathedral city in Britain, shrine of Wales's patron saint. Magnificent ruins of Bishop's Palace beside ancient cathedral nestling in hollow. Set in Pembrokeshire Coast National Park, with fine beaches nearby; superb scenery on nearby headland. Craft shops, sea life centres, painting courses; ideal for walking and birdwatching

CALL Holidays (0792) 645555

Guest Houses

Cwmwdig Water Guest House

Berea, St David's, Dyfed, SA62 6DW
Tel: (03483) 434
Converted from lovely old stone faced farmhouse and barns. Five miles from St David's with views of Aber Eiddi Bay from most rooms. Less than one mile sea and coastal path. Resident owners lounge with log fire, TV lounge. Guest kitchen. Tea/coffee facilities all rooms (some en-suite). High quality food. Credit cards accepted. Brochure on request. From Jan 1990 (0348) 831434.

H ✗ P TW ♞	SINGLE PER PERSON B&B		DOUBLE FOR 2 PERSONS B&B		🛏	11
	MIN £	MAX £	MIN £	MAX £	🏠	2
		13.00		26.00	OPEN 1-12	

Glan-y-Môr Guest House

Caerfai Road, St David's, Dyfed,
SA62 6QT
Tel: (0437) 721788
With magnificent views over St Bride's Bay. Glan-y-Môr is just a short walk from the Pembrokeshire coastal path or nearby St David's. All rooms have wash basins, shaver points and central heating. Glan-y-Môr is residentially licensed with TV and sun lounges, private parking, gardens and freezer pack service. Full fire certificate.

P	SINGLE PER PERSON B&B		DOUBLE FOR 2 PERSONS B&B		🛏	4
	MIN £	MAX £	MIN £	MAX £	🏠	
	12.00		24.00		OPEN 3-10	

The Mount

66 New Street, St David's,
Haverfordwest, Dyfed SA62 6SU   [L]
Tel: (0437) 720276
A 200 year old ex-farmhouse with character, situated in own grounds. A few minutes from the city centre. Double and family rooms. Hot and cold water and shaver points all bedrooms. Electric heating all rooms. Large lounge with colour television. Dining room with separate tables. Private car park behind house. Fire certificate granted.

P ♞	SINGLE PER PERSON B&B		DOUBLE FOR 2 PERSONS B&B		🛏	4
	MIN £	MAX £	MIN £	MAX £	🏠	
			18.00		OPEN 4-10	

Ramsey House

Lower Moor, St David's,
Pembrokeshire, Dyfed SA62 6RP
Tel: (0437) 720321
Superior accommodation with all amenities in quiet convenient location ½ mile from Cathedral and Coast Path, within easy reach of sandy beaches and all attractions. Renowned for our imaginative Welsh cooking and exceptional hospitality. Licensed bar. Tea/coffee facilities, packed lunches, easy private parking. Winter Leisure Breaks. AA/RAC Listed. Taste of Wales recognised.

H ✗ P TW ♞	SINGLE PER PERSON B&B		DOUBLE FOR 2 PERSONS B&B		🛏	7
	MIN £	MAX £	MIN £	MAX £	🏠	
		25.30		28.00	OPEN 1-12	

Rigsby's

Royal Terrace, 49 Nun Street,
St. David's, Dyfed
Tel: (0437) 720632
A comfortable guest house with some en-suite rooms available. Situated in St. David's convenient for shops and cathedral, 1½ miles to the beach. Colour TV's in rooms, radio, teasmade, hair dryer and irons. Disabled ground floor en-suite unit. Bus stop nearby. Good full breakfast. High reputation for food and accommodation. Enquiries to Mr Terry Armitage.

✗	SINGLE PER PERSON B&B		DOUBLE FOR 2 PERSONS B&B		🛏	5
	MIN £	MAX £	MIN £	MAX £	🏠	3
	11.00	13.00	22.00	26.00	OPEN 1-12	

Tŷ Newydd

Parc Bach, Llanrhian, Haverfordwest,   [L]
Dyfed SA62 5BH
Tel: (03483) 7733
Family home, high standard accommodation. ¾ mile from coast path, 100 yards coast road, 5 miles St. David's. 1 large family room, 1 double room. TV lounge. Tea/coffee facilities. Parking. Homely and friendly. Non smokers only please.

P ⌘ ✗	SINGLE PER PERSON B&B		DOUBLE FOR 2 PERSONS B&B		🛏	2
	MIN £	MAX £	MIN £	MAX £	🏠	
	8.50		17.00		OPEN 3-9	

Ty Olaf

Mount Gardens, St. David's,
Pembrokeshire, Dyfed, SA62 6BS
Tel: (0437) 720885
Family home in quiet position on edge of Britains smallest city in Pembrokeshire Coast National Park. Single, double and family rooms. Hot and cold. Shaver points. Tea making facilities. Television lounge. No stairs. Five minutes walk to Cathedral and excellent restaurants. Off road parking. Convenient for coastal path, boat trips, etc.

P ♞ ⌘	SINGLE PER PERSON B&B		DOUBLE FOR 2 PERSONS B&B		🛏	4
	MIN £	MAX £	MIN £	MAX £	🏠	
	10.00	12.00	20.00	24.00	OPEN 1-12	

Wyncliffe Guest House

Quickwell Hill, St. David's, Dyfed,
SA62 6PD
Tel: (0437) 720447
Wyncliffe is situated in a secluded position overlooking the cathedral and valley to the coast beyond in its own grounds away from traffic. Ample parking. Tea making facilities in bedrooms, with wash basins and central heating. Good home cooking and personal service. Please write for brochure and tariff.

H P ✗	SINGLE PER PERSON B&B		DOUBLE FOR 2 PERSONS B&B		🛏	4
	MIN £	MAX £	MIN £	MAX £	🏠	
	12.00	13.00	24.00	26.00	OPEN 3-10	

Y Glennydd Restaurant & Guest House

51 Nun Street, St. David's, Dyfed, SA62 6NU
Tel: (0437) 720576
Comfortable Victorian house with 10 spacious centrally heated rooms, 3 en-suite, all with H & C, teasmade, colour TV, many with splended views. We also offer a licensed restaurant, an elegant lounge and friendly service. Ideal centre for bird watching, walking, outdoor activities. Children welcome, AA & RAC listed. Routier recommended. WTB Two Crowns.

H	SINGLE PER PERSON B&B		DOUBLE FOR 2 PERSONS B&B		🛏	10
X					🏠	3
	MIN £	MAX £	MIN £	MAX £		
	12.50	14.00	25.00	27.00	OPEN 3-12	

Farmhouses

Bank House Farm

Croes-Goch, Haverfordwest, Dyfed, SA62 6XZ
Tel: (03483) 305 [L]

A friendly Welsh farmhouse welcome awaits you in quiet coastal countryside, situated 5 miles from St. David's and 10 miles from Fishguard Harbour, 1½ miles from coast a Aber Eiddi Beach. 3 comfortable bedrooms available, 1 double, 1 single, 1 family. Not more than 6 people taken. TV lounge, separate tables, bathroom for sole use of guests. Good home produced food served.

P	SINGLE PER PERSON B&B		DOUBLE FOR 2 PERSONS B&B		🛏	3
🐕					🏠	
X	MIN £	MAX £	MIN £	MAX £		
	9.00	10.00	16.00	18.00	OPEN 2-11	

Binchurn

Tre-fin, Haverfordwest, Pembrokeshire, Dyfed SA62 5AE
Tel: (03483) 264

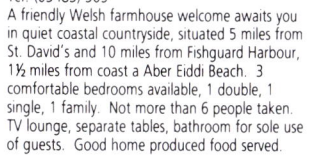

Superb 16th century farmhouse with panoramic land and sea views. Ideal for hikes, nature lovers, central sandy beaches, places of historical interest and natural beauty. WTB Farmhouse Award. Good home cooking. TV lounge for guests. Separate dining room. Tea/coffee facilities. Near coastal village of Tre-fin.

H	SINGLE PER PERSON B&B		DOUBLE FOR 2 PERSONS B&B		🛏	3
P					🏠	1
X	MIN £	MAX £	MIN £	MAX £		
	14.00		28.00		OPEN 4-10	

Torbant Farm Guest House

Croes-Goch, Haverfordwest, Pembrokeshire, Dyfed SA62 5JN
Tel: (0348) 831276

Relax in comfort in our friendly 300 year old farmhouse on a working mixed farm. Fully licensed bar, good home cooking. All bedrooms have H & C and heating, some en-suite. Substantial evening dinners available. The spectacular Pembrokeshire Coast is just 1½ miles away. Glorious beaches, abundant wildlife. Brochure from Mrs B B Charles. AA/RAC Listed. British Relais Routiers.

H	SINGLE PER PERSON B&B		DOUBLE FOR 2 PERSONS B&B		🛏	6
P					🏠	2
🐕	MIN £	MAX £	MIN £	MAX £		
	12.00	14.00	24.00	28.00	OPEN 3-10	

ST. NICHOLAS
Map Ref Jc3

Village on north coast of Pembrokeshire, a land of many hidden beaches. Walk the Coastal Path to enjoy this distinctive landscape. Woollen mill nearby and Fishguard within easy reach.

Farmhouses

New Mill

Tregwynt, St. Nicholas, Letterston, Dyfed, SA62 5UX
Tel: (03485) 637

Small traditional farm in picturesque valley ½ mile walk/drive from beaches of Abermawr/bach and coastal footpath off A487 Fishguard-St. David's road. Three double/twin rooms, two bathrooms, central heating. Lounge with colour television. Dining room, separate tables, excellent cuisine from organic grown home produced, meat, vegetables, eggs.

H	X	SINGLE PER PERSON B&B		DOUBLE FOR 2 PERSONS B&B		🛏	3
P						🏠	
🐕		MIN £	MAX £	MIN £	MAX £		
		12.00		24.00		OPEN 4-10	

TENBY
Map Ref Je6

Popular south Pembrokeshire resort with two wide beaches. Fishing trips from the attractive Georgian harbour, and boat trips to nearby Caldy Island. The Medieval walled town has fine old buildings, including Tudor Merchant's House (National Trust). Art galleries, pottery, museum, bowls, putting, golf. Regatta and carnival in August.

Hotels

Ocean Hotel

The Croft, Tenby, Dyfed, SA70 8AP
Tel: (0834) 2476

The hotel with marvellous views. The entrance to the beach is just opposite for bathing. A friendly, comfortable family run hotel, enjoying one of the finest positions in Tenby. Having beautiful views of the picturesque harbour. North Beach and Carmarthen Bay with combination of the highest standards of cuisine and comfort. Attractive lounge with colour television, bar. Reductions for children. Special terms early and late bookings. All bedrooms with tea/coffee facilities and colour television.

H	SINGLE PER PERSON B&B		DOUBLE FOR 2 PERSONS B&B		🛏	9
X					🏠	4
	MIN £	MAX £	MIN £	MAX £		
	11.00	14.00	22.00	28.00	OPEN 1-12	

Paragon Hotel

The Paragon, Tenby, Dyfed, SA70 7HL
Tel: (0834) 3022

Within town walls, seafront, magnificent views over Carmarthen Bay, Caldy Island and St Catherine's Island. Steps to the beach 20 yards from hotel. Gardens opposite. Our own car park. Licensed. Tea making facilities. Most rooms en-suite. Home cooking. Find us at the bottom of St Mary's Street which is opposite back gate of St Mary's Church.

H	🍴	SINGLE PER PERSON B&B		DOUBLE FOR 2 PERSONS B&B		🛏	10
P	X					🏠	7
🐕		MIN £	MAX £	MIN £	MAX £		
		12.00	14.00	24.00	28.00	OPEN 2-11	

Ripley St Mary's Hotel

St Mary's Street, Tenby, Pembrokeshire, Dyfed SA70 7HN
Tel: (0834) 2837

Highly recommended hotel in the quiet "Floral Street" in centre of Tenby. 75 yards seafront and Paragon Gardens. Lounge and bar lounge. Attractive bedrooms with TV, tea making, six with private bathrooms. Reductions for children and senior citizens. AA Listed. RAC acclaimed. Personally managed by Alan and Kath Mace. Our aim: to make your holiday a very enjoyable and memorable one with "Good home cooking and a friendly welcome".

H	SINGLE PER PERSON B&B		DOUBLE FOR 2 PERSONS B&B		🛏	14
🐕					🏠	6
X	MIN £	MAX £	MIN £	MAX £		
	14.00	14.00	28.00	28.00	OPEN 3-10	

TENBY

TENBY CONTINUED

Guest Houses

Coach House

Gumfreston, Tenby, Pembrokeshire,
Dyfed SA70 8RA
Tel: (0834) 3558

The coach house is situated in a quiet position has considerable charm and a relaxing atmosphere. Ample parking. All bedrooms have hot and cold, hot drinks facilities, heating. Lounge with TV, dining room with separate tables. Near Tenby, Saundersfoot, Manorbier beaches.

	SINGLE PER PERSON B&B		DOUBLE FOR 2 PERSONS B&B			2
						1
	MIN £	MAX £	MIN £	MAX £		
	10.00	11.00	20.00	22.00	OPEN 3-10	

Flemish Court

St Florence, Tenby, Dyfed
Tel: (0834) 871413

Lovely home of June ane Eric Taylor who will welcome you to spend your holiday with them. Most rooms have shower and toilet. All have colour TV, tea making and heating. Food will be excellent and varied. Within easy reach of National Park, attractions, beaches etc. Please telephone or write for brochure to find real value for money and that real Welsh hospitality.

	SINGLE PER PERSON B&B		DOUBLE FOR 2 PERSONS B&B			6
						4
	MIN £	MAX £	MIN £	MAX £		
	9.50	12.50	18.00	25.00	OPEN 1-12	

Glenholme

Picton Terrace, Tenby, Dyfed, SA70 7DR
Tel: (0834) 3909

Centrally situated. Minutes from town centre and South Beach. Nice outlook over bowling green. 6 bedrooms en-suite. Residential licence. Good home cooking, traditional and vegetarian. Personal attention from resident proprietors. Television lounge. Off season 3 day breaks available. Midweek at special rates. Each room is tastefully decorated and is provided with a complimentary tea tray.

	SINGLE PER PERSON B&B		DOUBLE FOR 2 PERSONS B&B			8
						6
	MIN £	MAX £	MIN £	MAX £		
			20.00	28.00	OPEN 1-12	

Glenthorne Guest House

Deer Park, Tenby, Dyfed, SA70 7LE
Tel: (0834) 2300

Situated 300 yards from Tenby's popular north beach. Convenient for railway station, coach station and car parks. Open all year. Hot and cold. Shaver points all bedrooms, single, double and family rooms available. Special rates for children. Good home cooking. Separate tables, licensed bar, television lounge. Fire certificate granted

	SINGLE PER PERSON B&B		DOUBLE FOR 2 PERSONS B&B			9
	MIN £	MAX £	MIN £	MAX £		
	10.00	12.00	20.00	24.00	OPEN 1-12	

Hidden Spring Guest House

Princes Gate, Narberth, Dyfed,
SA67 8TF
Tel: (0834) 861074

A warm friendly welcome awaits you, in the heart of the countryside. Panoramic views of the Preseli Hills. One acre of gardens. Only minutes away from beautiful Pembrokeshire coastline. Bedrooms tastefully decorated, H & C, shaver points, heating, drinks facilities, colour television all rooms. Double rooms en-suite, showers. Good home cooked food. Two Crowns, highly recommended.

	SINGLE PER PERSON B&B		DOUBLE FOR 2 PERSONS B&B			3
						2
	MIN £	MAX £	MIN £	MAX £		
	10.00	14.00	28.00	28.00	OPEN 1-12	

High Seas

8 The Norton, Tenby, Dyfed, SA70 8AA
Tel: (0834) 3611

Situated on the seafront overlooking the north beach and harbour close to the town centre. Many rooms with magnificent sea views across Carmarthen Bay. All bedrooms have colour TV, H & C, shaver points and tea making facilities. Reductions for children sharing parents room and for weekly bookings.

	SINGLE PER PERSON B&B		DOUBLE FOR 2 PERSONS B&B			7
	MIN £	MAX £	MIN £	MAX £		
	12.00	14.00	24.00	28.00	OPEN 4-10	

Morewood Guest House

Wooden, Saundersfoot, Pembrokeshire,
Dyfed SA69 9DY
Tel: (0834) 812098

A small easy going guest house situated along the A478 Kilgetty to Tenby road, two miles from Tenby and the Pembrokeshire coast. Licensed for residential guests. Lounge with TV. Bedrooms have hot and cold with hot drink making facilities. Evening dinner by arrangement, vegetables in season are produced from own garden. Children are welcome.

	SINGLE PER PERSON B&B		DOUBLE FOR 2 PERSONS B&B			3
	MIN £	MAX £	MIN £	MAX £		
			17.00	19.00	OPEN 3-10	

The Oaks

Gumfreston, Tenby, Dyfed, SA70 8RA
Tel: (0834) 2619

Welcoming couple offer bed and breakfast in detached country house in own grounds, 1½ miles from Tenby. Convenient for Wildlife Park, riding, swimming pool and excursions. Use of garden, free private parking. Separate breakfast/sitting room with colour TV. One double, one twin and one single bedroom. Private shower room and toilet for guests.

	SINGLE PER PERSON B&B		DOUBLE FOR 2 PERSONS B&B			3
	MIN £	MAX £	MIN £	MAX £		
	11.00	14.00	22.00	28.00	OPEN 4-9	

Sutherlands

3 Picton Road, Tenby, Dyfed, SA70 7DP
Tel: (0834) 2522

Small family guest house within easy reach of beaches, shops, car parks, golf course, putting and bowling greens. Shower room. H & C in all rooms. Tea/coffee making facilities, at no extra charge. Home cooking and a varied menu - traditional English breakfast or Continental. Friendly informal atmosphere.

	SINGLE PER PERSON B&B		DOUBLE FOR 2 PERSONS B&B			6
	MIN £	MAX £	MIN £	MAX £		
	9.50	11.50	19.00	23.00	OPEN 1-12	

Tides Reach

St Julian Street, Tenby, Dyfed,
SA70 7BD
Tel: (0834) 2614

Family run guest house situated near harbour with private steps onto Castle beach. Large bedrooms with superb sea views and showers, tea/coffee facilities. Centrally heated with large lounge overlooking Caldy Island. Colour TV. Bed, breakfast only. Fire certificate held. SAE Mrs Siân John.

	SINGLE PER PERSON B&B		DOUBLE FOR 2 PERSONS B&B			4
	MIN £	MAX £	MIN £	MAX £		
			21.00	28.00	OPEN 3-10	

Farmhouses

Beaconing Farm

Temple Bar Road, Kilgetty,
Pembrokeshire, Dyfed SA68 0RD
Tel: (0834) 813296

Traditional farmhouse on a working dairy farm, centrally situated within easy reach of beaches and amenities between Saundersfoot and Tenby. Ideal for adults and children alike. Games room with snooker table. Central heating. TV lounge. Separate tables in dining room. Ample parking. Phone or write for brochure now. Fishing and riding available nearby.

	SINGLE PER PERSON B&B		DOUBLE FOR 2 PERSONS B&B			2
	MIN £	MAX £	MIN £	MAX £		
	10.00	13.00	20.00	26.00	OPEN 4-10	

THE COASTLINE AND VALES OF DYFED

At Llandovery, you can stand in the cobbled old market square and still see why that 19th-century traveller and writer George Borrow described it as 'the pleasantest little town' in Wales. Llandovery's timeless charm epitomises the traditional town-and-country character of the Vales of Dyfed.

The landscape is dominated by the two great valleys carved by the Towy and Teifi rivers. Rich farmlands in the Vale of Towy are flanked by the brooding Black Mountain and the Brechfa Forest. Along the rushing Teifi, thick woods crowd down to the riverbanks where coracles are still used to fish for salmon and trout. This is an area of cattle and sheep markets – don't miss bustling Carmarthen on market day – and a magical coastline so vividly captured in the writings of Dylan Thomas (the Boathouse where he lived in sleepy Laugharne is open to the public).

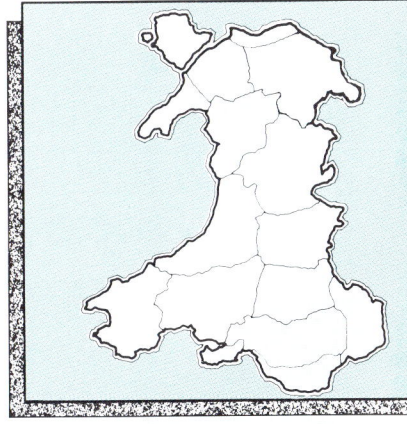

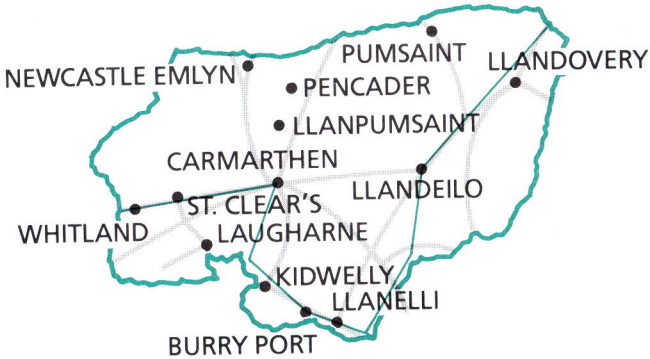

BURRY PORT
Map Ref Kd4

Small seaside town, once a busy commercial port now bustling with leisure and fishing craft. Pembrey Country Park and Cefn Sidan's 7 mile sandy beach provide excellent facilities for visitors. The Ashburnham Championship Golf Links nearby. Main line railway station and easy access to M4.

Guest Houses

Plas Kenrhos

Y Graig, Burry Port, Dyfed, SA16 0DG
Tel: (05546) 3742
Plas Kenrhos is over 200 years old, built in 1780. Situated in an elevated position overlooking the town and harbour of Burry Port. The views over the estuary to the Gower Peninsula are magnificent. Ideally situated for touring the Gower and West Wales. Golf, fishing, horse riding, walking nearby.

H	SINGLE PER PERSON B&B		DOUBLE FOR 2 PERSONS B&B		🛏	3
P	MIN £	MAX £	MIN £	MAX £		
X	13.50	13.50	27.00	27.00	OPEN 1-12	

CARMARTHEN
Map Ref Kc2

County town of Dyfed, lively market and shops, livestock mart. Carmarthen Castle was an important residence of the native Welsh princes but only the gateway and towers remain. Museum, golf, fishing, tennis and well-equipped leisure centre. Remains of Roman amphitheatre. Coracle fishing may still be seen on the Towy, meandering through the lush countryside.

Guest Houses

Gardde y Rebecca Guest House

High Street, Lower St. Clear's,
Carmarthen, Dyfed, SA33 4DY
Tel: (0994) 230617
17th century country house four miles from Carmarthen Bay and Dylan's "Sunhoneyed", Laugharne. Spacious rooms, washbasins, tea trolleys, TV lounge, central heating, ample parking. Fishing, rambling, trekking, wildlife, Preseli mountains, motor racing nearby. Garden fresh food. Once the home of Horniman who dealt in butter and tea and later of Huw Williams, the chartist and Rebecca Figurehead.

H	SINGLE PER PERSON B&B		DOUBLE FOR 2 PERSONS B&B		🛏	7
P	MIN £	MAX £	MIN £	MAX £		
X		10.50		19.00	OPEN 1-12	

Glasfryn Guest House

Brechfa, Carmarthen, Dyfed, SA32 7QY   L
Tel: (0267) 202306
Situated in the heart of the Brechfa Forest surrounded by moss covered hills. A small family owned country guest house. Ideally located for salmon and sewin fishing, pony trekking, walking, shooting, bird watching. 2 double rooms, 1 twin bedded room. Large dining room with separate tables. ½ hour from nearest town, 45 minutes from nearest beaches.

H X	SINGLE PER PERSON B&B		DOUBLE FOR 2 PERSONS B&B		🛏	3
P	MIN £	MAX £	MIN £	MAX £		
🐕	10.00	10.00	20.00	20.00	OPEN 1-12	

Neuadd Wen Country Guest House

Cwmduad, Carmarthen, Dyfed,
SA33 6XJ
Tel: (0267) 87438
Comfortable guest house, ideally situated for exploring West Wales, set in Duad Valley amid beautiful scenery. Single, twin, double and family rooms available all with H & C and shaver points and heating. Good rates for children sharing. Excellent home cooking, most diets catered for. Luxurious lounge with TV, residential licence. Bargain winter breaks. Brochure available.

H X	SINGLE PER PERSON B&B		DOUBLE FOR 2 PERSONS B&B		🛏	6
P	MIN £	MAX £	MIN £	MAX £		
🐕	9.00	11.00	18.00	22.00	OPEN 1-12	

Ystrad Farmhouse

Llansteffan Road, Johnstown,   L
Carmarthen, Dyfed SA31 3PE
Tel: (0267) 235073
Two miles from Carmarthen centre, 2 minutes leisure centre. Sauna, golf, riding, fishing, markets, castles, beaches etc. A warm welcome to enjoy your stay in former farmhouse full of character. Quiet position. Comfortable bedrooms. TV lounge, central heating, excellent breakfast. Shower in bathroom. Cot available. Double or family room. One twin.

P	SINGLE PER PERSON B&B		DOUBLE FOR 2 PERSONS B&B		🛏	2
🐕	MIN £	MAX £	MIN £	MAX £		
⚘	9.00		20.00		OPEN 1-12	

Farmhouses

Pant Farm

Meidrim, Carmarthen, Dyfed,
SA33 5QU
Tel: (0994) 230252
Working dairy farm in pleasant rural setting, elegantly decorated and lovingly furnished for style and comfort. Stunning views of unspoilt beauty overlooking the surrounding valleys far from the stresses of city life. Close to Laugharne - Dylan Thomas' country and centrally situated for touring the Pembrokeshire and Cardiganshire coast.

H ⚘	SINGLE PER PERSON B&B		DOUBLE FOR 2 PERSONS B&B		🛏	5
P X	MIN £	MAX £	MIN £	MAX £		3
🐕	14.00	14.00	28.00	28.00	OPEN 1-12	

Pantgwyn Farm

Whitemill, Carmarthen, Dyfed,   L
SA32 7ES
Tel: (0267) 290247
A warm welcome awaits you at our recently renovated 200 year old farmhouse. Relax in luxuriously appointed bedrooms. Residents inglenook lounge, large dining room. Superb home cooking. Children welcome at special rates. Games room. 4 miles Carmarthen, 8 miles sandy beach. Ideally situated for touring West Wales, historic sites, castles, gold mine, steam railway nearby.

H ⚘	SINGLE PER PERSON B&B		DOUBLE FOR 2 PERSONS B&B		🛏	4
P X	MIN £	MAX £	MIN £	MAX £		1
🐕	10.00	12.50	20.00	25.00	OPEN 1-12	

Plas Newydd Farmhouse

Blaenycoed Road, Carmarthen, Dyfed,   L
SA33 6EX
Tel: (0267) 87368
Plasnewydd is centrally situated for north, south and west coasts of Dyfed. Friendly small farm offering single, double, family rooms with special rates for children. Superb cooking. Many guests return, including one family from Scotland, 14 times!! Take A484 to Cynwyl Elfed. Turn left in village S P Blaenycoed. Turn right in Blaenycoed. Farmhouse one mile.

H X	SINGLE PER PERSON B&B		DOUBLE FOR 2 PERSONS B&B		🛏	3
P	MIN £	MAX £	MIN £	MAX £		
⚘	9.00	12.00	18.00	24.00	OPEN 1-12	

KIDWELLY Map Ref Kc3

Historic town 9 miles south of Carmarthen; its first charter was granted by Henry 1. With its ancient church, 14th century bridge and great castle, once stormed by the warrior-princess Gwenllian, it has a medieval air. Industrial museum on outskirts. Sited at the tip of the Gwendraeth Fach estuary, the town is close to the Cefn Sidan Sands and Pembrey Country Park.

CALL Holidays (0792) 645555

Farmhouses

Pen-y-Bac Farm
Mynyddygarreg, Kidwelly, Dyfed, SA17 4LR L
Tel: (0554) 891200
Comfortable farmhouse in beautiful secluded location near castle, beaches, country park, Industrial Museum, Welsh motor sports centre. Secure yard for parking, private fishing. Convenient touring base. Inglenook fireplace, exposed beams, log fires, good home cooking. Pets welcome. 2 family rooms, 2 double rooms. Private bathroom.

	SINGLE PER PERSON B&B		DOUBLE FOR 2 PERSONS B&B		🛏	4
H ✕	MIN £	MAX £	MIN £	MAX £		
P 🐾	12.00	14.00	26.00	28.00		OPEN 1-12

LAUGHARNE Map Ref Kb3

Atmospheric small town where poet Dylan Thomas lived in The Boathouse - the 'house on stilts' now a museum devoted to his memory. Local life inspired his classic radio play Under Milk Wood. 12th century castle. Interesting little shops and a pottery.

Farmhouses

Delacorse Farm Guest House
Taf Estuary, Ants Hill, Laugharne, Carmarthen, Dyfed SA33 4QP
Tel: (0994) 427647
Secluded 1800 AD farmhouse idyllically situated beside the beautiful Taf Estuary. Water ski-ing, sailing, windsurfing, fishing, bird watching available. All rooms have estuary views, wash-basins, tea making. Situated on the picturesque coastal footpath, 15 minutes walk from Laugharne and the Dylan Thomas Boathouse. Beaches, castles nearby. A perfect setting for holidays, weekend and mid-week breaks. Open all year. Brochure on request.

	SINGLE PER PERSON B&B		DOUBLE FOR 2 PERSONS B&B		🛏	3
P ✕	MIN £	MAX £	MIN £	MAX £		
🐾 ✕	8.50	11.50	17.00	23.00		OPEN 1-12

Halldown
Cross Inn, Laugharne, Dyfed, SA33 4QS
Tel: (0994) 427452
Halldown farmhouse 1 mile from the estuary at Laugharne just 2 miles off the A40 set in the quiet countryside yet within 15 minutes drive of the lovely Carmarthen Bay. Fishing, pony riding, bird watching, walking are available locally. 3 double bedrooms, heating, tea making facilities, lounge, colour TV. Good farmhouse food served. Friendly welcome assured.

	SINGLE PER PERSON B&B		DOUBLE FOR 2 PERSONS B&B		🛏	3
H ✕ P	MIN £	MAX £	MIN £	MAX £		
🐾	9.50	10.00	19.00	20.00		OPEN 1-12

LLANDEILO Map Ref Ga7

Farming centre at an important crossing on river Towy, and handy as touring base for Carreg Cennen Castle, impressively set on high crag, and remains of Dryslwyn Castle. Gelli Aur Country Park nearby has 90 acres, including a nature trail, arboretum and deer herd.

Guest Houses

Tŷ Gwyn Bach
Ffairfach, Llandeilo, Dyfed, SA19 6UY L
Tel: (0558) 823546
Spacious attractive and comfortable rooms. Central heating, H & C, morning tea etc. One bed-sitting room with en-suite shower. The house is set in an acre of landscaped gardens. Outdoor swimming pool, heated in summer. Ideally located for touring, walking, golf, birdwatching, fishing, etc. Within easy reach of Brecon Beacons, Gower Peninsula and M4.

	SINGLE PER PERSON B&B		DOUBLE FOR 2 PERSONS B&B		🛏	3
P ✕	MIN £	MAX £	MIN £	MAX £		1
	10.00	14.00	22.00	28.00		OPEN 1-12

LLANDOVERY Map Ref Gb6

An important market town on the A40 with a ruined castle; its Welsh name Llanymddyfri means "The Church Among the Waters" Nearby is the cave of Twm Sion Catti - the Welsh Robin Hood. Good touring centre for Brecon Beacons and Llyn Brianne area.

Hotels

The Plough Inn
Myddfai, Llandovery, Dyfed, SA20 0NZ L
Tel: (0550) 20643
200 year old stone built inn, situated in peaceful village in Brecon Beacons. Log fires, good home cooking, imaginative vegetarian dishes. Good area for fishing, walking, birdwatching, touring. Dogs welcome. Two double, two single bedrooms.

	SINGLE PER PERSON B&B		DOUBLE FOR 2 PERSONS B&B		🛏	4
H ✕ P	MIN £	MAX £	MIN £	MAX £		
🐾	10.00		20.00			OPEN 1-12

LLANDEILO

LLANDOVERY CONTINUED

Guest Houses

Llwyncelyn Guest House

Llandovery, Dyfed, SA20 0EP
Tel: (0550) 20566
AA/RAC listed. Delightful riverside setting. Town centre 10 minutes walk. Full central heating. Homely atmosphere. Good food. Licensed. Ample parking. Within 60 mile radius of Llwyncelyn, visitors would have almost complete coverage of Mid and South Wales, or you could relax on our lawn or laze beside our stretch of the River Towy.

P	SINGLE PER PERSON B&B	DOUBLE FOR 2 PERSONS B&B	🛏	6
✗	MIN £	MAX £	MIN £	MAX £	🚗	
				27.00	OPEN 1-12

Y Neuadd Guest House & Photo Holidays

Pentre Ty Gwyn, Llandovery, Dyfed, SA20 0RN
Tel: (0550) 20603
Small comfortable guest house and photography centre. All rooms own shower, toilet, tea/coffee. Attractive lounge with log fire. Secluded but easily accessible in hidden valley on edge of Brecon Beacons National Park. Ideal for touring Mid/South Wales, walking, birdwatching. Photobreak holidays, camera hire, evening meals, packed lunches, afternoon teas. Llandovery 3 miles.

P	SINGLE PER PERSON B&B	DOUBLE FOR 2 PERSONS B&B	🛏	3
🐕						3
✗	MIN £ 13.00	MAX £	MIN £ 26.00	MAX £		OPEN 1-12

Farmhouses

Cwmgwyn Farm

Llangadog Road, Llandovery, Dyfed, SA20 0EQ
Tel: (0550) 20410   L
Welcome to our 17th century modernised farmhouse overlooking the river Towy which provides a picturesque view of the Towy Valley. Peaceful, ideal for walking. A working livestock farm. Two miles from Llandovery market town on A4069 road. Ideal centre for touring. One family room and one double room. TV lounge and dinning room.

P	SINGLE PER PERSON B&B	DOUBLE FOR 2 PERSONS B&B	🛏	2
	MIN £ 10.00	MAX £ 11.50	MIN £ 20.00	MAX £ 23.00		OPEN 3-9

CALL Holidays (0792) 645555

Goyallt Farm

Halfway, Llandovery, Dyfed, SA20 0SD
Tel: (0550) 20604   L
One family room, one double room sharing bathroom. Central heating in all rooms. Sitting room with colour television. Excellent scenery with good walking area. Ample parking space. Working farm. Dogs accepted. Evening meal by arrangement.

H	✗	SINGLE PER PERSON B&B	DOUBLE FOR 2 PERSONS B&B	🛏	2
P					
🐕		MIN £ 9.00	MAX £ 10.00	MIN £ 18.00	MAX £	OPEN 3-12

LLANELLI   Map Ref Kd4

Bustling market town with good shopping and covered market. Pembrey Country Park, adjoining 7 miles of sandy beach, has a Visitor Centre and offers guided walks, pony trekking, new ski slope, adventure playground and much more. The Welsh Motor Sports Centre is nearby and Kidwelly Castle and Industrial Museum must be visited.

Guest Houses

Glenthorne Guest House

61 Queen Victoria Road, Llanelli, Dyfed, SA15 2TR
Tel: (0554) 751221   L
Centrally situated for the amenities of the town centre, indoor bowls, indoor swimming pool, parks and shops. Also within walking distance of the beach. Open all year. Single, double and family rooms. Tea and coffee facilities available. Traditional home cooking. Television lounge and sitting room with library. Redcued rates for children when they share.

H	✗	SINGLE PER PERSON B&B	DOUBLE FOR 2 PERSONS B&B	🛏	5
P					
⚒		MIN £ 9.00	MAX £ 10.00	MIN £ 18.00	MAX £ 20.00	OPEN 1-12

LLANPUMSAINT   Map Ref Fc7

Small village off the main A485 Carmarthen-Lampeter road, nestling in a quiet valley between Cwmduad and the western edge of Brechfa Forest.

Farmhouses

Fferm-y-Felin

Llanpumsaint, Carmarthen, Dyfed, SA33 6DA
Tel: (0267) 84498   👑👑
A warm welcome awaits you at this eighteenth century farmhouse in fifteen acres of conserved countryside. Oak beams, log fire, central heating. Bedrooms with en-suite facility or hot and cold. Enjoy splendid views over woodland and lake with ornamental waterfowl including black swans. Excellent home cooking, relaxed atmosphere. A delight.

H	✄	SINGLE PER PERSON B&B	DOUBLE FOR 2 PERSONS B&B	🛏	4
P	✗					2
🐕		MIN £ 14.00	MAX £ 14.00	MIN £ 28.00	MAX £ 28.00	OPEN 1-12

NEWCASTLE EMLYN   Map Ref Fb6

Market town on the river Teifi surrounded by rolling farmland and noted for its fine fishing. Felin Geri Mill for stoneground products. The Teifi Valley Railway is a nearby attraction. An attractive base for touring North Pembrokeshire and Teifi Valley. You may see coracle fishing at nearby Cenarth where the old mill is open to visitors.

WALES It's magic

Guest Houses

Glan Medeni

Betws Ifan, Beulah, Newcastle Emlyn, Dyfed SA38 9QJ
Tel: (023975) 8850   👑👑
Glan Medeni is a small Georgian mansion of great charm set in 4 acres of decidious woodland and mature gardens. 3½ miles from beaches. All rooms are tastefully decorated and furnished. TV, washbasins and tea/coffee making facilities, games room with pool/table tennis. Special rates for chidren. Brochure available.

H	✗	SINGLE PER PERSON B&B	DOUBLE FOR 2 PERSONS B&B	🛏	3
P						1
🐕		MIN £ 14.00	MAX £ 14.00	MIN £ 28.00	MAX £ 28.00	OPEN 1-12

Yr Hen Efail

Lon Derwen, Cwm Cou,
Newcastle Emlyn, Dyfed, SA38 9PB
Tel: (0239) 710092

L

Lovely country setting, 1½ miles west of Newcastle Emlyn. Views over open countryside with one acre garden. Many unspoilt beaches, Cenarth Falls working water mills and many other places of interest nearby. 2 double bedrooms. Tea and coffee facilities, TV lounge. Homely atmosphere with good hearty breakfast.

H ✕	SINGLE PER PERSON B&B		DOUBLE FOR 2 PERSONS B&B		🍴	2
P					🛏	
🐾	MIN £	MAX £	MIN £	MAX £		
	9.50	10.00	19.00	20.00	OPEN 1-12	

Farmhouses

Llain Farm

Felindre, Llandysul, Dyfed, SA44 5XT
Tel: (0559) 370683

L

Beautiful views surround our working dairy farm situated midway between Carmarthen and Cardigan. Ideal for touring South and West coast. Dining room, lounge TV, central heating. Within easy reach of the many beautiful sandy beaches of the Cardigan Bay coastline.

P	SINGLE PER PERSON B&B		DOUBLE FOR 2 PERSONS B&B		🍴	2
✕					🛏	
	MIN £	MAX £	MIN £	MAX £		
	8.50	9.00	17.00	18.00	OPEN 3-10	

PENCADER   Map Ref Fc6

Rural village, Brechfa forest. Carmarthen.

Farmhouses

Pen y Banc Farm

Pencader, Carmarthen, Dyfed, SA39 9AG
Tel: (0559) 384515

L

A homely welcome awaits you at this working farm set in the beautiful Welsh countryside. Full central heating, large comfortable bedrooms, residents lounge and dining room. Traditional farmhouse cooking using home produce, special meals by arrangement. Half an hour from the coast and market town of Carmarthen. Reduced rates for children under twelve.

H ✕	SINGLE PER PERSON B&B		DOUBLE FOR 2 PERSONS B&B		🍴	3
P ✕					🛏	
🐾	MIN £	MAX £	MIN £	MAX £		
	10.00	10.00	20.00	20.00	OPEN 3-10	

CALL *Holidays* (0792) 645555

PUMSAINT   Map Ref Ga5

Famous for the Roman gold mines at Dolaucothi - now a National Trust site open to visitors. The village is attractively sited near the Caeo Forest on the river Cothi. There are plenty of nature trails to enjoy and the ruins of Talley Abbey are 6 miles south.

Farmhouses

Llystroiddyn Home Farm

Pumsaint, Llanwrda, Dyfed, SA19 8YU
Tel: (05585) 482

L

Llystroiddyn Home Farm offers bed and breakfast with a friendly and personal touch. All rooms with handbasins and TV, central heating. Breakfast room, sitting room. Packed lunches. Pony trekking, fishing, Roman gold mines nearby. Local Inns. Splendid scenic forestry and hill walks abound in the area. All made welcome and nothing too much trouble.

H ✕	SINGLE PER PERSON B&B		DOUBLE FOR 2 PERSONS B&B		🍴	3
P ✕					🛏	
🐾	MIN £	MAX £	MIN £	MAX £		
	9.50	10.50	17.00	19.00	OPEN 1-12	

ST. CLEAR'S   Map Ref Kb2

Large village convenient for Carmarthen and Dylan Thomas's Boathouse in Laugharne.

Farmhouses

Castell Gorfod

Llangynin, St. Clear's, Dyfed, SA33 4JU   👑👑
Tel: (0994) 230835

Country house set in its own beautiful secluded valley on the banks of the Gynin River. Private trout fishing, riverside and woodland walks in 200 acres. We are a working sheep farm with forestry. Ideally situated for touring West Wales. Tenby and Saundersfoot are within easy reach.

H ✕	SINGLE PER PERSON B&B		DOUBLE FOR 2 PERSONS B&B		🍴	3
P ✕					🛏	2
🐾	MIN £	MAX £	MIN £	MAX £		
			28.00	28.00	OPEN 4-10	

WHITLAND   Map Ref Ka2

Market town with remains of 12th century abbey. Handy touring base for Pembrokeshire Coast National Park. Canolfan Hywel Dda is a visitors' centre, with thematic gardens, which tells the story of the Welsh King Hywel the Good, who devised a famous legal code.

Farmhouses

Maesgwyn Isaf Farm

Llanboidy, Whitland, Dyfed, SA34 0ET
Tel: (09946) 385

L

A working farm very centrally placed for touring Dyfed. We offer three double bedrooms, good home cooking and a warm welcome. Open Easter to October.

H	SINGLE PER PERSON B&B		DOUBLE FOR 2 PERSONS B&B		🍴	3
P					🛏	
✕	MIN £	MAX £	MIN £	MAX £		
	10.00	11.00	20.00	22.00	OPEN 4-10	

Maesylan

Cwmfelin Mynach, Whitland, Dyfed, SA34 0HT
Tel: (0994) 448335

L

Maesylan is a spacious country smallholding, situated in a delightful farming area with panoramic views over the surrounding countryside and westwards to the Preseli Mountains, offering a peaceful country holiday. Ideally situated for easy access to the Pembrokeshire and Cardiganshire coast. Rooms centrally heated, guests lounge with log fire and colour television.

H ✕	SINGLE PER PERSON B&B		DOUBLE FOR 2 PERSONS B&B		🍴	2
P					🛏	
🐾	MIN £	MAX £	MIN £	MAX £		
	10.00	12.00	20.00	24.00	OPEN 3-10	

WALES *It's magic*

BRECON AND THE BEACONS

Handsome Brecon is ideally located for exploring the 519-square-mile Brecon Beacons National Park. The grassy slopes of the Beacons themselves, rising above the town, are only one of four mountain ranges within this huge park. To the east, there are the borderland Black Mountains, to the west the lonely wilderness of Fforest Fawr and the challenging Black Mountain. This high, fresh country, rising to almost 3,000 ft, is watered by innumerable lakes and rivers – such as the remote Llyn y Fan Fawr or reedy Llangorse Lake near Brecon.

This great outdoors attracts walkers and pony trekkers, hang gliders and canoeists, anglers and golfers – even canal cruises along the peaceful Monmouthshire and Brecon Canal. The wide, open spaces up in the hills decline into sheltered valleys dotted with pretty places to stay – book-filled Hay-on-Wye, or the old stagecoach town of Crickhowell.

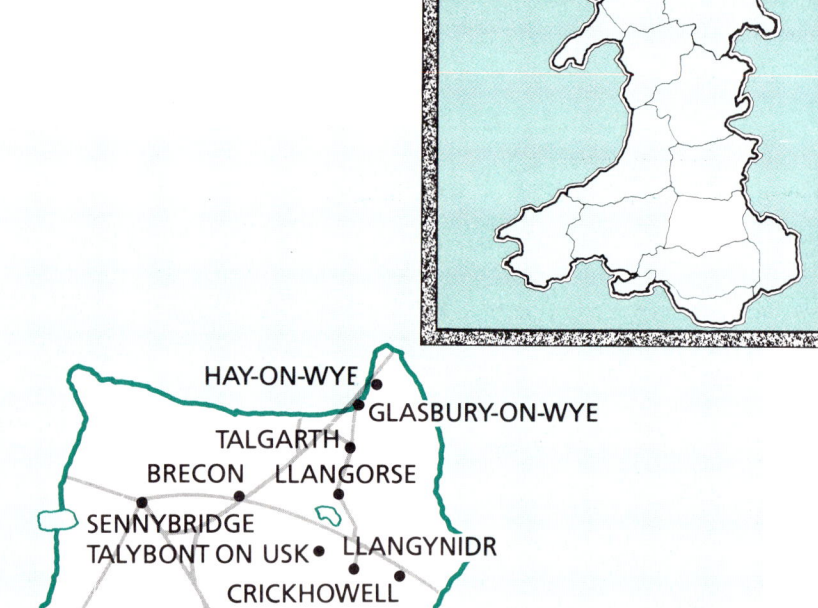

BRECON Map Ref Ge6

Main touring centre for the 519 square miles of the Brecon Beacons National Park. Castle, Cathedral, priory and interesting Brecknock and South Wales Borderers museums. Wide range of inns, guest houses and hotels, and good shopping. Centre for riding and pony trekking. Golf, fishing and canal cruising available. Very popular summer jazz festival.

Hotels

The Gremlin Hotel   L

The Watton, Brecon, Powys, LD3 7EG
Tel: (0874) 3829
A comfortable, family run public house approximately 200 yards from the town centre. Home cooked bar meals. A la Carte restaurant. Television lounge. Full central heating. Fire certificate. Wales Tourist Board Listed. Ideally situated for golf, walking, fishing, sailing, canoeing, surf boarding, pony trekking, caving and touring the magnificent Mid Wales countryside.

	SINGLE PER PERSON B&B		DOUBLE FOR 2 PERSONS B&B			8
	MIN £	MAX £	MIN £	MAX £		OPEN 1-12
	12.00	14.00	24.00	28.00		

Guest Houses

Aberyscir Old Rectory

Aberyscir, Brecon, Powys, LD9 9NP
Tel: (0874) 3457
Aberyscir Old Rectory is 2¾ miles from Brecon and stands in 5½ acres of its own secluded grounds. All rooms have handbasins, shaver points, colour TV's, tea and coffee making facilities and are centrally heated. Private lounge. Home cooking, diets catered for. It has glorious views of the Brecon Beacons. Golf, fishing, riding nearby.

	SINGLE PER PERSON B&B		DOUBLE FOR 2 PERSONS B&B			3
	MIN £	MAX £	MIN £	MAX £		OPEN 1-12
	14.00	14.00	22.00	26.00		

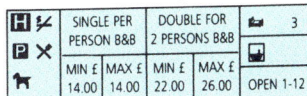

WALES
It's magic

Beacons Guest House

16 Bridge Street, Brecon, Powys, LD3 8AH
Tel: (0874) 3339
Friendly Georgian guest house situated close to town centre, River Usk and beautiful Brecon Beacons. Comfortable rooms with beverage trays, some rooms en-suite. Cosy bar, TV lounge and private parking. Ideal location to visit local attractions and outdoor activities. Groups, pets and children welcome. Excellent home cooking-Taste of Wales recommended. AA listed. Telephone for brochure.

	SINGLE PER PERSON B&B		DOUBLE FOR 2 PERSONS B&B			12
						6
	MIN £	MAX £	MIN £	MAX £		OPEN 1-12
	12.00	13.50	24.00	27.00		

Brooklands   L

Llanfihangel, Talyllyn, Brecon, Powys, LD3 7TL
Tel: (087484) 687
Situated 1½ miles from Llangorse Lake. Dining room with separate tables. Television lounge. Tea making facilities. Evening meals by arrangement. Friendly relaxing atmosphere. Popular area for all water sports. Market towns of Brecon and Abergavenny easily accessible. Baby sitting services. Laundry services. Hairdressing by appointment. Pony trekking, scenic views, beautiful walks.

	SINGLE PER PERSON B&B		DOUBLE FOR 2 PERSONS B&B			3
	MIN £	MAX £	MIN £	MAX £		OPEN 1-12
	12.00	14.00	24.00	26.00		

The Coach Guest House

Orchard Street, Llanfaes, Brecon, Powys LD3 8AN
Tel: (0874) 3803
Hotel standards at guest house prices. All six bedrooms are en-suite, four with shower, two with bath, and have colour television, hair dryer, clock radio, telephone and tea and coffee making facilities. Close to town centre, licensed, full central heating, private car park, fire certificate. Ideal base for touring in Brecon Beacons National Park.

	SINGLE PER PERSON B&B		DOUBLE FOR 2 PERSONS B&B			6
						6
	MIN £	MAX £	MIN £	MAX £		OPEN 1-12
			26.00	28.00		

Dolycoed

Talyllyn, Brecon, Powys, LD3 7SY
Tel: (0874) 84666
Midway between Brecon and Llangorse in a peaceful rural setting. This warm and friendly home offers two comfortable twin bedrooms, one with shower, both with hot and cold, shaver points, tea and coffee making facilities. Good centre for touring. Further details on request from Mary Cole.

	SINGLE PER PERSON B&B		DOUBLE FOR 2 PERSONS B&B			2
	MIN £	MAX £	MIN £	MAX £		OPEN 4-10
	10.00	10.00	20.00	20.00		

Flag and Castle Guest House

11 Orchard Street, Llanfaes, Brecon, Powys LD3 8AN
Tel: (0874) 5860
Former coaching inn opposite Christ College. Convenient all amenities, town and national park. Comfortable family run accommodation includes double, twin, family, single rooms with hot and cold, heating, tea/coffee facilities. Spacious bathroom has shower over sunken bath. Lounge with log fire has facilities for indoor games and reading. Varied diets accommodated. Residential licence. Parking.

	SINGLE PER PERSON B&B		DOUBLE FOR 2 PERSONS B&B			5
	MIN £	MAX £	MIN £	MAX £		OPEN 1-12
	11.00	12.00	20.00	22.00		

Glascwm Guest House

Talyllyn, Brecon, Powys, LD3 7SY
Tel: (087484) 649
Situated just 4 miles from Brecon near Llangorse Lake, Black Mountains, Brecon Beacons, Big Pit, caving, sailing, pony trekking, fishing, boating. Situated in lovely country surroundings. Tea/coffee making facilities, hot and cold in all rooms. Walking nearby.

	SINGLE PER PERSON B&B		DOUBLE FOR 2 PERSONS B&B			3
						1
	MIN £	MAX £	MIN £	MAX £		OPEN 1-12
	12.00	14.00	22.00	24.00		

The Old Rectory

Llanddew, Brecon, Powys, LD 3 9SS
Tel: (0874) 2058
Situated 1½ miles from Brecon with magnificent views of Brecon Beacons. Family run guest house, offering every comfort with personal hospitality and excellent home produced meals, special menus catered for. H & C, colour TV, tea/coffee facilities all rooms. Private lounge, central heating, ample parking, croquet on lawns, golf course, pony trekking, country walks nearby.

	SINGLE PER PERSON B&B		DOUBLE FOR 2 PERSONS B&B			3
	MIN £	MAX £	MIN £	MAX £		OPEN 1-12
	11.00	12.00	22.00	24.00		

Paris Guest House

28 The Watton, Brecon, Powys, LD3 7EF
Tel: (0874) 4205
Mal and Paul Hayes are happy to provide comfortable, friendly, licensed accommodation, 100 yards from Brecon town centre. A selection of evening meals are available. All rooms have hot drink facilities. Special rates for children. TV lounge, separate dining tables. Open all year. Ideal base for exploring the Brecon Beacons National Park.

	SINGLE PER PERSON B&B		DOUBLE FOR 2 PERSONS B&B			4
	MIN £	MAX £	MIN £	MAX £		OPEN 1-12
	12.00	14.00	24.00	28.00		

...ON CONTINUED

Guest Houses

Scethrog Tower

Scethrog, Brecon, Powys, LD3 7YE
Tel: (087487) 672 [L]

Medieval house in Usk valley, wonderful views of fields, river and mountains. Private fishing, lovely garden where you can picnic. Two very large comfortable rooms both with television, tea and coffee, one with en-suite, toilet and wash basin. Four miles from Brecon. Relaxed atmosphere, breakfast until eleven. Generous heating. Three nights discount. Steep stone staircase.

H	SINGLE PER PERSON B&B		DOUBLE FOR 2 PERSONS B&B		🛏	2
P	MIN £	MAX £	MIN £	MAX £	🏠	
	14.00		20.00	24.00	OPEN 3-12	

Tir Bach Guest House

13 Alexandra Road, Brecon, Powys, LD3 7PD
Tel: (0874) 4551 [L]

Comfortable homely, family run guest house. Quiet road overlooking the town, 2 minute walk from centre. Panoramic views of Brecon Beacons. Lounge with colour TV, central heating and car park. Plentiful hot water. Traditional British breakfast. Four bedrooms, family, twin, double and single. Special rates for children. Well travelled friendly hosts.

H	SINGLE PER PERSON B&B		DOUBLE FOR 2 PERSONS B&B		🛏	4
P	MIN £	MAX £	MIN £	MAX £	🏠	
🐕	9.00	10.50	18.00	21.00	OPEN 1-11	

Farmhouses

Brynfedwen Farm

Trallong Common, Sennybridge, Brecon, Powys, LD3 8HW
Tel: (0874) 82505 👑👑

Brynfedwen is 118 acre livestock farm with lovely views over the Usk Valley and Brecon Beacons. Well situated for all country pursuits or relaxing. Period, centrally heated farmhouse, TV lounge with log fire. 2 family rooms en-suite. Twin bedded flat designed for disabled, self catering or B & B. Good home fare. Children welcome.

H X	SINGLE PER PERSON B&B		DOUBLE FOR 2 PERSONS B&B		🛏	3
P	MIN £	MAX £	MIN £	MAX £	🏠	3
🍴	12.00	14.00	24.00	28.00	OPEN 1-12	

CALL Holidays (0792) 645555

Cefncoedbach Farm

Sarnau, Brecon, Powys, LD3 9PT
Tel: (0874) 3548 👑

With beautiful views of Black Mountains and Brecon Beacons. Ideally situated for visiting main attractions. Centrally heated farmhouse with 2 double bedrooms and washbasins, 1 twin bedded room en-suite. TV lounge available. Offers all modern comforts in friendly family atmosphere. Tea making facilities in all bedrooms. Four miles from cathedral town of Brecon.

H	SINGLE PER PERSON B&B		DOUBLE FOR 2 PERSONS B&B		🛏	3
P	MIN £	MAX £	MIN £	MAX £	🏠	1
🍴	12.00	12.00	24.00	24.00	OPEN 1-12	

Cwm Uchaf

Crai, Brecon, Powys, LD3 8YN
Tel: (087482) 703 [L]

17th century farmhouse in the centre of glorious Brecon Beacons. Excellent facilities for all outdoor activities. Experienced guides available for walking etc. Friendly family atmosphere with good home cooking. Transport available from Swansea. Tea making facilities in all rooms.

H X	SINGLE PER PERSON B&B		DOUBLE FOR 2 PERSONS B&B		🛏	3
P	MIN £	MAX £	MIN £	MAX £		
🍴	10.00		20.00		OPEN 1-12	

Cwrt-y-Castell

Libanus, Brecon, Powys, LD3 8NR
Tel: (087482) 8108 [L]

Situated in the heart of the Brecon Beacons National Park. Ideal base for touring or rambling. Enjoy the wildlife, birds or our Norman Castle site. Friendly, homely with excellent country cooking. All rooms prettily furnished in country style. A marvellous area for any outdoor activities. Telephone now for a free brochure.

H 🍴	SINGLE PER PERSON B&B		DOUBLE FOR 2 PERSONS B&B		🛏	2
P X	MIN £	MAX £	MIN £	MAX £		
🐕			18.00	22.00	OPEN 1-12	

Llanbrynean Farm

Llanfrynach, Brecon, Powys, LD3 7BQ
Tel: (087486) 222 [L]

Quiet country situation in relaxed and informal Victorian farmhouse. 3 miles from Brecon. Beautiful views. Sitting room with TV. Ideally located for Beacons, River Usk, Brecon, Monmouth Canal, Llangorse Lake and pony trekking. 2 double bedrooms (one en-suite), 2 twin bedrooms. Competitive rates for five days visit or more. Working farm with large garden.

H 🍴	SINGLE PER PERSON B&B		DOUBLE FOR 2 PERSONS B&B		🛏	4
P	MIN £	MAX £	MIN £	MAX £		1
🐕	9.00	9.50	20.00	22.00	OPEN 3-10	

Lodge Farm

Talgarth, Brecon, Powys, LD3 0DP
Tel: (0874) 711244 👑👑

Lodge Farm is a cattle and sheep farm situated 1½ mile east of Talgarth set on a quiet country road in delightful rural surroundings. The late 18th century farmhouse offers comfortable cosy accommodation, with H & C, one with shower, tea making facilities. Good interesting farm fare served and a warm welcome awaits you. Pony trekking arranged.

P	SINGLE PER PERSON B&B		DOUBLE FOR 2 PERSONS B&B		🛏	3
🐕	MIN £	MAX £	MIN £	MAX £		
X	11.00	12.00	22.00	24.00	OPEN 3-10	

Morfa

Llandefalle Hill, Brecon, Powys, LD3 0NU
Tel: (0874) 85436 [L]

You will receive a warm welcome at Morfa. An attractive stone farmhouse quietly situated in beautiful unspoilt countryside, 7 miles from Brecon. Relaxing atmosphere with good home cooking. All the facilities for a countryside holiday such as walking, fishing, trekking, etc, are within easy reach. Good base for exploring Mid, South Wales.

H X	SINGLE PER PERSON B&B		DOUBLE FOR 2 PERSONS B&B		🛏	3
P	MIN £	MAX £	MIN £	MAX £		
🐕	9.50	10.50	19.00	21.00	OPEN 3-10	

Trehenry Farm

Felinfach, Brecon, Powys, LD3 0UN
Tel: (0874) 754312

A mixed working farm of 200 acres, 6 miles east of Brecon. The farmhouse with inglenook fireplaces, exposed beams, offers all comforts. Good farmhouse cooking, cosy sitting room, colour TV, separate dining tables, 3 bedrooms, one en-suite all with hot and cold, tea and coffee, central heating. Award winner. Separate brochure on request.

H	SINGLE PER PERSON B&B		DOUBLE FOR 2 PERSONS B&B		🛏	3
P	MIN £	MAX £	MIN £	MAX £		1
X	14.00	24.00	24.00	28.00	OPEN 3-11	

Wernfawr Farm

Penpont, Brecon, Powys, LD3 8ET
Tel: (087482) 429 [L]

Three miles from Brecon, Wernfawr is peacefully situated overlooking the Usk Valley with walks, wildlife, lake and fishing. Ideal base for touring Wales. Close to Brecon Beacons, show caves, steam railway, wildlife park, pony trekking, swimming pools, etc. One family and one double room. Lounge for guests. Children welcome. A warm welcome awaits you.

P	SINGLE PER PERSON B&B		DOUBLE FOR 2 PERSONS B&B		🛏	2
🐕	MIN £	MAX £	MIN £	MAX £		
X	9.50	11.00	19.00	22.00	OPEN 4-12	

CRICKHOWELL
Map Ref Hb7

Small, pleasant country town beautifully situated on the river Usk. Walking, fishing, pony trekking and riding facilities. Remains of Norman castle, 14th century Tretower Court and earlier castle worth a visit.

Hotels

Dragon House Hotel
High Street, Crickhowell, Powys, NP8 1BE
Tel: (0873) 810362
Fax: (0873) 811868
Enjoy our charming 18th century hotel in a picturesque market town amid glorious scenery. Within the Brecon Beacons National Park. Ideal for business or pleasure. Rooms have telephones and tea/coffee facilities. Colour TV and hairdryers in en-suite rooms. Some non smoking rooms. Our cosy bar and restaurant with real log fire serves freshly prepared meals. Residents lounge. Car park.

H X	SINGLE PER PERSON B&B		DOUBLE FOR 2 PERSONS B&B		🛏	17
P					🍴	9
⚒	MIN £ 14.00	MAX £	MIN £ 28.00	MAX £		OPEN 1-12

GLASBURY-ON-WYE
Map Ref Ha5

Three miles from Hay, Glasbury is the haunt of fishermen and farmers. Pony trekking popular in this area.

Guest Houses

The Forge
Glasbury-on-Wye, Hay-on-Wye, Powys, HR3 5LN
Tel: (04974) 237
17th century Welsh longhouse, with interesting features near River Wye beach. Civilised comforts available all bedrooms. Activities arranged include Canadian and Kayak canoeing, pony trekking, gliding, caving, bird watching, walking. Black Mountains, Brecon Beacons nearby. Hay-on-Wye bookshops and superior restaurants nearby. Safe parking, drying facilities. Diet catering. Quiet village location with shaded or sunny sitting-out areas in secluded gardens.

H ⚒	SINGLE PER PERSON B&B		DOUBLE FOR 2 PERSONS B&B		🛏	4
P X					🍴	1
🐕	MIN £ 10.00	MAX £ 13.00	MIN £ 20.00	MAX £ 24.00		OPEN 1-12

HAY-ON-WYE
Map Ref Hb5

Small market town on the Offa's Dyke path, nestling below the Black Mountains on a picturesque stretch of the river Wye. A mecca for book lovers - there are second-hand bookshops, some huge, all over the town.

Guest Houses

Lynwood
Llanigon, Hay-on-Wye, Hereford, HR3 5PU
Tel: (0497) 820716
1 double, 1 twin bed, 1 single, 1 bathroom with shower. Two miles Hay-on-Wye.

H ⚒	SINGLE PER PERSON B&B		DOUBLE FOR 2 PERSONS B&B		🛏	3
P X					🍴	
🐕	MIN £	MAX £ 10.00	MIN £	MAX £ 20.00		OPEN 3-10

York House
Hardwick Road, Cusop, Hay-on-Wye, Powys HR3 5QX
Tel: (0497) 820705
Peter and Olwen Roberts welcome you to their traditional Victorian guest house, quietly situated in beautiful gardens on the edge of Hay-on-Wye. Sunny mountain views enjoyed by the well equipped rooms (some en-suite). Ideal base for a relaxing holiday browsing the bookshops, exploring the National Park and Kilvert country. Private parking and AA listed.

P X	SINGLE PER PERSON B&B		DOUBLE FOR 2 PERSONS B&B		🛏	6
🐕					🍴	1
⚒	MIN £ 12.00	MAX £ 12.00	MIN £ 24.00	MAX £ 24.00		OPEN 1-12

LLANGORSE *Map Ref Ha6*

Village in lovely lakeside setting in Brecon Beacons National Park. Set at northern edge of Llangorse Lake, with Mynydd Tan-Troed rising above. Much used by climbers, pony trekkers, walkers and sailors. Caravan and activity holidays available.

Guest Houses

Lake View Guest House
Llangorse, Brecon, Powys, LD3 7UG
Tel: (087484) 223
Licensed cosy establishment with friendly relaxed atmosphere overlooking beautiful Llangorse Lake and Brecon Beacons, on edge of picturesque village with charming pubs. Delightful bedrooms with tea/coffee, H & C, lounge with TV, piano, log fire. Dining room facing Black Mountains, organic vegetable garden, orchard, lawns, parking. Excellent for many varied outdoor pursuits or simply relaxing.

H X	SINGLE PER PERSON B&B		DOUBLE FOR 2 PERSONS B&B		🛏	4
P					🍴	
🐕	MIN £ 10.00	MAX £ 13.00	MIN £ 22.00	MAX £ 24.00		OPEN 1-12

LLANGYNIDR
Map Ref Ma1

This village in the Brecon Beacons National Park is approached from the south along a snaking road with breathtaking views. Pleasure boats ply along the nearby Monmouthshire and Brecon Canal. Good fishing.

Farmhouses

Upper Pencomyn Farm
Forge Lane, Llangynidr, Crickhowell, Powys, NP8 1LU
Tel: (0874) 730666
Comfortable recently renovated 16th century farmhouse in picturesque village in Usk Valley. Within walking distance of canal and River Usk. Television lounge, oak panelled guest dining room. Bedrooms are oak beamed with en-suite facilities. Full central heating. Stabling available. An ideal area for touring National Park. Home cooked evening meals available by arrangement.

H X	SINGLE PER PERSON B&B		DOUBLE FOR 2 PERSONS B&B		🛏	2
P					🍴	2
⚒	MIN £ 14.00	MAX £ 14.00	MIN £ 24.00	MAX £ 26.00		OPEN 1-12

CALL Holidays (0792) 645555

TALGARTH Map Ref Ha6

Small market town between Brecon and Hay-on-Wye, in foothills of the Black Mountains. Centre for walkers, pony trekkers and anglers.

Farmhouses

Penyrheol Farm

Pengenffordd, Talgarth, Brecon,
Powys LD3 0EY   L
Tel: (0874) 711409

Penyrheol is a hill farm of 140 acres in the Brecon Beacons National Park, between the Black Mountains and Llangorse Lake, 2½ miles from Talgarth off the A479 road. All bedrooms have wash basins. Travellers Britain listed. We have a TV, cot and children's pony for guests. Enquiries to Mrs Ann Powell, send SAE please.

H P ♞	SINGLE PER PERSON B&B		DOUBLE FOR 2 PERSONS B&B		🛏 2
	MIN £	MAX £	MIN £	MAX £	
	8.00	11.00	16.00	22.00	OPEN 3-10

TALYBONT ON USK
Map Ref Ge7

Village in picturesque setting on banks of river Usk and Monmouthshire-Brecon Canal. Within the Brecon Beacons National Park, the surrounding hills are perfect for walking and pony trekking.

Guest Houses

Abercynafon Lodge

Abercynafon, Talybont on Usk, Brecon,
Powys   LD3 7YT   L
Tel: (087487) 342

Situated 5 miles from Talybont on Usk in the Brecon Beacon National Park. Ideal for touring, walking, pony trekking, bird watching or fly fishing on Talybont Reservoir (according to season). Mrs Jill Carr extends a warm welcome and excellent home cooked food. Pack lunches available on request. Reduced rates for children under 12.

H ✗ P ✗ ♞	SINGLE PER PERSON B&B		DOUBLE FOR 2 PERSONS B&B		🛏 3
	MIN £	MAX £	MIN £	MAX £	
	10.00	11.00	20.00	22.00	OPEN 1-12

Farmhouses

Llanddetty Hall Farm

Talybont on Usk, Brecon,
Powys, LD3 7YR
Tel: (087487) 267

200 acres family farm between River Usk and Brecon Canal in National Park. Accessible to Brecon Beacons and Black Mountains. On bus route. Villages within walking distance. O S maps available. Use of canoe on canal. Colour TV. Mrs Marjorie Morris welcomes you with good food and comfortable accommodation in 17th century farmhouse. Brochure available SAE.

P ♞ ✗	SINGLE PER PERSON B&B		DOUBLE FOR 2 PERSONS B&B		🛏 3
	MIN £	MAX £	MIN £	MAX £	
			22.00	28.00	OPEN 4-11

BRECON BEACONS

SWANSEA, MUMBLES AND GOWER

Swansea's stylish marina and Maritime Quarter have won accolades for the way in which they have brought new life to the waterfront of this city-by-the-sea. Swansea also has its traditional side — visit Wales's finest fresh-foods market, where you can buy that peculiar Welsh delicacy, laverbread, and fresh cockles direct from the pickers of Penclawdd.

The Gower Peninsula, only a stone's throw from the city, was the first part of Britain to be declared an 'Area of Outstanding Natural Beauty'. It is a lovely promontory with sheltered, south-facing bays — at Langland, Caswell, Oxwich and Port-Eynon. The peninsula comes to an end in spectacular fashion along the precipitous Worms Head and the endless beach at Rhosili, where surfers ride the waves. At Gower's approach stands The Mumbles, a strangely named, attractive little sailing and water sports centre guarded by one of this area's many castles at Oystermouth.

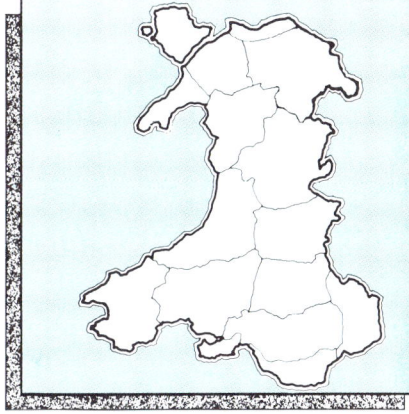

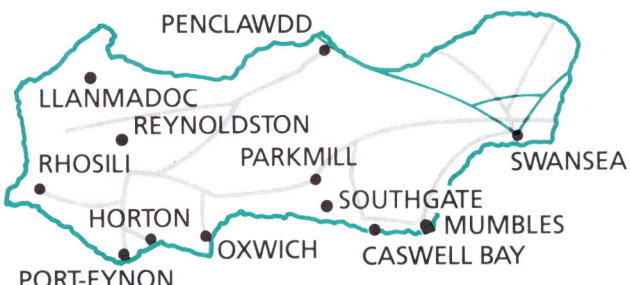

LLANMADOC
Map Ref Kd5

Village on north-west coast of Gower Peninsula with easy access to beaches.

Guest Houses

Riverside
Cheriton, Gower, West Glamorgan, SA3 1DA
Tel: (044127) 601 [L]

Beamed cottage in peaceful coastal village surrounded by beautiful countryside with golden sandy beaches. Ideally situated for swimming, surfing, horse riding, walking and bird watching. Large garden with superb views overlooking Whiteford Burrows. Children and pets welcome. Open all year. Centrally heated.

	SINGLE PER PERSON B&B	DOUBLE FOR 2 PERSONS B&B	🛏	3
H ✂ P 🐕	MIN £ 12.00	MAX £ 12.00	MIN £ 18.00	MAX £ 18.00	OPEN 1-12

CALL Holidays (0792) 645555

MUMBLES
Map Ref La4

Small resort on Swansea Bay with attractive waterfront; centre for all watersports and sailing. On fringe of Gower peninsula, a designated Area of Outstanding Natural Beauty. Oystermouth Castle and Clyne Valley country park and gardens nearby.

Guest Houses

The Coast House
708 Mumbles Road, Mumbles, Swansea, West Glamorgan SA3 4EH
Tel: (0792) 368702   👑👑

Small family owned guest house with a relaxed atmosphere with panoramic views overlooking Swansea Bay. En-suite room available. Tea making facilities and colour TV in all bedrooms.

🐕	SINGLE PER PERSON B&B	DOUBLE FOR 2 PERSONS B&B	🛏	5
	MIN £	MAX £	MIN £ 22.00	MAX £ 28.00	1 / OPEN 1-12

Mumbles Hotel
650 Mumbles Road, Mumbles, Swansea, West Glamorgan SA3 4EA
Tel: (0792) 367147   👑👑

Family run hotel located on the Mumbles sea front overlooking Swansea Bay. Most rooms have en-suite facilities. All rooms have colour TV and licensed restaurant offers good value, light snacks and main course meals. Ideal for a pleasant relaxed break. Good parking facilities. AA Listed. Les Routiers recommended.

SINGLE PER PERSON B&B		DOUBLE FOR 2 PERSONS B&B		🛏	8
MIN £ 14.00	MAX £ 14.00	MIN £ 25.00	MAX £ 28.00	OPEN 1-12	4

OXWICH
Map Ref Kd7

Gower peninsula beach with three miles of glorious sand and extensive dunes; easily accessible. Nature trail and visitor centre.

Guest Houses

Little Haven Guest House
Oxwich, Gower, Swansea, West Glamorgan SA3 1LS
Tel: (0792) 390940 [L]

Family run guest house situated in Oxwich village. Located near beach which is ideal for most water sports. Evening meal by prior arrangement. Reduction for weekly bookings, also for senior citizens and children under twelve years. No pets allowed.

H P ✗	SINGLE PER PERSON B&B	DOUBLE FOR 2 PERSONS B&B	🛏	3
	MIN £ 9.50	MAX £ 11.50	MIN £ 16.00	MAX £ 20.00	OPEN 1-12

PARKMILL
Map Ref Ke5

Gower Peninsula village, easy access to beaches and Swansea.

Farmhouses

Lunnon Farm
Parkmill, Swansea, West Glamorgan, SA3 2EJ
Tel: (0792) 371205 [L]

Working diary farm. 2 double rooms. Central heating. Public bathroom. Separate toilet. TV lounge. Shaving points. Shower. Easy reach of Three Cliffs Bay and all other Gower Bays. Delightful walks. Fresh farm produce, good breakfast. Traditional 15th century Gower farmhouse. Easy location for Swansea and Mumbles. Parking space. Welsh welcome always.

P ✂ ✗	SINGLE PER PERSON B&B	DOUBLE FOR 2 PERSONS B&B	🛏	2
	MIN £ 10.00	MAX £ 12.00	MIN £ 20.00	MAX £ 24.00	OPEN 3-10

Parc Le Breos
Parkmill, Gower, West Glamorgan, SA3 2HA
Tel: (0792) 371636 👑👑

Spacious 18th century farmhouse in the heart of beautiful Gower Peninsula. A quiet scenic setting within easy reach of magnificent cliffs and beaches and all amenities. Perfect for walking (footpaths to Three Cliffs Bay, Cefnbryn etc). Ideal base for a wide range of holiday activities around Gower. Riding holidays and day rides available, paddock rides for children. TV lounge, gamesroom, safe lawn play area. Homegrown and cooked food, warm welcome. BHS approved. AA listed. SAE for colour brochure.

H ✗ P 🐕	SINGLE PER PERSON B&B	DOUBLE FOR 2 PERSONS B&B	🛏	9
	MIN £ 11.50	MAX £ 14.00	MIN £ 23.00	MAX £ 28.00	OPEN 1-12	4

REYNOLDSTON
Map Ref Kd5

Gower peninsula village near sandy beaches. Good walking. Easy access to Swansea.

Farmhouses

Greenways
Hills Farm, Reynoldston, Gower, West Glamorgan, SA3 1AE
Tel: (0792) 390125 [L]

In beautiful countryside near main road. Central to all Gower bays. Working farm with home cooking and own produce. Hot and cold in bedrooms and separate tables, central heating. TV lounge. Evening meal by arrangement. Pets by arrangement. Car park. Send SAE please.

P 🐕 ✗	SINGLE PER PERSON B&B	DOUBLE FOR 2 PERSONS B&B	🛏	4
	MIN £ 12.00	MAX £ 14.00	MIN £ 22.00	MAX £ 24.00	OPEN 3-10

Sunnyside Farm

Llanddewi, Reynoldston, Gower,
West Glamorgan, SA3 1RU
Tel: (0792) 390194
Family holiday on working farm. One family room and twin bedded room. Reduced rate for children. Sandy beaches and pony trekking nearby. Easy reach of Swansea. Farm produce and home cooking. Guests are welcome to look around. Plenty of parking space.

	SINGLE PER PERSON B&B		DOUBLE FOR 2 PERSONS B&B			2
	MIN £	MAX £	MIN £	MAX £		
		10.00		20.00		OPEN 1-12

RHOSILI Map Ref Kc5

Gower peninsula village set on headland above stunning 3 miles of sandy beach. Good surfing, hang gliding. Strange formation known as Worms Head juts into the sea.

Guest Houses

Broad Park Guest House

Rhosili, Gower, West Glamorgan,
SA3 1PL
Tel: (0792) 390515
Situated in an area of outstanding natural beauty. Friendly family run guest house with panoramic coastal views. Ideally placed for pony trekking, hang gliding, walking or just relaxing. Full fire certificate, hot and cold water in all bedrooms. Ample parking. Children welcome. 30 minutes drive from Swansea.

	SINGLE PER PERSON B&B		DOUBLE FOR 2 PERSONS B&B			9
	MIN £	MAX £	MIN £	MAX £		
	10.50	10.50	21.00	21.00		OPEN 1-12

Sunnyside

Rhosili, Gower, Nr Swansea,
West Glamorgan, SA3 1PL
Tel: (0792) 390596
Small guest house with sea views close to the sandy beaches. Hand-basins and tea/coffee making facilities in all bedrooms. Separate dining tables, TV lounge. Parking. Dogs welcome. Special diets by arrangement. Local activities include surfing, hang gliding, pony trekking and walking.

	SINGLE PER PERSON B&B		DOUBLE FOR 2 PERSONS B&B			3
	MIN £	MAX £	MIN £	MAX £		
	9.00	10.00	18.00	20.00		OPEN 4-10

SOUTHGATE Map Ref Ke5

Gower Peninsula village; fine beaches at Three Cliffs Bay and Oxwich, and popular Caswell and Langland bays just to the east. Close to Swansea, with its Leisure Centre, Maritime Quarter, museums and shopping.

Guest Houses

Heatherlands

1 Hael Lane, Southgate, Gower,
Swansea, West Glamorgan, SA3 2AP
Tel: (044128) 3256
Delightful situation. Haeatherlands is a modern residence, standing in its own secluded garden near National Trust land. Cliff walk to beautiful beaches. Three double bedrooms with hot and cold and shaver points. Spacious television lounge. Separate tables in dining room. Ideal base for rest of Gower. Glorious walks. Parking. Bed and breakfast only. Send SAE please.

	SINGLE PER PERSON B&B		DOUBLE FOR 2 PERSONS B&B			3
	MIN £	MAX £	MIN £	MAX £		
	11.00	11.50	20.00	21.00		OPEN 4-9

SWANSEA Map Ref La4

Gateway to the Gower, Britain's first designated Area of Outstanding Natural Beauty. Superb new marina complex and Maritime Quarter - excellent leisure centre, with Industrial and Maritime Museum nearby. Art galleries. Good shopping. Covered market with distinctively Welsh atmosphere; try the cockles, laverbread and Gower potatoes. Swansea Festival and "Fringe" Festival in October. Theatres and cinemas, parks and gardens, restaurants and wine bars.

Guest Houses

Driftwood Guest House

Oxwich, Gower, Swansea,
West Glamorgan SA3 1LS
Tel: (0792) 390405
Welcome to Driftwood, our homely 200 year old converted cottage, situated approximately 5 minutes walk from the beautiful safe beach of Oxwich. Ideal for walking, swimming and fishing. All bedrooms with hot and cold, bedside lights and shaver points. Lounge, colour TV. Dining room with separate tables. Ample car parking space. Restaurant nearby.

	SINGLE PER PERSON B&B		DOUBLE FOR 2 PERSONS B&B			3
	MIN £	MAX £	MIN £	MAX £		
	13.00		23.00	26.00		OPEN 3-10

Malbork Guest House

2 Bonville Terrace, Uplands, Swansea,
West Glamorgan, SA1 4QS
Tel: (0792) 473420
Situated quiet residential area convenient for shops, beach, buses, marina. All rooms with TV, radio, tea/coffee making facilities, central heating, H & C basins, shaver points. Lounge with colour TV, books. Breakfast menu daily. Shower and bath available. Payphone. Children welcome. Colour brochure on request. Welcome home from home. Car parking adjacent. Pensioners special discount.

	SINGLE PER PERSON B&B		DOUBLE FOR 2 PERSONS B&B			3
	MIN £	MAX £	MIN £	MAX £		
	10.00	10.00	20.00	20.00		OPEN 1-12

Mirador Guest House

14 Mirador Crescent, Uplands,
Swansea, West Glamorgan SA2 0QX
Tel: (0792) 466976
Comfortable, family guest house, close to city, parks, university, leisure centre, marine, Gower. B & B, H & C, heated, razor points. TV lounge. Fire certificate. Hygiene certificate. No parking restrictions.

	SINGLE PER PERSON B&B		DOUBLE FOR 2 PERSONS B&B			7
	MIN £	MAX £	MIN £	MAX £		
	11.00	14.00	22.00	28.00		OPEN 1-12

Woodside Restaurant

Oxwich, Gower, Swansea,
West Glamorgan, SA3 1LS
Tel: (0792) 390791
Located 200 yards from beach and nature reserve. We offer a warm welcome. Wash basins, shaver points and TV in all rooms. Licensed restaurant bar with log fire burning in inglenook fireplace. Fire certificate. Good value food. Les Routiers recommended. Regret no pets. For further information contact Diane Workman.

	SINGLE PER PERSON B&B		DOUBLE FOR 2 PERSONS B&B			2
	MIN £	MAX £	MIN £	MAX £		
			24.00	28.00		OPEN 2-11

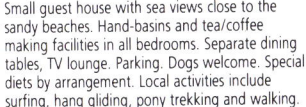

CARDIFF AND THE SOUTH WALES COAST

Cardiff has now come into its own – and deservedly so – as a popular visitor centre. There's so much to enjoy and appreciate in this cosmopolitan capital – a much-praised Civic Centre, amazing city-centre castle (a Roman fort, Norman castle and fabulous Victorian mansion all rolled into one!), treasure-packed National Museum, St David's Concert Hall, superb shopping and entertainment. And if that's not enough, there's the Welsh Folk Museum at St Fagans on the city's outskirts, where the Wales of bygone times lives on. It's all so easy to get to – less than two hours by train from London, or a short, swift drive along the motorway.

On its doorstep is the Vale of Glamorgan, an area of rich farmlands dotted with charming villages. And fringing this greenery is a coastline of great variety that includes the towering cliffs of the Glamorgan Heritage Coast. Penarth has a delightful Victorian pier and modern marina, while the lively resorts of Barry Island and Porthcawl offer traditional seaside fun.

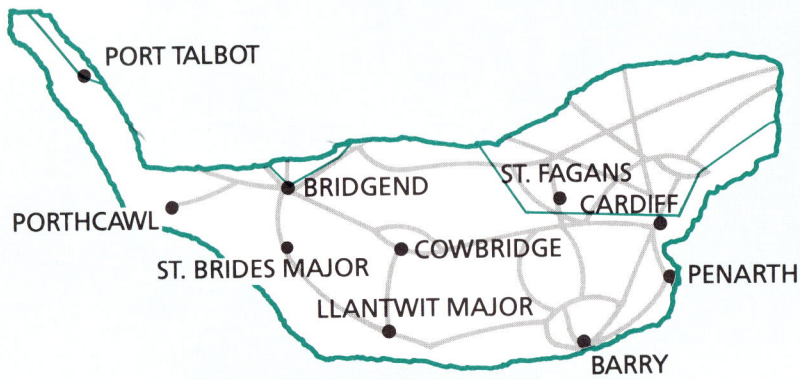

BRIDGEND   Map Ref Ld5

Bustling industrial and market town in the rural Vale of Glamorgan. Lively resorts and bays nearby. Ewenny Priory is said to be one of the best examples of church architecture in Wales. Three ruined Norman castles in the area - Coity, Newcastle and Ogmore.

Guest Houses

St Andrews Guest House

21 West Farm Road, Brig-y-Don Hill, Ogmore-by-Sea, Nr Bridgend, Mid Glamorgan CF32 0PS
Tel: (0656) 880183   L

Secluded position overlooking sea. Family, double and single bedrooms with vanity units and shaving points, all centrally heated with tea and coffee making facilities. Dining room, TV lounge. Easy access to beach, golf course, fishing, pony trekking, leisure centres and cultural facilities. Easy access to M4. Proven reputation for good food and excellent accommodation.

H / P / ✘	SINGLE PER PERSON B&B		DOUBLE FOR 2 PERSONS B&B		🛏	3
	MIN £	MAX £	MIN £	MAX £		OPEN 1-12
	11.00	11.00	22.00	22.00		

CARDIFF   Map Ref Mb5

Capital of Wales, business, trade and entertainment centre. Splendid civic centre, lovely parkland, modern pedestrianised shopping centre, good restaurants, theatres, cinemas, clubs and sports facilities, including ice rink. Visit St David's Hall for top-class entertainment. National Museum of Wales has fine collection of Impressionist and Post-Impressionist paintings. Cardiff Castle well worth a visit; nearby National Stadium is home of Welsh rugby. Wide range of accommodation at all prices. Llandaff Cathedral close by and fascinating collection of old farmhouses and other buildings in Welsh Folk Museum at St. Fagans.

Hotels

Austins

11 Coldstream Terrace, City Centre, Cardiff, South Glamorgan CF1 8LJ
Tel: (0222) 377148

Situated in the centre of Cardiff, 300 yds from the Castle. 7 single and 5 twin bedrooms. 5 rooms with private shower. All with hot and cold, shaver points, fixed heating, tea and coffee, colour TV. Full English breakfast. Evening meal by arrangement. 10 minutes from bus and train station. Fire certificate held. Warm welcome offered to all nationalities.

H / ✱ / ✘	SINGLE PER PERSON B&B		DOUBLE FOR 2 PERSONS B&B		🛏	12
						3
	MIN £	MAX £	MIN £	MAX £		OPEN 1-12
	13.00	14.00	26.00	28.00		

Clare Court Hotel

46-48 Clare Road, Grangetown, Cardiff,
South Glamorgan CF1 7QP
Tel: (0222) 344839

Just refurbished family run hotel. Nine bedrooms all with bathrooms en-suite, tea and coffee making facilities, remote control colour TV. Spacious family rooms, sky TV. Evening meals, licensed bar. TV lounge. Strolling distance from town centre, main bus and railway stations, castle, leisure centre etc.

✘ / H / P	SINGLE PER PERSON B&B		DOUBLE FOR 2 PERSONS B&B		🛏	9
						9
	MIN £	MAX £	MIN £	MAX £		OPEN 1-12
	14.00		28.00			

Clayton Hotel

65 Stacey Road, Cardiff,
South Glamorgan, CF2 1DS
Tel: (0222) 492345

Situated less than 200 yards from main bus route and short distance to city centre. This hotel provides a hearty British breakfast and home cooked meals tastefully prepared by the owners. Several rooms with shower and all rooms centrally heated, providing tea and coffee making facilities Television lounge. Car park and bar service. service.

H / P / ✘	SINGLE PER PERSON B&B		DOUBLE FOR 2 PERSONS B&B		🛏	9
	MIN £	MAX £	MIN £	MAX £		OPEN 1-12
	12.00	14.00	24.00	28.00		

Guest Houses

Acorn Lodge

182 Cathedral Road, Cardiff,
South Glamorgan, CF1 9J3   L
Tel: (0222) 221373

A fine large Victorian house of great character situated in a conservation area. Ideally located central to all attractions and within a few minutes walk of City centre. All rooms are to high standard and have tea and coffee and colour television. Full breakfast. Car Park. Shops, diners, restaurants close by. Friendly personal service.

H / P	SINGLE PER PERSON B&B		DOUBLE FOR 2 PERSONS B&B		🛏	9
						1
	MIN £	MAX £	MIN £	MAX £		OPEN 1-12
	14.00	14.00	24.00	28.00		

Albany Guest House

191-193 Albany Road, Roath, Cardiff,
South Glamorgan
Tel: (0222) 494121

Situated approximately 2 miles from Cardiff's beautiful city centre, Albany Guest House is a family run concern where your stay is our concern. Near to famous Roath Park Lake, you can enjoy boating and walking. We are close to all shops and a good variety of diners and restaurants to suit all tastes.

H / P / 🐾	SINGLE PER PERSON B&B		DOUBLE FOR 2 PERSONS B&B		🛏	15
	MIN £	MAX £	MIN £	MAX £		OPEN 1-12
	13.00	13.00	19.00	22.00		

Amberley Guest House

22 Plasturton Gardens, Pontcanna,
Cardiff, South Glamorgan CF1 9HP   L
Tel: (0222) 374936

The house is situated within easy reach of the city centre and all amenities, such as shops, theatres, Cardiff Castle, new Ice Rink and National Sports Centre for Wales. A warm friendly atmosphere is provided for guests who are made as comfortable as possible in rooms that have central heating, TV, tea/coffee making facilities.

P	SINGLE PER PERSON B&B		DOUBLE FOR 2 PERSONS B&B		🛏	3
	MIN £	MAX £	MIN £	MAX £		OPEN 1-12
	11.00	11.00	21.00	21.00		

Glan-y-Dwr

157 Lake Road West, Cardiff,   L
South Glamorgan, CF2 5PL
Tel: (0222) 758126

Glan-y-Dwr means Water's Edge. Friendly welcome in Edwardian family house overlooking Roath Park lake. Rooms have gas fires, washbasins, TV, tea and coffee making facilities, fruit, biscuits. Special rates for huge family room sleeping five. Full british breakfast. Pleasant walks around park. Strong North American links. French, Spanish, German, Welsh spoken. Good parking. Convenient bus.

✱	SINGLE PER PERSON B&B		DOUBLE FOR 2 PERSONS B&B		🛏	2
	MIN £	MAX £	MIN £	MAX £		OPEN 1-12
	12.00	12.00	21.00	21.00		

Plas-y-Bryn

93 Fairwater Road, Llandaff, Cardiff,   L
South Glamorgan, CF5 2LG
Tel: (0222) 561717

Comfortable house set in quiet part of Cardiff near train halt and buses. Also short walk from pretty shopping village of Llandaff and Cathedral. All home comforts, central heating, TV, and good service.

✱	SINGLE PER PERSON B&B		DOUBLE FOR 2 PERSONS B&B		🛏	3
	MIN £	MAX £	MIN £	MAX £		OPEN 1-12
	10.00	14.00	20.00	25.00		

CARDIFF CONTINUED

Guest Houses

The Preste Gaarden

181 Cathedral Road, Cardiff,
South Glamorgan, CF1 9PN
Tel: (0222) 228607

Situated in conservation area on main bus route, a few minutes walk from the town and National Sports Centre, rugby stadium, cinemas and theatres. A small family run establishment offering personal and friendly service and value for money. All rooms comfortably furnished, centrally heated, colour TV and tea/coffee facilities. En-suite rooms also available.

H	SINGLE PER PERSON B&B		DOUBLE FOR 2 PERSONS B&B		🛏	9
✗	MIN £	MAX £	MIN £	MAX £	🅿	2
	13.00		25.00		OPEN 1-12	

Sophia House

48 Ryder Street, Cardiff,
South Glamorgan, CF1 9BU
Tel: (0222) 394338   [L]

1 twin, 2 single, central heating, TV in rooms. Ample parking. Central for city centre, National Sports centre. Small homely run guest house.

H	SINGLE PER PERSON B&B		DOUBLE FOR 2 PERSONS B&B		🛏	3
🐕	MIN £	MAX £	MIN £	MAX £	🅿	
✗	10.00		19.00		OPEN 1-12	

The Sycamore

St Nicholas, Cardiff, South Glamorgan,
CF5 6SH   [L]
Tel: (0446) 760542

Situated in the beautiful Vale of Glamorgan, 6 miles west of Cardiff. You are assured of a friendly welcome at the Sycamore. 2 double bedrooms with tea/coffee facilities. Television lounge and pleasant dining room. Convenient for Folk Museum, Dyffryn Gardens, the historic town of Cowbridge, the airport, and the M4 motorway.

P	SINGLE PER PERSON B&B		DOUBLE FOR 2 PERSONS B&B		🛏	2
🍴	MIN £	MAX £	MIN £	MAX £	🅿	
✗	12.00	14.00	24.00	28.00	OPEN 2-11	

Tŷ Gwyn

7 Dyfrig Street, Pontcanna, Cardiff,
South Glamorgan CF1 9LR
Tel: (0222) 239785

A warm welcome awaits within this friendly beautifully decorated Victorian house. Just half a mile from Cardiff Castle. All original features have been restored. Central heating, wash hand-basins, shaver points, private showers. Bath in a Victorian bath with original brass fittings or relax in the tastefully refurbished lounge. Full English breakfast. Vegetarians welcome.

H	SINGLE PER PERSON B&B		DOUBLE FOR 2 PERSONS B&B		🛏	3
P	MIN £	MAX £	MIN £	MAX £	🅿	3
🐕	12.50	14.00	21.00	28.00	OPEN 1-12	

White Barn House

Rhydlafar, St Fagans, Cardiff,
South Glamorgan CF5 6JH
Tel: (0222) 843152

A warm welcome awaits you at this charming oak beamed converted barn adjacent farm land, just five miles from city centre. Close to Welsh Folk Museum. Ideal base for touring South Wales. Children welcome. Excellent breakfast. Central heating. Colour TV. Parking. Tea/coffee making facilities in all rooms. Attractive lounge and dining room. Pretty bedrooms.

H	SINGLE PER PERSON B&B		DOUBLE FOR 2 PERSONS B&B		🛏	3
P	MIN £	MAX £	MIN £	MAX £	🅿	
🐕	12.00	12.00	24.00	24.00	OPEN 1-12	

Hostel

Cardiff Y M C A Housing Association

The Walk, Roath, Cardiff,
South Glamorgan CF2 3AG
Tel: (0222) 489101
Fax: (0222) 471826

Cardiff YMCA is a modern residential hostel close to the city centre. Consisting of 72 single study bedrooms with a unlimited number of twin rooms. Accommodation is available to males and females for long and short stays. Children welcome. Part board available.

H	SINGLE PER PERSON B&B		DOUBLE FOR 2 PERSONS B&B		🛏	72
P	MIN £	MAX £	MIN £	MAX £	🅿	
✗	10.50		19.00		OPEN 1-12	

COWBRIDGE Map Ref Le6

Pictureque town with wide main road and pretty houses - the centre of the Vale of Glamorgan farming community. Fine old inns, shops selling high-class clothes and country wares. Fourteenth century town walls. Good touring centre for South Wales.

Guest Houses

Stembridge Farm Guest House

Llandow, Cowbridge,
South Glamorgan, CF7 7NT
Tel: (065679) 389

A centuries old house of character in the beautiful Vale of Glamorgan. Set in landscaped gardens with splendid open views, close to Heritage Coast and 30 minutes drive from Cardiff. Oak beamed dining room and comfortable lounges. Three well appointed spacious bedrooms with colour TV and private bathrooms. One en-suite.

P	SINGLE PER PERSON B&B		DOUBLE FOR 2 PERSONS B&B		🛏	3
🍴	MIN £	MAX £	MIN £	MAX £	🅿	1
	28.00		28.00		OPEN 1-12	

Farmhouses

Cartreglas Farm

Welsh St Donats, Cowbridge,
South Glamorgan, CF7 7SX   [L]
Tel: (0446) 772368

Warm welcome awaits you on our family dairy farm in the beautiful Vale of Glamorgan, conveniently situated for M4, Cardiff coast and mountains. Family, double, twin bedrooms, two bathrooms. TV lounge, tea/coffee making facilities provided in spare kitchen, which can also be used for cooking own evening meal. Adjoining barn as games room.

P	SINGLE PER PERSON B&B		DOUBLE FOR 2 PERSONS B&B		🛏	4
🐕	MIN £	MAX £	MIN £	MAX £	🅿	
🍴	12.00	14.00	24.00	28.00	OPEN 1-12	

Treguff Farm

Llantrithyd, Cowbridge,
South Glamorgan, CF7 7LT   [L]
Tel: (0446) 750210

AA approved. In unspoilt Vale of Glamorgan. Castles, beaches, country and coastal walks. Picturesque villages. Near Welsh Folk Museum, city of Cardiff, Wales Airport, St Donats Castle. Relax in the comforts of a listed Elizabethan country house, tastefully furnished, spacious bedrooms, warm hospitality in the country. Prices do not reflect excellent food and accommodation. (Featured in "Style" Magazine).

P	SINGLE PER PERSON B&B		DOUBLE FOR 2 PERSONS B&B		🛏	3
🍴	MIN £	MAX £	MIN £	MAX £	🅿	
✗			28.00		OPEN 1-12	

Tŷ Gwyn

Maendy, Cowbridge, South Glamorgan, CF7 7TG   L
Tel: (0446) 3258
Small holding with delightful cottage, car parking. Cat boarding available. Lovely scenery situated in unspoilt Vale of Glamorgan. Two double bedrooms, central heating, public bathroom, TV lounge. Excellent home cooking. One mile from market town of Cowbridge. Area rich with castles, beaches, gardens, heritage coast walks. Pretty villages, old inns, restaurants, leisure centres. Ideal touring centre for South Wales.

P ✗	SINGLE PER PERSON B&B		DOUBLE FOR 2 PERSONS B&B		🛏	2
	MIN £	MAX £	MIN £ 20.00	MAX £ 24.00	OPEN 3-10	

LLANTWIT MAJOR
Map Ref Lc6

Intriguing old town with narrow streets, a square, and a church with Celtic crosses and other relics of a long Christian tradition. The small Col-huw beach lies on the attractive Heritage Coast. Nearby is St. Donat's Castle, now the International Atlantic College.

Guest Houses

The Curriers

Wine Street, Llantwit Major,   L
South Glamorgan, CF6 9RZ
Tel: (04465) 3506
We offer clean comfortable centrally heated accommodation with TV lounge, tea/coffee making facilities, hot and cold in most rooms and ample car parking in our olde worlde guest house in this small historical town on the Heritage Coast. Swimming, surfing, beach is 1½ miles away with many beautiful walks in the immediate area.

P	SINGLE PER PERSON B&B		DOUBLE FOR 2 PERSONS B&B		🛏	6
	MIN £ 12.50	MAX £ 14.00	MIN £ 25.00	MAX £ 28.00	OPEN 1-12	

Heron House

Bakers Lane, Llantwit Major,   👑👑
South Glamorgan
Tel: (04465) 3564
Gillian and Mike welcome you to Heron House, situated in Llantwit Major village by the heron pond. One mile to beach, close to shops, swimming pool. One room en-suite, televisions, tea/coffee making facilities in all bedrooms, also television lounge. Excellent area for exploring South Wales. Cardiff, Barry, St. Donat's castle all within easy reach.

P ✗ 🐕 ✗	SINGLE PER PERSON B&B		DOUBLE FOR 2 PERSONS B&B		🛏	4
	MIN £ 12.00	MAX £ 14.00	MIN £ 24.00	MAX £ 28.00	OPEN 1-12	1

PENARTH   Map Ref Mb5

Small resort near Cardiff offering boating, yachting, fishing, water-skiing and cliff walks. Victorian pier and promenade. New marina.

Guest Houses

Alandale Guest House

17 Plymouth Road, Penarth,   L
South Glamorgan, CF6 2DA
Tel: (0222) 709226
The guest house is 5 minutes from seafront, railway station 2 minutes away. Large bedrooms, with colour TV, full central heating, hot and cold, shaver points, car park. Reduced rates for weekly bookings. Evening meals if required, Cardiff 10 minutes away by train or car. St Fagans, Castle 15 minutes away, spoil yourself with a holiday with good food and accommodation.

H ✗ P ✗ 🐕	SINGLE PER PERSON B&B		DOUBLE FOR 2 PERSONS B&B		🛏	10
	MIN £ 13.00	MAX £ 14.00	MIN £ 26.00	MAX £ 28.00	OPEN 1-12	2

Ardwyn

53 Cog Road, Sully, Penarth,   👑👑
South Glamorgan, CF6 2TE
Tel: (0222) 530103
Cliff and Margaret Robinson welcome you to Ardwyn, our friendly free and easy home in the coastal village of Sully. Convenient for Cardiff, Penarth, Barry and Vale of Glamorgan. All rooms colour TV, wash hand basins, hot drinks, hair dryers, heating, visitors lounge with colour TV, parking. Pleasant gardens with views over surrounding countryside.

H ✗ P ✗ 🐕	SINGLE PER PERSON B&B		DOUBLE FOR 2 PERSONS B&B		🛏	3
	MIN £ 12.00	MAX £	MIN £ 24.00	MAX £	OPEN 1-11	

Starcross Guest House

1 Archer Road, Penarth,   L
South Glamorgan, CF6 2HW
Tel: (0222) 702718
Attractive Victorian house set in quiet residential area near town centre and railway station. Within walking distance of beach and Cosmeston Country Park. Single, double and family rooms with special rates for children. Lounge with colour TV, full central heating. Standard and vegetarian meals. Home-made bread available. Welcoming and friendly atmosphere.

H ✗ P ✗	SINGLE PER PERSON B&B		DOUBLE FOR 2 PERSONS B&B		🛏	4
	MIN £ 12.00	MAX £	MIN £ 24.00	MAX £	OPEN 1-12	

Trelawne

4 Albert Crescent, Penarth,   L
South Glamorgan, CF6 1DA
Tel: (0222) 709184
Victorian house overlooking park and bowling green. Beach and medieval village with country lakes close by. Cardiff 5 miles. Ideal base for touring South Wales. St Fagans Castle and Folk Museum, Castell Coch, Cardiff Castle and Caerphilly Castle within 20 miles. The pretty Vale of Glamorgan villages and Porthcawl within ½ hours drive.

H P	SINGLE PER PERSON B&B		DOUBLE FOR 2 PERSONS B&B		🛏	3
	MIN £ 10.00	MAX £ 10.00	MIN £ 20.00	MAX £ 20.00	OPEN 1-12	

PORT TALBOT
Map Ref Lb4

Extensive sands of Aberavon beach - bathing and surfing. Afan Lido sports centre. Margam Country Park has a deer herd, sculpture park, orangery, maze and children's fairytale village. The fascinating Welsh Miner's Museum is in Afan Argoed Country Park.

Guest Houses

Ty'n-y-Caeau

Margam Village, Port Talbot,   👑👑
West Glamorgan, SA13 2NW
Tel: (0639) 883897
Country guest house set in four acres fields and walled gardens. Close to junction 38 M4, Margam Park and South Wales coast. Private parking and childrens play area. Comfortable large lounge and dining room. Fresh home cooked meals with garden produce in season. Double, twin or family rooms. Brochure from Mrs Rhiannon Gaen.

P ✗ 🐕 ✗	SINGLE PER PERSON B&B		DOUBLE FOR 2 PERSONS B&B		🛏	3
	MIN £ 13.00	MAX £	MIN £ 22.00	MAX £ 28.00	OPEN 1-12	

CALL *Holidays*
(0792) 645555

103

PORTHCAWL
Map Ref Lc6

Traditional seaside resort - beaches, funfair, promenade, golf. Summer entertainment at the Grand Pavilion. Sailing and windsurfing. Convenient for visiting the unspoilt Vale of Glamorgan with its attractive villages set amid leafy country lanes.

Hotels

Minerva Hotel
Esplanade Avenue, Porthcawl,
Mid Glamorgan, CF36 3YU
Tel: (065671) 2428
A comfortable, licensed, AA Listed hotel run personally by the owners Rosemarie and Tony Giblett. Occupying a central position close to the promenade and shops. Our rooms are centrally heated, have tea and coffee making facilities and colour televisions. Some have bathrooms en-suite. Reduced rates for weekly bookings, children under 12 charged half price.

	SINGLE PER PERSON B&B		DOUBLE FOR 2 PERSONS B&B		🛏	8
✕	MIN £	MAX £	MIN £	MAX £		4
	12.00	12.00	24.00	24.00	OPEN 1-12	

Penoyre Private Hotel
29 Mary Street, Porthcawl,
Mid Glamorgan, CF36 3YN
Tel: (0656) 714550
In the heart of Porthcawl within 100 yards of shopping centre and beach. This small hotel offers excellent home cooking, with public car park opposite. Tea and coffee, colour television in all bedrooms. Bar facilities are provided for residents. Ann and Jim Ormiston extend a warm welcome and personal attention is assured. RAC listed.

H	SINGLE PER PERSON B&B		DOUBLE FOR 2 PERSONS B&B		🛏	5
🐕	MIN £	MAX £	MIN £	MAX £		
✕	12.00	13.00	24.00	26.00	OPEN 1-12	

Guest Houses

The Oasis
2 South Road, Porthcawl, [L]
Mid Glamorgan, CF36 3DG
Tel: (0656) 716276
Comfortable spacious Victorian house with large garden, close to the town and beaches. Good home cooking, special diets catered for. Ground floor en-suite room for disabled guests, good wheelchair access throughout ground floor and garden. Ideal accommodation too for small groups of ramblers or golfers. Riding and fishing nearby. Bookable in advance.

H ✕	SINGLE PER PERSON B&B		DOUBLE FOR 2 PERSONS B&B		🛏	4
P ✕	MIN £	MAX £	MIN £	MAX £		1
🐕	11.50	13.00	23.00	26.00	OPEN 1-12	

Rockybank Guest House
15 De Breos Drive, Porthcawl,
Mid Glamorgan, CF36 3JP
Tel: (065671) 5823
Within walking distance of town, beaches, restaurants, funfair, country walks, bus station. Children's park 50 yards away. Situated between two excellent golf courses, close to nature reserve. Parking. TV, teasmade. Family double room en-suite with balcony, twin and double room next door to bathroom, H & C, razor point, dining room, central heating. Special rates for children.

H	SINGLE PER PERSON B&B		DOUBLE FOR 2 PERSONS B&B		🛏	3
P	MIN £	MAX £	MIN £	MAX £		1
✕	14.00	14.00	24.00	28.00	OPEN 1-12	

Rosedale Guest House
48 Esplanade Avenue, Porthcawl,
Mid Glamorgan, CF36 3YU
Tel: (0656) 5356
A comfortable family run guest house offering a warm welcome. Good home cooking and friendly service. Situated within 100 yards of beach, promenade and shops. All rooms centrally heated with tea/coffee facilities and TV's. TV lounge available to all guests. Special rates for children. Fire certificate held.

✕	SINGLE PER PERSON B&B		DOUBLE FOR 2 PERSONS B&B		🛏	6
	MIN £	MAX £	MIN £	MAX £		1
	12.00	12.00	24.00	24.00	OPEN 1-12	

ST. BRIDES MAJOR
Map Ref Ld6

Small picturesque village in the Vale of Glamorgan on B4524. Close to Bridgend and ideal for visiting Ogmore Castle and Ewenny Priory. Golf at Southerndown.

Guest Houses

Bryn Cerrig
17 Lon-yr-Eglwys, St. Brides Major, [L]
Bridgend, Mid Glamorgan CF32 0SH
Tel: (0656) 880611
Situated close to heritage coast, 1 mile Southerndown Bay midway between Cardiff and Swansea. Easy distance to Welsh Folk Museum, Dan yr Ogof Caves, Brecon Beacons, Gower Coast, Barry and Porthcawl. A spacious modern bungalow in quiet area with large garden, separate dining room, lounge with television, tea making facilities, local produce, home made bread.

H	SINGLE PER PERSON B&B		DOUBLE FOR 2 PERSONS B&B		🛏	2
P	MIN £	MAX £	MIN £	MAX £		
	10.00	12.50	20.00	25.00	OPEN 1-12	

VALE OF USK AND WYE VALLEY

This is a tale of two rivers – the meandering Usk and the languid Wye. The stretch of the Wye between Monmouth and Chepstow – an 'Area of Outstanding Natural Beauty' – provides the leafy setting for the mellow ruins of Tintern Abbey praised by poet William Wordsworth. Both rivers are famous for their fishing as well as their beauty. The Usk, which follows a pastoral course southwards from Abergavenny to Newport, flows past Caerleon where the Romans established a major base. Their amphitheatre, amazingly well-preserved after all these years, stands close to remains of a barracks and a recently excavated bath-house complex.

This green, history-laden border country has Britain's first stone-built castle at Chepstow. Raglan is the home of one of the later breeds of castle, when fortresses were evolving into more comfortable homes. At Newport, there's home comfort on a grand, glided scale at opulent Tredegar House, a 17th-century mansion set in a splendid country park.

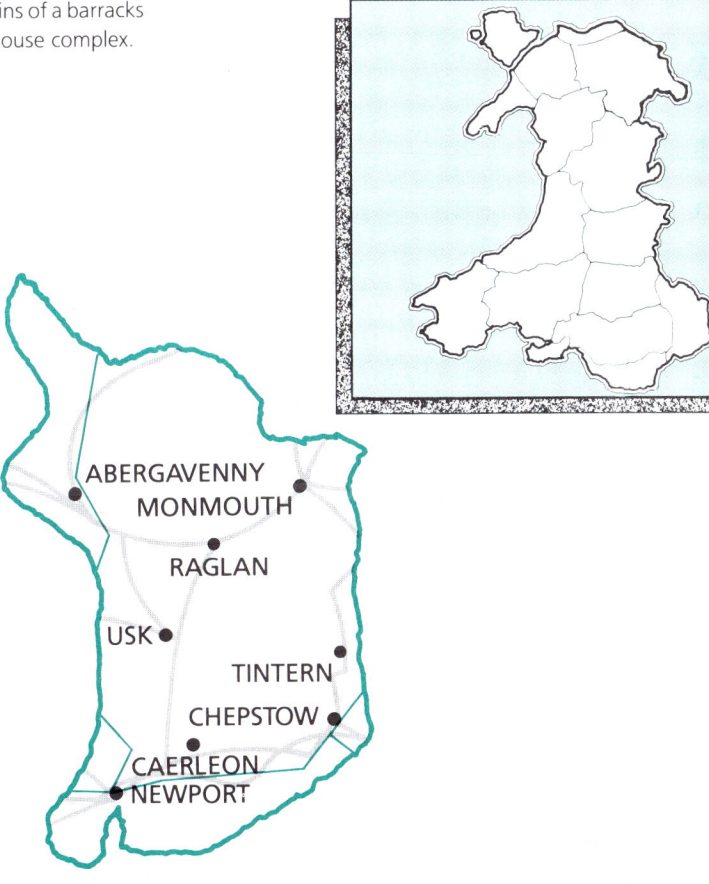

ABERGAVENNY
Map Ref Mc2

Flourishing market town with backdrop of mountains. Leisure centre. Pony trekking in nearby Black Mountains. Castle with museum. The Monmouthshire and Brecon Canal runs just to the west of the town. Excellent touring base for lovely Vale of Usk and Brecon Beacons National Park.

Guest Houses

Belchamps Guest House
1 Holywell Road, Abergavenny, Gwent, NP7 5LP
Tel: (0873) 3204
Worldwide recommendations for comfort, good food, personal attention. Rooms tastefully furnished, vanity basins, tea, coffee making facilities, power, razor points. Guests TV lounge, bathroom and toilet, separate shower room and toilet. Access at all times. Guestaccomm Good Room Award. AA approved. Full fire certificate. Excellent touring centre for historic and beautiful countryside.

H ✗ P ✿	SINGLE PER PERSON B&B		DOUBLE FOR 2 PERSONS B&B		🛏 5 🛁
	MIN £	MAX £	MIN £	MAX £	
	12.00	14.00	24.00	28.00	OPEN 1-12

The Cloisters
Llanvihangel Crucorney, Abergavenny, Gwent, NP7 8DH
Tel: (0873) 890738
17th century former coachman's house set in 1 acre of gardens, 100 yards from the oldest pub in Wales; The Skirrid Inn. One double room with en-suite facilities. One family room with double bed and either single beds or double bed settee. Bathroom attached. Full english breakfast or vegetarian.

P ✗ ✿ ✌	SINGLE PER PERSON B&B		DOUBLE FOR 2 PERSONS B&B		🛏 2 🛁 2
	MIN £	MAX £	MIN £	MAX £	
	13.00	13.00	26.00	26.00	OPEN 2-10

Ingleside
61 Monmouth Road, Abergavenny, Gwent, NP7 5HR
Tel: (0873) 5262
Victorian house within easy walking distance of town centre, bus and train stations. Three double bedrooms with modern amenities and tea/coffee making facilities, television lounge. Full English or Continental breakfast. Ideal base for touring, walking, fishing and riding.

P ✌	SINGLE PER PERSON B&B		DOUBLE FOR 2 PERSONS B&B		🛏 3 🛁
	MIN £	MAX £	MIN £	MAX £	
			24.00	26.00	OPEN 4-10

Park Guest House
36 Hereford Road, Abergavenny, Gwent, NP7 5RA
Tel: (0875) 3715
A warm friendly welcome, personal attention and home cooking of the highest quality are assured in this family run early Georgian guest house. Recently tastefully redecorated and refurbished and comprising six bedrooms (doubles, twins, family and single), two bathrooms, lounge and dining room, full central heating, fully licensed. Fire certificate and ample private parking.

H P ✗	SINGLE PER PERSON B&B		DOUBLE FOR 2 PERSONS B&B		🛏 6 🛁
	MIN £	MAX £	MIN £	MAX £	
	14.00	14.00	24.00	24.00	OPEN 1-12

Pentre Cottage
Brecon Road, Llanwenarth, Abergavenny, Gwent, NP7 7EW L
Tel: (0873) 3435
Pretty small country house situated on the turning to the Sugar Loaf Mountain. Large garden, plenty of parking space, lovely grounds. Three bedrooms available, bathroom and separate shower room. Sitting room with television, very comfortably furnished. Pony trekking and lovely walks. The River Usk just down the lane. Brochure available, world wide recommendations.

P ✿	SINGLE PER PERSON B&B		DOUBLE FOR 2 PERSONS B&B		🛏 3 🛁
	MIN £	MAX £	MIN £	MAX £	
	12.00	14.00	20.00	24.00	OPEN 1-12

Farmhouses

Great Tre-rhew Farm
Llanvetherine, Abergavenny, Gwent, NP7 8RA L
Tel: (0873) 86268
Warm welcome on our 240 acre working family farm. Good home cooking. Quiet situation, ideal for touring Wye Valley, Black Mountains, Brecon Beacons. Near to Offa's Dyke, ancient castles, fishing in farm stream and River Trothy.

H ✌ P ✗ ✿	SINGLE PER PERSON B&B		DOUBLE FOR 2 PERSONS B&B		🛏 2 🛁
	MIN £	MAX £	MIN £	MAX £	
	10.00	12.00	20.00	24.00	OPEN 1-12

Little Treadam
Llantilio Crossenny, Abergavenny, Gwent, NP7 8TA
Tel: (060085) 326
16th century farmhouse in beautiful gardens. Quiet setting Welsh warmth and hospitality. Good food with local produce. Situated between B4233 and B4521 with views towards the Black Mountains, within walking distance of White Castle and Offa's Dyke path. All rooms have private toilets and wash basins. Two rooms en-suite. Table licence.

H ✗ P ✿	SINGLE PER PERSON B&B		DOUBLE FOR 2 PERSONS B&B		🛏 4 🛁 2
	MIN £	MAX £	MIN £	MAX £	
	13.00	15.00	22.00	28.00	OPEN 1-12

Pen-yr-Heol Farm
Cymro Road, Gilwern, Abergavenny, Gwent NP7 0HH L
Tel: (0873) 830406
Welcome to our traditional farmhouse 4 miles from Abergavenny with views overlooking the Usk Valley. Good home cooking, dining room and lounge with TV. 1 en-suite and one double bedroom. Within walking distance, caving, pony trekking, canoeing, walking and climbing. Historic sites include Big Pit, Tretower Court, Llanthony Abbey, Iron Works, Abergavenny and Crickhowell.

H P ✗	SINGLE PER PERSON B&B		DOUBLE FOR 2 PERSONS B&B		🛏 2 🛁 1
	MIN £	MAX £	MIN £	MAX £	
	10.00	12.00	20.00	24.00	OPEN 1-12

CAERLEON
Map Ref Mc4

Historical associations with ancient Rome and Arthurian legend. Once the chief fortress of the Second Augustan Legion, it held 6,000 troops In the fort of AD74. Amphitheatre and Roman Baths well worth visiting as is the Legionary Museum.

Guest Houses

Ashburton House
66 Caerleon Road, Newport, Gwent, NP9 7BY L
Tel: (0633) 211140
Two family rooms with hand basin and TV, one twin, 1 single. All rooms with tea making facilities and clock radio. Two toilets, two showers, one bathroom. TV lounge. Central heating.

H ✌	SINGLE PER PERSON B&B		DOUBLE FOR 2 PERSONS B&B		🛏 4 🛁
	MIN £	MAX £	MIN £	MAX £	
	12.00	14.00	24.00	28.00	OPEN 1-12

CALL Holidays
(0792) 645555

CHEPSTOW Map Ref Me4

Attractive hilly town with substantial remains of Strongbow's great stone castle above the Wye. Fortified gate still stands in main street and medieval walls remain. Good shopping, Sunday market, fine racecourse, excellent walks - beginning of Wye Valley Walk and Offa's Dyke Path. Ideal for touring beautiful Wye Valley.

Guest Houses

Hazelhurst Guest House

Gloucester Road, Tutshill, Chepstow, Gwent NP6 7DB
Tel: (0291) 622266

Small friendly guest house Central heating, hot and cold, tea making and colour TV in bedrooms. Children and pets welcome. Evening meals and special diets catered for. Family, twin, singles and double rooms available.

H×	SINGLE PER PERSON B&B	DOUBLE FOR 2 PERSONS B&B	🛏	3
P			🖼	
🐾	MIN £ / MAX £	MIN £ / MAX £	OPEN 1-12	
	10.00 / 12.00	20.00 / 24.00		

Lower Viney Farm Guest House

Viney Hill, Blakeney, Gloucestershire, GL15 4LT
Tel: (0594) 516000

Spacious period house just west of Gloucester in the Royal Forest of Dean. All guest rooms have modern facilities and are comfortably furnished. All have hot and cold water, shaver points, tea/coffee making facilities and with full central heating. Evening meals are available if required. AA listed.

H ✱	SINGLE PER PERSON B&B	DOUBLE FOR 2 PERSONS B&B	🛏	5
P ×			🖼	5
🐾	MIN £ / MAX £	MIN £ / MAX £	OPEN 1-12	
	12.50 / 14.00	25.00 / 27.50		

Farmhouses

Cribau

The Cwm, Llanvair Discoed, Chepstow, Gwent NP6 6RD
Tel: (02917) 528

Six miles south of Severn Bridge, two miles A48. 16th century modernised farmhouse with comfortable facilities in traditional settings. 2 rooms, one double bedded, one twin bedded with own patio. Both have shower rooms en-suite. Very quiet position, no traffic. Beautiful countryside. Variety of animals kept.

H	SINGLE PER PERSON B&B	DOUBLE FOR 2 PERSONS B&B	🛏	2
P			🖼	2
	MIN £ / MAX £	MIN £ / MAX £	OPEN 1-12	
	14.00 / 14.00	24.00 / 24.00		

Great Llanmelyn Farm

Llanvair Discoed, Chepstow, Gwent, NP6 6LU
Tel: (02917) 210

Welcome to our large historical farmhouse. Working farm of 200 acres. Spacious bedrooms, tea and coffee making, centrally heated, hot and cold. Family room en-suite. Peaceful setting in beautiful countryside. Ideal touring Wye Valley, Caldicot Medieval Banquets, near St Pierre Golf Club, 6 miles junction 22, Severn Bridge, 1 mile A48, pub food nearby. AA listed.

H	SINGLE PER PERSON B&B	DOUBLE FOR 2 PERSONS B&B	🛏	3
P			🖼	1
🐾	MIN £ / MAX £	MIN £ / MAX £	OPEN 4-10	
	11.00 / 11.00	24.00 / 26.00		

Home Farm

Shirenewton, Chepstow, Gwent, NP6 6RL
Tel: (02917) 334

Atttractively situated on edge of picturesque village five miles from Severn Bridge. Spacious and comfortable 17th century farmhouse, five twin bedded rooms, all H & C, three bathrooms. One en-suite. Large lounge. Separate TV room. Full central heating. Ideally placed for touring Wye Valley, Bath, Brecon Beacons, Bristol, Cardiff. Many local inns available for evening meal.

H	SINGLE PER PERSON B&B	DOUBLE FOR 2 PERSONS B&B	🛏	5
P			🖼	1
	MIN £ / MAX £	MIN £ / MAX £	OPEN 1-12	
	12.00 / 12.00	24.00 / 24.00		

Parsons Grove

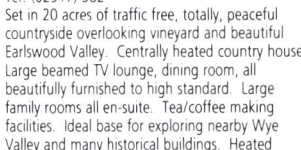

Earlswood, Chepstow, Gwent, NP6 6RD
Tel: (02917) 382

Set in 20 acres of traffic free, totally, peaceful countryside overlooking vineyard and Earlswood Valley. Centrally heated country house. Large beamed TV lounge, dining room, all beautifully furnished to high standard. Large family rooms all en-suite. Tea/coffee making facilities. Ideal base for exploring nearby Wye Valley and many historical buildings. Heated swimming pool. WTB Farmhouse Award.

H×	SINGLE PER PERSON B&B	DOUBLE FOR 2 PERSONS B&B	🛏	2
P			🖼	2
🐾	MIN £ / MAX £	MIN £ / MAX £	OPEN 1-12	
		26.00 / 26.00		

MONMOUTH Map Ref Me1

Historic market town in picturesque Wye Valley - birthplace of Henry V and Charles Rolls (of Rolls-Royce). Interesting local history museum with collection of Nelson memorabilia. Rare fortified gateway still spans the river Monnow. Good centre for touring.

Guest Houses

Church Farm Guest House

Mitchel Troy, Monmouth, Gwent, NP5 4HZ
Tel: (0600) 2176

A 16th century former farmhouse with oak beams and inglenook fireplaces, set in large attractive garden with stream. Easy access to A40 and only 2 miles from historic Monmouth. Excellent base for Wye Valley, Forest of Dean and Black Mountains. Central heating, some en-suite bedrooms, tea/coffee making facilities. Tasty alternatives to English breakfast available.

P	SINGLE PER PERSON B&B	DOUBLE FOR 2 PERSONS B&B	🛏	6
✱			🖼	2
×	MIN £ / MAX £	MIN £ / MAX £	OPEN 1-12	
	11.00 / 14.00	22.00 / 28.00		

Lugano

Llandogo, Monmouth, Gwent, NP5 4TL
Tel: (0594) 530496

Lugano set in pleasant gardens off the main A466, halfway between Monmouth and Chepstow in the picturesque village of Llandogo. Ideal touring centre, a walkers paradise. Single, double (one with en-suite bathroom), family/twin bedded rooms all with hot and cold, tea and coffee making facilities and colour TV. Access to bedrooms and gardens at all times. Brochure available.

P	SINGLE PER PERSON B&B	DOUBLE FOR 2 PERSONS B&B	🛏	3
✱			🖼	1
	MIN £ / MAX £	MIN £ / MAX £	OPEN 2-11	
	12.00 / 14.00	22.00 / 28.00		

Priory House

98 Hereford Road, Monmouth, Gwent, NP5 3HH
Tel: (0600) 5896

Detached residence set in attractive gardens. Bright bedrooms with country views. Ample private parking. Evening meal optional. One single, one double, one twin, one family. Bathroom with modern shower. Just a few minutes from Monmouth town centre on the A466 road to Hereford.

H×	SINGLE PER PERSON B&B	DOUBLE FOR 2 PERSONS B&B	🛏	4
✱			🖼	
	MIN £ / MAX £	MIN £ / MAX £	OPEN 1-12	
	12.00 / 12.00	24.00 / 24.00		

MONMOUTH CONTINUED

Guest Houses

St. Thomas Lodge

14 St Thomas Square, Monmouth, Gwent, NP5 3ES
Tel: (0600) 6520 [L]
Andrew and Marilyn Wright welcome you to St. Thomas Lodge, a Georgian house situated in the historic town of Monmouth. Friendly family home with single, double and family accomodation. Evening meal by arrangement.

P ⚒ ✗	SINGLE PER PERSON B&B		DOUBLE FOR 2 PERSONS B&B		🛏 🏠	2
	MIN £	MAX £	MIN £	MAX £		
	10.00	10.00	20.00	20.00		OPEN 1-12

Wye Avon

Dixton Road, Monmouth, Gwent, NP5 3PR
Tel: (0600) 3322 👑
Spacious Victorian house with lovely views and within easy walking distance of Monmouth town centre. Excellent walking country. Ideal touring centre for the Wye Valley, Forest of Dean, Welsh border castles, Cardiff, Hereford and Gloucester. Washbasin and shaver point in all rooms. Central heating, tea coffee making facilities. Choice of breakfast. No smoking please!

P 🐕	SINGLE PER PERSON B&B		DOUBLE FOR 2 PERSONS B&B		🛏	3
	MIN £	MAX £	MIN £	MAX £		
	11.00	12.00	22.00	24.00		OPEN 1-12

Farmhouses

The Grange

Penrhos, Raglan, Gwent, NP5 2LQ
Tel: (0600) 85202 [L]
Traditional mixed farm in quiet unspoilt countryside, away from crowds, on Offa's Dyke path. Share our fantastic views 120 acres of trees, streams, animals. Local golf, fishing, places to visit. A good centre for touring and children love it. Large conmfortable rooms newly converted, two en-suite. Good home cooking. Riding for children by arrangement.

H ⚒ P ✗ 🐕	SINGLE PER PERSON B&B		DOUBLE FOR 2 PERSONS B&B		🛏 🏠	3 2
	MIN £	MAX £	MIN £	MAX £		
	12.50	16.00	21.00	28.00		OPEN 1-12

NEWPORT   Map Ref Mc4

Busy industrial, commercial and shopping centre. Interesting murals in main hall of Civic Centre. Newport Museum and Art Gallery in John Frost Square (named after Chartist leader) and new Leisure Centre with wave machine. On the outskirts, magnificently restored Tredegar House with extensive country park.

CALL Holidays
(0792) 645555

Guest Houses

Chapel Guest House

Church Road, St Brides, Wentloog, Newport, Gwent NP1 9SN
Tel: (0633) 681018 [L]
Comfortable accommodation in a converted chapel near the centre of a charming country village between Newport and Cardiff. Pleasant walks and sea fishing, country pub and restaurant adjacent. Family, double, and twin rooms, most en-suite. Guest lounge. Children welcome, special rates. Leave M4 junction 28 follow B4239 (3 miles) Coastal Road towards Cardiff. Ample parking.

H ⚒ P ✗ 🐕	SINGLE PER PERSON B&B		DOUBLE FOR 2 PERSONS B&B		🛏 🏠	5 4
	MIN £	MAX £	MIN £	MAX £		
	12.00	14.00	24.00	28.00		OPEN 1-12

Langtree Guest House

49 Cardiff Road, Newport, Gwent, NP9 2EN
Tel: (0633) 213832 [L]
Perfectly situated for commercial visitors or tourists. Ideal centre for touring beauty spots, 5 minutes walk town centre and leisure/entertainment complex. Tea making and TV all rooms, full central heating. Children welcome at reduced rates. 25 yards main bus routes. Personal attention of proprietor. 2 miles from M4 junction 28.

H ✗ P ⚒	SINGLE PER PERSON B&B		DOUBLE FOR 2 PERSONS B&B		🛏	4
	MIN £	MAX £	MIN £	MAX £		
	12.00	12.00	20.00	24.00		OPEN 1-12

Westwood Villa Guest House

59 Risca Road, Cross Keys, Gwent, NP1 7BT
Tel: (0495) 270336 [L]
Five miles M4 close to Newport, Cardiff, Wye Valley. Friendly, family run, home cooking english breakfast. Single, double, family rooms. Central heating, television lounge, separate dining room. H & C, tea/coffee provided all rooms. Children and pets welcome. Scenic drives, walks, sport, leisure, entertainment, restaurants. Open Christmas. A warm welcome awaits you all year from Bob and Maureen.

P 🐕	SINGLE PER PERSON B&B		DOUBLE FOR 2 PERSONS B&B		🛏 🏠	5
	MIN £	MAX £	MIN £	MAX £		
	12.00	14.00	20.00	24.00		OPEN 1-12

Widecombe

Old Chepstow Road, Langstone, Newport, Gwent, NP6 2ND
Tel: (0633) 413311 [L]
Small friendly family home in half acre pleasant garden. Comfortable accommodation in twin, double, and single rooms with tea making facilities. Clock radio, shaver points, hot and cold, good home cooking, lounge, sun lounge. Ideal base for touring. Just off A48 ¾ mile junction 24, M4 and A449 3½ miles east Newport town centre.

P ✗ 🐕 ⚒	SINGLE PER PERSON B&B		DOUBLE FOR 2 PERSONS B&B		🛏 🏠	4
	MIN £	MAX £	MIN £	MAX £		
	12.50	13.50	25.00	27.00		OPEN 1-12

TINTERN   Map Ref Me2

Riverside village in particularly lovely stretch of Wye Valley. Impressive ruins of Tintern Abbey. The former railway station has a visitors' interpretative centre and a picnic site with refreshments. Excellent walks and good fishing.

Guest Houses

Millfield

Mill Hill, Brockweir, Chepstow, Gwent NP6 7NW
Tel: (0291) 689484 [L]
Large modern bungalow situated in small village between Monmouth and Chepstow with outstanding views across valley. Guests enjoy a relaxing and friendly atmosphere with separate dining room and large lounge, colour TV, central heating and parking facilities. Well appointed bedrooms with views across the Wye Valley. A warm welcome awaits our guests.

H ✗ P 🐕	SINGLE PER PERSON B&B		DOUBLE FOR 2 PERSONS B&B		🛏	3
	MIN £	MAX £	MIN £	MAX £		
	12.00	12.00	24.00	24.00		OPEN 1-12

The Old Rectory

Tintern, Chepstow, Gwent, NP6 6SG
Tel: (0291) 689519 [L]

A free and easy atmosphere awaits the visitor to this 18/19th century house. Accommodation in 5 bedrooms, 3 overlooking the River Wye with H & C hand basins. Lounge with stone fireplace and dining room serving good home cooked food. Situated on the border between England and Wales, it makes a perfect base for touring.

P	SINGLE PER PERSON B&B		DOUBLE FOR 2 PERSONS B&B		🛏	5
🐕	MIN £	MAX £	MIN £	MAX £		
✕	10.50	10.50	21.00	21.00	OPEN 1-12	

The Smithy

Trellech Grange, Llanishen, Chepstow,
Gwent NP6 6QN [L]
Tel: (0600) 860027

Ideal touring centre for castles, Wye Valley, Brecon Beacons. Bath within one hour. Recently renovated blacksmiths/carpenters workshop. Small comfortable rooms, most with hot and cold. Set in small farming community. All rooms tea/coffee facilities. Reductions and packed lunches for extended stays. Warm relaxed family atmosphere. Good imaginative home cooking. Television and telephone available.

P	SINGLE PER PERSON B&B		DOUBLE FOR 2 PERSONS B&B		🛏	4
✕	MIN £	MAX £	MIN £	MAX £		
	12.50	13.50	20.00	21.00	OPEN 1-12	

Tanglewood

Tintern Post Office, Tintern, Chepstow,
Gwent, NP6 6SE
Tel: (0291) 689242

Comfortable family home situated in the heart of the Wye Valley, overlooking the River Wye with panoramic views of Tintern woods and the famous cistercian Abbey. Ideal base for walking and sightseeing. Colour television, tea and coffee making facilities in all rooms.

H	SINGLE PER PERSON B&B		DOUBLE FOR 2 PERSONS B&B		🛏	2
🐕	MIN £	MAX £	MIN £	MAX £		
🍴				25.00	OPEN 4-11	

USK Map Ref Md3

Ancient borough on river Usk; excellent salmon fishing and inns catering for anglers. Good walks. Great castle of Raglan 5 miles north; convenient for farm museum at Wolvesnewton. Sailing and other watersports on nearby Llandegfedd reservoir. Good central location for sight-seeing in Gwent.

Farmhouses

Pentwyn Farm

Little Mill, Pontypool,
Gwent, NP4 0HQ
Tel: (049528) 249

On the edge of the Brecon Beacons National Park, Pentwyn is a typical 16th century Welsh Longhouse surrounded by a large garden and swimming pool. Our reputation for good food and hospitality is of prime importance and the reason so many guests return. Three bedrooms (2 en-suite) prettily decorated with tea making facilities. Licensed.

H	SINGLE PER PERSON B&B		DOUBLE FOR 2 PERSONS B&B		🛏	3
P	MIN £	MAX £	MIN £	MAX £		2
✕			23.00		OPEN 2-10	

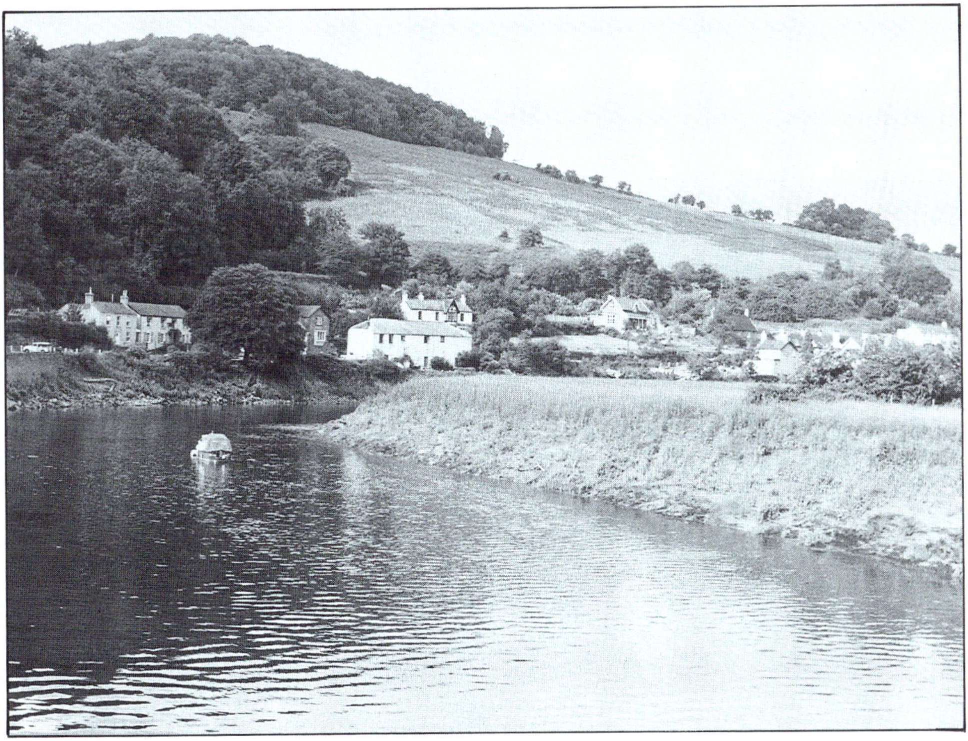

RIVER WYE

SOUTH WALES VALLEYS

First-time visitors to this part of Wales are invariably surprised – first by the unexpected natural beauty of the Valleys, and also by their wealth of attractions. This is an area of country parks, forest walks and panoramic hilltop views across untouched moorland. The Royal National Eisteddfod, Wales's most important cultural gathering, takes place this August at the Bryn Bach Country Park, Rhymney. And nearby Ebbw Vale is already preparing for the 1992 Garden Festival, which will be held on a site embracing valley, mountain and lake.

The Valleys' many and varied attractions include a dry ski slope at Pontypool and narrow-gauge railway at Merthyr Tydfil, a wildlife park near Neath, and – at Caerphilly – one of Europe's great castles. The Valleys' fascinating industrial past as a coal- and iron-producing area is not forgotten. Visitors are taken on conducted underground tours at the Big Pit Mining Museum, Blaenavon. And there are more memories of 'King Coal' at the Welsh Miners' Museum, near Cymmer, and the exciting new Rhondda Heritage Park.

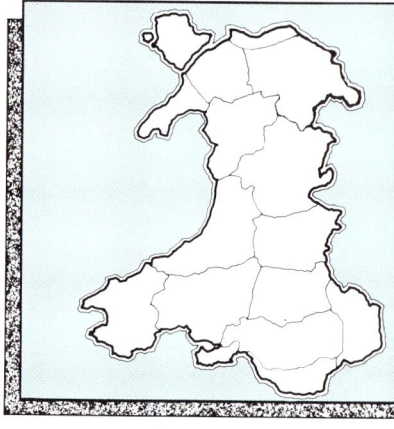

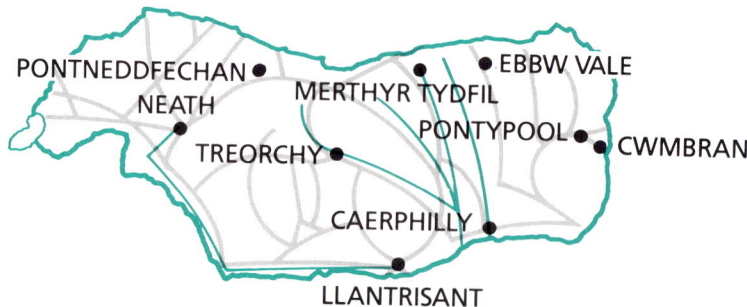

CAERPHILLY
Map Ref Ma4

A sight not to be missed - Caerphilly Castle, a fine example of medieval military architecture. The extensive ruins of this 13th century castle, only 7 miles north of Cardiff, have a famous leaning tower - the result of some gunpowder work by the Roundheads. Golf course, shopping; excellent centre for exploring Valleys and visiting Cardiff. Caerphilly Mountain offers pleasant walks and fine views. Caerphilly cheese made at the Old Courthouse.

Guest Houses

The Cottage Guest House
Pwllypant, Caerphilly, Mid Glamorgan, CF8 3HW
Tel: (0222) 869160
The owners of this 300 year old cottage offer a warm homely welcome. All bedrooms centrally heated and hot and cold water, tea/coffee making facilities, television lounge and car park. Owner a registered Wales and Cotswolds Guide and provides free touring advice. Good convenient restaurants in town. Perfect centre for castles, coast and mountains.

H	SINGLE PER PERSON B&B		DOUBLE FOR 2 PERSONS B&B		🛏	3
P					🚗	
MIN £	MAX £	MIN £	MAX £		OPEN 1-12
14.00	14.00	26.00	28.00		

Farmhouses

Wern Ganol Farm
Nelson, Treharris, Mid Glamorgan, CF46 6PS
Tel: (0443) 450413
Wern Ganol Farm is a 60 acre dairy farm on main A472 at Nelson with pleasant views. Easy access to Brecon Beacons, Cardiff, South Wales coast. Clay pidgeon shoot and ski-slope nearby. 2 double rooms, 1 family room, all en-suite and TV, tea and coffee making facilities available. Friendly and homely atmosphere.

H	✱	SINGLE PER PERSON B&B		DOUBLE FOR 2 PERSONS B&B		🛏	3
P						🚗	3
🐴		MIN £	MAX £	MIN £	MAX £		OPEN 1-12
		12.00	14.00	24.00	28.00		

CWMBRAN Map Ref Mc4

A 'new town' and administration centre of Gwent. Good sports and leisure facilities. Shopping precinct and sports centre with international athletics stadium. Theatre and cinemas. Good touring centre for the Vale of Usk and the South Wales Valleys.

Guest Houses

The Glebe
Trehouber Road, Croesyceiliog, Cwmbran, Gwent NP44 2DE
Tel: (0633) 49251
This friendly Welsh home welcomes your visit. Perfectly situated for business people and tourists, 6 minutes drive from M4 Junction 26, A4042. Overlooking this lovely corner of rural Wales. Highly recommended by home and overseas visitors. Convenient stopover for Irish ferry. AA listed. Mrs Beryl Watkins.

H	SINGLE PER PERSON B&B		DOUBLE FOR 2 PERSONS B&B		🛏	3
P					🚗	
✱	MIN £	MAX £	MIN £	MAX £		OPEN 1-11
	12.50		24.00			

Springfields Guest House
371 Llantarnam Road, Llantarnam, Cwmbran, Gwent NP44 3BN
Tel: (06333) 2509
Established 17 years. 4 miles from M4, 1 mile Cwmbran. Large car park. TV, tea making, shaver points all rooms. 2 double (en-suite), 2 double, 1 family, 2 twin, 1 family en-suite by March 1990, 1 twin en-suite, 1 single, central heating. Separate dining room and lounge. Children 4-12 half price, under 3 years free. We enjoy our work and feel sure you will enjoy your visit. Good centre for touring. Joan Graham.

P	✱	SINGLE PER PERSON B&B		DOUBLE FOR 2 PERSONS B&B		🛏	10
🐴							3
✱		MIN £	MAX £	MIN £	MAX £		OPEN 1-12
		12.50	14.00	25.00	27.00		

EBBW VALE Map Ref Ma2

Industrial town - steel and coal. Fine sports complex and Penyfan Pond Country Park six miles south has extensive recreational facilities.

Guest Houses

Lamb House
West Side, Blaina, Gwent, NP3 3DB
Tel: (0495) 290179
Close to Heads of the Valleys, ideally situated for visiting South Wales, tourist attractions, i.e. Big Pit Mining Museum, Brecon Beacons, scenic forest drive etc. Impressive scenery, good mountain walks. Twin and double rooms. Sepcial rates for children. H & C in all rooms, full central heating, colour TV in lounge. Personal service in friendly family atmosphere.

H	✱	SINGLE PER PERSON B&B		DOUBLE FOR 2 PERSONS B&B		🛏	3
P						🚗	
✱		MIN £	MAX £	MIN £	MAX £		OPEN 3-12
		11.50		22.00	22.00		

LLANTRISANT
Map Ref Le5

Small hilltop town in the lower reaches of the Ely Valley, 8 miles from Cardiff. Once the home of Dr William Price, Victorian eccentric who practised cremation when this was still illegal. Best known now for a more prosaic reason - the Royal Mint is here.

Farmhouses

Llwynau Farm Riding Centre   L
Castellau, Llantrisant, Mid Glamorgan, CF7 8LP
Tel: (0443) 229021/403891
Welcome to one of the few remaining 600 year old Welsh Longhouse farmhouses, tastefully modernised to include colour TV in every room, central heating. Retaining many original features, inglenook fireplaces, oak beams etc. Riding lessons, trekking, archery, clay pigeon shooting, outdoor heated swimming pool. Ideally situated for Cardiff or Rhondda Valleys. Brochure on request.

H	✱	SINGLE PER PERSON B&B		DOUBLE FOR 2 PERSONS B&B		🛏	3
P						🚗	
🐴		MIN £	MAX £	MIN £	MAX £		OPEN 1-12
		14.00	14.00	28.00	28.00		

MERTHYR TYDFIL
Map Ref Le2

Once the "iron capital of the world"; the museum in Cyfarthfa Castle, built by the Crawshay family of ironmasters and set in pleasant parkland, tells of those times. Visit the birthplace of hymn-writer Joseph Parry. The narrow-gauge Brecon Mountain Railway makes the most of the town's location on the doorstep of the Brecon Beacons National Park. Excellent road to Cardiff.

CALL Holidays (0792) 645555

Guest Houses

Hillside House
1 Sunnybank, Tirphil, New Tredegar, Gwent NP2 6EL
Tel: (0443) 834460 　L

A small family run guest house situated in the historic Rhymney Valley. Personal attention, relaxed atmosphere and home cooked food, with fresh produce from the garden whenever possible. Vegetarians welcome. Cosy TV lounge, central heating, fitted carpets and double glazing throughout. Car parking. Tea/coffee making facilities. Ideal base for touring South Wales.

P ⚹ ✗	SINGLE PER PERSON B&B		DOUBLE FOR 2 PERSONS B&B		🛏 2
	MIN £	MAX £	MIN £	MAX £	
		12.00		24.00	OPEN 1-12

Rose Cottage
6 Grawen Houses, Cefn Coed,
Merthyr Tydfil,
Mid Glamorgan CF48 2NL
Tel: (0685) 59309 　L

A warm welcome awaits you in our delightful stone cottage overlooking front garden. Very comfortable bedrooms provided with tea and coffee facilities. Dinner available. Situated off main road, this is an ideal place to stay for touring the South Wales valleys and the Brecon Beacons. Highly recommended.

P ✗	SINGLE PER PERSON B&B		DOUBLE FOR 2 PERSONS B&B		🛏 2
	MIN £	MAX £	MIN £	MAX £	
	10.00	10.00	20.00	20.00	OPEN 4-10

NEATH
Map Ref Lb3

Busy town, now emerging as a tourist centre. The Vale of Neath has a wide variety of tourist attractions including an abbey, Penscynor Wildlife Park and Aberdulais Falls and Canal Basin. Superbly located for a choice of activities, surrounded by forests.

Guest Houses

3 Main Road
Cadoxton, Neath, West Glamorgan,
SA10 8AP
Tel: (0639) 639423 　L

Three small welsh cottages converted into unique accommodation. Family run B & B, guest sitting room, colour TV, coffee/tea making facilities in sitting room. One mile Penscynor Wildlife Park, Aberdulais Waterfalls, canal tow path walks. One mile from town centre. Children welcome. Restaurant and public house two doors away.

H P	SINGLE PER PERSON B&B		DOUBLE FOR 2 PERSONS B&B		🛏 3
	MIN £	MAX £	MIN £	MAX £	
	9.50	9.50	19.00	19.00	OPEN 1-12

PONTNEDDFECHAN
Map Ref Lc2

On the edge of the Brecon Beacons National Park, close to Rheola Forest, Ystradfellte and Henrhyd waterfalls (2 of many in the area). A wealth of industrial heritage in the surrounding area.

Guest Houses

Briony Guest House
Ystradfellte Road, Pontneathvaughan,
Glynneath, West Glamorgan
SA11 5UG
Tel: (0639) 720679

Attractive accommodation, ideally situated at the foothills of the Brecon Beacons, overlooking the Vale of Neath within the picturesque waterfall area of Pontneddfechan. Central heating, hot and cold, shaver points, TV, tea/coffee making facilities in rooms. Two doubles, one twin. Special rate for children. Ideal for walking, touring. Fishing, golf, horse riding arranged. Friendly, homely atmosphere.

P	SINGLE PER PERSON B&B		DOUBLE FOR 2 PERSONS B&B		🛏 3
	MIN £	MAX £	MIN £	MAX £	
	10.00	14.00	22.00	22.00	OPEN 3-10

PONTYPOOL
Map Ref Mc3

Industrial town on Torfaen Trail of History, which includes Valley Inheritance Centre, and Big Pit, Blaenavon. Sailing and fishing at Llandegfedd reservoir. Ski Slope.

Farmhouses

Tŷ Isha
Mamhilad, Pontypool, Gwent, NP4 0JE
Tel: (049528) 573 　L

Close to M4/M50. Rural position, peaceful, lovely views. Well equipped comfortable double rooms, bathroom and shower. Central heating, English or continental breakfast in traditional Welsh inglenook living room, supper available on request. Morning tea. Convenient base for walking in Brecon National Park and Usk Valley, Offa's Dyke path. Close to Monmouth/Brecon Canal.

H ⚹ P ✗ 🐕	SINGLE PER PERSON B&B		DOUBLE FOR 2 PERSONS B&B		🛏 2
	MIN £	MAX £	MIN £	MAX £	
	12.00	14.00	24.00	28.00	OPEN 1-12

WALES It's magic

BRECON MOUNTAIN RAILWAY

WE'RE HERE TO HELP

When you arrive in Wales, call in at a Tourist Information Centre. Staff will be only too pleased to assist with enquiries and offer advice on where to go and what to see both locally and further afield, suggest scenic routes and so on. "What's On" events information will also be available, together with a wide range of tourist literature including all Wales Tourist Board publications.

Our network of over 90 centres cover all major resorts, towns and key points in Wales.

TOURIST INFORMATION CENTRES

NORTH WALES

OPEN ALL YEAR

Beddgelert, Gwynedd LL55 4YA
The National Trust Information Point,
Llewelyn Cottage
Tel: (076686) 293

Caernarfon, Gwynedd LL55 2PB
Wales Tourist Information Centre,
Oriel Pendeitsh
Tel: (0286) 672232 BB BABA

Colwyn Bay, Clwyd LL29 8BU
Wales Tourist Information Centre/
Colwyn Borough Council,
Station Road
Tel: (0492) 530478 BB BABA

Holyhead, Gwynedd LL65 1DR
Wales Tourist Information Centre,
Marine Square, Salt Island Approach
Tel: (0407) 2622 BB BABA

Llandudno, Gwynedd LL30 2YU
Wales Tourist Information Centre,
Chapel Street
Tel: (0492) 76413 BB BABA

Llanfair P.G., Gwynedd LL61 5UJ
Wales Tourist Information Centre,
Station Site
Tel: (0248) 713177 BB BABA

Llangollen, Clwyd LL20 5PD
Wales Tourist Information Centre,
Town Hall
Tel: (0978) 860828 BB BABA

Porthmadog, Gwynedd LL49 9LP
Wales Tourist Information Centre,
High Street
Tel: (0766) 512981 BB BABA

Rhyl, Clwyd LL18 5NL
Wales Tourist Information Centre/
Rhuddlan Borough Council,
Central Promenade
Tel: (0745) 355068 BB BABA

Ruthin, Clwyd LL15 1BB
Wales Tourist Information Centre,
Craft Centre
Tel: (08242) 3992 BB BABA

OPEN SUMMER ONLY

Abersoch, Gwynedd
Village Hall
Tel: (075881) 2929

Bangor, Gwynedd LL57 2TL
Wales Tourist Information Centre,
Theatr Gwynedd,
Deiniol Road
Tel: (0248) 352786 BB BABA

Betws y Coed, Gwynedd LL24 0AH
Wales Tourist Information Centre/
Snowdonia National Park,
Royal Oak Stables
Tel: (06902) 426/665 BB BABA

Colwyn Bay, Clwyd
Colwyn Borough Council,
Coach Park Information Point,
Princes Drive
Tel: (0492) 534432

Colwyn Bay, Clwyd
Colwyn Borough Council/
Tourist Information Centre,
The Promenade, Rhos On Sea,
Tel: (0492) 48778 BB

Conwy, Gwynedd
Wales Tourist Information Centre,
Conwy Castle Visitor Centre
Tel: (0492) 592248 BB BABA

Criccieth, Gwynedd LL52 0EY
Criccieth Trade & Tourism Association,
The Sweet Shop, 47 High Street
Tel: (0766) 523303

Halkyn, Clwyd CH8 8DF
Wales Tourist Information Centre,
Little Chef Services A55
Tel: (0352) 780144 BB BABA

Llanberis, Gwynedd LL55 4UB
Wales Tourist Information Centre,
Amgueddfa'r Gogledd/Museum of the North
Tel: (0286) 870765 BB BABA

Mold, Clwyd CH7 1AB
Wales Tourist Information Centre,
Mold Town Council, Town Hall
Tel: (0352) 59331 BB BABA

Prestatyn, Clwyd LL19 9LH
Wales Tourist Information Centre,
Scala Cinema
Tel: (07456) 4365 BB BABA

Pwllheli, Gwynedd LL53 6HE
Wales Tourist Information Centre,
Y Maes
Tel: (075861) 3000 BB BABA

Wrexham, Clwyd LL12 7AG
Wales Tourist Information Centre,
Memorial Hall
Tel: (0978) 357845

TOURIST INFORMATION ON NORTH WALES ALSO AVAILABLE AT

Chester, Cheshire CH1 2HF
Town Hall, Northgate Street
Tel: (0244) 313126/317962/324324
BB BABA

Manchester, M22 5NY
Manchester International Airport,
International Airways Hall,
Greater Manchester
Tel: (061) 436 3344
BB BABA

Oswestry, Salop
Mile End Services
Tel: (0691) 662488
BB BABA

Sandbach, Cheshire CW11 0TD
Sandbach Service Area,
M6 Northbound
Tel: (0270) 760460
BB BABA

MID WALES
OPEN ALL YEAR

Aberystwyth, Dyfed SY23 2AR
Ceredigion District Council Information
Centre, Terrace Road
Tel: (0970) 612125/611955
BB BABA

Knighton, Powys LD7 1EW
Offa's Dyke Association Information
Centre, The Old School
Tel: (0547) 528753 BABA

Llandrindod Wells, Powys LD1 6AA
Radnor District Council/Wales Tourist
Board Information Centre
Tel: (0597) 2600/822600 BB BABA

Machynlleth, Powys SY20 8EE
Wales Tourist Information Centre,
Canolfan Owain Glyndwr
Tel: (0654) 2401/702401 BB BABA

Welshpool, Powys SY21 7DD
Wales Tourist Information Centre,
Vicarage Gardens Car Park
Tel: (0938) 552043 BB BABA

OPEN SUMMER ONLY

Aberaeron, Dyfed SA46 0BT
Ceredigion District Council Information
Centre, The Harbour
Tel: (0545) 570602 BB BABA

Aberdovey, Gwynedd LL35 0EO
Snowdonia National Park Information
Centre, The Wharf
Tel: (0654) 72321 BB BABA

Bala, Gwynedd LL23 7AB
Snowdonia National Park Information
Centre, High Street
Tel: (0678) 520367 BB BABA

Barmouth, Gwynedd LL42 1LU
Barmouth Tourist Information Centre,
The Old Library
Tel: (0341) 280787 BB BABA

Blaenau Ffestiniog,
Gwynedd LL41 3HD
Snowdonia National Park Information
Centre, High Street
Tel: (0766) 830360 BABA

Builth Wells, Powys LD2 3BL
Builth Wells Tourist Information Centre,
Groe Car Park
Tel: (0982) 553307 BB BABA

Cardigan, Dyfed SA43 1JY
Ceredigion District Council Information
Centre, Theatre Mwldan, Bath House Road
Tel: (0239) 613230

Corris, Gwynedd SY20 9RF
Corris Craft Centre
Tel: (0654) 244 BB BABA

Dolgellau, Gwynedd LL40 1LF
Snowdonia National Park Information
Centre, The Bridge
Tel: (0341) 422888 BB BABA

Elan Valley, Powys LD6 2YA
Elan Valley Visitor Centre
Tel: (0597) 810898 BB BABA

Harlech, Gwynedd LL46 2YA
Snowdonia National Park Information
Centre, High Street
Tel: (0766) 780658 BB BABA

Llanfyllin, Powys SY22 5DB
Llanfyllin Tourist Information Centre,
High Street
Tel: (069184) 8868 BB BABA

Llanidloes, Powys SY18 6ES
Llanidloes Tourist Information Centre,
Longbridge Street
Tel: (05512) 2605 BB BABA

Newtown, Powys SY16 2PW
Newtown Tourist Information Centre,
Centre Car Park
Tel: (0686) 625580

New Quay, Dyfed SA45 9NZ
Ceredigion District Council Information
Centre, Church Street
Tel: (0545) 560865 BB BABA

Presteigne, Powys
Presteigne Tourist Information Centre,
Market Hall
Tel: (0544) 260193 BB BABA

Rhayader, Powys LD6 5AB
Rhayader Tourist Information Centre,
The Old Swan
Tel: (0597) 810591 BB BABA

Tywyn, Gwynedd LL36 9AD
Tywyn Tourist Information Centre,
High Street
Tel: (0654) 710070 BB BABA

SOUTH WALES
OPEN ALL YEAR

Bagle Brook, West Glamorgan
SA12 8DS
Wales Tourist Information Centre,
Beefeater Restaurant,
Sunnycroft Road, Baglan
Tel: (0639) 823049 BB BABA
(written and telephone enquiries on the
whole of South Wales)

Brecon, Powys LD3 8ER
Brecon Beacons National Park Centre,
The Mountain Centre, Libanus
Tel: (0874) 3366

Cardiff, South Glamorgan CF1 2EE
Wales Tourist Information Centre,
8-14 Bridge Street
Tel: (0222) 227281 BB BABA

Merthyr Tydfil, Mid Glamorgan
CF47 8AU
Wales Tourist Information Centre,
14a Glebeland Street
Tel: (0685) 79884 BB BABA

Newport, Gwent NP9 1HZ
Wales Tourist Information Centre,
Newport Museum & Art Gallery,
John Frost Square
Tel: (0633) 842962 BB BABA

Pont Abraham, Dyfed SA4 1FP
Wales Tourist Information Centre,
Pont Abraham Services,
Junction 49, M4, Nr. Cross Hands
Tel: (0792) 883838 BB BABA

Pontypridd, Mid Glamorgan CF37 3PE
Pontypridd Historical & Cultural Centre,
The Old Bridge
Tel: (0443) 402077 BB BABA

Sarn, Mid Glamorgan CF32 9SY
Wales Tourist Information Centre,
Sarn Park Services,
Junction 36, M4 Nr. Bridgend
Tel: (0656) 654906 BB BABA

Swansea, West Glamorgan SA1 3QN
Tourist Information Centre,
Singleton Street
Tel: (0792) 468321 BB BABA

Tredegar, Gwent
Wales Tourist Information Centre,
Bryn Bach Country Park
Tel: (0495) 711816 BB BABA

OPEN SUMMER ONLY

Abercraf, Powys
Dan Yr Ogof Showcaves,
Upper Swansea Valley
Tel: (0639) 730284

Aberdulais, West Glamorgan SA10 8ED
Wales Tourist Information Centre,
Aberdulais Basin, Nr. Neath
Tel: (0639) 633531 BB BABA

Abergavenny, Gwent NP7 5HH
Wales Tourist Board &
Brecon Beacons National Park Information
Centre, Swan Meadow, Cross Street
Tel: (0873) 77588 BB BABA

Barry, South Glamorgan CF6 8TT
Wales Tourist Information Centre,
The Promenade, Barry Island
Tel: (0446) 747171 BB BABA

Blaenavon, Gwent NP4 9XP
Wales Tourist Information Centre,
Big Bit Mining Museum
Tel: (0495) 790122 BB BABA

Brecon, Powys, LD3 7DE
Wales Tourist Information Centre,
Cattle Market Car Park
Tel: (0874) 2485 BB BABA

Brecon, Powys LD3 7DE
Brecon Beacons National Park Centre,
Watton Mount
Tel: (0874) 4437

Broad Haven, Dyfed SA62 3JH
Pembrokeshire Coast National Park Centre,
Car Park
Tel: (043783) 412

Caerphilly, Mid Glamorgan CF8 1AA
Wales Tourist Information Centre,
Old Police Station, Park Lane
Tel: (0222) 851378 BB BABA

Carmarthen, Dyfed SA31 3AQ
Wales Tourist Information Centre,
Lammas Street
Tel: (0267) 231557 BB BABA

Chepstow, Gwent NP6 5LH
Wales Tourist Information Centre,
The Gatehouse, High Street
Tel: (02912) 3772 BB BABA

Cwmcarn, Gwent SA65 9HL
Wales Tourist Information Centre,
Cymcarn Forest Drive, Visitor Centre,
Nr. Cross Keys
Tel: (0495) 272001 BB BABA

Fishguard, Dyfed SA65 9HL
Wales Tourist Information Centre,
4 Hamilton Street
Tel: (0348) 873484 BB BABA

Haverfordwest, Dyfed SA62 6SD
Wales Tourist Board and
Pembrokeshire Coast National Park
Information Centre, 40 High Street
Tel: (0437) 763110 BB BABA

Hay on Wye, Powys HR3 5AE
Tourist Information Centre,
The Car Park
Tel: (0497) 820144

Kilgetty, Dyfed SA68 0YA
Wales Tourist Board and
Pembrokeshire Coast National Park
Information Centre,
Kingsmoor Common
Tel: (0834) 813672 BB BABA

Llandovery, Dyfed SA20 0AB
Wales Tourist Board and
Brecon Beacons National Park Information
Centre, Broad Street
Tel: (0550) 20693 BB BABA

Monmouth, Gwent NP5 3BX
Wales Tourist Information Centre,
National Trust Shop, Church Street
Tel: (0600) 3899 BB BABA

Newcastle Emlyn, Dyfed SA83 9AE
Wales Tourist Board Information Centre,
Market Hall
Tel: (0239) 711333 BB BABA

Newport, Dyfed SA42 0SY
Pembrokeshire Coast National Park Centre,
East Street
Tel: (0239) 820912

Pembroke, Dyfed
Pembrokeshire Coast National Park Centre,
Drill Hall
Tel: (0646) 682148

Pen y Cae, West Glamorgan SA9 1GL
Craig y Nos Country Park,
Swansea Valley
Tel: (0639) 730395

Pont Nedd Fechan,
West Glamorgan SA11 5NR
Wales Tourist Information Centre,
Nr. Glynneath
Tel: (0639) 721795 BB BABA

Porthcawl, Mid Glamorgan CF36 3DT
Wales Tourist Information Centre,
The Old Police Station, John Street
Tel: (065671) 6639 BB BABA

Saundersfoot, Dyfed SA69 9HE
Tourist Information Centre,
The Harbour
Tel: (0834) 811411

St. David's, Dyfed SA62 6SB
Pembrokeshire Coast National Park Centre,
City Hall
Tel: (0437) 720392

Swansea, West Glamorgan SA3 4DQ
Tourist Information Centre,
Oystermouth Square, Mumbles
Tel: (0792) 361302 BB BABA

Tenby, Dyfed SA70 8AP
Tourist Information Centre,
The Norton
Tel: (0834) 2402

Tintern, Gwent NP6 8TE
Wales Tourist Information Centre,
Abbey Entrance,
Tintern Abbey
Tel: (0291) 689431 BB BABA

BRITISH TOURIST AUTHORITY OVERSEAS OFFICES

Your enquiries will be welcome at the offices of the British Tourist Authority in the following countries:

AUSTRALIA

British Tourist Authority, 4th Floor,
171 Clarence Stret, Sydney, NSW 2000.
Tel: (02) 298627
Fax: (02) 2821414

BELGIUM

British Tourist Authority, Rue de la Montagne,
Bergstraat 52, B2-1000 Brussels.
Tel: 02/511 43 90
Telex: 23108 GBRAIL B

BRAZIL

British Tourist Authority, Avenida Nilo Pecanha
50 – Conj. 2213, Edificio de Paoli, 20040 Rio
de Janeiro – RJ.
Tel: 220 1187
Telex: (21) 34031 IPCOPR (attn. BTA)

CANADA

British Tourist Authority,
94 Cumberland Street, Suite 600, Toronto,
Ontario, M5R 3N3.
Tel: (416) 925 6326 BRITOURIST TOR
Fax: (416) 9612175

DENMARK

British Tourist Authority, Mantergade 3,
1116 Copenhagen K.
Tel: 01 1207 93
Telex: 15370 ETACPH DK

FRANCE

British Tourist Authority,
63 rue Pierre-Charron, 75008 Paris.
Tel: 42 89 11 11
Telex: TAGBAND 649 138 F MINITEL:
3616 code OTGB

GERMANY

British Tourist Authority, Taunusstraße,
52-60, 6000 Frankfurt 1.
Tel: 069-23 80 711
Telex: 4185 209 BTA D
Fax: 069-2380717 Btx: 22 00 20

HONG KONG

British Tourist Authority, BTA, Suite 903,
1 Hysan Avenue, Causeway Bay,
Hong Kong.
Tel: 5-764366 Telex: 80201 BTAHK
Fax: 5-8950049

IRELAND

British Tourist Authority, 123 Lower Baggot
Street, Dublin 2.
Tel: 614188 Telex: 91419

ITALY

British Tourist Authority, Corsa Vittorio
Emanuele II No 337,00186 Rome.
Tel: 654 0821 or 554 0464
Telex: 622690 BTA ROM I

JAPAN AND KOREA

British Tourist Authority, 246 Tokyo Club Bldg,
3-2-6 Kasumigaseki, Chiyoda-KU, Tokyo 100.
Tel: (03) 581 3603 or (03) 581 3604
Telex: 2223235 Fax: (03) 581 5797.
Installation of new telephone system may
affect number.

NETHERLANDS

British Tourist Authority, Aurora
Gebouw (5th Floor), Stadhouderskade 2,
1054 ES Amsterdam.
Tel: 020-85 50 51 Telex: ETABR NL
Fax: 020-186868

NEW ZEALAND

British Tourist Authority, Third Floor, Dilworth
Building, Corner Queen & Customs Streets,
Auckland 1.
Tel: (09) 3031 446
Fax: (09) 776 965

NORWAY

British Tourist Authority, FR, Nansens Plass 9,
0160 Oslo 1 (Visitors only),
Postboks 1554, Vika, 0117 Oslo 1 (Post only).
Tel: (2) 41 18 49
Telex: 76748 BTA N
Fax: 2 33 53 79

SINGAPORE

British Tourist Authority,
24 Raffles Place, 17-04 Clifford Centre,
Singapore 0104.
Tel: 5352966, 5352967 (24 hr ansaphone)
Telex: RS28493 BTA 5IN
Fax: 5344703

SPAIN

British Tourist Authority, BTA, Torre de Madrid
6ª of 7, Pza España 18, 28008, Madrid.
Tel: 241 13 96 Telex: 49295 M BTA E

SWEDEN

British Tourist Authority, Box 7293, S-103 90
Stockholm (post only), Malmskillnadsgatan 42,
1st floor (Visitors only).
Tel: 08-21 24 44
Telex: 11537 BTA S

SWITZERLAND

British Tourist Authority, Limmatquai 78,
CH-8001 Zurich.
Tel: 01/47 42 77/97
Telex: (HS) 817832 BTA CH
Fax: 01/251 44 56

UNITED STATES OF AMERICA

CHICAGO – British Tourist Authority,
875 N Michigan Avenue, Chicago, IL 60611.
Tel: (312) 787 0490
Fax: (312) 787 7746

DALLAS – British Tourist Authority,
Cedar Maple Plaza, Suite 240, 2305, Cedar
Springs Road, Dallas, TX 75201.
Tel: (214) 720 4040
Fax: (214) 871 2665

LOS ANGELES – British Tourist Authority,
Room 450, 350 South Figueroa Street,
Los Angeles, CA 90071.
Tel: (213) 628 3525
Telex: 466695 BTA LSA CI
Fax: (213) 687 6621

NEW YORK – British Tourist Authority,
40 West 57th Street, New York,
NY 10019-4001.
Tel: (212) 581 4700
Telex: 237798
Fax: (212) 265 0649

PRONUNCIATION OF WELSH

There are some sounds in spoken Welsh which are very different from their English equivalents. The following is a basic guide:

WELSH			ENGLISH EQUIVALENT
c	cath = *cat*		cat (never as in receive)
ch	chwaer = *sister*		loch
dd	yn dda = *good*		them
f	y fam = *the mother*		of
ff	ffenestr = *window*		off
g	gardd = *garden*		garden (never as in George)
h	het = *hat*		hat (never silent as in honest)
ll	llaw = *hand*		There is no equivalent sound. Place the tongue on the upper roof of the mouth near the upper teeth, ready to pronounce l; then blow rather than voice the l
th	byth = *ever*		Three (never as in English the)

The vowels in Welsh are a e i o u w y; all except 'y' can be long or short:

long a	tad *father*	similar to England hard
short a	mam *mother*	similar to England ham
long e	hen *old*	similar to English sane
short e	pen *head*	similar to English ten
long i	mis *month*	similar to English geese
short i	prin *scarce*	similar to English tin
long o	môr *sea*	similar to English more
short o	ffon *walking stick*	similar to English fond
long w	sŵn *sound*	similar to English moon
short w	gwn *gun*	similar to English look

y has two sounds:

1 – CLEAR
dyn *man*, — a long 'ee' sound almost like English geese

cyn *before*, — a short 'i' sound almost like English tin

2 – OBSCURE
something like the sound in English run
Examples:
y *the*; yn *in*; dynion *men*.

It is well to remember that in Welsh the accent usually falls on the last-syllable-but-one of a word, e.g. cadair *chair*.

A FEW GREETINGS

Bore da	Good morning
Dydd da	Good day
Prynhawn da	Good afternoon
Noswaith dda	Good evening
Nos da	Good night
Sut mae?	How are you
Hwyl	Cheers
Diolch	Thanks
Diolch yn fawr iawn	Thanks very much
Croeso	Welcome
Croeso i Gymru	Welcome to Wales
Da	Good
Da iawn	Very good
Iechyd da!	Good health

USEFUL TRANSLATIONS

Aber	Estuary
Llan	Church
Caer	Fort
Mynydd	Mountain
Afon	River
Pont	Bridge
Castell	Castle

Tourism Wales
The Wales Tourist Board is the statutory authority for the promotion and development of Tourism in Wales. For further information about the Board and its services please write to:-
Wales Tourist Board, Department H.C.T.A., Davis Street, Cardiff CF1 2FU

BOOKING CONDITIONS

1. Payment — A deposit of £25 per person per week is required on bookings or 20% of the total cost when booking a self catering unit or caravan. if required, your premium for holiday cancellation insurance will be added to the sum required as a deposit. The balance is payable 42 days prior to departure. If the booking is made within 42 days of departure full payment is required at that time.

2. Cancellation by You — Cancellation of your holiday may be made at any time by the person who signed the booking form. It must be submitted through the office at which the booking was made. Your deposit will be retained to cover our administration costs, and there will be additional cancellation charges in accordance with the following scale.

Cancellation notice received in writing before departure	Cancellation Charge
More than 42 days (6 weeks)	Deposit
29-42 days	30%
15-28 days	45%
1-14 days	60%
Departure date or after	100%

NB: If you have taken our Holiday Insurance through HWL, you may be able to recover these amounts subject to the reason for cancelling being covered under the policy.

3. Alteration or Cancellation by Us. — Circumstances may arise where we have no alternative but to cancel your holiday. If such an exceptional situation should occur, we will make a complete refund to you or offer a suitable alternative holiday.

In the event that we have to cancel your holiday at any time, we will be liable only for any money paid to us at the time of cancellation. Holidays Wales Limited accepts no further liability whatsoever.

4. VAT — is included in all prices at the current rate of 15%, where applicable. In the event of any changes in the VAT regulations, these will be passed on to the client (only applicable if VAT has been included in the price).

5. Outside Agencies — All bookings for accommodation and other facilities are made by us as agents for the establishment concerned upon the understanding that we shall not accept any liability whatsoever for any injury, loss, damage, accident or delay caused by or in any way connected with the acts of defaults of any Company or person engaged in carrying out the bookings or or any proprietor or servant, or any liability whatsoever arising in any way directly or indirectly in connection with the making of the booking.

6. Holidays Wales Limited cannot accept liability for losses, additional expenses or any claim whatsoever due to changes in accommodation establishment, sickness, weather, strikes or any other cause. All such losses, additional expenses or claims will be borne by the client.

Note: Bookings other than through Holiday Wales Limited are subject to the operator's own booking conditions.

HOLIDAY INSURANCE

Holiday Insurance brings peace of mind and we recommend that everyone in your party takes advantage of the special scheme we have arranged through **Accident & General Ltd,** with **Municipal General Insurance Ltd.** A full Statement of cover will be sent to you with your confirmation of booking which also includes claims notification procedure. If a specimen copy of this statement is required prior to booking, we will be happy to send one on request.

Premiums per person which must be included with the deposit:

	Serviced Accommodation	Self Catering Accommodation
Up to 3 nights	£3.75	£2.75
Up to 7 nights	£4.50	£3.50
Up to 14 nights	£6.00	£5.00
Each additional week	£3.00	£3.00

Once the booking is accepted, no refund of premium can be allowed. The cover and limits are:
1. Cancellation and curtailment up to holiday cost (excluding insurance premium).
2. Personal accident up to £5,000.
3. Personal baggage up to £1,000 (single article limit £200/valuables limit £200).
4. Personal money up to £200.
5. Personal liability up to £500,000.

Claims under sections 1, 3 and 4 are subject to an excess of £15.00 except loss of deposit where no deduction is made.

ABERGLASLYN PASS, SNOWDONIA

WALES – BED & BREAKFAST GUIDE 1990
BOOKING FORM

Send this booking form to the accommodation of your choice
Note to applicants and establishments using this form.
It must be clearly understood that the Wales Tourist Board is in no way connected with the booking and accepts no liability whatsoever in any way connected with, arising out of the booking, or the use of this form. In the case of direct bookings applicants (or their agents as the case may be) should check direct with operators as to any Terms of Booking.

Booking Ref.

Client's Name and Address (or Agent's Stamp).

Tel No:

Details of Party

Mr/Mrs Miss	Initials	Surname	Age if Under 16

Total Number in party ☐   Number of children ☐
Number of adults ☐   Number of children (under 2) ☐
Pets ☐

Accommodation

Accommodation name_____
Accommodation address_____

Date of arrival __/__/__   Length of stay ☐ Nights

Type of accommodation required

HOTELS, MOTELS, GUEST HOUSES AND FARMHOUSES
Enter number in box.

Single room(s)	Double-bedded room(s)	Twin-bedded room(s)	Family room(s)
With bath/shower ☐	With bath/shower ☐	With bath/shower ☐	With bath/shower ☐
Without bath ☐	Without bath ☐	Without bath ☐	Without bath ☐

Special Requirements_____

Payment

Payment Method ☐ Cheque ☐ Postal Order ☐
Cheque/Postal Order Number [   ]

If you wish to pay by credit card, please tick the appropriate box and enter your account number below.

Please check that the establishment of your choice accepts your particular credit card.

☐ American Express   ☐ Diners Card
☐ Access   ☐ Visa

[ ][ ][ ][ ][ ][ ][ ][ ][ ][ ][ ][ ][ ][ ][ ][ ]

Note to Travel Agents:
Unfortunately we are unable to accept ABTA Credit Card Vouchers.

Basic Cost £ [   ]
Supplements £ [   ]
Holiday Insurance £ [   ]
Total Cost £ [   ]
Less Deposit £ [   ]
Balance Payable £ [   ]

I agree to the terms of the Booking Conditions of the operators concerned as advised to me at the time of booking.

I enclose a deposit of £ [   ]

Signed_____ Date_____

Telephone:
0792 645588 Agents
0792 645555 Holidaymakers

BOOKING FORM  1990 HOLIDAYS

PO BOX 40, SWANSEA, WEST GLAMORGAN, SA1 1PX

NOTE: This booking form to only be used for holidays booked through Holiday Wales Reservation Service

Client Name & Address (or Agents stamp)

Tel No: _____

Details of Party

Mr/Mrs Miss	Initials	Surname	Age if Under 16

Total Number in Party ☐   Number of Children ☐
Number of Adults ☐   Number of Children (under 2) ☐
Pets ☐

Accommodation

Accommodation Name _____
Accommodation location _____
Date of Arrival __/__/__   Length of Stay ____ Nights

Mark NO in this box if holiday insurance is not required ☐

Type of Accommodation Required

Hotels, Motels, Guest Houses and Farmhouses (Enter number in box)

SINGLE ROOM(S)   DOUBLE-BEDDED ROOM(S)
With bath/shower ☐   With bath/shower ☐
Without bath ☐   Without bath ☐
TWIN-BEDDED ROOM(S)   FAMILY ROOM(S)
With bath/showwer ☐   With bath/shower ☐
Without bath ☐   Without bath ☐

Self-Catering

Type of Units _____
Sleeping _____
No. of Units Required ☐

Supplements (where applicable)
Linen hire ☐   T.V. ☐ _____

Special Requirements _____

Rail Tickets

Tickets required No. ADULTS ☐ No. CHILDREN 5-15 years ☐
Travelling via London YES ☐ NO ☐
Travelling from _____ station
           in _____ county
Travelling to _____ station
           in _____ county

Touring Holidays (Pre-Booked)

	Night	Hotel	Date of Arrival	Nights
1				
2				
3				
4				
5				
6				

Payment Method   Cheque ☐   Postal Order ☐
Cheque/Postal Order Number _____

If you wish to pay by credit card, please tick the appropriate boxes, enter your account number and sign below.
I authorise Holidays Wales Ltd. to charge to my account
☐ Full cost of holiday now   ☐ or my initial payment only
Please tick appropriate box.
☐ Access ☐ VISA (No other credit cards are acceptable)
No. ☐☐☐☐☐☐☐☐☐☐☐☐☐☐
Card Holder's Name
Card Holder's Signature _____

Basic Cost	£
Supplements	£
Holiday Insurance	£
Total Cost	£
Less Deposit (plus Insurance)	£
Balance Payable	£

I understand that the BALANCE must be received at least 42 days before the holiday is due to start. I have read the conditions as of booking and agree on behalf of all persons named above to abide by these conditions.

Signed _____ Date _____

RHUDDLAN CASTLE

NEVER GO WITHOUT A GUIDE

If you're still undecided on a place to stay, or you want to know more about an area, then take a look at our colourful, informative range of publications. Our guides are designed to help you get the most out of your holiday in Wales, offering plenty of useful information and advice. To order any of the publications listed simply write, enclosing the appropriate remittance in the form of a cheque, postal/money order to:

Wales Tourist Board, Dept CB, Davis Street, Cardiff CF1 2FU

WALES: HOTELS AND GUEST HOUSES GUIDE 1990 – £2.95

A comprehensive guide to over 400 hotels, guest houses and farmhouses in Wales.

WALES: SELF-CATERING GUIDE 1990 – £2.75

Guide to over 350 self-catering properties in Wales including cottages, flats and chalets, caravan holiday home parks and touring caravan and camping parks.

WALES: BED AND BREAKFAST GUIDE 1990 – £2.50

Guide to budget accommodation in Wales, featuring over 600 hotels, guest houses and farmhouses, all with one thing in common — they offer bed and breakfast at an all inclusive price of £14.00 or under per person per night.

All publications include 5 mile to the inch full colour maps of Wales.

WALES TOURIST MAP – £1.45

A real best-seller. Detailed 5 mile/1 inch scale, also includes a wealth of tourist information, town plans, suggested tours and information centres.

WALES: CASTLES AND HISTORIC PLACES – £6.95

This full colour guide is a joint publication produced by the Wales Tourist Board and Cadw: Welsh Historic Monuments. More than 140 sites are covered in the extensive gazetteer, including castles, abbeys, country houses, Roman and prehistoric remains — all regularly open to the public. An historic introduction sets the scene, and 12 pages of maps help visitors to plan their routes.

MOUNTAIN BIKING NEAR LLANWRTYD WELLS

VIDEOS

Three videos are available.

THE WONDER OF WALES VIDEO (VHS)* – £10.50

A new 24 minute video encapsulating the breathtaking beauty and myriad attractions of Wales. Narrated by Siân Phillips, the film features prominently the cultural and architectural heritage of Wales and includes the most recent visitor attractions in the Principality.

HERITAGE OF A NATION VIDEO (VHS/BETA)* – £10.00

Narrated by Richard Burton, this 25 minute video presents the Heritage of Wales from prehistoric times through to the present day. Wales as a holiday country is vividly depicted with some memorable sequences.

SOUTH WALES VALLEYS VIDEO (VHS/BETA)* – £10.00

"The South Wales Valleys" (approx 15 minutes) is a lively short presentation of the culture and heritage of the area.

POSTERS

North Wales scenes	£1.30
Rhosili Beach, Gower	£1.30
Tal-y-Llyn	£1.30
Llangrannog Beach	£1.20
Great Little Trains	£1.30
Coracle Fisherman	£1.20
Mid Wales scenes	£1.30
Pembrokeshire Coast	£1.30
South Wales scenes	£1.30

NOTE: All prices quoted include postage and packaging.

*Please indicate clearly video format required when ordering.

PLACES	PAGE						
Aberaeron	59	Goodwick	79	Nefyn	32		
Aberdaron	30	Harlech	56	New Quay	63		
Aberdovey	52	Haverfordwest	80	New Radnor	74		
Abergavenny	106	Hay-on-Wye	95	Newcastle Emlyn	90		
Abergele	24	Holyhead	20	Newport (Dyfed)	81		
Abersoch	30	Holywell	45	Newport (Gwent)	108		
Aberystwyth	59	Kidwelly	89	Newtown	68		
Amlwch	19	Lake Vyrnwy	66	Neyland	82		
Bala	52	Lampeter	62	Northop	47		
Bangor	35	Laugharne	89	Oxwich	98		
Barmouth	53	Little Haven	80	Parkmill	98		
Beaumaris	19	Llan Ffestiniog	40	Pembroke	82		
Beddgelert	35	Llanarth	62	Penarth	103		
Bethesda	36	Llanberis	40	Pencader	91		
Betws Garmon	36	Llanbrynmair	66	Penmaenmawr	42		
Betws-y-Coed	36	LLandeilo	89	Penybontfawr	47		
Blaenau Ffestiniog	38	Llandinam	66	Pont Nedd Fechan	112		
Borth	61	Llandovery	89	Pontrhydfendigaid	64		
Brecon	93	Llandrillo	45	Pontypool	112		
Bridgend	101	Llandrindod Wells	72	Port Talbot	103		
Broad Haven	77	Llandudno	26	Porthcawl	104		
Brynsiencyn	19	Llandysul	63	Porthmadog	32		
Builth Wells	72	Llanelli	90	Prestatyn	28		
Burry Port	88	Llanerchymedd	20	Presteigne	74		
Caerleon	106	Llanfair Caereinion	66	Pumsaint	91		
Caernarfon	38	Llanfair P.G.	21	Pwllheli	33		
Caerphilly	111	Llanfairfechan	41	Reynoldston	98		
Capel Curig	40	Llanfyllin	67	Rhayader	74		
Cardiff	101	Llangefni	21	Rhos-on-Sea	28		
Cardigan	61	Llangollen	45	Rhoscolyn	22		
Carmarthen	88	Llangorse	95	Rhosili	99		
Cemaes Bay	20	Llangrannog	63	Rhyl	28		
Chepstow	107	Llangurig	67	Ruthin	48		
Colwyn Bay	24	Llangynidr	95	Saundersfoot	83		
Conwy	25	Llanidloes	67	Solva	83		
Corwen	44	Llanmadoc	98	Southgate	99		
Cowbridge	102	Llanpumsaint	90	St. Asaph	48		
Criccieth	31	Llanrhaeadr Ym Mochnant	47	St. Brides Major	104		
Crickhowell	95	Llanrwst	41	St. Clear's	91		
Croes-Goch	77	Llantrisant	111	St. David's	84		
Crymych	77	Llantwit Major	103	St. Nicholas	85		
Cwmbran	111	Llanwrtyd Wells	73	Swansea	99		
Dale	78	Machynlleth	67	Tal-y-Llyn	56		
Denbigh	44	Maenclochog	80	Talgarth	96		
Dinas Cross	78	Marloes	81	Talybont on Usk	96		
Dinas Mawddwy	54	Meifod	68	Tenby	85		
Dolgellau	54	Menai Bridge	21	Tintern	108		
Dyffryn Ardudwy	55	Merthyr Tydfil	112	Trawsfynydd	56		
Ebbw Vale	111	Milford Haven	81	Trearddur Bay	22		
Erwood	72	Mold	47	Trefriw	42		
Fairbourne	55	Monmouth	107	Tregaron	64		
Fishguard	78	Montgomery	68	Tywyn	57		
Flint	44	Morfa Nefyn	31	Usk	109		
Freshwater East	79	Mumbles	98	Valley	22		
Glasbury-on-Wye	95	Mynachlog-Ddu	81	Welshpool	69		
Glyn Ceiriog	44	Narberth	81	Whitland	91		
Glynyfrdwy	45	Neath	112	Wrexham	49		

MAPS OF WALES

The maps which follow divide Wales into twelve sections, each with a slight overlap. The grid overlaying each map will help you find the town or village of your choice for against the entry of each of them in this book is a reference number indicating the section of map and grid square. Simply turn up the appropriate map sheet, look for the grid square quoted in the code and pick out the place itself in that square. The maps are at 5 miles or 8 kilometres to one inch scale.

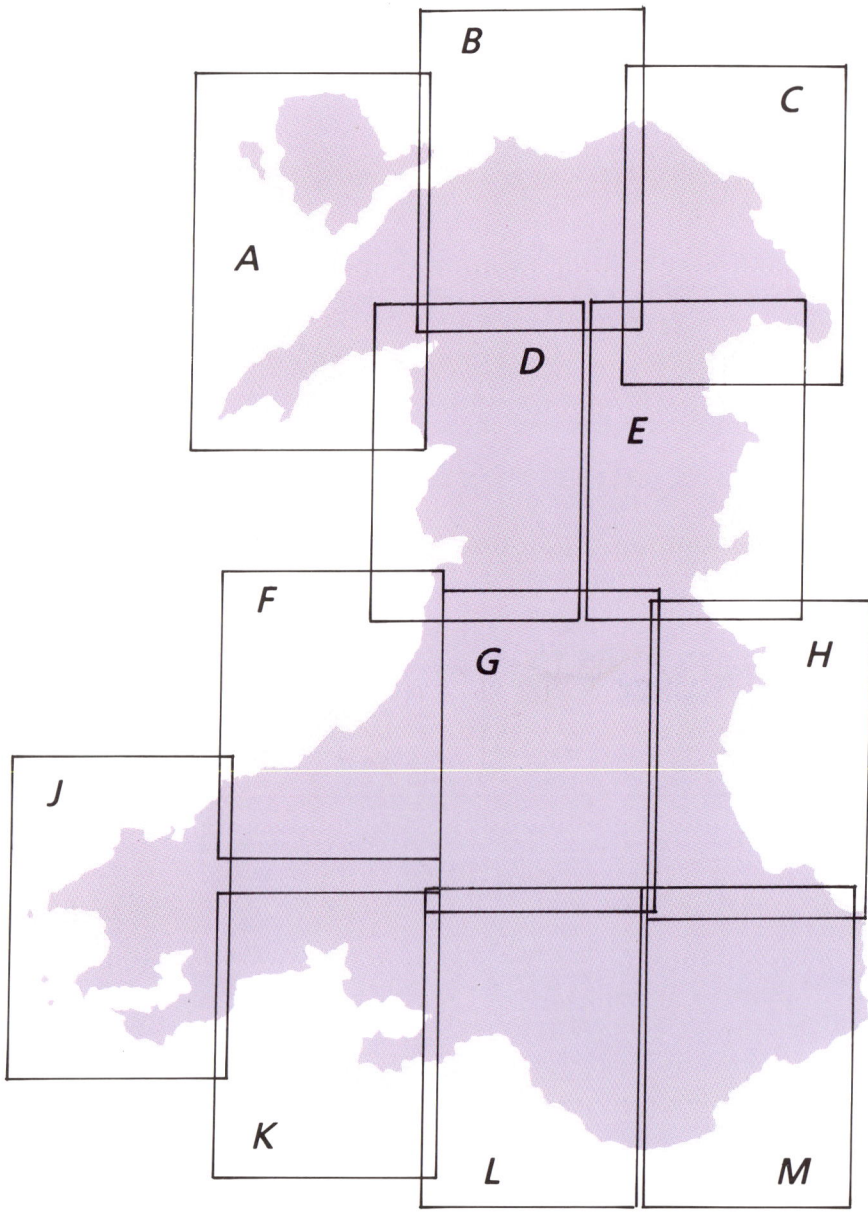

Map A

Map B

Map C

Map D

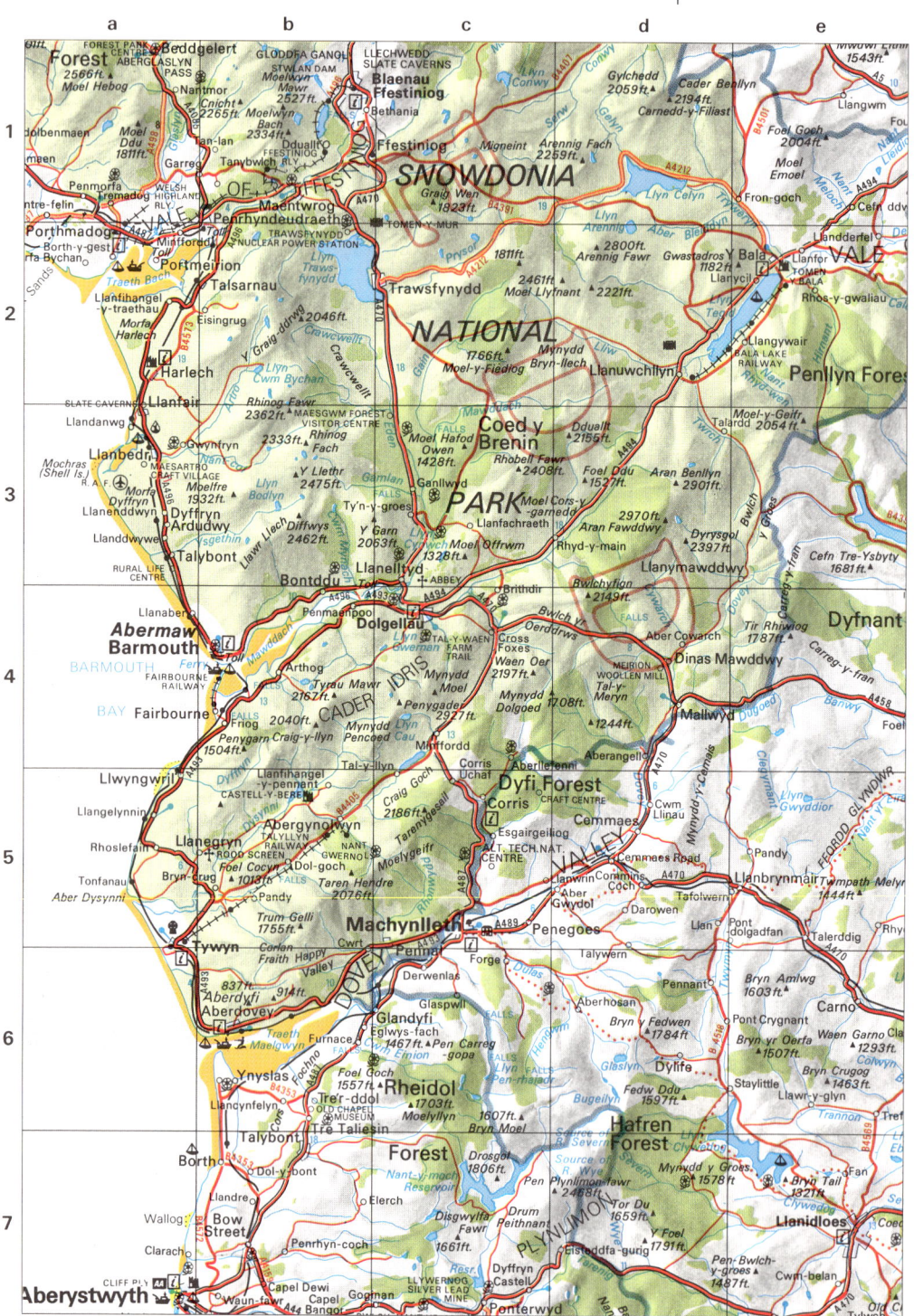

Map E

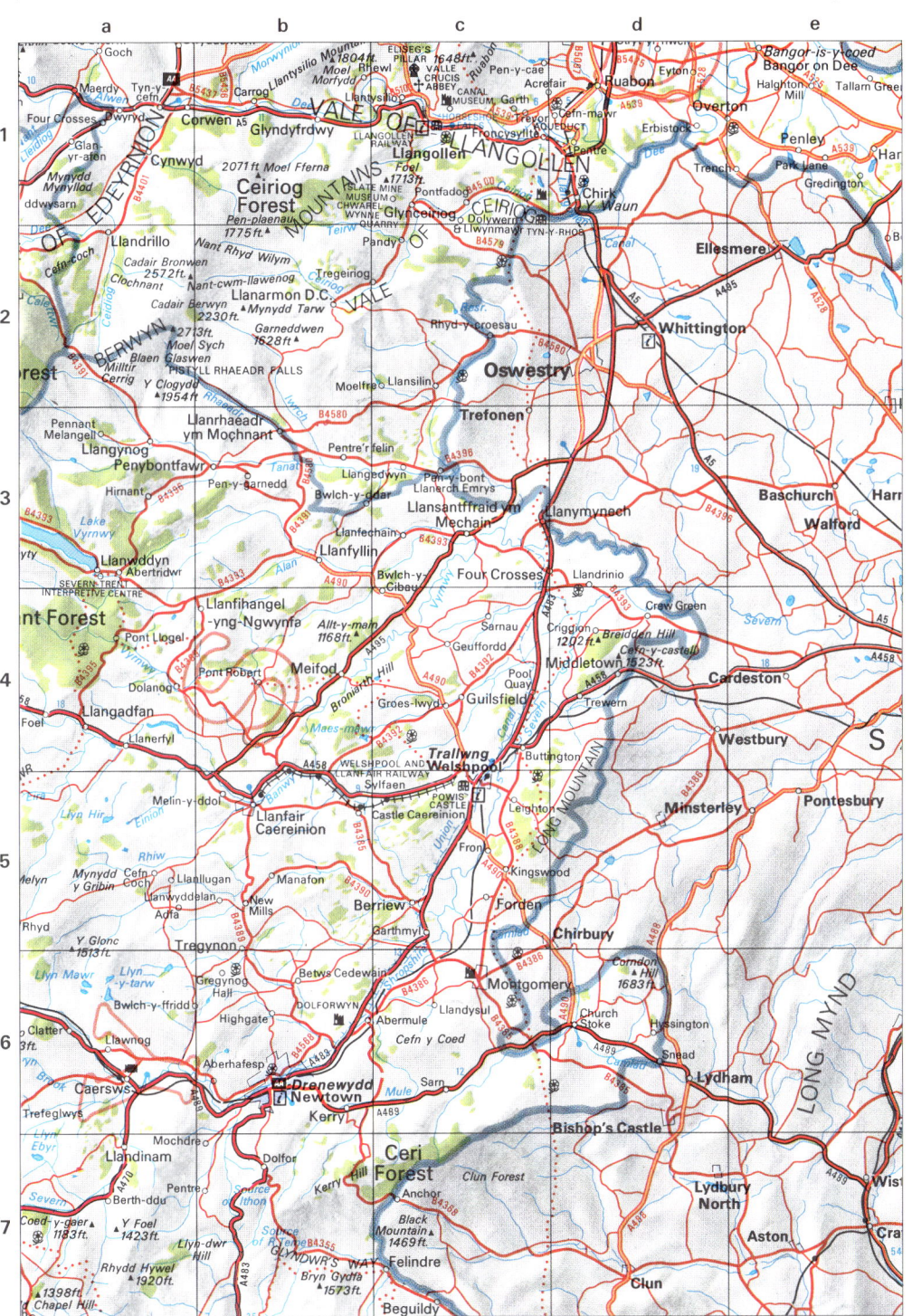

Map F

Map G

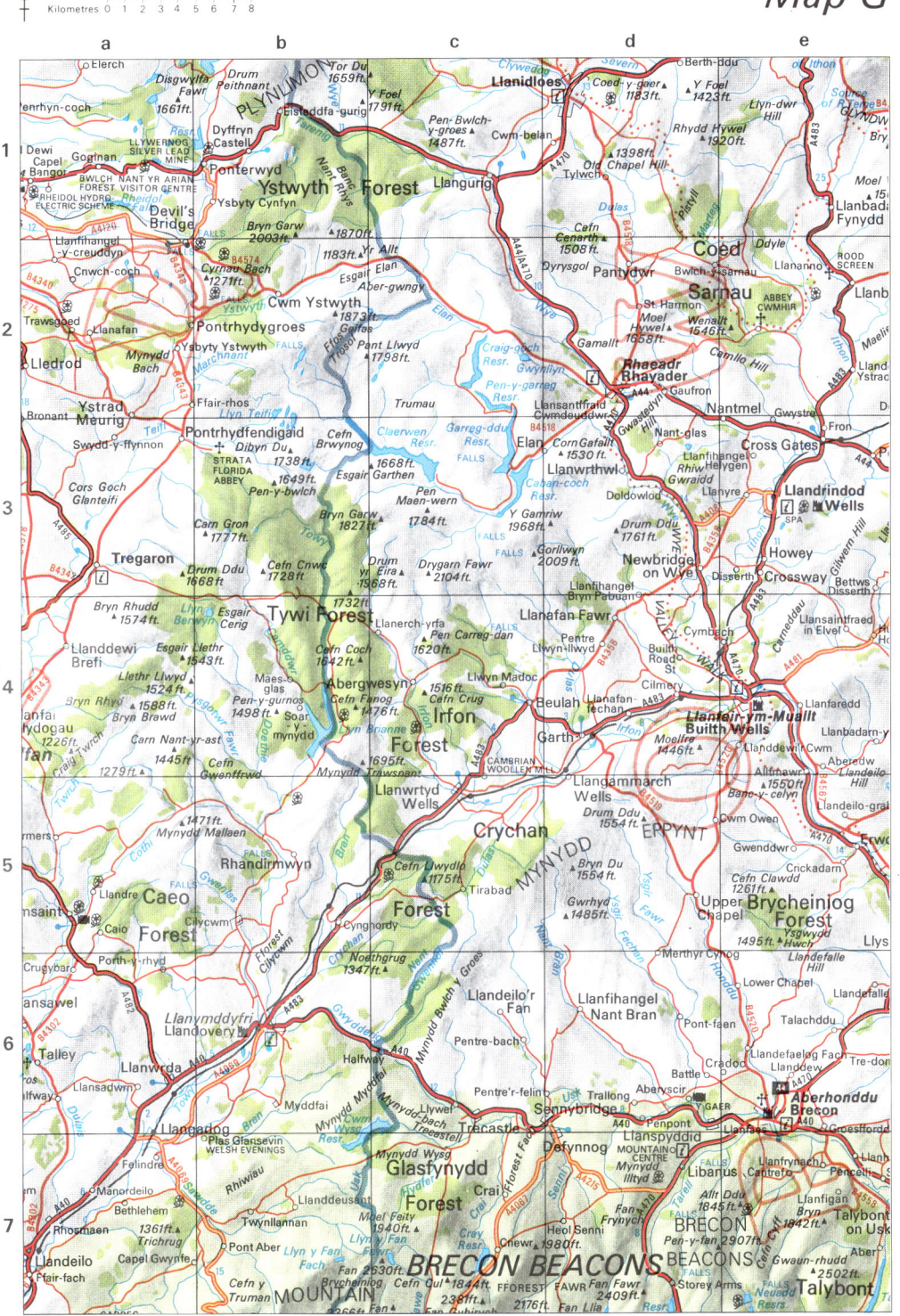

Map H

Map K

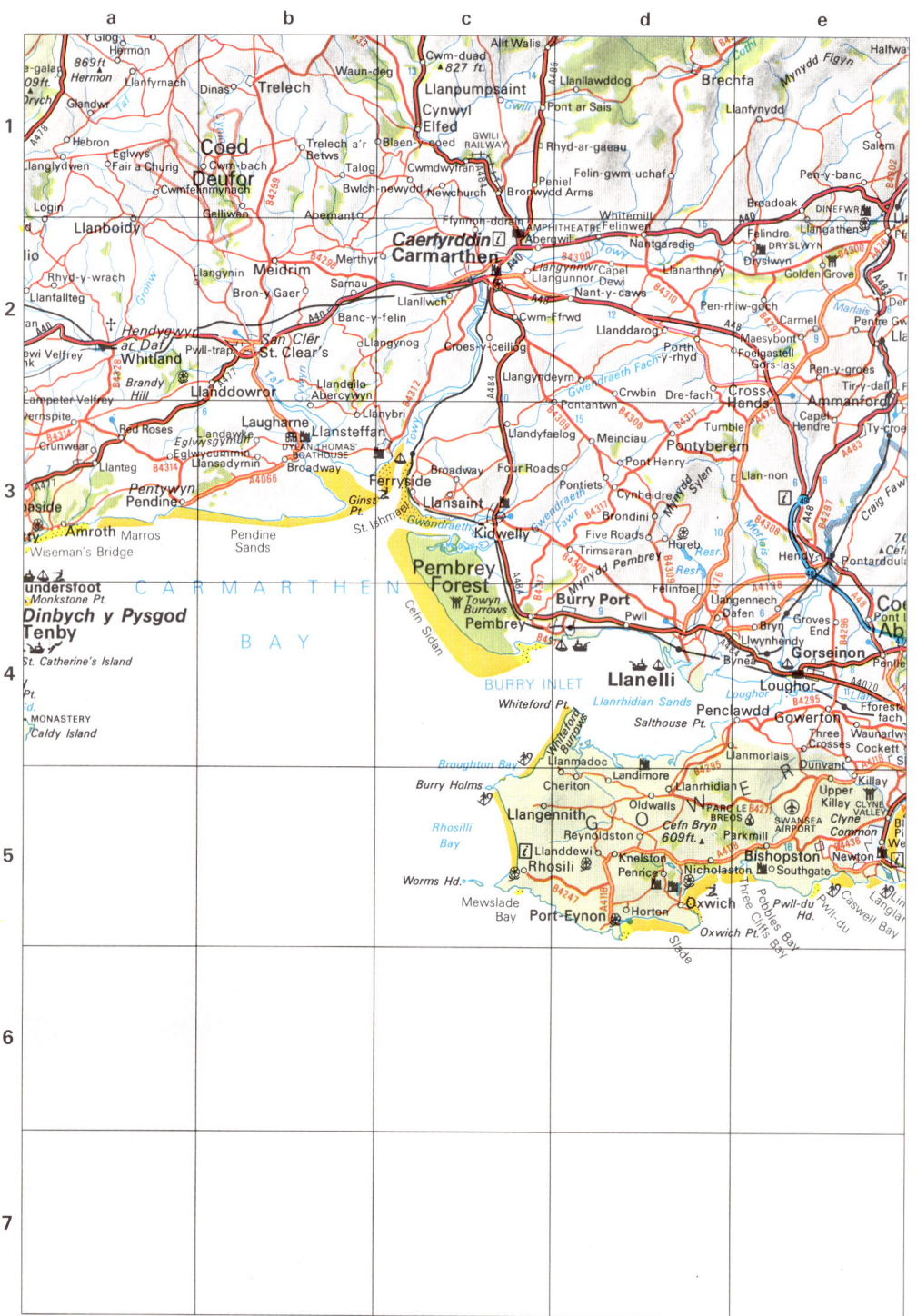

Map M

Map L

N
Miles 0 1 2 3 4 5
Kilometres 0 1 2 3 4 5 6 7 8

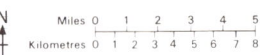

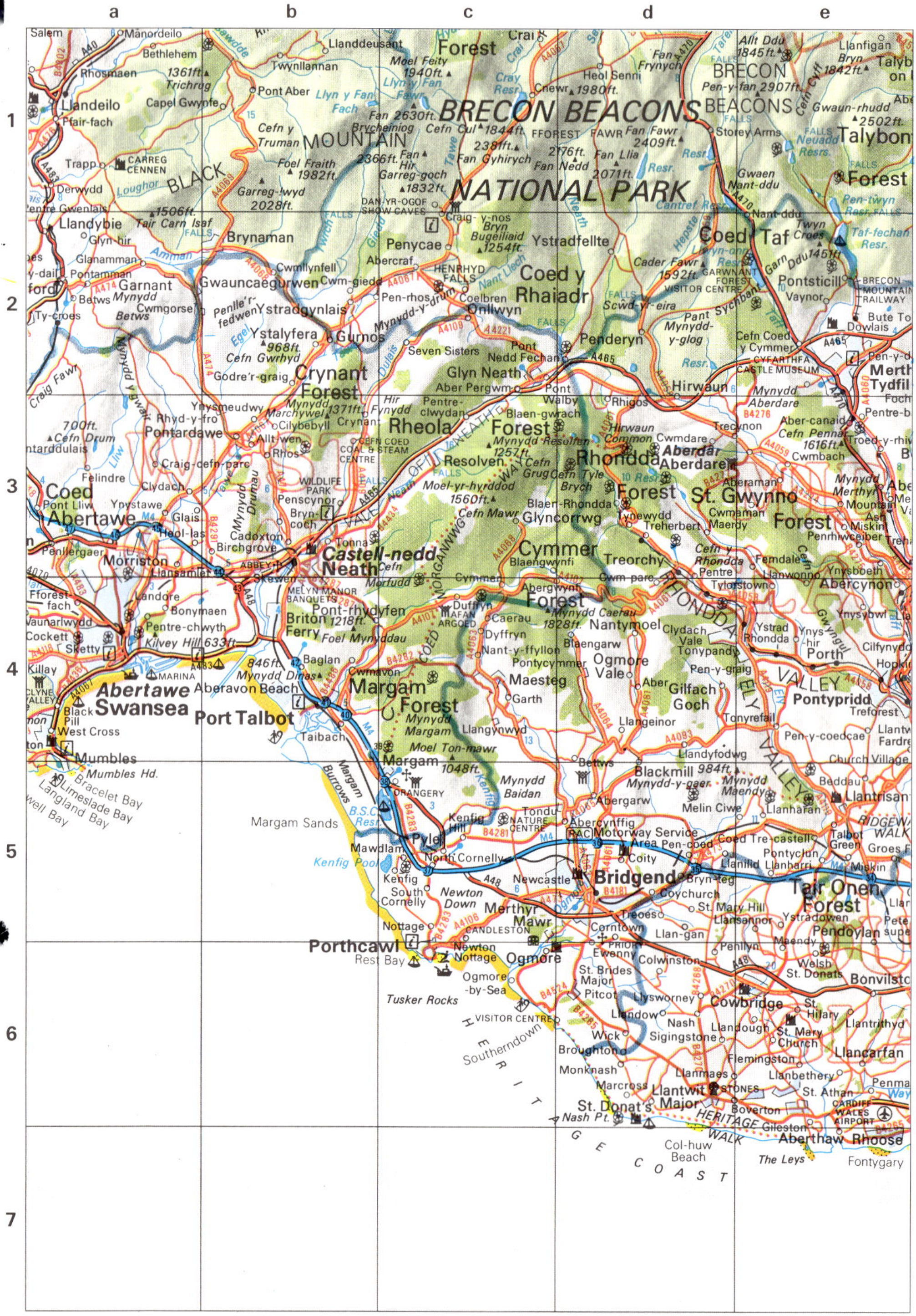
a
b
c
d
e
1
2
3
4
5
6
7
Salem
Manordeilo
Bethlehem
Llanddeusant
Forest
Crai
Rhosmaen
1361ft.
Trichrug
Twynllannan
Moel Feity
1940ft.
Llyn y Fan Fawr
Cray Resr.
Heol Senni
Fan Frynych
Allt Ddu
1845ft.
Llanfigan
Bryn
1842ft.
BRECON
Pen-y-fan 2907ft.
Llandeilo
Capel Gwynfe
Pont Aber
Llyn y Fan Fach
Chewr
1980ft.
Pfair-fach
Fan 2630ft.
BRECON BEACONS
BEACONS
Gwaun-rhudd
2502ft.
Cefn y Truman
MOUNTAIN
Brycheiniog
Cefn Cul
1844ft.
FFOREST FAWR
Fan Fawr
2409ft.
Storey Arms
Talybont
Trapp
CARREG CENNEN
BLACK
Foel Fraith
1982ft.
2366ft.
Fan Hir
238ft.
Fan Gyhirych
2176ft.
Fan Nedd
Fan Llia
2071ft.
Neuadd Resrs.
Derwydd
Loughor
Garreg-lwyd
2028ft.
Garreg-goch
1832ft.
NATIONAL PARK
Gwaen Nant-ddu
Forest
Pentre Gwenlais
1506ft.
Tair Carn Isaf
DAN-YR-OGOF SHOW CAVES
Cantref Resr.
Pen-twyn Resr.
Llandybie
Brynaman
Craig-y-nos
Bryn Bugeiliaid
1254ft.
Ystradfellte
Coed Taf
Nant-ddu
Twyn Croes
Taf-fechan Resr.
Glyn-hir
Penycae
Glanamman
Amman
Abercraf
Cwmllynfell
HENRHYD FALLS
Coed y Rhaiadr
Cader Fawr
1592ft.
GARWNANT FOREST VISITOR CENTRE
Garn Ddu
1451ft.
Pontamman
Garnant
Gwauncaegurwen
Cwm-giedd
Pen-rhos
Coelbren
Nant Llech
Pontsticill
BRECON MOUNTAIN RAILWAY
Betws
Mynydd Betws
Cwmgorse
Pen-lle'r-fedwen
Ystradgynlais
Onllwyn
Scwd-yr-eira
Vaynor
Ty-croes
Ystalyfera
968ft.
Gurnos
Mynydd-y-drum
Pant Sychbant
Mynydd-y-glog
Cefn Coed y Cymmer
Bute Town
Dowlais
Cefn Gwrhyd
Seven Sisters
Pont Nedd Fechan
Penderyn
Craig Fawr
Godre'r-graig
Crynant Forest
Glyn Neath
Aber Pergwm
Pont Walby
Hirwaun
CYFARTHFA CASTLE MUSEUM
Pen-y-darren
Merthyr Tydfil
Ynysmeudwy
Mynydd Marchywel
1371ft.
Hir Fynydd
Pentre-clwydau
Blaen-gwrach
Rhigos
Mynydd Aberdare
Pentre-bach
700ft.
Cefn Drum
Rhyd-y-fro
Pontardawe
Cilybebyll
Crynant
Rheola
Forest
Hirwaun Common
Cwmdare
Trecynon
Aber-canaid
Cefn Pennar
1616ft.
Troed-y-rhiw
Pontarddulais
Alltwen
Rhos
CEFN COED COAL & STEAM CENTRE
Mynydd Resolfen
1257ft.
Aberdar
Aberdare
Cwmbach
Craig-cefn-parc
Resolven
Cefn Grug
Cefn Tyle Brych
Rhondda
Felindre
Clydach
Mynydd Drumau
WILDLIFE PARK
Moel-yr-hyrddod
1560ft.
Forest
Aberaman
Mynydd Merthyr
Coed
Pont Lliw
Ynystawe
Penscynor
Bryn-coch
Cefn Mawr
Blaen-Rhondda
St. Gwynno
Mountain Ash
Abertawe
Glais
Heol-las
Cadoxton
Glyncorrwg
Tynewydd
Treherbert
Cwmaman
Maerdy
Forest
Miskin
Penllergaer
Birchgrove
Tonna
Castell-nedd
Neath
Cymmer
Penrhiwceiber
Morriston
Llansamlet
ABBEY
Cefn Morfudd
Blaengwynfi
Treorchy
Cefn y Rhondda
Ferndale
Pentre
Llanwonno
Ynysboeth
Abercynon
Forest-fach
Landore
Skewen
MELYN MANOR BANQUETS
Cymmer
Abergwynfi
Forest
Cwm-parc
Tylorstown
Bonymaen
Pont-rhydyfen
AFAN ARGOED
Duffryn
Caerau
Mynydd Caerau
1828ft.
Nantymoel
RHONDDA
Clydach Vale
Ystrad Rhondda
Ynysybwl
Waunarlwydd
Pentre-chwyth
Briton Ferry
1218ft.
Foel Mynyddau
Dyffryn
Tonypandy
Ynys-hir
Cockett
Kilvey Hill 633ft.
Nant-y-ffyllon
Blaengarw
Porth
Cilfynydd
Sketty
Baglan
Pontycymmer
Ogmore Vale
Pen-y-graig
Killay
846ft.
Mynydd Dinas
MARINA
Cwmavon
Maesteg
VALLEY
Abertawe
Swansea
Aberavon Beach
Margam Forest
Aber
Gilfach Goch
Pontypridd
Black Pill
Garth
Treforest
West Cross
Port Talbot
Mynydd Margam
Llangynwyd
Llangeinor
Tonyrefail
Llantwit Fardre
Oystermouth
Taibach
Moel Ton-mawr
1048ft.
Pen-y-coedcae
Mumbles
Margam
Bettws
Blackmill
984ft.
Llandyfodwg
Church Village
Mumbles Hd.
Bracelet Bay
Limeslade Bay
Langland Bay
Caswell Bay
Margam Burrows
ORANGERY
Mynydd Baidan
Mynydd-y-gaer
Mynydd Maendy
Beddau
Llantrisant
Margam Sands
B.S.C. Resr.
Kenfig Hill
Tondu
NATURE CENTRE
Abergarw
Melin Cwe
Llanharan
RIDGEWAY WALK
Pyle
Aberkenfig
Motorway Service Area
Pen-coed
Coed Tre-castell
Talbot Green
Groes Faen
Mawdlam
Kenfig Pool
North Cornelly
Coity
Pontyclun
Llanilid
Llanharri
Miskin
Kenfig
South Cornelly
Newton Down
Newcastle
Bridgend
Bryn-teg
Tair Onen Forest
Coychurch
Merthyr Mawr
St. Mary Hill
Llansannor
Nottage
CANDLESTON
Treoes
Ystradowen
Pendoylan
Porthcawl
Rest Bay
Newton Nottage
Ogmore
Corntown
Llan-gan
Maendy
PRIORY
Ewenny
Penllyn
Colwinston
Welsh St. Donats
Bonvilston
Ogmore-by-Sea
St. Brides Major
Pitcot
Tusker Rocks
Llyswormey
Cowbridge
St. Hilary
VISITOR CENTRE
Llandow
Nash
Llandough
Llantrithyd
Southerndown
Wick
Sigingstone
St. Mary Church
Broughton
Flemingston
Llancarfan
Monknash
Llanmaes
Llanbethery
Penmark
Marcross
Llantwit Major
STONES
St. Athan
St. Donat's
Boverton
CARDIFF WALES AIRPORT
Nash Pt.
HERITAGE WALK
Gileston
Aberthaw
Rhoose
Col-huw Beach
The Leys
Fontygary
HERITAGE COAST